Mrs. S. L. Heaps
312 E. Central Blvd.
Kewanee, Illinois.

Our
YOUNG FAMILY
in America

RANDOLPH FRIENDS MEETING HOUSE

THE RANDOLPH MEETING HOUSE, earlier called the Mendham Meeting House, still standing in the outskirts of Dover, N. J., but no longer in use, was erected in 1758 and was a branch of the Woodbridge Meeting House. Here our Young family of eight children said their prayers. The adjoining burial ground contains, in accordance with the early custom of the Quakers, unmarked graves. Probably here lie John, Morgan and Elizabeth Young, and others of our forbears. The grave of Margaret, sister of John, was recently marked with a memorial stone that reads:

DANIEL CARREL

MARGARET YOUNG CARREL

DANIEL CARREL, JR.
Aug. 30 1745
Oct. 19 1839

JANE CLUTTER CARREL
Mar. 13 1765
Feb. 22 1843

Our YOUNG FAMILY in America

COMPILED BY PROF. EDWARD HUDSON YOUNG, DURHAM, N. C.

PUBLISHED BY

SANBORN AND RUTH YOUNG, LOS GATOS, CALIFORNIA

RUTH YOUNG ORB, CHICAGO, ILLINOIS

HELEN YOUNG HARDY, BARRINGTON, ILLINOIS

AND THE COMPILER

PRINTED AT

DURHAM, NORTH CAROLINA, U.S.A.

1947

OUR YOUNG FAMILY

1722 ~ 1947

Morgan from Scotland, sailing to the Colonies,
Little lad of nine, with wonder in his gaze;
Growing up, marrying, founding the family,
Guiding his descendants in the new world ways.

John, Jacob, Aaron, and Hannah and Tryphena,
Blacksmiths and merchantmen, tillers of the soil,
Care-cumbered housewives, preachers and teachers,
Head and hand diligent in sober toil.

Minute Men, Lexington, gaunt wraiths at Valley Forge;
The Alamo, Gettysburg, serving in dark years;
Manila Bay, Argonne, Pearl Harbor, Anzio,
Rivers of men's blood and seas of women's tears.

Pony Express to transatlantic telephone;
Crawling covered-wagons to arrow swift trains;
Pianoforte to radio, spinning wheel to ready-made;
Atomic bombs, television, soaring planes.

Seventeen twenty-two, nineteen forty-seven,
Still unforgotten thro' the past's pale haze . . .
Morgan from Scotland, sailing to the Colonies,
Little lad of nine, with wonder in his gaze . . .

Ruth Comfort Mitchell
(Mrs. Sanborn Young)

OUR YOUNG FAMILY

[illegible]

[illegible] from Norway, landing to the Colonies,
[illegible] with [illegible]
[illegible]
[illegible]

[illegible]

[illegible]

[illegible]

[illegible] in the Colonies,
[illegible]

[illegible]

Introduction

The title of the present volume indicates a limitation that was imposed on me by the fact that research in foreign lands was impossible during the years of World War II. I am hoping that the following-up of the clue in Record #2 will reveal the birthplace in Scotland and the names of the parents of our immigrant ancestor "who arrived in America from the North of Scotland, Nov. 11 1722, at the age of nine years." My compilation, limited to America, covers ten generations, about 250 years.

The gathering of this domestic material, in the midst of a busy life, has been a stupendous but fascinating task. My sufficient reward is that I now have my own family tree as it was planted and grown in America, and also the trees of several hundreds of my kith and kin. Two trips to the Pacific coast States, following the trail blazed by our adventuresome pioneers, have been made during vacation periods; numerous shorter excursions to centers where our forefathers planted their crops and labored a time on their westward march have been taken; and endless letters have been written to obtain the data in this volume. Our records come from the leaves of old family Bibles, scrap books of old newspaper clippings, old letters, from church and cemetery records, county histories, city directories, census reports and other official documents, and from personal interviews.

I have emphasized the fact that our eight immigrant brothers and sisters were Quakers because this affiliation has greatly aided me in distinguishing them and their children from four other Young families who were their neighbors in colonial New Jersey. Just now I am proud that we are of Quaker origin because the Society of Friends in Great Britain and the United States is celebrating the 300th anniversary of its founding by George Fox, the inspired weaver, and is receiving as a birthday gift the Nobel Peace Prize. Perhaps our ancestors were not good Quakers since they bore arms, as their war records show, during the Revolution and because none of their descendants, so far as I know, is today a Quaker. Nevertheless, I find a peculiar pleasure in dating my work in the year 1947. This does not mean that the records of all the branches of our family have been brought to date.

My special effort has been to trace the descendants of Morgan and Israel Young who were of no kin but were my own paternal and maternal ancestors. While doing this I have collected considerable data about the descendants of the seven brothers and sisters of Morgan and I have thought well to preserve it by incorporating it in this compilation. I have also given space to data about certain Young families who settled near Morgan Young, jr. in Adams County, Ohio, whom I suspect but cannot prove to have been his kin. I have also endeavored to trace the marriages of the Young girls and in some instances their families have been carried down to the near present and their husbands' ancestry taken back to their immigrant ancestors. A family tree has become a family grove!

Enough has been found about our pioneering ancestors to know that they were men and women of character and capacity. They were first settlers in the Northwest Territory, the present States of Ohio, Indiana, Illinois, Michigan, and Wisconsin, and they were leaders there in the social, religious, educational, commercial and political development of their communities (Records #6, 9, 14, 15, 18, 28, 34). They were homesteaders in Iowa, Kansas and Missouri and in the farther west as the lands were opened for settlement. R. A. Young was a member of the first legislature of Nevada (Record #308). E. P. Young was the first school teacher in Whiteside County, Ill. (#48). A. N. Young was an early member of the Chicago Board of Trade (#118). John and C. S. Young were concerned with the welfare of the Indians (#6, 301).

The maps of the early and the present political divisions of Ohio will make for a better understanding of some seemingly contradictory land deeds that have been quoted. The portraits, which are largely of those who saw service in World Wars I and II, are of both the paternal and maternal lines and cover several branches of the family beginning with the third generation in America. One of these, Allan W. Taylor, was killed in action. There are items of general interest in the records of all of the first generation (Records #1, 2, 295, 313, 318, 319, 320, 321, and 322), and also in Records 6, 8, 34, 38 and 84.

Every possible effort has been made to avoid unforgivable errors. It may, however, be foreseen that defects will be found. I appeal to my readers for help in making the necessary corrections and also for information that will fill the lacunae. I especially wish to learn why John Young was so generous to so many Loseys in his will. I shall feel happy if my labor of love is appreciated.

EDWARD H. YOUNG.

Summary of the Eight Immigrant Children and Their Children

1. JOHN YOUNG, Bachelor. Will, 1774.

2. ROBERT YOUNG m. Mary ———
    - a. James m. Sarah Benjamin
    - b. Morgan
    - c. Robert m. Elizabeth Morris
    - d. ? Sarah m. Isaac Hathaway
    - e. Jean m. Asher Lyon

3. MORGAN YOUNG m. Elizabeth Mills
    - a. William m. Miriam Drake Throckmorton
    - b. Charity m. Jacob Drake
    - c. Anne m. Abraham Drake
    - d. John m. Hannah Mitchell
    - e. James
    - f. Robert m. Sarah Bryant
    - g. Morgan m. Jane Losey

4. THOMAS YOUNG m. Thankful Robarts
    - a. Arthur
    - b. Margaret
    - c. Elizabeth m. James Lum
    - d. Phebe
    - e. Thomas, Jr.
    - f. Thankful
    - g. Morgan m. Eizabeth ———
    - h. Daniel m. ———
      m. 2nd Dorcas Coonrod
    - i. Mary
    - j. Hannah
    - k. David

5. ANNY YOUNG m. John Clark
    - a. John Clark, Jr.

6. HERCULES m. Sarah Philips
    - a. Names of children unknown

7. MARGARET YOUNG m. Daniel Carrel
    - a. James
    - b. Hercules m. Sara Wheeler
    - c. John
    - d. Thomas m. Elizabeth Richey
    - e. Sarah m. ——— Clawson
    - f. Daniel m. Jane Clutter
    - g. Mary m. Moses Kerr
    - h. Hannah
    - i. Elizabeth

8. MARY YOUNG m. Adam Miller
    - a. Conrod
    - b. Catherine
    - c. Anna
    - d. John
    - e. Robert
    - f. Elizabeth
    - g. James
    - h. Margaret
    - i. Conrod
    - j. Thomas

The Will of John Young—Record 1

The will of John Young is the foundation of this compilation. It is the most important single document bearing on our Young family that has been found and is therefore shown here in its entirety, and followed by an important note. This copy of the original will which is filed in the office of the Secretary of State, Trenton, N. J. (File 623N) was made by the compiler. An abstract of the will is printed in the "New Jersey Archives, 1st Series, Vol. XXXV."

In the Name of God Amen, this twenty-third day of March in the year of our Lord One Thousand Seven Hundred and Seventy Four, I John Youngs of the County of Morris in the Province of New Jersey, in good health and sound in mind and memory:—calling to mind the frailty of man, and that it is appointed for all mankind to die, do make and ordain this my last Will and Testament, that is to say, Principally and first of all I recommend my soul into the hands of God who gave it me, and my body to the earth to be buried in a decent and Christian like manner at the discretion of my Executors. And as touching such worldly estate wherewith it hath pleased God to bless me in this life, I give, devise and dispose of the same in the following manner:

Imprimis, it is my will, and I do order that all my just debts and funeral charges be paid.

Item, I give to James Youngs (the son of Robert Youngs) the sum of twenty pounds money at eight shillings the ounce to be paid him by my Executors hereinafter named.

Item, In like manner I give to Elizabeth the wife of Morgan Youngs the sum of ten pounds.

Item, I give and bequeath to James Puff Losey, in like manner, the sum of twenty pounds.

Item, I give and bequeath in like manner to John Losey (the brother of James) the sum of ten pounds.

Item, I give to Philip Losey, in like manner, the sum of ten pounds.

Item, I give to Jacob Losey (the son of James Losey), when he arrives to the age of twenty one years, the sum of ten pounds, in manner as aforesd.

Item, In like manner I give to Samuel Tuthill (the son of Samuel Tuthill, Esq.r/the sum of ten pounds at my decease, to be paid him by my Executors hereafter mentioned as af/d.

Item, I give to Jacob Tuthill (the son of Samuel Tuthill, Esq.r/the sum of five pounds to be paid him in the manner as last aforesaid.

Item, I give to Samuel Converse (to whom I learnt the weavers trade) if living at the time of my decease, the sum of twenty pounds to be paid him by my Executors as first aforesaid, and if not living, then this twenty pounds is to be paid to James Losey, the son of Timothy Losey, when he arrives to the age of twenty one years.

Item, I give to Nathaniel Doty the sum of ten pounds to be paid him by my Executors.

Item, in like manner I give to Timothy Losey the sum of five pounds.

Item, in like manner to Thomas Carryl (the son of Daniel Carryl) the sum of ten pounds.

Item, in like manner I give to Thomas Youngs (the son of Thomas Youngs) the sum of ten pounds.

Item, in like manner I give to John Burwell (the son of John Burwell of Rockaway) the sum of ten pounds whenever he arrives to the age of twenty one years.

Item, I give to Elizabeth, the daughter of John Losey deceased, the sum of ten pounds, to be paid her by my Executors.

Item, in like manner I give the three daughters of Daniel Carryl, viz— to Mary, to Peggy, and to Hannah five pounds each.

Item, I give to John, to Robert, and to Morgan Youngs (the sons of Morgan Youngs) to each of them, the sum of ten pounds, in the manner as afore'd.

Item, I give to Morgan and to Robert Youngs (the sons of Robert Youngs) to each of them the sum of twenty pounds, in manner as afore'd.

Item, I give to John Clark (the son of my sister Anny) the sum of twenty pounds, in manner as afore'd.

Item, I give to John Miller (the son of Adam Miller) the sum of twenty pounds, in manner as afores'd.

Item, I give to the children of my brother Hercules Youngs the sum of twenty pounds to be equally divided among them, share and share alike, to be paid as afores'd.

Item, I give to Jean, the wife of Asher Lyon, the sum of ten pounds in manner afores'd.

Item, I give to Daniel, and to Hercules Carryl, to each of them, the sum of ten pounds, in manner as afores'd, viz. the sons of Daniel Carryl.

Item, I give to Charity, the wife of Jacob Drake, the sum of ten pounds, in manner as afores'd.

Item, I give to Anne, the wife of Abraham Drake, the sum of ten pounds, in manner as afores'd.

Item, I give to Morgan Youngs (the son of Thomas Youngs) the sum of five pounds.

Item, It is my will and I do order that in case of the decease of anyone or more of the above persons to whom I have made bequests before they arrive to the full age of twenty one years, that in such case the sum so ordered to be paid to him or them, shall be equally divided among the survivors, share and share alike, excepting Samuel Tuthill and Jacob Tuthill as before excepted.

Item, I do give and bequeath to the Members of the Quaker Meeting in the Township of Mendham, the sum of twenty pounds, to be paid them by my Executors as afores'd.

Item, I do give and bequeath to each and every of the children of my brother Robert Youngs, of my brother Thomas Youngs, deceased, and of my brother Hercules Youngs, of my sister Anny, my sister Margaret, and my sister Mary as though here particularly called by name, the sum of five pounds.

Item, It is my will, and I do further order that if yet there remains any part of my estate, it shall be equally divided, share and share alike among my legatees af'd. And in order to enable my Executors hereafter to be named to pay the several before recited bequeaths, I do hereby fully empower and order my Executors, or in case of the decease of one or more of them, the surviving Executor or Executors to sell all and singular my real and personal estate, and to execute good and sufficient conveyances in the law for the same, as tho' I were present; and my will is further that my Plantation laying on both sides of the Rockaway river be sold at ten years credit with the lawfull interest being paid from date of sale and the principal well and sufficiently secured to the satisfaction of my Executors, and the interest well and faithfully paid every year. The bond to be given payable in one year, but to say the term of ten years as af'd if the interest is punctually paid and my Executors think the money still lays safe.

Item, I constitute, make and ordain Samuel Tuthill, Esq.r., Moses Tuttle, Esq.r, and Hartshorn Fitz Randolph the sole executors of this my last Will and Testament. And I do hereby utterly disalow, revoke and disannul, all and every other Testaments, Wills, Legacys & Bequests, and Executors by me in anywise before willed, named and bequeathed. Ratifying and confirming this and no other to be my last Will and Testament. In witness whereof I have hereunto set my hand and seal the day and year first above written. Signed, sealed and published, pronounced and declared by the said John Youngs as his last Will and Testament in the presence of: Peter Mackie Jno. Doughty James Ford, jr.

John Youngs

The following oath is attached to the Will:—

"Peter Mackie, one of the witnesses to the foregoing Will, hereto annexed, being duly sworn, did depose and say that he saw John Young, the Testator therein named, sign and seal the same, and heard him publish, pronounce and declare the foregoing writing to be his last Will and Testament, and that at the doing thereof the said Testator was of sound and disposing mind and memory as far as this deponant knows and as he verily believes, and that Jno. Doughty and Jacob Ford, Jun., the other subscribing witnesses were present at the same time, and signed their names as witnesses to the said Will together with this deponent in presence of the said Testator.

Signed—Peter Mackie

Sworn at Morris Town
this 8th day of July 1784
before me

Jos. Lewis Sur.tt.

NOTES ON THE WILL

Youngs—with an s—and Yong were common variants of Young in official documents of colonial New Jersey. Our Quaker ancestors from Scotland, when they signed their name did not add the s. John's amanuensis signed for John and John made his mark. Yong was "phonetic" and bad spelling rather than a variant of the English Yonge. Youngs, however, was the spelling used by the family of the Rev. David Youngs who was settled in Morris County, N. J., at the time of our John Young. This may have been the source of the spelling of John's scribe.

The will of John Young was probated, July 8, 1784, at Morristown, N. J., in the presence of but one of the three who witnessed its making. There are no accompanying papers to show what disposition of the estate was made by the executors. A natural assumption from this situation would be to think that two of the witnesses were beyond reach, that John died shortly before the date of the probation and that the accompanying papers were lost. According to the following official records John, in less than three months after making his will, sold his plantation which he had requested his executors to sell in order to satisfy his legacies, and John died previous to April 8, 1776.

"1774 June 1. John Youngs, of Roxbury, sells to John Losey, of Mendham, for 475 Pounds, his property on the Rockaway river between the two great mountains, 91.37 acres that he bought from David Ogden, Nov. 6 1750; and a second tract that he bought from Richard H. Morris, 25 March 1763; *all* his land except 4 acres that he has sold to James Losey. Witness: Joseph Lewis." (County Deed Bk. B; p. 140, Morristown, N. J.) By the purchase of the above land John became John Youngs of Roxbury. See record No. 1. By the sale of the plantation the legacies in John's will were annulled, and both the witnesses to the will and the Court might regard the will, as they seemingly did, of small importance.

On April 8, 1776, Letters of Administration were issued, at Morristown, N. J., to Adam Miller, James Puff Losey, James Young and Thomas Millidge, as administrators of the property of John Youngs, of Roxbury Township in Morris County, N. J. These Letters are now on file in the office of the Secretary of State, at Trenton, N. J. (No. 587N). On the back of these Letters of Administration there is written the oath that was taken by the administrators. We quote: "Morris County, N. J. Adam Miller, James Puff Losey and James Young, Administrators with the Will annexed of John Youngs, deceased, being of the people called Quakers, did truly affirm and declare . . . that they will make and exhibit into the Prerogative Office at Perth Amboy, a true and perfect inventory of all the goods, chattels and credits of the deceased, and render a just and true account when thereunto lawfully required. Sworn and affirmed this 8th day of April 1776, before me, Abraham Ogden, Surr. Signed: James Puff Losey, Adam Miller, James Young." The name of Thomas Millidge does not appear on the back of the Letters.

It is the studied opinion of the writer that the will annexed to the above Letters of Administration was the will of our John Youngs (File 623N, Trenton, N. J.) and not that of another John Youngs of Roxbury. These Letters of Administration seem to have been issued because the will of our John Youngs had been annulled by his selling his plantation. John was legally intestate and hence these Letters of Administration annexed with the will. The administrators named by the Court to carry out the Letters of Administration are not the executors of the will of John but administrators *with the will annexed,* and they are all relatives of our John Youngs, as will be shown under their records. John and the administrators were Quakers. No record of the administrator's report to Perth Amboy can be found. The will probably became separated from the Letters of Administration during the settlement of the personal estate and was probated some eight years later before one witness as a matter of form.

An oddity in the will of John is his two bequests to all "the children of my brother Hercules" while none is named.

John Miller, son of Mary, is identified as the son of Adam Miller. Charity and Anne Drake, daughters of Morgan and Elizabeth (the only spouse of a brother or sister made a legatee) are not identified as nieces. Jean Lyon probably was a daughter of Robert, brother of John.

Doty and Doughty are variants of the same name. An unverified tradition says that Nathaniel Doty married the widow Anne Clark. John Clark, husband of Anny Young, perhaps was related to Henry Clarke, of Brookside, near Mt. Freedom, N. J., whose daughter married Nathaniel Doty, Jr.

The relationship of John Young to the several Loseys who are legatees has not been satisfactorily established. If Jane, wife of John Losey (Will, 1765) was a sister of John Young the list of nephews and nieces made legatees would be enlarged. What is known is that Morgan Young, Jr. married Jane (b. 1758), daughter of John and Jane Losey, near the end of the Revolution.

John Burwell, son of John of Rockaway, was also the son of Catherine Losey, sister-in-law of Morgan Young, Jr.

EDW. H. YOUNG.

THE JERSEY SETTLEMENT IN WAYNE TOWNSHIP, KNOX COUNTY, OHIO

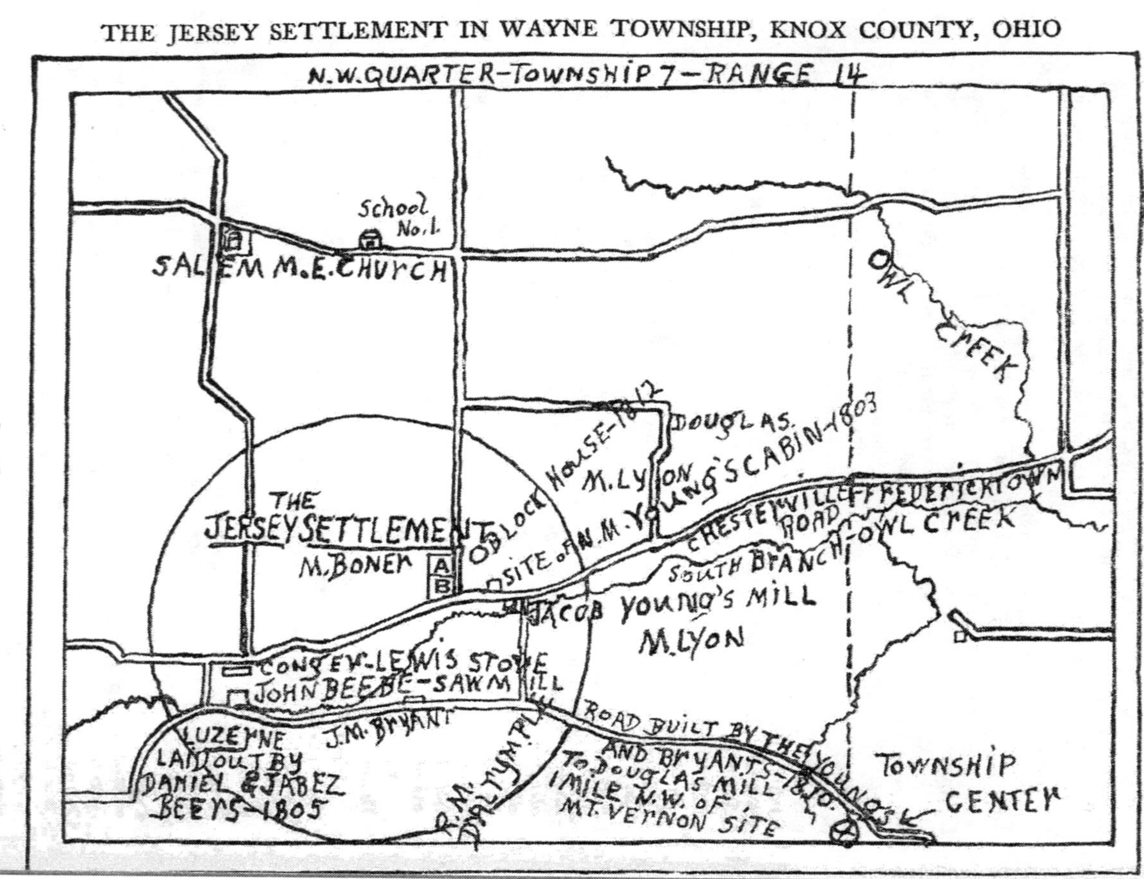

THE JERSEY SETTLEMENT IN WAYNE TOWNSHIP KNOX COUNTY, OHIO

A This CEMETERY contains the remains of NATHANIEL MITCHELL YOUNG, the first permanent settler within the present limits of Knox County. He built his cabin within a few hundred yards of his present resting place in Wayne cemetery in the Spring of 1803. JACOB YOUNG, his brother, and ABRAHAM and SIMEON LYON came in the Spring of the following year. Later in the same year ELIPHALET and JOHN LEWIS and JAMES BRYANT joined the settlers. Since these pioneers were all from New Jersey the settlement became known as the "Jersey Settlement."

B The WAYNE BAPTIST CHURCH was organized by the Lewises in 1810. William, John and Eliphalet Lewis, together with a revolutionary soldier, by the name of Ackerman, were the first members. The first church was built in 1815. It was used until 1837 when a new church was erected. The SALEM M.E. CHURCH was organized in 1830. "Original members were: Daniel Lyon, Daniel Beers, Henry Wider, James Beebe and their wives, Mrs. Jeffers, Aaron Jackson and Mr. John Young."

Knox County was created from Fairfield in 1808; Fairfield was created from Franklin in 1800; and Franklin from Ross in 1803. Ross, the great grandfather of Knox County, was carved from the old Northwest Territory in 1798, five years before the State of Ohio was created. The earliest U. S. Census of Knox County that has been preserved is that of 1830, alas! The Census of 1820 is the earliest for any section of Ohio. The Census of Richland County, 1820, places Noah Young (Rec. 28) in Washington Township, Jacob Young (Rec. 15) in Orange, Aaron (Rec. 18) and John Young (Rec. 17) in Troy Township. A John Halderman, possibly John Halterman, husband of Hannah Young (Rec. 19), with a phonetic spelling, is in Troy Township.

John Young
and the
Generations of Morgan Young

1 JOHN YOUNG

John Young is supposed to have been born in Scotland. See Record 2. He probably was the eldest of the eight brothers and sisters whom he mentioned by name in his will. His parents are unknown. What little that is known about John comes from his will and from other official and public records. From his will we know that he was a weaver by trade who became a farmer in Mendham (earlier Roxiticus) and Roxbury townships, Morris County, N. J. An earlier residence has not been found. The earliest records about the family are in the Quaker archives of the Kennett (Newark) Monthly Meeting which was held at Kennett Square, Chester County, Pa. In these archives, preserved at the Friends Headquarters in Philadelphia, Pa., the marriages of Anny Young, in 1742, to John Clark, and of Hercules Young, Feb. 17 1745, to Sarah Philips, are recorded. It is also recorded that Hercules and Sarah were transferred, in 1749, to the Woodbridge (N. J.) Meeting. The record of the marriage of Mary, 9th month, 6th day, 1746, to Adam Miller stands in the Woodbridge records. The Mendham Meeting was established as a branch of the Woodbridge Meeting in 1758. Two of the witnesses to the Deed by which Robert Schooley transferred land to the Mendham Meeting were William Schooley and Sarah Young. (? Wife of Hercules Young)

The earliest record about John is in the "Alexander (Lord Stirling) Papers," now in possession of the N. Y. Historical Society. Here is shown that a survey of 94.56 acres of land on the Rockaway river, between the two great mountains, near Green Swamps, was made, Nov. 7 1750, by Ebenezer Byram for John Young, and the results sent to James Alexander, Surveyor General, at Perth Amboy, N. J. In the "land records of the Board of Proprietors of East Jersey," John Young is listed as having purchased, Nov. 10 1750, 91.37 acres on the Rockaway river between the two great mountains (Bk. 3, p. 98). This land is described in a report of an inspection to the Proprietors of East Jersey as follows: "On Friday, Oct. 22 1772 (20 years after John's purchase), we set out from Morristown to view the land in the valley (Berkshire), and passed through the land sold to Mr. Faisby which we viewed on both sides of the road to Mt. Hope. From thence we proceeded to Middle Forge, and passed the mountain. We then proceeded to Kenny's Forge, passing John Young's house, and went on foot and viewed John Young's 91 acre tract, along the south of Green Mountains. This tract takes in much valuable timber, by which the mountain is made useless to anybody else. Had these locations been carried up the mountain, as they ought to have been, the general interest would not suffer, as it must, and has, by these irregular surveys" (Hist. of Morris Co., N. J., p. 333, W. W. Munsel, N. Y., 1882).

The records at Perth Amboy (Bk. S –3, p. 241) show that, in April 1752, John added to his first purchase "3.20 acres on the westerly side of the Rockaway river," and that, March 26 1763, he bought an additional "127.23 acres on a branch of the Rockaway river from Robert H. Morris." Morgan and Thomas Young, brothers of John, also bought at this period on the Rockaway. John's property is further described in two advertisements which he had printed about a year before he made his will and before he sold the land. The same advertisement appeared in the N. Y. Journal and Advertiser, March 18 1773, and in the N. Y. Gazette and Weekly Mercury, March 22 1773: "To be sold at public vendue, on Wednesday, the 21st day of April next, the well known excellent farm of John Young, situate in Buckshear-Valley (Berkshire), adjoining the Green Pond Meadow, in the township of Roxbury, in the county of Morris, on which farm is a convenient small dwelling, a good barn, and contains about 240 acres of choice arable meadow, timber, and pasture land, with a beautiful small river of water running through the said plantation, within a few rods of the house; it is very advantageously situated for the raising of cattle of all kinds, from the benefit of a most extensive range of unimproved lands adjoining it, and the very best market may be had at the door, for all kinds of produce, from its contiguity to the iron works; the payments will be made easy to the purchaser, as upon proper security being given, little or none of the money will be wanted; and an indisputable title will be given by John Young, the present owner, of whom for further particulars enquire, or of Samuel Tuthill, or William D. Hart, Esquires, at Morristown." For the sale of the property and the death of John, see "Notes on the Will of John Young." John was, from all evidence, a bachelor, and was buried in the yard of the Meeting House to which he left a legacy.

2 MORGAN YOUNG

Morgan Young was the progenitor in America of that branch of our Young family with which this compilation is mainly concerned. He "arrived in America, Oct. 11 1722, at the age of nine years, from the Highlands of Scotland," says the "Generations of Daniel Beers Young" without noting the source of information. The "Generations of Daniel Beers Young" was compiled by Jacob Clark Young and Tryphena Johnson from family records found in Ohio and New Jersey. It was completed about 1890 and widely distributed amongst the descendants of Daniel in typewritten form. This record says nothing about the parents of Morgan or about any of his fellow voyagers. Morgan's year of birth, fixed in the above quotation as 1713, is approximately confirmed by an inscription which tops a list of three generations on a family monument in the cemetery at Newton, N. J. This notation reads: "Morgan Young, Died Nov. 20 1792, Aged 75 years. Elizabeth Mills, His wife, Died Sept. 24 1791, Aged 71 years." This inscription except for the family name of Elizabeth came from the family records of William, eldest child of Morgan and Elizabeth, and it was published, June 23 1917, by William I. Young, in the Newark (N. J.) Evening News. Morgan probably was buried in the cemetery adjoining the Mendham (Randolph) Quaker Meeting House on the outskirts of Dover, N. J. It was to this Meeting House that John, brother of Morgan, left a legacy. Our progenitor's name which is often spelled Morgin in the early tax lists of Mendham and other official documents suggests that his mother was a Morgan and a descendant of the Clan Morgan, one of the most ancient clans of Scotland.

Morgan Young was a Quaker. When the will of Thomas Young, brother of Morgan, was proved in 1769, the usual wording of the oath was effaced because Morgan and his fellow witness "being two of the people called Quakers did severally declare and affirm" etc. (Office of the Secr. of State, Trenton, N. J.). Hugh D. Vail says that "several members of the Mendham Quaker Meeting came from Craigforth, Aberdeen County, Scotland." (N. Y. Gen. & Biog. Record, Vol. 7, p. 176). Records on the parentage of Morgan may be found in Aberdeen when the World War is ended.

Morgan Young perhaps was related to his namesake, Morgan Young, who belonged to the Philadelphia Quaker Meeting and whose wife, Mary, bore him a daughter, Mary, Dec. 25 1690, (W. H. Hinshaw, Encyclopedia of American Quaker Gen.," Vol. 2, p. 440). The probability of a relationship is indicated by the fact that the earliest records of our family are found near Philadelphia in the files of the Kennett Square (Chester County, Pa.) Meeting of Friends. Here are recorded the marriages of Anne and Hercules Young, sister and brother of our Morgan. The Morgan Young who was settled near Philadelphia in 1690 probably arrived in America with the earliest pioneering Quakers who sailed up the Delaware river and settled first at Upland (now Chester, Pa.) and at Salem and Burlington, N. J., and he was followed to the same vicinity by our family of eight brothers and sisters. This assumption does not seem unreasonable.

The earliest official date relating to Morgan locates him in 1750, in Mendham Township, Morris County, N. J. Mendham was created from Roxbury Township in 1749 and in that year began to keep records. Under the heading of "Registration of Earmarks," one name appears in 1749,

Eliphalet Lewis (Rec. 14), and the first name in 1750 is that of "Morgin" Young. The next official date referring to Morgan is May 10 1754. By a Deed dated Aug. 6 1784, recorded Jan. 20 1786, at Morristown, N. J., Morgan Young, of Mendham, sold to John Young, of Hanover Township, 149 acres of land that he bought, May 10 1754, from John Kirkbride, of the Falls, County Bucks, Province of Pennsylvania. A note appended to the Deed designates Morgan and John as blacksmiths. (Book A, p. 106). A recording of the purchase in 1754 has not been found. John was the eldest son of Morgan. Morgan's name disappears from the Mendham tax list in 1786. (State Library, Trenton, N. J.)

Morgan and his son John were blacksmith-farmers. Blacksmithing in colonial N. J. was a widely practiced craft because in the hills of Morris County were locked vast quantities of rich iron ore. Mining this ore and welding the iron was big business. It was so big that it made this region the most industrial sector of the country. Even today, the mines are being worked for the benefit of the war program. The blacksmith of colonial days was a smith who worked in black metal and made various utensils, parts of machines, guns etc. Nathaniel Young, grandson of Morgan, and first white settler north of Mt. Vernon, in what is today Knox County, Ohio, was also a blacksmith-farmer. His specialty was axes. To the Indians, he became the "Axe-man." (A. B. Norton, "Hist. of Knox County, O. 1779-1862). The rapid prosperity of the Quaker colony in N. J. is accounted for by the fact that a majority of the Quakers were Master craftsmen. These farmers used their farms as a source of food supply but they expected their craft to be the chief source of money revenue.

The following quotation from two New York City newspapers, dated Aug. 28 1778, describe Morgan's land, and suggest that he may have been in the hotel business: (See Record #3)

"To be sold, by public vendue, in three months from date, or at private sale any time before, 150 acres of good land, situate in Mendham, Morris County, whereon the subscriber now lives, where a public house has been kept, with two good frame houses and kitchens adjoining the same, and good cellars under both, with two good frame barns, three very good orchards, about 30 acres of good meadow, and more may easily be made. The above premises is well watered and timbered. It being so well known, there needs no particularizing. Conditions will be made known and due attendance will be given by me. Signed: Morgan Young." (N. J. Archives, Newspaper Extracts, Vol. 2, 1779, p. 430). See Record #319.

Morgan Young served his country in the Revolutionary war as a Wagon-master. (Stryker, "Jerseymen in the Revolution," p. 855). The following record in the office of the Adjutant General, Trenton, N. J. may refer to our progenitor or to his nephew, Morgan, son of Robert Young: (Morgan, jr. and Morgan, son of Thomas Young received pensions as privates) "Young, Morgan. Sergeant. Received Certificate #134 and #902, dated May 3 1784, for 3 Pounds, 2 Shillings and 8 Pence depreciation of his Continental pay for services as Sergeant in the Morris County Militia."

Morgan married, May 25 1741, Elizabeth Mills of Long Island, N. Y. The Mills family settled at Southold, L. I. in 1660. Timothy and Samuel, sons of Samuel Mills of Long Island, moved to Morris County, N. J. in 1740, and a daughter of Samuel married Isaac Drake, Jan. 27 1740. Elizabeth Mills may have been another daughter of Samuel. She was born in 1720. The children of Morgan and Elizabeth, all born in Morris County, N. J., were: (Family records of William, son of Morgan)

3. i. William, b. March 16 1742
4. ii. Charity, b. Sept. 24 1744
5. iii. Anne, b. Sept. 25 1747
X 6. iv. John, b. Nov. 30 1750
7. v. James, b. Apr. 19 1754
8. vi. Robert, b. Feb. 13 1756
9. vii. Morgan, b. Jan. 3 1762

3 WILLIAM YOUNG

Eldest child of Morgan and Elizabeth Mills Young, born, March 16 1742, some twelve years before his father bought land in that part of Mendham which became Randolph Township, Morris County, N. J., died, July 21 1819, aged 77 years. He left vital statistics of the family which include the marriage and death dates of his parents, and the names and birth dates of his brothers and sisters but he failed to locate any of the events. The records of William were published in the genealogical column of the Newark, N. J. Evening News, #5742, June 23 1917. The graves of William and his wife have not been found. Their birth and death dates appear on the family monument at Newton, N. J. but there are no headstones for them as there are for other members of the family who are known to be buried here.

A voucher found amongst the papers of William showed that he paid a "Congress tax," Dec. 20 1775, in the township of Mendham, Morris County, N. J. The County records reveal that he, with Thomas Carrel and Andrew Briant, witnessed the will of Jonathan Oliver, in 1777, and his name follows that of his father on the Ratables for Mendham for 1778, (State Lib., Trenton, N. J.). On the tax list for 1779 he has 'Esquire' after his name. William perhaps kept the public house of which his father spoke when he advertised his property as for sale. (Record #2). This seems indicated by the following advertisement dated at Woodbridge, N. J., April 8 1778: "Any person finding a pocket-book and giving information to James Fitz-Randolph, inn-keeper at Short Hills, or to Edward Fitz-Randolph in Woodbridge, or to William Young, inn-keeper near Succasunny Plain, so that the owner can have it again, shall be entitled to twenty dollars reward by me." Signed: Robert Miller.

William Young moved his family, about 1790, to Wantage Township, Sussex County, N. J. where he bought a farm adjoining that of Jacob DeWitt. (Record #4). In 1796 William was Executor of the estate of Wm. Jones, sr. whose will was witnessed by Jacob DeWitt and Elizabeth Crane, in Wantage. The inventory was made by William Mitchell. Documents such as this are cited not merely to locate our subject but also because they contain the names of families allied by marriage to the Youngs, and referred to elsewhere in the records. A voucher in the hands of the compiler shows that William was a cooper-farmer and that he was practicing his trade in Wantage Township, Feb. 16 1814. The County records at Newton, N. J. indicate that he and his wife Miriam sold their Wantage farm, May 19 1815.

James and Morgan Young, sons of Morgan, sr. and Thomas respectively, of Mendham, N. J., were granted pensions for services as privates during the Revolution. Each in his pension application stated that he had served under a Captain William Young. The military files, acknowledged to be incomplete, show no record of a Captain Wm. Young. However, the files at Trenton, N. J. show an Ensign Wm. Young, who was promoted to be Lieutenant, and it is further stated that Lt. Wm. Young commanded, part time, Capt. Ezekiel Crane's Company. This temporary captain doubtless was the officer to whom James and Morgan referred, and he may have been the subject of this record. This Lt. Wm. Young was appointed, Oct. 10 1777, for recruiting for the Continental Line, to rendezvous at Morristown, by a Committee of the Council and Assembly.

William Young married, Feb. 2 1764, Miriam (Drake) Throckmorton, (died, Nov. 24 1824, aged 89 yrs. 4 mos.), widow of Thomas Throckmorton, sr. of Roxbury, N. J. (Will proved 3 May 1763). Miriam was a sister of Jacob and Abraham Drake who married, respectively, Charity and Anne Young, sisters of William. She was also a sister of Catherine Drake Leforge. (Catherine's will, Dec. 4 1790). Hercules Young, uncle of our subject, helped make the inventory of the estate of Thos. Throckmorton, son of Job and Frances (? Stout) Throckmorton, of Shrewsbury, N. Y. The children of William and Miriam Young:

10. i. Elizabeth, b. Nov. 5 1764
11. ii. Charity, b. Apr. 5 1766
12. iii. "Caty," b. Aug. 15 1769
 iv. Miriam, b. Nov. 29 1771
 v. Ann, b. Sept. 16 1773, d. Jan. 11 1774
 vi. Mary, b. Nov. 8 1774
 vii. Sarah, b. Feb. 7, 1777, d. March 19, 1777
 viii. William, b. Aug. 25 1778, d. March 16 1785
13. ix. Robert, b. Dec. 12 1781

4 CHARITY YOUNG

born, Sept. 24 1774, in that part of Roxbury which became Mendham Township, Morris County, N. J., died Oct. 26 1776, and was buried beside her husband in the Presbyterian Churchyard at Succasunna, N. J. The inscription on her gravestone reads: "To the Memory of Mrs. Charity Young, Relict of Jacob Drake, Esq., Who departed this life, 26 Oct. 1776, Age 32 years." Charity married Col. Jacob Drake^{5} (Abraham^{4}) b. Apr. 21 1732, at Piscataway, N. J., d. Sept. 18 1823. Abraham Drake, brother of Jacob, md. Anne Young, sister of Charity. The sisters were legatees of John Young, record #1. William Young, brother of Charity and Anne, md. Miriam, sister of Jacob and Abraham Drake. After the death of Charity, Col. Drake md., Dec. 13 1781, Esther Dickerson (b. Apr. 2 1757, d. Oct. 13 1819), widow of George King, and daughter of Peter Dickerson. The children of Jacob and Esther were: Clarissa H. Woodruff, Jacob B., George King, Silas, Peter D., and Eliza Drake. They lived at Drakeville, now Ledgewood, N. J. Jacob and Charity Young had one child, Rachel, who md., Oct. 10 1782, Samuel Howell (d. Dec. 8 1829), son of Charles whose will, proved Aug. 9 1759, at Morristown, N. J., contains family names allied by marriage to different branches of our Young family: Timothy Mills (Record #2), Daniel Losey, Samuel Bayles, John Lindsley, and Matthew Lum. The children of Samuel and Rachel Howell are listed by T. F. Chambers in his "Early Germans and Other Early Settlers in New Jersey," p. 425. Mr. Chambers says that Abigail Young, unidentified, bought the Drake mill property at Drakeville in 1819.

5 ANNE YOUNG

The inscription on her gravestone in the Presbyterian Churchyard at Succasunna, N. J. reads: "In memory of Anne, wife of Abraham Drake deceased, who departed this life, July 18 1809, Age 62 years. 9 mo. 18

days." Anne was born Sept. 25 1747. (Record #3). Anne married, March 17 1763, Abraham[5] Drake (b. March 21 1730, Sarah Rude Bible, d. Feb. 7 1806) son of Abraham.[4] The children of Abraham and Anne, named in the former's will, were: Wm. Y. Drake, said to have gone to Illinois; Morgan, d. Nov. 13 1806, age 41 yrs. 10 mos. 2 days; Elizabeth who md. 1st. Abraham Slack, and 2nd. a Mr. Easton; Jacob, d. Nov. 27 1843, age 74 years; and Catherine Drake.

6 JOHN YOUNG

was born, Nov. 30, 1750 (Record #3), the year when his father registered his "Earmarks" in the one year old Mendham Township, Morris County, N. J. He was a nephew and legatee of John Young, Record #1, and may have been named for him. John died, Feb. 16 1826, and was buried in Wayne Township Cemetery, Knox County, Ohio (on Highway #95, near Fredericktown) where his wife Hannah Mitchell joined him two years later. An account of the death of John was told the writer in 1942 at Albert Lee, Minn. by Mrs. Margaret Young (Geo. A.) King. She said, "My father Bonar Young who was born near Fredericktown, O. told me that when he was a young boy his father, Ebenezer Pierson Young, bought a farm in what is now Troy Township (7th Range), Richland County, O. From their farm they used to haul produce to Lake Erie (Sandusky) to exchange it for supplies needed at home. One day when David had gone to the lake, his grandparents, John and Hannah Young, arrived at the farm for a few hours visit with their son and family. Late afternoon came and the grandparents were about to start back home in their buggy when David drove into the yard. "Ellzy" persuaded his parents to stay for supper and hear the news from Sandusky. Sarah (wife of Ellzy) prepared the meal and they sat down to eat. After the Blessing had been asked, John took up his cup of coffee and the cup fell from his hand, and he started to fall to the floor but Ellzy caught him. He had suffered a stroke, and he died without regaining consciousness." "John," Mrs. King continued, "was very popular with the Indians. He used to make a variety of tools for them. When it came time to move the Sandusky Indians to Indiana, the Indians who were very suspicious about the moving, said that they would go provided John Young went with them. John went and remained with them for about two years."

Little is known of John's life in New Jersey. It has been shown under Morgan's record (#3) that John bought his father's Mendham farm in 1784, and in the Deed gave his residence as in Hanover township. John sold his Hanover land April 1 1788. A witness to the Deed was Wm.

Mitchell, brother of John's wife. John and his wife Hanah, together with his son Nathaniel M. Young and his wife Mary, sold, March 17 1798, the Mendham property that John had bought from his father (Bk. F, p. 246, Morristown, N. J.). It was not long after this that John moved his family to Fallowfield township, Washington County, Pa. and settled near his brother Morgan and near his wife's mother, Abigail (Harris) Mitchell who with her brothers had come to Washington County in 1787 (Census 1790).

John and his son Nathaniel were involved in 1794 in an unhappy land dispute the result of which has not been found. There was recorded Dec. 30 1810, in the Deed records, at Mt. Vernon, O., the following "Agreement" between John Young, of Mendham, N. J., and Nathaniel Mitchell Young, of the same place, which bound them to Nathaniel Shotwell for 70 Pounds Sterling with which sum they wish to sue James Young, jr. to recover land which John Young claims to own and on which James is living. The witnesses to the Agreement were Elizabeth (Mitchell) Kent, sister of John's wife, and Benjamin Lyon (Record 9). The relationship between Benjamin and Asher Lyon who married Jean Young has not been found. John Kent, father of John, husband of Elizabeth Mitchell, moved from Ohio to Whiteside County, Ill. in 1839 (Bents, Hist. Whiteside Co., Ill.).

John Young, jr., Aaron Jackson, James Beebe and wife, Daniel Lyon and wife, Daniel Beers and wife were original members of the Salem M.E. Church that was organized in the Jersey Settlement in 1830.

John Young served as a private and a corporal in the Revolution under Capt. Josiah Hall of the Eastern N. J. Battalion, Morris County Militia (J. P. Crayon's, Rockaway Records). John's name appears in the classing of companies, May 1788, in the 14th class, and is again on the list of those who served in Jan. 1781, against the revolt of the Penn Line Troops (Adjutant General's Office, Trenton, N. J.).

John married, Nov. 30 1768, in Morris County, N. J., Hannah Mitchell, b. Aug. 26 1753, d. Sept. 21 1828, near Fredericktown, O. and was buried in Wayne Township cemetery. Hannah was a daughter of Nathaniel and Abigail (Harris) Mitchell. Nathaniel Mitchell (1728-1773) was a son of Jacob and Hannah Halstead Mitchell, and a grandson of James and Mary Mitchell who came to America from Scotland about 1683. Hannah Halstead was a daughter of Timothy and Abigail, and a granddaughter of Timothy and Hannah (Williams) Halstead. William Mitchell (d. Aug. 12 1848, age 83, buried at Mt. Vernon, O.), brother of Hannah, married, Nov. 4 1789, Phebe Southard (d. Feb. 24 1861, age 91). Three children of William and Phebe Southard Mitchell, Mary, Naomi and Silas, married, respectively, Aaron, James L., and Elizabeth Young, grandchildren of our subject. (Mrs. Lena (Mitchell) Welker, Howard, O.). The children of John and Hannah Young:

14. i. Nathaniel Mitchell, b. Mar. 31 1770
X 15. ii. Jacob, b. Nov. 27 1774
16. iii. Mary, b. Oct. 26 1777
17. iv. John, jr., b. May 17 1785
18. v. Aaron, b. Nov. 14 1788
19. vi. Hannah, b. July 30 1791
vii. Elizabeth, b. Jan. 28 1795, d. Apr. 1813
20. viii. Ebenezer Pierson, b. May 5 1798, called "Ellzy"

7 JAMES YOUNG

son of Morgan and Elizabeth Mills Young was born, April 19 1754, in that part of Mendham which in 1805 became Randolph Township, Morris County, N. J. (Rec. 3). James and his brother William were two of Morgan's children who were not legatees of their uncle (Rec. 1). James gave his father and Andrew Bryant (?his father-in-law, record 8) a mortgage, April 24 1786, on 85 acres of land (County records, Morristown, N. J.). This was the year that Morgan Young sold his farm to his son John and this may be the land that was in dispute in 1794, two years after the death of Morgan (Rec. 6). No other information about James has been verified. There were at least three with the name of James Young in Mendham when our James was living there. A James Young, jr. whose name is on the Tax List of Mendham for 1778 (State Lib., Trenton, N. J.) between the names of William and Morgan Young, jr. perhaps was the son of Robert Young, brother of Morgan, sr. A not infrequent use of the term 'junior' was to distinguish two persons of the same name living near each other. This James Young, jr. registered his 'earmarks' at Mendham in 1759.

A James Young who perhaps was the son of Morgan applied from Randolph township, Morris Co. N. J. May 21 1833, for a pension for service during the Revolution, giving his age as 79 years. This fixes his birth in the year that James, son of Morgan was born, and locates him in 1833 where he is the sole James Young on record. (Gen'l. Accounting Office, Washington, D. C., Certificate #9984, N. J. Agency). No descendant of James has been found to verify our guess. In his pension papers, James said that he had served under a Capt. Robert Young (unidentified in the military files) and also that he was living near a Robert Young with whom he had served but who was not Capt. Robert Young. There were 3 Robert Youngs in our Young family: Robert, sr., and his son Robert, jr., and

Robert, son of Morgan. To which of the two Roberts James referred cannot be decided. Capt. Robert Young may have been his cousin, son of Robert, sr.

James Young was granted his pension. He died, a widower, June 30 1836, in Randolph township, Morris Co., N. J. and the final pension payment was made on behalf of his children Nov. 11 1842. The first three of his children in the list that follows died before March 22 1842:—Charity Lanning, Daniel Young, Lois Cowin, Eunice, Abraham, Silvamer, Ann Young, Rachel Lewis and Elizabeth Chapman, the latter living "in the lake district" (Pension papers, Nat'l. Archives, Washington, D. C.).

A James Young, unidentified, who may have been a member of our Young family, applied for a pension for service in a N. J. Company as a Teamster from Lackawanock township, Mercer Co., Pa., Sept. 1 1832, stating that he was 72 years old. He died, Aug. 6 1841, leaving a widow, Prudence Young, who said that the family had moved in 1798 from Washington Co., Pa. to Mercer Co. (Nat'l. Archives, Washington, D. C.). The U. S. Census for 1800 shows this James, his wife and six children, in Washington Co. The Census also lists Morgan Young and other members of our family in the same county.

8 ROBERT YOUNG

was, like his father and brother John, a blacksmith-farmer and a Quaker. He was born, Feb. 13 1756, and died, Jan. 29 1840, in Randolph Township, Morris County, N. J. (Record #3; Pension papers, Nat'l. Archives, Washington, D. C.). He left a widow Sarah Young to whom the arrears of his pension were paid, Oct. 22 1840, through her attorney, Lewis Condit. John Young, record #1, identifies him as a son of Morgan and Elizabeth Young, and makes him a legatee. Robert is identified in the military files at Trenton, N. J. by this notation: "Born 1756. Private in Morris County Militia under Capt. Robert Young (unidentified); also served in the 1st Regiment, Somerset County Militia Monthly Tours from 1776 until the end of the war. Resident of Mendham. Resided in Randolph Township, Morris County, July 30 1832. A son of Morgan."

Robert applied for a pension for services during the Revolution, March 29 1829, and said that his wife was 63 years old and infirm, that his daughter, Malinda, was single, 18 years of age, and was keeping house for his wife and himself; he was a cripple due to a bayonet wound in his thigh received at the Battle of Stony Point; that he had not owned land since 1814 and was living on a lot of 16 acres of mountain land belonging to his son Elias Briant Young. The tax list for Mendham for 1805 shows Robert holding

16 acres of land (State Lib., Trenton, N. J.), and the County Records reveal that Robert and Sarah Young sold, Apr. 20 1806, their land in Randolph to Elias and Jacob Briant. In his pension papers, Robert enumerated his war services thus: "enlisted in the Fall of 1775 at Succasunna, for one year, in the Company of Capt. Mitchell, 1st N. J. Regiment, and after service in N. Y. State was stationed in 1776 at Flatbush, L. I., was in the Mud Rounds through N. J. to Elizabethtown; re-enlisted for a second year taking the place of Robert Logan in Capt. Patterson's Company, 3rd N. J. Regiment, Col. Dayton, Continental Establishment; discharged at Valley Forge by General Washington, 1779; was in the battles of Long Island, White Plains, Trenton, Princeton, Germantown, Brandywine and Monmouth; assisted in carrying off the field General Lafayette at Brandywine; after the regular service, did Monthly Tours under Capt. Freylinghausen; before the war was in the Militia under Capt. Bigelow and Col. Munson." Robert also stated that their family had consisted of 11 sons and 5 daughters, of whom 4 sons and 2 daughters were dead in 1829. The names of these children with their birth dates and that of their mother are given here through the generosity of Mrs. Mattie Briant Parsons (Eugene J.) Cooper, of Dover, N. J., who has also supplied from her family Bible and records valuable information about our allied Parsons and Dalrymple families.

Robert Young married Sarah Briant, b. Jan. 17, 1767, dau. of Andrew and Rachel (Meeker) Briant of Randolph Township, Morris County, N. J. The children of Robert and Sarah:

i. Samuel, b. Feb. 13 1785

ii. William, b. June 1 1786, perhaps md. Nov. 15 1807 Esther Bruen, of Lyons Farm, and for whom a child of Robert was named.

21. iii. James, b. May 19 1788

iv. Robert, jr., b. Apr. 8 1790

22. v. Elias B., b. Sept. 13, 1791

vi. John, b. Oct. 19, 1793

23. vii. Jacob, b. Aug. 5 1796

viii. Andrew, b. Feb. 26 1797

24. ix. Simeon, b. Sept. 29 1798

x. Elizabeth, b. March 8 1801

xi. Stephen, b. Feb. 15 1803

xii. Charles, b. Sept. 25 1804, md.? Sarah Abner, Randolph, Oct. 1826 (N. J. Gen. Mag.)

xiii. Mahala, b. July 9 1807, d. Apr. 20 1891, age 83; widow of Jabez Beers, b. July 9 1807, d. Jan. 1858, age 54, son of Joseph (Hist. of 1st Presby. Church, Morristown, N. J. p. 279). Joseph was a bro. of Daniel Beers, Rec. 15.

xiv. Malinda, b. June 24, 1808, md. a Mr. Kennedy

25. xv. Esther Bruen, b. March 27 1810

THE BRYANT AND YOUNG FAMILIES

The descendants of Pieter Corneliss Breyandt(Briant, Bryant) who came to America from Holland in 1690 and of Morgan Young were often allied by marriage or by business in the early days of New Jersey and Ohio. The marriage of Robert Young and Sarah Bryant probably was the first of these alliances.

Andrew (1737-1821) and Rachel (Meeker) Briant (1744-1829), parents of Sarah, moved in 1780 from Springfield, N. J. to Randolph Township, Morris County, N. J. where Morgan Young and family were settled. Robert Young and Sarah Bryant met, married, and their first child Samuel was born in 1785. The names of 15 of their 16 children were supplied from the records of Mrs. Cooper through her daughter, Miss Caroline Parsons Cooper, of Dover, N. J. Miss Cooper is a great grandchild of Robert (1805-1864) and Esther Bruen (Young) Parsons and a great[2] grandchild of John (1762-1835, brother of Sarah of this record) Bryant who married Mary Ayres.

The records at Morristown, N. J. show that Andrew Briant and Morgan Young, the two fathers-in-law, in 1786, took together a mortgage from James, son of Morgan. Did James Young (Record 7) marry a daughter of Andrew Briant, as did his brother Robert?

Simeon (1710-1784) and Hannah (Searing) Briant (1718-1785), great[3] grandparents of Miss Lena Briant (b. 1860) of New York City, and grandparents of our Sarah, had two sons, Elias and Jacob who, in 1803 and again in 1806, purchased land in Randolph, Morris County, N. J. from Robert and Sarah Bryant with Samuel and Simeon Bryant as witnesses to the Deeds. Simeon and Hannah also had a son James who after service in the Revolution moved his family to western Pennsylvania. This James perhaps was the father of James (b. 1754) who married Anna Lewis (1774-1828) whose gravestone in Wayne Cemetery, Fredericktown, O. reads: "Anna, Consort of James Bryant, Died 1828." Anna, daughter of James (1747-1819) and Abigail Douglass Lewis (1747-1830), and granddaughter of Edward (from Wales about 1717, "Lewisiana," Vol. 3, p. 184, N. Y. Pub. Lib.) and Sarah Morris (daughter of Daniel, son of Stephen) was a sister of Mary Lewis who married Nathaniel Mitchell Young. N. M. Young was son-in-law of James Lewis and brother-in-law of James Bryant.

Two of the children of James and Anna Bryant were William H.

(1795-1877) who witnessed the will of N. M. Young in 1828, and Samuel, b. 1799. William H. Bryant md. 1st. Elizabeth Norton. They had three children all of whom moved to Illinois; Anna, b. 1819; James, b. 1821; and William, b. 1830. Wm. H. Bryant married 2nd. Maria McGinis (1810-1891) and is buried beside her in Wayne Cemetery, Fredericktown, O. They had three children: David M., b. 1832; Jacob Mitchell b. 1837, and Rebecca Bryant, b. 1839. David M. Bryant married, 1st. Abigail Struble, and 2nd. Abigail Foote. William Preston Bryant (1874-1937), son of Jacob M., married Ada Taylor (b. 1874), now living in Fredericktown, O. Their son William Paul Bryant and his family are living on the old homestead established in 1804 near Fredericktown.

Abraham Bryant also settled near Fredericktown, O. He bought Nov. 25 1805, a lot in the 17th Range, 7th Township and 2nd Quarter from Nathaniel M. Young (Lancaster, O. records, Bk. F. p. 327).

David Bryant, wife Catherine Wooley (Newark Evening News, Jan. 31 1903) was in Washington County, Pa. in 1790 (Census report). He or his son David bought land near Fredericktown, O. from William and Jacob Mitchell, brothers of Hannah, wife of John Young, also members of this Jersey Settlement in Ohio. Samuel Bryant (b. 1790), son of David, sr. married in Indiana for his third wife a widow, Sally (Davis) Young, first husband unidentified. Samuel spent his last years in Ohio with his step-son John Young. A daughter of Samuel and his second wife, Joanna Bryant married Edward R. Beebe whose relationship to John Beebe, son-in-law of N. M. Young (record 14) has not been established.

Ethlinda Bryant md., March 22 1821, Edward Young (Chillicothe, O. records). Edward perhaps was the son of Edward Young whose marriage to Rachel Miller in 1803 is recorded at Lancaster, O. (Bk. A. 154). Edward and Ethlon sold to their son Wilson a piece of land, Feb. 19 1957, with A. H. Bryant as witness. Edward bought land, July 19 1836, from Nancy Briant, and from Andrew Lemmons (? Timmons) and Jane Briant Lemmons, heirs of John Briant(Chillicothe, records).

Stephen C. Bryant in 1862 witnessed the will of Silas Young (Morristown, N. J. records).

9 MORGAN YOUNG, JR.

was one of four relatives with the same name who lived near each other in Morris County, N. J. in 1774 when John Young (Rec. #1) wrote his will. John Young distinguishes our subject in these words: "to John, Robert and Morgan Young, sons of Morgan," and makes him one of his legatees. In the will, the mother of Morgan, jr. is spoken of as "Elizabeth, the wife of Morgan."

Morgan Young, jr. was born, Jan. 3, 1762, in Mendham (now Randolph) Township, Morris County, N. J. (Rec. 3). In his application for a pension for services during the Revolution, Morgan confirmed the year of his birth, 1762, as given by his brother William, and added the place of birth. He also said that he re-enlisted for service in 1778 "when about 16 years of age." Mrs. Lydia (Wade) Young (1805-1897), wife of Henry, son of Morgan, jr., in 1892, in a letter to her nephew Delevan Young, of Lagrange, Ind., speaking of the family wrote that Morgan was born, Jan. 4 1762, that he was, at first, during the war a water-boy for General Washington and his officers when but 14 years old, and that when winter came Morgan was sent home because of his scanty clothing, and that upon his arrival home, his mother took cloth from the loom, made him clothes and sent him back to the army. (Rec. #34). Morgan died in the home of his son Losey (Rec. 35), on Pretty Prairie, Lagrange, Ind. and was buried in Pretty Prairie cemetery where memorial stones with the following inscriptions mark the graves of his wife and himself:

MORGAN YOUNG
Died
Jan. 21 1852
In his 97th year
A Revolutioneer
Formerly of New Jersey

JANE
Wife of Morgan Young
Died
Nov. 25 1847
In her 90th year
"Peace be unto us"

Morgan's age on the gravestone is wrong. His own word in his pension application, dated at Norwalk, O., Feb. 27 1832, shows this. (Nat'l. Archives, Washington, D. C.). That Morgan Young of Lagrange, Ind. was Morgan, jr. was proven to the compiler by Mrs. Diantha (Miller) Lilly (1857-1943) in her home at Sturgis, Mich. in 1941. Mrs. Lilly was the daughter of Daniel Miller who was raised in that part of Adams County, O. that is now Highland County, and who married Elizabeth Young (1827-1874), daughter of Losey, in whose home Morgan died. The Millers, like the Youngs, came from N. J. to Ohio where they were neighbors. A relationship between Daniel Miller and Adam Miller who married Mary Young, sister of Morgan, sr. has not been established. The family records of Mrs. Lilly also showed that her grandfather Losey Young was a cousin of Simeon (Rec. #24), son of Robert Young (Rec. #8). Mrs. Lilly gave the writer a table scraf that was made by Jane Young from flax that had been grown on their farm on Pretty Prairie.

PRINCIPAL LAND SUBDIVISIONS IMPOSED ON PRESENT MAP OF OHIO

Reproduced by permission of the Hon. J. T. Ferguson,
Auditor of the State of Ohio.

Morgan first appears in a public document on the Tax List for Mendham, Morris County, N. J., in 1778. (State Lib., Trenton, N. J.) The names Morgan, William, James, jr., and Morgan jr. (the last two without acreage) appear together and in this order which may indicate that they were of one household and that the last three were sons of Morgan. James was perhaps called "jr." to distinguish him from his neighbor and cousin James, son of Robert Young. See Record 7. The next official appearance of Morgan is in the county records at Morristown, N. J. On Aug. 29 1788, James and Sarah Young sold to Stephen Jackson land on the Rockaway river that was conveyed to James, Oct. 13 1785, by Morgan Young, jr., with Johnathan Young, son of James, as a witness to the sale. Rec. 314.

Morgan moved his family from New Jersey to Fallowfield Township, Washington County, Pa. between the birth of his son Noah in 1788 and the taking of the first U. S. Census in 1790. This census places his family in Washington County, and shows it to have consisted of father, mother, one son and two daughters. In his pension application Morgan said that "several years after the war, I moved to Red Stone Old Fort (now Brownsville), Pa. where I lived about 18 years." His name with the title Ensign appears on a general return of an election of officers of the militia for the First Washington Brigade, Dec. 5 1793. (Penn. Archives, 6th series, Vol. 4, page 326). Morgan was not the first of our Youngs and their allied families to reach Fallowfield in Washington County, Pa. The records of Hercules, Silas and John (was he the founder of Youngstown, O.?) Young will show that they were there in 1784 (P.R.P. Vol. 23, State Lib., Harrisburg, Pa.). Mrs. Abigail Harris (Nathaniel) Mitchell, mother-in-law of John Young, Rec. #6, reached Washington County, Pa. in 1787. The 1790 Census also lists some of the children of Margaret Young (Daniel) Carrel, sister of Morgan, in Washington County, Pa. (Rec. 319)

Morgan was living in Washington County, Pa. in 1800 (U. S. Census) and his family consisted of his wife, two boys and one girl under ten, and one boy and two girls between ten and sixteen years old. He moved his family to near West Union, Ohio about 1807. In a "List of Resident-Proprietors of Adams County, O. in 1810" (State Lib., Columbus, O.), Morgan is shown as owning and living on 150 of the 1100 acres of land originally granted to Nathaniel Massie who was the first to survey this part of the Northwest Territory, which became in 1784 the Virginia Military Lands. Adams County was created from this military land in 1797 and then consisted of what are now 8 counties and parts of 12 others. The Deed by which Morgan purchased this land was not recorded at West Union, O. until Sept. 27 1814 (Bk. 8, Deed 257). It reads: "Henry Spears and Rebecca, his wife, of Fallowfield Township, Washington County,

Ohio County Boundaries

Pa., sell 150 acres of land on Brush Creek, Adams County, O., to Morgan Young, of Green Township, Adams County, O., from land that was patented from Washington, D. C. Witnesses: Thos. Carron (? Carroll) and James Young." See Rec. 7. Morgan remained on his Brush Creek property until about 1827. Unclaimed letters for Morgan, Henry and Uriah Young were advertised, Jan. 1st and 28th 1828, in the "Village Register" of West Union, O., which seems to indicate that the family moved to northern Ohio before the farm was sold, Aug. 6 1829, to Hosea Moore. Mitchell Morrison Young (1854-1942) of near West Union, Ohio, told the compiler in 1941 that he was living on Morgan Young's land and drinking water from a well that was dug by Morgan's sons. He also said that the farm had not been out of the name of a Young except for the brief period that Hosea Moore owned it.

Morgan bought, Oct. 29 1829, from Daniel A. Green, a farm in Lyme Township, Huron County, O., near where his son Noah had been living for some years. He did not remain long in Huron County. He sold his land there, Jan. 22 1831, in equal parts, to his sons Noah and Henry, each paying $160.00 for his share (Deed Bk. 6, p. 472, Norwalk, O.). While living in Lyme Township Morgan applied for his pension. About 1835 he and his wife moved to near Lagrange, Ind. to be near their youngest child, Losey. In order to receive the arrears of his pension in Indiana, Morgan certified, Sept. 30 1851, that he had been living for 16 years in Greenfield Township, Lagrange County, Ind. and that previously he had lived in Sandusky (earlier Huron) County, O. (Gen'l. Acct. Office, Washington, D. C.)

Morgan's service during the Revolution introduces again the mysterious Capt. Robert Young who, at times, commanded for Capt. Crane. Morgan lists his services as: "One Monthly Tour in 1776 with the N. J. Troops in Capt. Ezekiel Crane's Company, Col. Stark's Regiment; nine months in Capt. Crane's and Capt. Robt. Young's Companies; three months in guarding prisoners at Morristown, N. J.; in 1778, having re-enlisted, he served three months under Capt. Robt. Young; was nine months at Elizabethtown and Morristown under Capt. Robt. Young during the Revolt of the Penn. Line Troops; during the winter of 1780, he was two weeks with Gen'l. Stirling on Staten Island; in 1781 he served three months under Capt. Robt. Young. He was in the Battles of Hackensack, Springfield, Elizabethtown, New Brunswick, Spottswood and Minissink on the Delaware; he was on the expedition against the British the hard winter of 1779-80 and went over the ice; he was discharged by General Winds." His pension was $73.88 annually.

Morgan Young, jr. married, near the end of the Revolution, Jane

Losey, (b. 1758, Gravestone record), daughter of John and Jane Losey, of Mendham, N. J. This marriage perhaps was not the first such alliance between the two families. It does not seem a sufficient explanation for the fact that John Young (Rec. #1) left legacies to five of John Losey's children and to three of his grand children. John Young also sold his plantation on the Rockaway river to James Puff and John Losey, two children of John Losey, sr. Perhaps Jane, wife of John Losey, sr. was his second wife and a sister of John Young. John Losey, in his will (made June 4 1765, probated, July 2 1765, State files, Trenton, N. J.), mentioned his wife Jane as living, and gave the names of his children. He noted that Elizabeth and Jane were the youngest daughters and that Philip and Jane were under age. One of the witnesses to the will was James, son of Robert Young whose farm adjoined that of John Losey. The eldest child of John Losey, James Puff, was born in 1718 (d. Jan. 10, 1809, age 90 yrs. 7 mos., Rockaway Records), forty years before Jane (Morgan Young) was born. John Losey may have married twice. James Puff Losey married when he was 48 yrs. old, 1766, Hannah Burwell, born 1750 (Morristown, N. J. records). The Loseys were of Dutch origin, and the middle name of James suggests that there was a family alliance with Jurgen and Maria Puff whose daughter Elizabeth was born and baptized in 1722 (Luth. Ch. on the Raritans records). This Elizabeth Puff perhaps was the Elizabeth "Buff" who married, Apr. 13 1743, David Moor (Moore). (Morristown, N. J. records).

The names of the children of Morgan and Jane Young are from the family Bible of Losey Young, (their youngest child), owned in 1940 by Mrs. Nellie (Atfield) Walton, of Wakita, Okla. The order of birth is somewhat uncertain.

26. i. Susannah, eldest child
27. ii. Sallie,
28. iii. Noah, b. April 1788
29. iv. Jane,
30. v. Abraham,
31. vi. John,
32. vii. George,
33. viii. Moses, b. May 11 1802
34. ix. Henry, b. Feb. 21 1805
35. x. Losey, b. Feb. 9 1809

10 ELIZABETH YOUNG

born, Nov. 5 1764, in Roxbury Township, Morris County, N. J., married there, Dec. 23 1782, Aaron Stark, jr. They probably were buried in the Stark Burying Grounds, Flanders, Morris County, N. J. Their children:

i. Aaron, 3rd. b. Oct. 10 1783
ii. Miriam, b. Sept. 24 1785
iii. Amos, b. Apr. 16 1789, d. March 22 1796
iv. William, b. July 18 1791
v. Amy, b. Dec. 11 1793
vi. Elizabeth, b. Sept. 15 1796
vii. John, b. Sept. 5 1798

11 CHARITY YOUNG

born, Apr. 5 1766, died, Jan. 19 1814, and was buried near her husband in Old Clove cemetery, Wantage Township, Sussex County, N. J. (N. J. Gen. Mag. Vol. 2, #2). She md. Aug. 30 1792, Jacob[5] DeWitt who died, May 24 1862, age 87 yrs. 8 mos. 24 days. The will of Jacob[4] DeWitt who bought his farm in Sussex County, Oct. 10 1761, from the East Jersey Proprietors, and which he gave to his sons in 1802, was witnessed by John Wintermoot (Wintermute) and Benjamin Middaugh, families allied with the Youngs. Samuel, a son of Jacob[4] DeWitt, emigrated west. Jacob and Charity had one child, Miriam, b. Apr. 6 1793. The information of William Young (Rec. #3) about his daughter Charity is confused. She seems to have md. twice. Her first husband probably was John Darby (Darbe) by whom she had a son, John Darby, jr., b. Sept. 30 1790. (James P. Read, N. J. Gen. Soc.).

John DeWitt (d. March 15 1866) and his wife Mary (Washer) DeWitt (d. Aug. 22 1864, age 81 yrs. 7 mos. 2 days) are buried in Rivercliff cemetery, Mt. Gilead, O. They moved in 1818 from Sussex County, N. J. to Knox County, O. where they became members of the Jersey Settlement in Ohio. A son, John V. (b. Jan. 23 1810) md. in 1835 Jane Dalrymple, daughter of John and Jerusha (Sylvester) Dalrymple (Hist. of Morrow County, O. 1880). Another son, Isaac A. (d. July 13 1843, Age 49 yrs. 4 mos. 4 days) and Lenor his wife, are buried at Mt. Gilead.

12 "CATY" YOUNG

born, Aug. 16 1769, married, June 5 1788, Benjamin Middaugh (Maddaugh). Children:

i. Elizabeth, b. Oct. 27 1789
ii. Phebe, b. Nov. 3 1792
iii. John, b. Sept. 7 1794
iv. Salicy, b. Nov. 23 1796
v. Miriam, b. Aug. 3, 1801

13 ROBERT YOUNG

born, Dec. 12 1781, in Morris County, N. J., died July 7 1857. These dates appear on the tombstone of his son Silas, at Newton, N. J. He probably was not buried here. He married, June 1 1801, Sarah Wintermute, b. Jan. 9, 1780, d. Aug. 29 1885, age 75 yrs. 8 mos. Branches of the Wintermute and Young families settled in the Wyoming Valley, Pa. and inter-married there. These records have not been traced. Robert and Sarah had nine children.

36. i. Silas, b. March 10 1802
ii. Harriett, b. June 2 1804, md. ? David G. VanHorn, of Johnsonburg, N. J., Nov. 28 1838.
iii. Phebe, b. Oct. 17 1806
iv. William, b. May 12 1809, md. ? Margaret, dau. of G. B. Drake, and moved to Canada.
v. John D., b. July 12 1811, d. Apr. 22 1814
vi. Miriam, b. Feb. 4 1814
vii. Mary, b. Jan. 30 1816
viii. Coe S., b. Feb. 22 1821
ix. Sarah, b. July 1 1824, md. W. Desieux Hunt.

Mrs. Chas. Munson Young, of Waverly, N. Y., says, 1944, that Robert had two more children: Hulda Shaw and Millicent Wilson, both buried at Waverly, N. Y.

14 NATHANIEL MITCHELL YOUNG

The "Axe-man," as the Indians called him, Founder of the so-called "Jersey Settlement in Ohio," born in Morris County, N. J., was named after his maternal grandfather James Mitchell who came to N. J. about 1683 from Scotland. The inscriptions on the gravestones of Nathaniel and his wife in Wayne Cemetery near Fredericktown, O. read: "In Memory of Nathaniel M. Young, Who died Feb. 18, 1828, Age 57 yrs. 10 mos. 28 days," and "Mary, Consort of Nathaniel M. Young, Who died July 15 1830, Age 58 yrs. 11 mos. 28 days." On the flyleaf of the "Plot Book of

Wayne Cemetery," (located on Highway #95, near Luzerne), it is written: "This cemetery contains the remains of Nathaniel Mitchell Young, the first permanent settler within the present limits of Knox County. He built his cabin within a few hundred yards of his present resting place, in the Spring of 1803. Jacob Young, his brother, and Abraham and Simeon Lyon joined him in the Spring of the following year. Later in the same year Eliphalet and John Lewis, and James Bryant, joined the settlers. Since all these settlers were from N. J., the settlement was known as the Jersey Settlement." The will of Nathaniel Young, dated five days before his death, witnessed by his brother Ellzy Pierson Young and William Bryant, gave his gun and his desk to his son, ten dollars to each of his daughters and the rest of his property to his wife (Filed at Mt. Vernon, O.).

Abraham Lyon (b. 1749 in N. J., died in March 1848 in Allen County, O.) had a son Simeon who moved to Ohio in 1805 ("Lyon Memorial"). Abraham Lyon registered his cattle's earmarks at Mendham, N. J. in 1770, and Simeon did likewise in 1798. Eliphalet Lewis registered his there in 1749. N. M. Young and Mary, his wife, sold to Abraham Lyon of Clinton Township, Fairfield County (later Wayne Township, Knox County) Ohio, Nov. 25 1805, lot 11, in the 14th Range, 7th Township and 2nd Quarter, touching the land of James Lewis (Deed Bk. F, p. 327, Lancaster, O.). The earliest, 1820, Ohio Census shows Abraham, Simeon, Ephraim Lyon, John and William Lewis, and William Bryant as neighbors in the Mt. Vernon Area of Knox County, O. (National Archives, Washington, D. C.). See list of Burials in Wayne Cemetery, page 27.

N. M. Young bought, April 30 1800, from Ebenezer and Mary Drake of Mendham, N. J., 500 acres of wilderness land in what was then the U. S. Military Tract (1796) in the Northwest Territory. This was before the State of Ohio was created, in what was once Adams County, later Ross, still later Fairfield and finally Knox County. The land was originally sold to Benjamin I. Moore, of N. J. The deed by which Mr. Young purchased his land was one of the earliest recorded (May 7 1800) at Chillicothe, first capital of Ohio. It marked the beginning of the Jersey Settlement. On the same day, at the same place and from the same owner that Nathaniel bought his land which was located on the west side of Owl Creek in the present township of Wayne, Knox County, James Lewis, also of Mendham, N. J., bought land adjoining that of Nathaniel, described as in the 7th Township, 14th Range, 2nd Quarter of the U. S. Military Lands. The deed was signed by John Frelinghausen, as Clerk of Somerset County, N. J.

The following deed illustrates how political boundaries were changing in Nathaniel's day: "Nathaniel M. Young and Mary, his wife, of the Township of Clinton, County of Fairfield, O., sold, Nov. 25 1805, to Abraham

Lyon, of the same place, for $200.00, Lot 11 etc." Witnesses to the Deed were: Ziba Jackson and Jacob Young. The records at Mt. Vernon, O. show that Nathaniel sold, Feb. 2 1824, for $2025.00 part of his 500 acres to Noah Young, his cousin and his son-in-law, who was living in Richland County. (Rec. 28).

A. B. Norton, in his "History of Knox County, O., 1862," p. 9, says: "The first white settler north of Mt. Vernon was Nathaniel M. Young, from Pennsylvania, who in 1803, built a cabin on the south fork of the Vernon river, three miles west of Fredericktown. In the winter of 1805-6, Mr. Young, James Lewis and James Bryant caught 41 wolves in steel traps and pens. After many years of solitary residence on the beautiful Ko-Ko-sing, the solitude of Andrew Craig, the first white man to locate within the present boundaries of Knox County, is broken by the entrance of a lone Jerseyman who penetrates some ten miles farther into the wilderness. This follower of the trade of Vulcan, Mr. Young, soon gets ready to blow and to strike, and sets about supplying the sons of the forest the first axes they had ever seen. Mr. Young carried the sobriquet of "Axe-man," given him by the Indians, for many years. The old axe-maker is followed by some of his relatives and friends who start what has been ever since known as the Jersey Settlement in Ohio." Fredericktown, originally Kerr's Mill, was platted in 1807. (Rec. 319).

Nathaniel M. Young married Mary Lewis in New Jersey. Their first child was born in 1794. The inscription on Mary's gravestone fixes her birth in July 1771. She was the first child of James (b. 1747, d. Nov. 8 1819) and Abigail (Douglass) Lewis (b. 1747, d. Aug. 5 1830). In the "Lewis Letters" (Lewisiana, Vol. XII, p. 100, #142, N. Y. Pub. Library) Mary is noted as having "d. young" which contradicts a second notation which calls N. M. Young the son-in-law of James Lewis. "Md. Young" would have been accurate. A. A. Graham, in his "History of Knox County, O.," p. 616, writing about James Bryant, calls him "the brother-in-law of N. M. Young." The Lewis Letters speaking of Anna, daughter of James Lewis, says that she was born, Jan. 17 1774, died June 4 1828, and married a Mr. Bryant. Her gravestone, Wayne Cemetery reads, "Anna, Consort of James Bryant, Died 1828." Mrs. Sarah J. (Harris) Keifer, in her "N. J. Branch of the Harris Family," p. 9, says: "Nathaniel M. Young married a Miss Lewis." The "Lewis Letters" correctly list the other children of James and Abigail Lewis as: William (1772-1829); John (b. Nov. 23 1778, d. Apr. 5 1822; Eliphalet (b. 1781, d. Apr. 30 1823); and Sally who md. a Mr. Lindley and had no children.

To quote again from the Lewis Letters: "The three sons of James Lewis, William, John and Eliphalet, married three sisters by the name of

Conger, descendants of John Koeniger, a Hugenot, who settled in Middlesex, N. J. March 18 1669. William and Rhoda (Conger) Lewis, John and Hannah (Conger) Lewis, Eliphalet and Charlotte (Conger) Lewis are buried in Wayne Cemetery.

Mary Lewis was the great granddaughter of Samuel, progenitor of the Lewis family of Somerset County, N. J., who is said to have been born in Glamorgan, Wales, and to have arrived in America in 1717. She was the granddaughter of Edward (b. Aug. 8 1722, d. June 22 1792) and Sarah (Morris) Lewis (b. 1728, d. Nov. 6 1808) who were married, May 30, 1745. Edward and Sarah are interred at Basking Ridge, N. J. Sarah was the daughter of Daniel (son of Stephen) Morris who lived in Basking Ridge, N. J. in 1744 ("Lewisiana," Vol. 3, p. 184).

Several descendants of the Lewis family are buried in the Quaker cemetery near Fredericktown, O.

The names and birth dates of the children of N. M. and Mary Lewis Young were copied from the family Bible and records of William Mitchell Young, now (1945) owned by his son, Carl Dwight Young, of Delaware, O.

37. i. Anne, b. March 23 1794
38. ii. Elizabeth, b. June 9 1795
39. iii. James Lewis, b. Aug. 3 1797
40. iv. Hannah, b. March 13 1799

SOME BURIALS IN WAYNE CEMETERY

Knox County, Ohio

The following list of burials in Wayne Township Cemetery in which Wayne Baptist Church stood until it fell in ruins in 1938 is thought to be nearly complete. It was compiled in 1912 from the cemetery book supplemented by information furnished by descendants of those who had been interred in the cemetery. The numeral before a name indicates the row in the cemetery ground. The cemetery, no longer in use, is located on Highway #95, about three miles from Fredericktown, near the village of Luzerne, and not far from Salem cemetery. Both cemeteries were in the area of the Jersey Settlement, of which a map is shown.

Row	
6	Alworth, Elizabeth (Alward)
	Alworth, Samuel
	Alworth, Elizabeth
	Alworth, Eli
	Alworth, Dellia
	Alworth, Samantha
1	Ball, Rose Anna
	Ball, David
2	Beebe, Roxy

Row	
	Beebe, Rinda
	Beebe, Sarah
	Beebe, William
	Beebe, Infant
	Beebe, Infant
13	Beers, Alonzo
14	Beers, Ezekiel
	Beers, Mary
	Beers, Mary C.
16	Bloxham, Aurilla
6	Bockover, Peter
2	Bonar, T. B.
10	Bonar, Dr. R. S.
	Bonar, Lucy Ann
	Bonar, William
18	Bonar, Matthew
14	Bonar, John
	Bonar, Sarah
13	Bonar, Gilbert
	Bonar, Daniel
	Bonar, Jane
11	Bonar, Charlotte
15	Bonar, William
	Bonar, Anna
12	Bruce, Joel
	Bruce, Abigail
	Bruce, Hannah M.
1	Brown, Lewis
	Brown, Rachel
6	Bryant, Elizabeth
11	Bryant, James
	Bryant, Anna
16	Bryant, Wm. H.
	Bryant, Marie
	Bryant, Lela A.
2	Carter, A.
12	Case, Daniel
	Case, Anna
9	Conger, Sarah
	Conger, Mary
	Conger, Daniel

Row	
	Conger, Jane
	Conger, Elizabeth
9	Cooper, Hannah
	Cooper, Elias
	Cooper, Phebe A.
	Cooper, Phebe J.
	Cooper, Aaron
	Cooper, Jane
9	Dalrymple, Robert
	Dalrymple. Mary
	Dalrymple, Jacob
	Dalrymple, Phebe
13	Dalrymple, Herbert M.
	Dalrymple, Aurilla
4	Denman, James W.
	Denman, Joseph
	Denman, Mary
	Denman, Jonathan
13	Denman, Elizabeth
	Denman, Mary
	Denman, Lucy
	Denman, William
15	Denman, Lucille
	Denman, Gussie
14	Denman, John
2	Doty, Freeman
4	Dunham, Benjamin
	Dunham, Jane
	Dunham, Benj. W.
5	Dunham, Mary E.
4	Dunham, Ephraim
	Dunham, Jonathan
14	Elkins, Erastus
	Elkins, Jane
	Elkins, Harry
11	Farghar, Mary
14	Gardner, Henry
	Gardner, Samuel
	Gardner, Sarah
	Gardner, Infant
14	Gordon, Mary

Row		Row	
2	Hall, H.	8	Lyon, Daniel
2	Hammond, Permelia		Lyon, Hannah
	Hunt, Lewis	9	Lyon, Marianne
	Hunt, Phebe	15	Lyon, Benjamin
5	Ink, Acio		Lyon, Amy
	Ink, Ann	16	Lyon, James
14	Johnson, Salome	1	McGee, T. E.
2	Keyes, Hiram		McClelland, R. G.
	Keyes, Amy		McClelland, Harriet
13	Laycock, Abraham	15	Mettler, R.
	Laycock, Nathan	4	Mozier, Elizabeth
12	Laycock, Joseph	5	Mozier, Joseph
	Laycock, Elizabeth		Mozier, Miller
4	Lee, G. W.		Mozier, Harriet
	Lee, Mary		Mozier, John
	Lee, Phebe	6	Norton, Bartlett
9	Lefever, Olive May		Norton, Elizabeth
11	Lewis, Eliphalet		Norton, David
12	Lewis, John		Norton, Infant
9	Lewis, James	6	Proctor, Thomas
	Lewis, William	15	Randall, James
	Lewis, Rhoda	14	Reeder, Maria
10	Lewis, Clarissa	13	Royce, R.
	Lewis, James		Royce, Hulda
	Lewis, Abigail		Royce, Elizabeth
	Lewis, John	16	Rush, Adaline
	Lewis, Hannah	4	Shafer, Rebecca
	Lewis, Harriet	15	Shipman, Mary
	Lewis, Rachel	4	Slack, Nicholas
	Lewis, William	1	Smith, Solomon
1	Logan, Maurice	11	Stevens, J. W.
	Logan, John		Stevens, Delilah
	Logan, Jane		Stevens, Joseph
1	Louppe, Jacob		Stevens, Susan
5	Lyon, Abraham		Stevens, Wm. Nelson
	Lyon, Marcus		Stevens, Charley
	Lyon, Daniel	1	Stover, Mary F.
	Lyon, Erastus	4	Stover, Martha
	Lyon, John F.		Stover, James M.
	Lyon, George	6	Trowbridge, Lucy
	Lyon, Marshall		Trowbridge, Hannah

Row

Tulloss, Aurilla B.
Tulloss, George W.
5 Watkins, Joseph
Watkins, James
Watkins, Prudence
Watkins, Rodger
Watkins, Mary D.
4 Wayt, Elizabeth
14 Weston, Mary A.
Weston, Lydia
1 Whiteland, Priscilla

Row

Whiteland, Aquilla
Whiteland, Alice
15 Woodruff, Elmer
7 Young, Mary
Young, Nathaniel M.
4 Young, Jacob
Young, Tryphena
Young, Jacob D.
Young, Hannah
10 Young, Hannah Mitchell
Young, John

15 JACOB YOUNG

Farmer in New Jersey, Pioneer Developer of Wilderness Lands and Community Interests in the infant State of Ohio, Banker and Judge, was born, Nov. 27 1774, in Morris County, N. J., probably in Hanover Township where his parents lived until his father bought the Mendham property in 1784 from Morgan Young sr. Jacob died in Wayne Township, Knox County, O., and was buried in Wayne cemetery (Rec. 14) where a monument to his memory stands, with the following inscriptions: "Jacob Young, died March 6 1846, In the 72nd year of his life"; "Tryphena, his wife, died Feb. 2nd 1864, In her 84th year"; "Hannah, daughter of Jacob and Tryphena Young, died Aug. 14 1822, Age 4 years, 22 days"; Jacob D., son of J. & T. Young, died July 25 1830, Age 9 yrs. 4 mos. 22 days."

Jacob, as a resident of Byram Township, Sussex County, N. J., bought, Apr. 9 1805, from Abraham and Prudence Roll of the same place, for $750.00, 500 acres of land in the same Quarter, Township and Range of the U. S. Military Tract of the Northwest Territory in which his brother Nathaniel had bought in 1800. His purchase touched the northern boundary of James Lewis' land (Vol. E, p. 121, County records, Lancaster, O.). Jacob witnessed the deed by which his brother sold, Nov. 25 1805, to Abraham Lyon, land adjoining that of James Lewis. Through his wide interests and activities, Jacob quickly became one of the most prominent pioneers of the area. The county records at Mt. Vernon and at Mt. Gilead contain numerous accounts of his real estate dealings in the counties of Knox and Morrow. "Youngs Addition" to Mt. Gilead is pictured in Plat Book, #1, at Mt. Gilead. A few of the activities of Jacob are enumerated by A. B. Norton in his "History of Knox County, 1779-1862": "Nathaniel and Jacob Young were two of the Clerks of the 1st election for State and

Memorial Monument at Newton, N. J.
Showing lineage of Five Generations
from Morgan Young, Immigrant
Record 95

Family Memorial Monument
(Pyramid Stone)
North Monroeville, Ohio
JOSIAH YOUNG. Record 298

Gravestones of NATHANIEL MITCHELL AND MARY LEWIS YOUNG
Old Wayne Cemetery, Fredericktown, O. Record 14

JACOB YOUNG
Record 15

MARY YOUNG DALRYMPLE
Record 16

Delevan Paul Young
Record 192 and 9
Great grandson of Morgan Young

Memorial Stone
Jane Losey Young
Pretty Prairie Cemetery, Lagrange, Ind.
Record 9

John Young, Jr.
Record 17

Elizabeth Logan Young
Record 17

NOAH AND ANN YOUNG YOUNG
Record 28.

Henry Young
Record 34

Lydia Wade Young

Robert and Esther B. (Young) Parsons
Record 25

Aaron Pitney, John H., N. Mitchell, and Daniel Beers Young.
Record 15.

David Jackson, Sr.

Record 42.

Inscription on original photo

"Feb. 14 1872, David Jackson, sr., born 1786. Lived with one woman 62 years, has 15 children, 54 grandchildren, 50 great grand-children." "I have made my peace with God and all mankind."

JOHN YOUNG
Record 60.

County offices, held in the Township of Wayne, Oct. 11 1808"; "Jacob, in 1813, was appointed Associate Judge of Knox County"; "in 1816, he became a banker and was named Manager of the Owl Creek Bank at Mt. Vernon"; "he and Daniel Beers were a Committee of Arrangement for the 4th of July celebration in 1817 at Fredericktown, O."

Certain land sales of Jacob are interesting because of the allied family names which they contain. Jacob, June 17 1837, then of Knox County, sold land to Silas Miller. Two branches of the Young family, seemingly of no kin, are brought together in one of Jacob's last sales. On July 13 1842, he sold a lot in Mt. Gilead, then in Marion County, for $1.50 to Isaac DeWitt, husband of Martha, daughter of Josiah and Mary Barden Young who emigrated to Ohio, 1836, from Vermont (Marion records, Bk. 6, p. 483). Judge Henry Ustick, second husband of Abigail Young, daughter of Jacob, witnessed this deed.

Jacob served his country in the War of 1812 as Captain of an Ohio Company in which Noah Young (Rec. #28) was a corporal and several members of allied families were privates: Joseph Talmage, Jacob Shur, John Cramer, Israel Dalrymple, William Drake, Nathaniel Mitchell, Samuel Lewis, Daniel Ayers, and John Logan who was a sergeant (Evans, History of Knox County, O.).

The will of Jacob Young, made Feb. 19 1845, names his wife and his brother N. M. Young as executors, and lists the following children: Abigail Ustick, Daniel B., Charity Ann Jackson, Nathaniel M., Susan L. Talmage, John H., Elizabeth Mitchell, and Aaron Pitney Young. Three sales of land between May 1859 and Sept. 1862, recorded at Mt. Gilead, O., show additional heirs of Jacob: Phebe A., wife of John H. Young; Lydia, wife of A. P. Young; Susan and Tryphena Venum; Phebe Lane; Amanda Lewis; Elizabeth Rugg, daughters of Charity (Young) Jackson; L. J., F. J., J. Y., and S. M. Jackson, sons of Charity, all of Whiteside County, Ill. In one sale deed, T. H. Dalrymple, acting as attorney for Amanda and Lafayette Jackson, is called their ancestor. (Rec. 16).

Jacob Young was married by the Rev. John J. Carle, of Rockaway, N. J., Dec. 25 1796, to Euphemia Beers (her name is so written in the marriage record at Morristown, N. J.), daughter of Daniel and Azuba (Pitney) Beers. The children of Jacob and Tryphena (Euphemia) were: (Mrs. Cora Y. Logan, Los Angeles, Calif.)

41. i. Abigail, b. Oct. 29 1798
X 42. ii. Daniel Beers, b. Sept. 16 1800
43. iii. Charity Ann, b. June 21 1802
iv. Tryphena, b. Nov. 7 1804
44. v. Nathaniel Mitchell, b. Aug. 19 1807

45. vi. Susan L., b. Nov. 27 1810
46. vii. John H., b. Feb. 12 1813
47. viii. Elizabeth, b. Sept. 19 1815
ix. Hannah, b. July 6 1818, d. Aug. 14 1822
x. Jacob D., b. March 3 1821, d. July 25 1830
48. xi. Aaron Pitney, b. Feb. 17 1824

The Beers and Young Families

Jabeth Beers (Will, 1777, Morristown, N. J.) and his wife Catherine had two sons, Daniel and Joseph. Joseph had a son, Jabeth (1804-1858), who married Mahala Young (Record 8), granddaughter of Morgan and Elizabeth Mills Young. Daniel Beers (b. Dec. 30 1752, Will dated, June 3 1790, Mendham, N. J.) had a daughter, Euphemia (Tryphena), who married Jacob grandson of Morgan and Elizabeth Young. One administrator of Daniel's will was John Mills.

Daniel Beers married, Apr. 1 1774, Azuba Pitney, b. Nov. 27 1755, daughter of Benjamin (Will, 1793, d. 1795) and Abigail Byram Pitney. Benjamin Pitney registered the earmarks of his cattle at Mendham, N. J. in 1768. His brother James registered his in 1750. The children of Daniel and Azuba were: Elizabeth, b. Nov. 29 1775; Abigail, b. Sept. 28 1778; Tryphena, b. June 27 1780; Catherine, b. Dec. 10 1782, d. June 3 1874, age 91 yrs. 5 mos. 24 days, buried Rivercliff cemetery, Mt. Gilead, O., md. Joseph Talmage (1780-1837), son of Abraham and Phebe Fairchild Talmage; Daniel, jr., b. Dec. 30 1784; Benjamin Pitney, b. Feb. 29 1787; Byram, b. Sept. 17 1789; and Susan, b. Jan. 20 1795, md. a Mr. Lafever.

Catherine Beers Talmage, writing from Mt. Gilead, O. to her sister Tryphena Young at Morrison, Ill., May 30, year not shown, (after 1845 when Elmay Cooper died), recalls "the many associations when we were young, when we lived in the wilderness (Knox County, O.), eating our own corn bread and wild meat, those were happy days! no one to find fault with what we did! I sometimes stay with my son and sometimes with Nancy (Henry Snyder). Susan (Lafever) can tell you about all our friends. Write and tell me if you enjoy life. We are almost home. My hope is sure and steadfast, so come Lord Jesus. My health is good for my age. I thought of coming to see you and of going to Nancy Miller's (see below) but they have moved too far away, so I shall not come. Write and tell me if you are better content now than here. Byram is living in a new house on the old farm. His daughter Pheny lives in the old one. I send you a piece of sister Beers and Elmay Cooper's shroud" (Letter now owned by Mrs. S. L. Chesley, Fargo, N. D.). Byram Beers witnessed, June 17

1837, a sale of land by Jacob Young to Silas Miller (Marion, O. records).

Nancy Losey Miller, b. 1798, married in 1824, Jacob, son of Abraham and Catherine (Denman) Miller. She was the daughter of John and Hannah (Pierson) Losey who married about 1795, and the granddaughter of Cornelius and Abigail (Dunham) Losey. Cornelius is widely accepted as the son of John (Will, 1765, Morristown, N. J.) and Jane Losey of Mendham, N. J. but Stelle F. Randolph, of Grand Rapids, Mich., in a letter to the N. J. Historical Society, says that Cornelius was the son of James Puff Losey (1718-1809) and a first wife whose name is not known. To find the name of this first wife of James might be to solve the mystery of legacies to so many Loseys by John Young. (Rec. 1) Mary and Jane, daughters of John and Jane Losey, married respectively Jonathan Pitney (Will, Oct. 10 1778, Morristown, N. J.) and Morgan Young, jr. Mr. Pitney, in his will, calls James Puff Losey his brother-in-law. The relationship between this Miller family and that of Adam Miller who married Mary Young, sister of Morgan, sr., and that of Daniel Miller who married Elizabeth Young, daughter of Losey (Record 35) has not been traced.

16 MARY YOUNG

was b., Oct. 26 1777, in Morris County, N. J., died, Sept. 25, 1823, at Fredericktown, O. and was buried beside her husband in Wayne Cemetery, near Lucerne, O. Their tombstone carries the name of one of their sons, Jacob, and of his wife, Phebe (Lewis) Dalrymple. Mary md., Jan. 19 1794, in N. J., Robert Dalrymple (b. Nov. 4 1759, d. March 3 1836) son of Joseph and Jane (Boyles) Dalrymple.

The brothers and sisters of Robert Dalrymple were: Andrew, b. March 25 1746, father of Bruce who md. Susan Struble (b. 1788, dau. of Daniel and Mary (Couse) Struble who had a son, Andrew, (b. 1808, N. J., d. 1874, Knox County, O.); Solomon, b. Apr. 6 1749, d. 1829, md. Eunice Parsons and had a granddaughter, Emily Dalrymple, who md. John Lewis Carrel, grandson of Daniel and Margaret (Young) Carrel; Susannah; Sarah; William; Mary; John (registered his earmarks with his brother Solomon at Mendham N. J. in 1798); Robert; James; Elizabeth; Margrate; Ann; and Jane Dalrymple, b. July 26 1767. (Sources: Mrs. Ella Dalrymple (Geo. L.) Baird, Dover, N. J.; Lew M. Dalrymple, Bedford, O.; Histories of Knox and Morrow Counties, O). Mary Couse Struble died, July 11 1846, Age 88 yrs. 9 mos. 13 days, is buried in Forest Cemetery, Fredicktown, O. Robert and Mary had nine children.

i. Charles, b. June 8 1795, d. Feb. 22 1874, Morrow County, O., md. 1821, Nancy Hance, b. July 10 1800. Eight children: Mary, md. Mr. Lewis; Thomas H., of Mt. Gilead,

O. acted as att'y for Amanda and Lafayette Jackson in settlement of Jacob Young's estate (Mt. Gilead, O. records), was buried at Mt. Gilead, O. beside his wife, Anna (1833-1869); Ambrose; Martha, md. Mr. Douglass; Hannah, md. Mathew Boner (Bonar); William H., b. June 17 1834, Morrow County, O., md. 1871, Mary Busoul, b. Apr. 24 1844, and had a son Edward; C. Hannibal; and Jacob W. Dalrymple.

ii. Jacob, b. March 29 1797, d. May 17 1889, bur. Wayne Cemetery, near Fredericktown, O. md., Dec. 15 1821, Phebe, dau. of William and Rhoda (Conger) Lewis. Eight children, all born on the homestead farm near Fredericktown, O. (Mrs. Eva Dalrymple (C. J.) McGugin, Fredericktown, O.). Rhoda, b. Dec. 4 1822, md. Mr. Ogden; Aaron, b. Aug. 18 1824, d. Oct. 27 1900; William, b. Apr. 7 1827, d. Dec. 27 1885, had four children: Charles, Kitty, Lewis and Mary E.; Mitchell Young, b. Jan. 17 1830, d. Sept. 2 1870; Robert M., b. June 28 1833, d. Aug. 31 1924, md. Apr. 11 1861, Nancy Sabina Struble (dau. of Halsey) and had two children, born near Lucerne, O.; Lorin E., b. Dec. 27 1861, d. Nov. 26 1924, md. Nov. 17 1886, Nellie S. Truesdale and had two children: Eva, b. Nov. 4 1891, md. Clarence Joe McGugin (two children: Helen L., b. Feb. 18 1913, md., Aug. 9 1931, Lloyd Stinemetz, and Lena Alice McGugin, b. Nov. 26 1915), and Jennie Marie, b. Sept. 9 1899, md. Sept. 4 1924, Mr. Baker; and Lew M. (bro. Lorin E.), b. Aug. 15 1864, living 1946 at Bedford, O.; Sarah, 6th child of Jacob, b. 1837, md. Mr. Ball; Charles Lafayette, b. 1841; and Mary E. Dalrymple. Chas. Lafayette Dalrymple practiced medicine in Mt. Vernon, O. He md. 1st. Maggie Doty in 1845, and had six children: Aaron; Rhoda; Ogden; Robert; Chas. L. jr.; and Minnie Douglass Dalrymple.

iii. George, b. Mar. 29 1797, d. July 1 1818

iv. Abigail, b. July 20 1803, d. Oct. 5 1879, md. Mr. Clutter

v. Hannah, b. Apr. 4 1806, d. Jan. 24 1875, md. Daniel Lyon

vi. John, b. July 24 1809, d. Sept. 13 1891

vii. Albert, b. July 24 1814, d. Dec. 9 1814

viii. Phebe Ann, b. Aug. 15 1816, d. Feb. 22 1856, md. Mr. Struble
ix. Robert, jr. b. Mar. 2 1829, d. Dec. 12 1866

17 JOHN YOUNG, JR.

according to the inscription on his tombstone in Oakwood Cemetery, DeKalb, Ill., was "born May 17 1785 in New Jersey, died, Sept. 30 1869, Age 84 yrs. 4 mos. 13 days." It is also engraved on his tombstone that "Hannah, daughter of J. and E. Young, died Aug. 6 1866, Age 51 yrs. 1 mo. 22 days," and that "William Young, died, March 17 1864, Age 64 yrs." John was born in Randolph Township, Morris County, N. J. and spent most of his life farming in Troy Township, Richland County, O. where his wife died and was buried in Fairview Cemetery, near Mansfield, O. The inscription on her gravestone reads, "Elizabeth, wife of John Young, died May 17 1857, Age 73 yrs. 3 mos. 25 days," placing her birth in 1784. After the death of his wife, John went to live with his daughter Sarah (W. Harrison) Day in DeKalb, Ill. and died there.

John Young served during the War of 1812 in Capt Greer's Knox County Company. He was a Justice of the Peace and married, Dec. 26 1816, Mary Logan, his wife's sister, to James Harris, buried in Pleasant Hill Cemetery, Richland County, O., son of John and Mary Hamilton Harris. On Aug. 13 1814 John bought 42 acres of land for $84.00 in Range 19, Troy Township, Sect. 9 from his brother Aaron and Mary Mitchell Young. He sold land in the same Range in 1813 to Andrew Perkins, husband of his niece Elizabeth Young. Mr. Perkins bought from John Young, jr. and Elizabeth, the N. E. Quarter of Sect. 25 in Troy Township, March 17 1819. (Bk. 1, 643, Mansfield, O. records).

John Young, jr. married, Sept. 15 1807, Elizabeth Logan, both residents of Randolph Township, Morris County, N. J. (Morristown, N. J. records). Elizabeth probably was the daughter of John Logan, an inventory for whose estate in Morris County, N. J., Morgan Young, sr. helped to make and for whom Robert Young, son of Morgan, served during the Revolution. John Logan[2] lived near the Youngs in Washington County, Pa. in 1810 (Census report) and he served as Sergeant in Capt. Jacob Young's Company, made up of residents of Knox and Richland Counties, during the War of 1812 (Norton's, "History of Knox County, O."). John and Jane Logan (d. Feb. 14 1854, age 67 years 1 mo. 13 days) were buried in Wayne Cemetery, Fredericktown, O. John and Elizabeth Young had six children, all born in Richland County, O.

49. i. James Logan, b. Sept. 18 1808
50. ii. William, b. March 31 1810
51. iii. Mary Ann, b. Feb. 10 1812
iv. Hannah, b. June 14 1815, d. Aug. 6 1866, in the home of her sister Sarah Day at DeKalb, Ill.
52. v. Sarah, b. June 8 1817
53. vi. Ellzy Pierson, b. Jan. 26 1819

18 AARON YOUNG

Born, Nov. 14 1788, in Morris County, N. J., died April 19 1856, and probably was buried in the old cemetery at Mt. Gilead, O. His will, dated April 12 1856, filed at Mt. Gilead, gives his residence as Morrow County. His estate was left to his wife Mary and his seven children. His wife and John Logan, his son-in-law, were his executors. The land deals of Aaron are recorded at Mt. Vernon, Mansfield and Mt. Gilead, O. They testify to the changing county boundaries during his day. In 1813, Aaron sold land to Jacob Mitchell, his brother-in-law (Mansfield, O. records).

Aaron married, March 17 1812, his second cousin Mary Mitchell, both being residents of Wayne Township, Knox County, O. (Mt. Vernon records). Mary Mitchell, b. Aug. 15 1796, d. March 21 1868, Age 71 yrs. 7 mos. 6 days, was buried in Harrisburg Cemetery, Sauk County, Wis. (Gravestone record). She was the daughter of William and Phebe (Southard) Mitchell, niece of Hannah Mitchell (John) Young, sister of Naomi, md. Lewis Young (son of N. M. Young) and of Silas Mitchell, md. Elizabeth, daughter of Jacob Young. The children of Aaron and Mary, all born in Richland County, O., became pioneers in Missouri and Wisconsin. (Miss Estella E. Stevenson, from family Bible of Elizabeth Young, Rec. 54)

54. i. Elizabeth, b. Aug. 17 1813
55. ii. William M., b. Mar. 14 1815
56. iii. Phebe, b. Apr. 10 1817
57. iv. Hannah, b. May 8 1819
58. v. Pierson, b. June 11 1821
59. vi. Abigail, b. Apr. 12 1824
60. vii. John, b. July 20 1826

19 HANNAH YOUNG

No family record gives more than the date of her birth, July 30 1791. Hannah married John Halterman, in Richland County, O. where they raised a large family according to descendants of one child that has been found, Daniel H. Halterman, born, near Mansfield, O., Oct. 7 1812, died, Feb. 3 1885. Daniel had 3 brothers, Christopher, Joseph and Jacob. D. H. Halterman md. 1st., Jan. 6 1839, Elizabeth Glassburn, b. Oct. 31 1814, d. Feb. 7 1849. He md. 2nd., May 6 1849, Rebecca Yerian, b. Sept. 17 1882, d. June 13 1898. Children of Daniel and Elizabeth Halterman (Daniel Butler, Lucasville, O.).

i. Lucy, b. Oct. 2 1839, md. Ferdinand Rose.
ii. Susannah, b. Apr. 22 18—, md. William Mickle.
iii. John, b. Jan. 21 1843
iv. G. W., b. Dec. 17 1844
v. Jacob, b. Sept. 24 1846
vi. Lewis, b. Oct. 13 1848

Children of Daniel and Rebecca Halterman (both buried near Beaver, O.).

i. Eliza, b. Apr. 28 1851, md. Henry Clay Butler, b. Apr. 12 1843, d. July 19 1927, near Beaver, O. Two of their children are: Daniel, b. June 16 1883, our informant, and Mrs. Lee Yeoger, of near Richwood, O. A daughter of Daniel Butler is Mrs. Roger McLaughlin, of near Lucasville,O.

ii. William Jackson, b. Dec. 11 1852, md. Mary Hannah Riley (b. June 22 1861), at Limerick, O. After the death of William, Mary md., 2nd., a Mr. White. She now lives in the home of Dr. Baab, at Utica, O. William was buried in Jackson Co., O. Wm. and Mary had 4 children, three of whom died in infancy. The 4th child, Arthur Edwin Halterman, b. July 4 1896, Jackson Co., O., is with the Pioneer Rural Electric Co-operative, Piqua, O. He md. Aug. 31 1920, Opol Geneva Woods, at Lafayette, O., and has two children: Robert Woods, b. Aug. 4 1921, at W. Lafayette, O., md. March 1944, Mary Katherine Meline, at Kirkville, Mo. and is practicing medicine at London, O., and Opol Jeanine Halterman, b. Jan. 25 1931, at Maysville, O.

iii. Mary, b. Oct. 17 1854, md. Hiram Blakeman.

iv. Effaline, b. March 6 1857, md. Oct. 26 1884, Wm. Henry Sprague, at Beaver, O. He died, June 21 1939, in the home of his daughter, Viola Acord, at Richmond Dale, O. Children of Wm. and Effaline Sprague: Mary, b. Nov. 16 1885, md. ——— Maple. She lives near Chillicothe, O.;

Della, June 6, 1887, d. May 22 1910, md. Mr. Weaver; Elizabeth, b. Sept. 24 1889, d. June 12 1942, md. Mr. Boyer; Viola b. March 29 1893, md. Floyd Acord and lives at Richmond Dale, O.; Wm. O., b. Nov. 16 1894, d. Jan. 16 1924; and James, b. May 13 1896 md. Emma Cash, Nov. 6 1924

v. Daniel D., b. Apr. 28 1859, d. Apr. 3 1896
vi. Elizabeth, b. June 25 1861, d. Oct. 14 1883
vii. Catherine, b. Jan. 11 1864, md. A. H. Alexander and is living, 1946, with her son, H. W. Alexander who is with the American Sterilizer Co. at Erie, Pa.
viii. Anna, md. James S. Sprague
ix. Louise, b. June 19 1866

20 EBENEZER PIERSON YOUNG

"Elzy," as he was commonly called, was born, May 5 1798, of Quaker parentage, in Morris County, N. J. He was brought by his parents from Washington County, Pa. to Kerr's Mill (now Fredericktown), O. in 1809, and joined the "Jersey Settlement," founded by his brother Nathaniel Mitchell Young. Led by his innate spirit of pioneering he moved on in 1852 to Richland City, Wis. where he remained until 1856 when he settled in Richland Center and became active in local affairs. He was a ruling elder of the Presbyterian Church both in Ohio and Wisconsin. The high point in his career occurred when he anticipated Carrie Nation and conducted a one man crusade up and down the main street of Richland Center, wielding an axe upon every whiskey barrel his gaze fell upon. The local papers emphasized the dramatic aspect of his long white whiskers streaming in the breeze as he demolished barrel after barrel. He died, June 24 1870, at Gotham, Wis. and was buried in nearby Bulton Cemetery (Mrs. Margaret Young King, Albert Lea, Minn.).

Ellzy's given names take us back to the Rev. Ebenezer Pierson, one of the founders of New Ark (Newark), N. J. He was married, Feb. 17 1820, by James Scott, V. D. M. to Sarah E. Bonar (Mt. Vernon, O. records). Sarah was born, Apr. 30 1799, died, Apr. 2 1847, Age 47 yrs. 11 mos. 2 days, and was buried in Forest Cemetery, Fredericktown, O. Beside her tombstone are two stones marking the resting places of two daughters: "Margareta, daughter of E. P. and Sarah Young, Died June 27 1848, Age 21 yrs. 9 mos. 1 day," and "Sarah Amanda, died March 6 1845, Age 1 yr. 6 mos. 6 days."

Bonar is sometimes spelled Boner. Sarah Bonar was a distant relative of Horatius Bonar, the well known Scotch hymn writer.

Ellzy married, Aug. 24 1852, for his second wife, Caroline A. Collins, a widow, daughter of Col. R. D. Simons (Mt. Vernon, O. records). After Ellzy died, Caroline married the Rev. Mr. Barnes, a Presbyterian minister.

Ellzy sold in 1841 his Knox County farm to Daniel Beers, jr. and moved to Richland County, O. In 1846, he was living in Ridgefield Township, Huron County, O. when he bought a farm in Oxford Township, same county, near Courtland Center. (Sandusky, O. records). His children and the dates of their birth are from the family Bible of David Bonar Young: (Mrs. G. A. King).

61. i. David Bonar, b. March 26 1821
62. ii. Elizabeth, b. Sept. 4 1822
iii. Margaret Ann, b. Sept. 26 1826, d. June 27 1848
63. iv. Mary, b. Sept. 26 1828
64. v. Isabel, b. Aug. 26 1830
65. vi. Martha, b. Sept. 4 1835
vii. Sarah Amanda, b. Aug. 29 1843, d. March 6 1845

21 JAMES YOUNG

born, May 19 1788, Randolph Township, Morris County, N. J., died in 1824. (Record 8). He md., 1812, Margaret Clarke. Only one child of James and Margaret has been found, Lucinda Young (1814-1887) who md. Moses Lee, son of George W. and Kate (Lay) Lee. (File of Harry C. Haggerty of New Haven, Conn. at Nat'l Office of S.A.R. #26033, Washington, D. C.). Moses Lee may have been of the same family as Lucinda Young Lee whose birth (July 30 1797) and death (June 25 1821) are recorded in the Register of the First Presbyterian Church, Morristown, N. J. Lucinda was daughter of William Lee.

22 ELIAS BRIANT YOUNG

dated his will, March 20 1837, at Chester, N. J. (Morristown, N. J. records). He died, "June 12 1837, Age 45 yrs. 8 mos. 29 days" (Tombstone, Chester, N. J.). In his will, witnessed by Zachariah DeCamp, Wm. F. Woodruff and James Emmans, he names his wife and all his children except Malina who died before 1837. Elias died on his farm located between Chester and Chester Cross Roads. His father spent his last years on part of his farm. The name in written Youngs on his gravestone.

Elias married Sarah E. Condit, b. Aug. 8 1796, d. Sept. 10 1862, Age 66 yrs. 1 mo. 2 days (Gravestone record). After the death of Elias, Sarah md. Thomas Briant Stout as his third wife. (Warren Bryant Stout, So. Orange, N. J.). The children of Elias and Sarah:—

i. Malinda Condit, b. 1813, d. Jan. 25 1833, Age 19 yrs. 6 mos. (Gravestone record). She md. Joshua De Camp (1817-1859).

ii. Sarah Ann, b. 1817, d. Sept. 24 1859, buried Chester, N. J. She md., first, Robert Hughson, and second, Nathaniel T. Stout, bro. of Andrew Jackson Stout. See iv.

iii. Charlotte, md. Samuel Vanderveer.

iv. Napoleon Bonaparte, made his will, Sept. 2 1861 (proved, Sept. 19 1861), at Columbia, S. C. (recorded at Morristown, N. J.). In his will he gives the names of four children of his sister Sarah as: Matilda, Josephine, Charles and George Stout. He md. Catherine Shaw in N. J.

v. Charles A., died in N. J., did not marry.

vi. Elias Jacob, md. Loretta Moore and emigrated West.

66. vii. Robert Earle, b. 1830

67. viii. Ruth Ann, b. Aug. 30 1835

23 JACOB YOUNG

was born, Aug. 5 1796, in Randolph Township, Morris County, N. J. He married Minchey Morris in N. J. F. C. Hyer, of Newark, N. J., applying for membership in the S.A.R. states that his parents were Lewis S. and Jane (Young) Hyer, his grandparents Jacob and Minchy (Morris) Young, and his great grandparents Robert and Sarah Briant Young. No confirmation has been found.

24 SIMEON YOUNG

born, Sept. 29 1798, in the present Randolph Township, Morris County, N. J., died about 1865 at Shipshewanna, Ind. and was buried there. He was one of those of whom his father (Rec. 8) said, "they have gone to New York State and Ohio." Simeon's name is on the Tax List of Randolph for 1822 (State Lib., Trenton, N. J.). He went to Pennfield, N. Y. when he left N. J. and in 1845, he joined his several relatives in Lagrange County, Ind., and engaged in farming.

Simeon married four times. (Family Bible, owned 1943 by Mrs. Milo Zook, Sturgis, Mich.). He md. (1), Feb. 16 1825, Hylinda Luce of N. Y.

State. She was born May 10 1806 and died Nov. 8 1835, when her daughter Sarah was three days old. Sarah Young was raised by her grandmother Luce. Simeon md. (2), May 29 1836, Wealthy Luce, (b. Jan. 10 1804, d. Sept. 12 1839), sister of Hylinda. There were no children by the second marriage. Simeon md. (3), Nov. 3 1839, Eliza Sargent (b. Aug. 17 1805), at Howe (Lima), Ind. Simeon md. (4), a widow by the name of Sarah Banghart, in Michigan, according to a granddaughter, Mrs. Rheuama Young Woodworth, of Kalmazoo, Mich. Sarah B. Young died in southern Michigan. After the death of Simeon, she md. (3), Alec Cole, a farmer in Lagrange County, Ind.

The children of Simeon and Hylinda Young: (Zook Bible)

i. Linsley B., b. Dec. 16 1825, near Pennfield, N. Y.
ii. Sarah (Sally), b. May 14 1827
iii. Chester, b. Mar. 28 1829, d. June 28 1829.
iv. Wealthy Jane, b. May 28 1831
v. Joseph W., b. Mar. 23 1833, d. Apr. 2 1834.
vi. Sarah Linda, b. Nov. 5 1835, md. George Hardy, and lived in Medina, N. Y.

The children of Simeon and Eliza Young: (Zook Bible)

68. vii. Charles Wesley, b. Dec. 15 1840, near Sturgis, Mich.
69. viii. Mary Abigail, b. June 19 1842
ix. Wilbur Luce, b. Sept. 2 1844, md. twice. By his second wife Ella ———, he had three children, a daughter Fannie and two sons. Wilbur was a photographer and lived in southern Florida, St. Louis, Mo., and Nashville, Tenn.

Only child of Simeon and Sarah Banghart Young:

70. x. Alfred Dayton, b. Mar. 27 1862, at Shipshewanna, Ind.

25 ESTHER BRUEN YOUNG

born, Mar. 27 1810, Randolph Township, Morris County, N. J., died, Oct. 27 1896, and was buried in the Methodist Churchyard at Millbrook, N. J. (Gravestone record). She md., July 3 1827, Robert Parsons, b. Oct. 4 1805, d. Mar. 12 1864. Robert was one of four children; Solomon, Robert, Eunice and Sarah Parsons. Charles O. Parsons (son of Robert) told his granddaughter, Caroline Parsons Cooper, Dover, N. J., that when he was in school the teachers pronounced his name *Pierson* and that his brother Solomon looked at the family records and found no such spelling of the name. Their sister, Eunice, had the same name as Eunice Parsons

(1755-1830) who md., Nov. 25 1782, Solomon Dalrymple (1749-1829) who was a brother of Robert who md. Mary Young (Rec. 16).

The compiler believes, without supporting proof, that William Young who was md., Nov. 15 1807, by the Rev. S. Thompson, of Lyon's Farms, N. J., to Esther Bruen was a brother of our subject and that Esther Bruen Young was named for her sister-in-law. The names and birth dates of the children of Robert and Esther are from the family Bible of Mrs. Mattie B. (Parsons) Cooper, Dover, N. J., all were born near Millbrook, N. J.

i. Mary J., b. Nov. 26 1828, d. Feb. 4 1890, md. Wm. D. Henderson, Dec. 1874.

ii. Solomon, b. Aug. 10 1832, d. Nov. 21 1897, at Patterson, N. J. He taught school at Succasunna and Mendham, N. J., graduated at Wesleyan University and in 1858 entered the Methodist ministry joining the Newark Conference with which he continued active relations until his death. The Rev. Solomon Parsons, D.D. was a strong advocate of temperance and was chosen as candidate for Governor of N. J. on the Prohibition ticket in 1883. He md. 1st., Nov. 10 1859, Mary M. Peck who d. Apr. 1864. He md. 2nd., S. Louisa Towt and had 8 children: Robert Young, d. in infancy, John W., Fletcher, Floyd Yard, Ralph, Susan, and Louise Parsons. A son of Floyd Y. and Belle (Paige) Parsons is Hugh W. Parsons, of Denver, Colo. who supplied helpful data. Hugh md. 1934 Mary Whitaker and has a daughter Susan Paige, b. 1940.

iii. Caroline, b. June 7 1834, d. July 13 1860, md. Apr. 2 1857, Daniel Lawrence Dalrymple.

iv. Eunice M., b. Apr. 23 1836, d. Feb. 1 1907, md. Feb. 2 1859, Nicholas Byram Briant (1830-1898). Three children: Etta, md. John Patterson; Carrie; and Stacy H. Briant. Carrie P. Briant (b. 1865, Randolph, Morris Co., N. J.) md., Sept. 14 1889, Irving Oscar Ball (1865-1941) at Morristown, N. J. Eleanor B., only child of I. O. and Carrie Ball, b. Dec. 16 1901, Washington, D. C., md. Dec. 23 1926, Frederick H. Untiedt. Three children: Ruth Adelaide, b. Oct. 1 1927; Carol Frances, b. Mar. 5 1929; and Frederick Irving Untiedt, b. Apr. 9 1934, Washington, D. C.

v. Charles, b. Nov. 9 1838, d. Jan. 4 1839.

vi. Mahlon M., b. June 30 1840, d. Mar. 6 1912, md. Isabella Meeks.

vii. Charles Ogden, b. Nov. 30 1842, d. Feb. 19 1923, md. Sept. 27 1866, Anna Marie Briant, b. Jan. 17 1842, d. Apr. 19 1924, dau. of James Madison and Marie (Crane) Briant. Mattie Briant (b. June 24 1869, living 1946 at Dover, N. J.), dau. of C. O. and Anna Parsons, md. Mar. 23 1888, Eugene Jefferson Cooper (b. May 7 1861, d. Aug. 8 1940) at Dover, N. J. Five children. Caroline Parsons, b. May 23 1888, Dover, N. J., is a Registered Nurse, living near Dover; Eugene Evart, b. Jan. 8 1891; Chas. S., b. Dec. 13 1893; Frances E., b. Apr. 26 1895, md. Andy Joanides and has a son Charles, b. Aug. 26 1927; Phoebe A., b. March 7 1899, md. Henry W. Burd, Oct. 17, 1927, and has 2 children, Betty Ann, b. Sept. 10 1932, and Eugene C. Burd, b. June 7 1935, Dover, N. J.

viii. James, b. Nov. 23 1844, d. Aug. 27 1845.

ix. George H., b. Mar. 20 1847, d. Dec. 28 1871, md. Hattie W. Searing.

x. Robert E., b. Feb. 16 1850, d. Feb. 2 1888, md. Jessie Smith.

xi. Frank, b. June 30 1852, d. Nov. 25 1878.

26 SUSANNAH YOUNG

is listed first in all family records of the children of Morgan and Jane Losey Young. In some records she is called the eldest child. The date of birth is not given but this must have been before 1788 when her brother Noah was born in Morris County, N. J. (Rec. 8). The U. S. Census for 1790 places the family in Fallowfield Township, Washington County, Pa. and shows that it then consisted of father and mother, one son (Noah), and two daughters. It is unknown whether Sarah or Jane was the second daughter. A Susannah Young who bought a lot in Enterprise, near Monroeville, O., in Nov. 1847, might have been our Susannah.

27 SARAH YOUNG

commonly called Sally was born either in New Jersey or at Red Stone Old Fort, Washington County, Pa. One family record shows Sarah as having married a Mr. Ralston in Adams County, O. This cannot be confirmed because most of the records of Adams County were destroyed by fire in 1910. In a single volume of records that was saved from the fire there are a few marriage records and one of these is that of the marriage, June 12 1806, of Betsy Young to Robert Ralston. Evans and Stiver, in their "History of Adams County, Ohio, 1900," page 57, list a few early marriages, and one of them is: "1807, Oct. 9, Henry McGarah and Sarah Young, married by James Moore." It will be shown under record #31 that John Young married Jane McGarah. Mitchell Morrison Young (1854-1942), of near West Union, O., who inherited the Morgan Young farm and lived most of his life there, told the writer that a daughter of Morgan whose name he could not remember married Henry McGarah. No descendant amongst the Ralstons of Adams County has been found.

28 NOAH YOUNG

son of Morgan and Jane Losey Young was married, March 20 1811, at No. Monroeville, O., by Samuel Kratzer, to Anna Young (Rec. 37), daughter of Nathaniel M. and Mary Lewis Young (Rec. 14). The marriage united two collateral lines of our Young family. Noah died, July 5 1858, on his farm about two miles east of New Haven, O., age 70 years, 3 months, (Gravestone record) and was buried, as was his wife, in the old cemetery at New Haven. He was born in April 1788 in Elizabeth Township, Essex County, N. J. (Family Bibles). He was living with his parents and two sisters in Fallowfield Township, Washington County, Pa. when the U. S. Census for 1790 was taken. When about 18 years old he was taken by his parents to near West Union, Adams County, O. from where he moved after a brief sojourn and joined his relatives who had settled near Fredericktown, O. The death record of Mahlon, first child of Noah and Anna Young, shows that he was born two miles east of Fredericktown, O. (Norwalk, O. records).

On Feb. 15 1815, Noah Young, of Knox County, O., bought from the Federal Government through the Wooster, O. office, a farm of 163.67 acres in Troy Township, Richland County, O. (Dep't. of Interior, Washington, D. C.). In 1833, Noah and Anna sold this land described as the SW1/4 Sect. 30, Township 20, Range 18, to Andrew Perkins, their brother-in-law (Rec. 38) (Mansfield, O. records). The Mansfield records, Vol. 3, p. 4, show that Noah in 1821 bought from Andrew Perkins a farm in Range 19, Twp. 20, S. 25. In 1828, about one year before his parents arrived from Adams County to become his neighbors, Noah bought a farm in Ridgefield Township, Huron County, O. In 1831, with his brother Henry he bought his parent's recently purchased farm (Rec. 9). On this farm in New Haven Township, Noah died. At one time, Noah owned a farm in Berlin Township, Huron County, O. which he sold in 1841 to

Elias Ellis (Norwalk, O. records). Before making his first land purchase in northern Ohio Noah is said to have inspected the farm land in Fentress County, Tenn. and to have bought a farm which is still recorded in his name at Jamestown. Enquiry about the record at Jamestown has failed to bring a reply from the recorder. Noah's wife refused to live in Fentress County, Tenn. because of the lack of schools. (Family records).

Noah served in the War of 1812 as a corporal in the 6th Regiment, Ohio Militia, in a Company commanded by his cousin, Capt. Jacob Young (Rec. 15).

The will of Noah, made June 22 1858, proved Aug. 23 1858, gave all his property to his wife Anna during her life, and ordered his son Morgan after the death of Anna to sell the property and divide the proceeds amongst the children. The will names four children: Elizabeth B. Hough, Chilon, Mary Ann House, and Jane Boardman. The witnesses were: E. C. Woodworth, J. H. Mills and Dashop Warren. Morgan sold the property consisting of 55 acres, part of the J. V. Vredenburgh partition, New Haven Township, Huron County, Ohio, May 10 1860 ("Norwalk, O. Reflector," Apr. 24 1860). The will of Anna Young mentions the fact that her property adjoins that of Uriah Young, unidentified, who left Adams County, Ohio with Morgan Young (see Rec. 9). Anna's will is on file at Norwalk, O. Children of Noah and Anna Young (Various family Bibles):

71. i. Mahlon, b. March 12 1812
72. ii. Elizabeth B.
73. iii. Nathaniel Mitchell,
74. iv. Parsons E., b. May 9 1817
75. v. Morgan, b. March 9 1819
76. vi. James Lewis, b. Sept. 26 1820
77. vii. Mary Ann, b. March 8 1822
78. viii. Jane N.,
79. ix. Chilon H., b. July 31 1830
x. Noah, died in infancy.

29 JANE YOUNG

All family records list the name of Jane as one of the three daughters of Morgan and Jane Losey Young but none gives more than her name. Jane was born before 1800 when the family was living in Washington County, Pa. and according to the U. S. Census consisted of father, mother, three sons, one daughter under 10 years, and two daughters between 10 and 16 years old. The Vital Statistics of Adams County, O. where the family was living in 1810 were lost by fire in 1910.

30 ABRAHAM YOUNG

died before Dec. 9 1817 when his widow Leah sold their property the purchase of which was recorded at West Union, O., March 9 1814. Noah's father was a Resident-Proprietor near West Union, O. in 1810 but his deed of purchase was not recorded until 1814, the same year in which the purchase of Abraham was recorded (Rec. 9). They probably bought land at the same time. Abraham must have been born between the Census of 1790 and that of 1800, and must have been a young man when he died.

31 JOHN YOUNG

was named after his uncle (Rec. 6). He was born in Washington County, Pa. according to the family records of his grand daughter, Nancy Belle (C. M.) Cooper, of Clarksville, Ia., who is our authority for many facts about John and his family. Mrs. Cooper was the youngest daughter of Noah, first child of our subject and Jane McGarrah Young. The family data of Mrs. Cooper is confirmed and supplemented by the records of Elizabeth Young Piatt (daughter of Noah), now 1946, in the hands of E. Agnes Piatt, of Bellevue, Ky. John was born between the Census of 1790 and that of 1800.

The death notice of John in the "Village Register" of West Union, Ohio, June 25 1827 (State Lib., Columbus, O.) reads: "Died, 18th June 1827, John Young, Esq., at Jacksonville, Ohio, postmaster at that place." Tradition says that John was a storekeeper.

The Vital Statistics of Adams County, O., for the most part, were lost by fire in 1910 but the Deed records were saved. The latter show "A Petition (recorded June 26 1829) against John Young deceased, his widow Jane, and his heirs, Noah, Willis, John G., and William McGarrah Young." This Petition, read in the light of the will of Margaret McGarrah, probated, Aug. 12 1859, at West Union, O., by Noah Young, sole Executor, confirms much of our information from private sources.

The will of Margaret A. McGarrah grants legacies "to my dear grandchild Noah Young," who is made sole Executor, and "to my dear great grand children Jane Young, Margaret Ann Young, Levi Barker Young, Luella Frances Young, and Harriet Sophrona Young." Deborah Jack, sister of Jane McGarrah Young, was also remembered in the will. Jane McGarrah, daughter of William and the maker of the will, married our subject, John Young, and their first child Noah was the Executor of Margaret McGarrah's will. The Young legatees were children of Noah.

The McGarrahs (McGary, McGeary), Storers and Youngs came to Adams County, O., from Washington County, Pa. Margaret McGarrah according to the Piatt family records was a Young by birth and was related to Morgan Young (Rec. 6). Elizabeth (Betsy), a third daughter of William and Margaret McGarrah, married in 1826, George Young, son of Daniel, of West Union, O. This marriage united two branches of the Young family to the McGarrah family.

After the death of John, his widow Jane married, 2nd., Robert McKown (McCowan), at West Union, O., and their daughter Jane McKown married Wilson Storer (born 1832). Wilson was a brother of Susan Storer who married Noah Young (Rec. 80), son of our subject. Lucinda Storer (born 1820) sister of Wilson and Susan, married Amos, grandson of Daniel Young, of West Union, O. Susan, Lucinda and Wilson were children of William and Elizabeth Barker Storer, grandchildren of Ezekiel and Susannah Storer of Washington County, Pa., and great grandchildren of Thomas and Elizabeth (? Forman) Storer, of New Jersey. Children of John and Jane Young:

80. i. Noah, b. July 19 1817
ii. Wilson, b. about 1820, married and went to Kansas where he is said to have settled.
81. iii. John G. ("Ivory"), b. May 28 1822
iv. William McGarrah, b. about 1824, md. Tina (Christina) Thatcher and went to Kansas.

32 GEORGE YOUNG

Mrs. Mary Jane Young (H. M.) Loomis (1828-1909), niece of George, writing from her home in Chicago, Ill. in 1892 to her nephew Delevan Young of Lagrange, Ind. said: "George Young had a large family but I know the names of only two of his children, Daniel and Jennie. The family lived at one time in Sandusky County, O., and later in Will County, Ill., near his brothers, Moses, Henry and Losey. I did not know the family of George very well." No descendant of George has been found.

The records at Joliet, Ill. show that George Young bought, Jan. 5 1852, from the Trustees of the Ill. and Mich. Canal Commission, 20 acres of timber land. The same records show that Daniel C. and Mariah E. Young bought land in Range 11 from the Commission (Deed Bks. W. 157 and X. 218).

The Census of 1840 shows George, age between 40 and 50 years, living with his family (wife, four sons and two daughters) near Sturgis, St. Joseph County, Mich.

The names of only two children of George are known.

i. Daniel
ii. Jennie

An Unidentified Morgan Young

Perhaps was a son of George, Rec. 32. Morgan Young, farmer, born, Jan. 30 1834, near Columbus, Bartholomew Co., Ind., died, Sept. 10 1908 at Vincennes, Ind. and was buried there. He married, 1st., Susan Orchard who died Nov. 24 1868. He md., 2nd., Sarah I. Parsons, daughter of John and Ellen Parsons, June 13 1874, at Vincennes. She died, Feb. 28 1929, at Vincennes (Pension records, Washington, D. C.). When Morgan enlisted as a private for Civil War service, Feb. 10 1865, at Springfield, Ill., he gave his age as 30 years, and said that he was born in Johnson Co., Ind., and that his residence was Normal, McLean Co., Ill. He served in Company F, 54th. Illinois Vol. Infantry, and was mustered-out, Oct. 15 1865, at Little Rock Ark. (Adjutant General, State of Illinois). Morgan applied for a pension, Feb. 22 1907, from Vincennes, Ind. and said that he had lived 3 years in Illinois since having been mustered-out and the balance of the time in Knox Co., Ind. The last pension payment was made to his widow, Sarah I. Young, at Vincennes.

Sarah I. (Parsons) Young was raised by Sarah Parsons Osbon (sister of John Parsons) who lived 10 miles east of Washington, Daviess Co., Ind. George Young, record 150, married Electa Osbon. Noah Young, record 28, named a son, Parsons E. Young. Family names, location and time suggest that this Morgan Young was a near relative if not a son of George Young.

33 MOSES YOUNG

born, May 11 1802, at Red Stone Old Fort (now Brownsville) Pa., died, Feb. 23 1870, and was buried at Wilton Center, Will County, Ill. (Commander W. P. Roop, U. S. N., Woodbury, N. J.). He was a miller and farmer. The family moved from Adams County to Erie County, Ohio and in 1852 to Will County, Ill. where Moses bought, Sept. 2 1854, land in the Indian Reservation, north of Range 11. (Joliet, Ill. records). In 1866 Moses gave his homestead near Manhattan, Ill. to his daughter Sarah Young Robbins.

Moses married, March 20 1823, at West Union, O., Euroia Hamilton, of Kentucky. Euroia was buried at Wilton Center, Ill. beside her sister-in-law Mary Drown Young. Children of Moses and Euroia, order of births unknown:

82. i. John
83. ii. Jane, b. Dec. 16 1825
84. iii. Charles E., b. 1830
85. iv. Morgan
v. William, b. 1835, d. 1895 at Lower Lake, Calif. not marry.
86. vi. James H., b. Feb. 28 1834
87. vii. Sarah A., b. July 3 1838
88. viii. Susan F., b. Oct. 18 1842

34 HENRY YOUNG

was born, Feb. 21 1804, Red Stone Old Fort, Washington County, Pa., and died, Jan. 1 1886, on his farm at Buck Lake, four miles west of Howe, Ind. He, as also his wife, was buried in Riverside Cemetery, Howe, Ind. Some family records say Henry was born in Union County, N. J. which may be correct although the Census for 1790 and for 1800 place his father's family in Washington County, Pa., and in 1810 his father was a Resident-Proprietor in Adams County, O. (State Lib., Columbus, O.). A family Bible, owned in 1941 by Mrs. H. E. Walton, Wakita, Okla., granddaughter of Losey, brother of Henry, and which probably was Henry's Bible, has written on the fly-page the names of Morgan Young and his daughter Susannah. Our dates about Henry and his family are from this Bible unless otherwise indicated. There is no data about Losey's family in the Bible.

Henry first appears in an official record at West Union, O. A single volume containing vital statistics of Adams County, O. was saved from a disastrous fire in 1910, and in it is recorded the marriage, May 7 1825, by Henry Young (unidentified), J. P., of Henry Young to Lydia Wade. Henry and his father left Adams County for Lyme Township, Huron County, O. about 1827 (Rec. 9), and in 1831, Henry with his brother Noah bought their father's farm in Perkins Township, Huron County, O. The records at Sandusky, O. show that Henry purchased land in Erie (earlier Sandusky, and still earlier Huron County) in 1840 and in 1845. During the scholastic year of 1843-4, Mary Jane, eldest child of Henry, taught in the public schools of Sandusky. (Official papers, owned by Delevan Young, Lagrange, Ind.).

"Henry Young was appointed Sgt. Major in the 4th Regiment, 11th Division of the Ohio Militia, July 4 1843. Signed, Col. H. Richmond." (Certificate owned by Delevan Young). "At the first war meeting held in Lima (Howe), Ind., April 15 1861, in response to President Lincoln's call for militia, Henry Young was made one of the members of the Committee on Resolutions" (Hist. of the Counties of Lagrange and Noble, Ind." F. A. Battey, Chicago, Ill. 1882). When Henry moved from Erie County, O. to Indiana, he settled first near his parents, brothers and other relatives and later moved to Buck Lake.

Lydia Wade Young, born, Feb. 11 1805, died, Jan. 17 1897, was one of the 16 children of Zephaniah and Mary Wade who came from Virginia to Adams County, O. with the surveying party of Nathaniel Massie. Morgan Young's land was a part of the grant to Mr. Massie. (State Archives, Columbus, O.). The children of Henry and Lydia Young:

89. i. Mary Jane, b. Feb. 2 1826

90. ii. John Losey, b. July 14 1828

iii. Ahaz Wade, b. June 23 1830, was drowned at sea when returning in 1853 from California where he went during the Gold Rush.

iv. Selina May, b. March 8 1833, Erie County, O., died, May 9 1870, and was buried in Riverside Cemetery, Howe, Ind. She married in 1856 A. P. Warren, a school teacher, at Howe, Ind. No children.

91. v. Henry Washington, b. March 4 1836

vi. Sarah Helen, b. Jan. 3 1839, d. 1840.

35 LOSEY YOUNG

born, Feb. 9 1809, on his parents farm on Brush Creek, Green Township, Adams County, O., was given his mother's maiden name as a first name. He died, Feb. 23 1881, age 74 years, 14 days, near Viola, Kan. and was buried there in Peotone cemetery (Tombstone date). His name on his gravestone is spelled Locey. John Losey of Mendham, N. J., his grandfather, in his will, spelled the name Losey (Rec. 9).

Losey Young was a homesteader in Indiana, Illinois and Kansas. After the death of his father in his home which then was near Pigeon Lake on what is now Route 2, Pretty Prairie, Lagrange County, Ind., Losey with his brothers George and Moses moved to Will County, Ill. where Losey bought, March 12 1853, 33 acres of land in Wilton Tp., Range 11, for $500.00. On April 8 1853 he enlarged his holdings by a purchase from W. T. Nelson (County records, Joliet, Ill.). W. T. Nelson and Cecilia, his wife, Sept. 8 1862, gave Losey a Quit Claim for $500.00. This Quit Claim suggests that Cecilia may have been a Young, perhaps one of the lost children of George, brother of Losey (Rec. 32). The name Nelson has been a frequent given name in the Young family from colonial days in N. J. until the present in Adams and Ross Counties, Ohio.

Losey moved to near Viola, Kan. in 1857 according to Emma Jane Young (Elmer) Stine of Casper, Wyo. After the death of her mother, Emma lived with Losey and his family at Viola. Before going to Kansas, Losey sold, Jan. 26 1856, to his son Henry, land in Range 11, Will County, Ill. for $1.00. The balance of his Illinois property, 160 acres in Range 12 Tp. 33, he sold, Aug. 21 1872, to his son Newton (Joliet, Ill. records).

Losey Young married twice. He first married Christina Myers, in Lagrange County, Ind. On her gravestone in Pretty Prairie cemetery, Lagrange County, is inscribed, "Christina, wife of Losey Young, died, Oct. 23 1849, aged 44 yrs. 6 mos. 24 days." He married, 2nd., in Will County, Ill., Christina Miller Gawthrop, a widow, on whose tombstone at Viola, Kan. is written: "Christina, wife of Locey Young, born, Feb. 23 1815, died July 8 1900, age 85 yrs. 4 mos. 15 days." She was a sister of Daniel Miller who married Elizabeth, daughter of Losey. Mrs. Gawthrop by her marriage to Losey became the stepmother of Elizabeth who was also her niece. Elizabeth Gawthrop, daughter of Losey's second wife by her first husband, married Benjamin Young (Rec. 32). Benjamin and Elizabeth Young emigrated from Will County, Ill. to Kansas and later to Carthage, Mo. James Gawthrop, brother of Elizabeth, married Sarah Young (Rec. 87). Losey had five children by his first wife and one by his second wife.

92. i. Elizabeth, b. Oct. 19 1827

ii. Susan, b. 1834 in Ohio, married James Mudge, in Lagrange County, Ind.

iii. Ahaz, enlisted for service in the Civil War, Aug. 6 1862, at Wilton, Ill. and was mustered into service Aug. 30 1862 at Joliet, Ill. He gave his age as 19; his occupation, a farmer; nativity, Lagrange County, Ind. and his residence as Wilton, Ill. He was assigned to Company H, 100th Infantry, and was killed in action, Sept. 19 1863, at Chickamauga, Ga. (Adj. General, Springfield, Ill.).

iv. Henry, No descendants have been found. His purchase of land from his father at a nominal sum is noticed above. He was born in Ohio in 1842.

93. vi. Newton, b. Feb. 7 1848

94. vi. Caroline, b. Aug. 8 1852

36 SILAS YOUNG

born, March 10 1802, in Wantage Township, Sussex County, N. J., died, March 15 1887, and was buried in his family lot at Newton, N. J. He was a prosperous farmer who was a member of the State Assembly in 1866, and President of the Dairyman's Assoc. of Brighton in 1880 (Snell's, Hist. of Sussex County, N. J.).

In the Hall of Records, at Newton, it is recorded that Silas in 1827 sold land to Peter Wintermute, with Isaac Wintermute as a witness. The mother of Silas was Sarah Wintermute Young. The same records show that Silas was a resident of Allamuchy, Warren County (earlier Sussex and still earlier Morris County) in 1866 when he bought land in Andover Township from his son William I. Young, of New York, N. Y.

The tombstone of Silas is covered on its four sides with information that delights the heart of a genealogist. On one side it gives the death dates and ages of Morgan and Elizabeth Mills Young (Rec. 2), William and Miriam Throckmorton Young (Rec. 3), and Robert and Sarah Wintermute Young (Rec. 13). There are no headstones. On a second side are the birth and death dates of Silas, his two wives and three daughters. There is a headstone for each of these. On the third side there is similar data about William I. Young, his wife and one son. For each of these there is a headstone indicating burial here. The last side has engraved upon it: "John Burch, born, May 6 1805, died, March 17 1878"; "Nancy Cromwell, wife of John Burch, died Aug. 17 1886, aged 75 years"; "Caroline Leland Wintermute, daughter of John and Nancy Burch, born, July 3 1831, died May 4 1899." John Burch was the father-in-law of W. I. Young. Caroline Leland Wintermute married, first, Robert Porter Leland, and second, Mr. Wintermute.

The will of Silas Young (Yong) of Andover Township, Sussex County, N. J. (dated Mar. 6 1887, probated, May 4 1887, at Newton, N. J.) names his wife, Mary V. Young, and his son, William I., as Executors, and lists the following children: Emily Roe, widow of David Roe; William I. Young; Amanda Slater, deceased, wife of James B. Slater, and mother of George A. Slater and Isabelle H. Wolfe, widow of Jacob A. Wolfe, of Huntsville, N. J.; Charles M. Young; Julia M. Duncan, deceased, wife of W. Livingston Duncan, of Franklin, N. J.; Sarah Hazen, wife of Aaron C. Hazen, of Newark, N. J.; Ann Duncan, wife of Henry B. Duncan; Mary Isabelle; and Lewis S. Young. Accompanying papers with the will list the heirs of Silas Young that had been found when the final settlement of the estate was made in 1917: Lewis S. Young, James B. Slater, George A. Slater, W. L. Duncan, Millie Mayhew, Wm. L. Hazen, Arthur S. Hazen, Mabel E. Hazen (all of whom are noted as being out of N. J.);

Jacob A. Wolfe, Dolly A. Van Sycle, Grace L. Hazen, Joseph K. Hazen, Anna B. Hazen, A. C. Hazen, Emma C. Hazen, and Harry W. Hazen.

Silas Young married, 1st, Hulda Lewis, b. July 27 1806, d. March 18 1858, buried Newton, N. J. He married, 2nd, Mary C. Vought, b. Aug. 3 1838, d. May 12 1917. Hulda was the mother of all the children except Charlotte and Lewis S. Young (Mrs. M. L. Hunt, Andover, N. J.).

i. Emily, md. David Roe and lived in Goshen, N. Y.

95. ii. William I., b. Oct. 1, 1830.

96. iii. Amanda

97. iv. Charles Munson, b. Sept. 11, 1834.

v. Julia Mibler, md. 1823 Livingston W. Duncan, of Franklin (now Nutley, N. J.), brother of Henry B. Duncan who md. Anna, sister of Julia M. Young. Julia had no children (W. L. Duncan, Caldwell, N. J.).

98. vi. Sarah, b. 1836

vii. Ann, b. Nov. 16 1836, d. Oct. 29 1842 (Tombstone, Newton, N. J.)

viii. Mary Isabelle, b. Jan. 4 1841, d. May 24 1913. She md. Joseph K. Van Bomel (H. S. Fitz-Randolph, La Jolla, Calif.).

99. ix. Anna M.,

x. Charlotte, b. Dec. 16 1860, d. Sept. 12 1862 (Tombstone dates).

100. xi. Lewis Stuyvesant, b. 1862.

37 ANNA YOUNG

By her marriage to Noah Young (Rec. 28) two collateral lines of our Young family were united. Her birth, March 23 1794, Morris Co., N. J., is recorded in her brother's Bible now owned by C. D. Young, of Delaware, Ohio. Her death April 26 1886, age 92, in Perkins Twn., Erie Co., O. is recorded at Sandusky, O.

38 ELIZABETH YOUNG

was born, June 9 1795, in Morris County, N. J. according to records in her brother's Bible. (Rec. 39) She died and was buried in Perkins Township, Erie County, O. Elizabeth married Andrew Perkins in Knox County, Ohio, the early records of which are scattered between Mansfield and Mt.

Vernon, and those at Mt. Vernon in 1942 were stored in the attic and inaccessible, according to officials! Deed records at Mansfield, O. reveal that Andrew Perkins in 1813 bought land from John Young, jr., and Jan. 13 1821 Noah Young (Rec. 28) sold land in Range 18 to Andrew Perkins. Also in 1821 Andrew and Elizabeth Perkins sold land in Troy Township, Richland County, to Noah Young. This places the marriage of Elizabeth before 1821. Three of the children of Andrew and Elizabeth were: Lewis, Elias, and Hannah Perkins. The latter married a Mr. Beech (Mrs. Bertha Curtiss Anderson, Los Angeles, Calif.). Andrew was a kinsman of the Hon. Elias Perkins, resident of New London, Conn. after whom the township of Perkins derived its name (Hist. of Erie County, O., Lewis C. Aldrich).

39 JAMES LEWIS YOUNG

born, Aug. 3 1797, in Morris County, N. J., died, March 24 1849, at Mt. Vernon, O., where he was buried in Mound View Cemetery. His parents came to Ohio in 1803 and settled on the west branch of Owl Creek near Mt. Vernon. The U. S. Census for 1820 places Lewis and his family in the Mt. Vernon area of Knox County, O. Lewis married here, June 4 1818, his second cousin, Naomi Mitchell, b. Dec. 26 1800, d. April 7 1885. After the death of Lewis, Naomi married in Knox County, Thomas Evans. Naomi was the daughter of William (died Aug. 12 1848, age 83 yrs. buried Mt. Vernon, O.) and Phebe Southard Mitchell (d. Feb. 24 1861, age 91). William Mitchell was a brother of Hannah who married John Young (Rec. 6). He settled near the Youngs at Fredericktown in 1808, coming there from Allegheny County, Pa. Two other children of William and Phebe Mitchell and their wives are buried in Mound View Cemetery: the Rev. John (b. Apr. 19 1806, d. Nov. 23 1863) and wife Ann Ogden Mitchell (b. May 19 1805, d. May 12 1888), and Silas Mitchell (b. Apr. 20 1814, d. Apr. 29 1899, age 85) and wife Elizabeth Young Mitchell, d. July 24 1896, age 82 (Rec. 15). Mary, sister of Naomi Mitchell, married Aaron Young (Rec. 18). Lewis and Naomi had three children.

i. Sarah, b. March 10 1819, near Fredericktown, O., d. Apr. 6 1864, and was buried at Fredericktown. She md. Edward Calkins, d. Apr. 2 1862, son of James R. Calkins, d. Dec. 30 1847 (Bible of Lewis Young).

ii. Nathaniel Mitchell, b. March 4 1821, d. Sept. 2 1824, buried in the old cemetery at Fredericktown, O.

101. iii. William Mitchell (Mitch), b. May 21 1830

40 HANNAH YOUNG

born, March 13 1799, in Morris County, N. J., died, Aug. 1 1880, in Huron County, O. She married John Beebe (? son of David living in Ridgefield, Ohio, 1840, age 93. U. S. Census.), a farmer at Cook's Corners, now North Monroeville, O. The U. S. Census of 1830 places the family, parents and five children, in Ridgefield township, Huron County, O. They moved about 1835 to Norwalk, O. where Mr. Beebe established a fanning mill factory which he managed for years, then sold it and moved to Cleveland, O. Mr. Beebe was related to the Beebe family some of whom (Roxy, Sarah, William) were buried in Wayne Township Cemetery, near Fredericktown, O., and also to William R. Beebe who with Julius House (b. Sept. 3 1786, at Glastonbury, Conn., d. March 12 1871, at Perkins, O.) bought land in 1815 in the "Firelands." (L. C. Aldrich, "Hist. of Erie Co., O."). Mary Young (unidentified) married, Oct. 14 1841, Roswell R. Beebe (Rec. Norwalk, O.). Mrs. Bertha C. Anderson (Rec. 167) supplied the names of the children of John and Hannah Beebe.

i. Althea, md. George W. Whitney, of Cleveland, O.

ii. Lydia, md. McDonough Carey. A daughter, Althea Carey md. Dr. Whaley, of Carey, O.

iii. Ambrose, moved to Salina, Kansas

102. iv. Anne, b. April 1 1829

v. Frank, lived in Kansas

vi. David, lived in Kansas

vii. Charles, lived at one time in Marion, Ind.

41 ABIGAIL YOUNG

born, Oct. 29 1798, in Byram Township, Sussex Co., N. J., died, Nov. 19 1862, and was buried in a rural cemetery in Ustick Township, Whiteside Co., Ill. (M. C. Ustick, Lyons, Nebr. quotes from "A Register of the Ustick Family," by Wm. U. Ustick, 1894, Dubuque, Ia.).

Abigail md., 1st., in Knox Co., O., in 1813, Daniel Bryant (b. Aug. 25 1793, Morris Co., N. J., d. July 20 1820, near Fredericktown, O.) probably a son of James and Ann Lewis Bryant (Rec. 8). Daniel and Abigail had three children: John, William and Elizabeth Bryant.

Abigail md., 2nd., July 3 1821, for his second wife, Henry Ustick, J. P., of Morrow Co., Ohio. He md., 1st., Nancy Smiley, Apr. 14 1812, at Mt. Gilead, O. Judge Ustick moved his family in 1839 to Whiteside Co., Ill. and with John A. Robertson laid out Unionville, about half of a mile from

Morrison on the opposite side of Rock Creek. Unionville was the center of life for the area until the railway was built on the Morrison side of the creek. Mr. Ustick was the Assessor for Ustick Township from 1852 until 1855. The Bryant children:

i. John, b. Feb. 22 1814, d. Oct. 22 18—. He lived some years at Earlville, Ill.

ii. William, b. Jan. 11 1816, d. Dec. 1 1834.

iii. Elizabeth, b. Oct. 2 1817, d. Sept. 9 1825. An Elizabeth Bryant was buried in Wayne Cemetery, Fredericktown, O.

The Ustick children:

iv. Elizabeth, md. Faskit H. Loomis (b. Oct. 1 1828, d. Feb. 28 1879), Jan. 1 1850, in Whiteside Co., Ill.

v. Jacob Young, b. May 26 1822, at Mt. Gilead, O., d. Aug. 30 1863, while serving in the U. S. Army.

vi. Nathaniel Mitchell, b. May 8 1824, at Mt. Gilead, O., d. Apr. 7 1892, at Hyde, Colo. He lived some years in Dallas Center, Ia.

103. vii. Henry, jr., b. Apr. 30 1826, Mt. Gilead, O.

viii. Abner, b. Apr. 8 1831, Mt. Gilead, O. He lived a time at Gowrie, Webster, Co., Ia.

ix. Edward Payson, b. 1836, d. March 3 1843.

x. Daniel Beers, b. Oct. 8 1838 ("History of Whiteside Co., Ill.," Charles Bent).

The Census for 1850 shows John Young (Rec. 17), Phebe Young and Mary Venum living in the home of Henry and Abigail Ustick in Whiteside County, Ill.

42 DANIEL BEERS YOUNG

born, Sept. 16 1800, Byram Township, Sussex Co., N. J., was given the name of his maternal grandfather. He died, Aug. 5 1885, in the home of James Cobleigh, at Morrison, Ill., and was buried in Grove Hill cemetery, at Morrison, beside his first wife. A monument shows the dates of the deaths and the ages of Daniel and Betsy, his wife. Betsy died, Jan. 13 1872, Age 66 yrs. 2 mos. 16 days. Under the dates is inscribed: "Her children arise up and call her blessed."

The children of Daniel and Betsy did rise up and call them blessed by their private and public lives which were replicas of the spirit and character of their parents. Daniel and Betsy were remarkably intelligent and enter-

ANCESTRY AND ALLIANCES OF DANIEL BEERS YOUNG

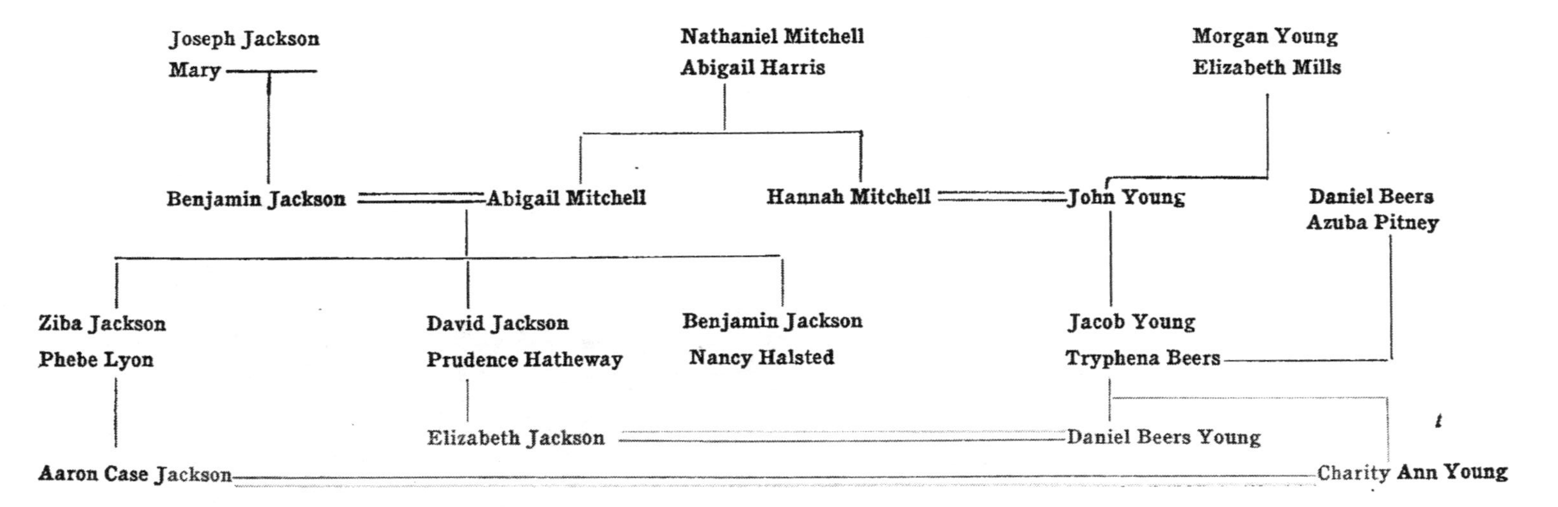

prising pioneers in the development of new lands, and both emphasized in this growth the importance of education. Hence came their own spiritual and material success, hence the respect and honors from their fellow pioneers, and hence their children rose up and called them blessed, and then exhibited, in their turn, the worthiness of their examples and their training.

When Daniel was five years old, his parents moved from New Jersey and joined the Jersey Colony in the forest covered lands of Knox County, O. They settled in that part of the county which became Marion and later Morrow County, on land that touched that of James Lewis whose acreage bordered that of N. M. Young, brother of Jacob, the newcomer. Here, near Mt. Gilead, O., were born the first seven children of Daniel and Elizabeth.

In 1838 the inborn spirit of pioneering was aroused by their large family and the liberal land grands in Illinois and Daniel moved his family to Whiteside County after a trip of inspection. He bought a claim of 640 acres in what became Union Grove Township. With him in the township before 1840 were Henry Ustick, Silas Mitchell (brothers-in-law), John A. Robertson (son-in-law), and Porteus Robertson (History of Whiteside County, Ill., Chas. Bent). They laid out the village of Unionville in 1841. Daniel Young, in 1839, was elected the first Probate Judge of Whiteside Co. and served until 1842. He was also the first School Commissioner serving from 1840 until 1842. From 1852 until 1857 he was Justice of the Peace of Union Grove, and in 1858 he represented the township on the Board of Supervisors. At the age of 65, he sold his farming interests and moved to Morrison. After the death of Betsy, his wife, he lived with his daughter Tryphena Johnson until he married for the second time.

Family relationships are reflected in the two following land records. On Aug. 8 1837, D. B. Young, and Betsy, his wife, sold land in Marion Co., O. to Ustick Miller. See Records 15 and 41. On Dec. 31 1842, D. B. Young and wife Betsy, of Whiteside Co. Ill. sold a lot at Mt. Gilead, Morrow Co., O. to Wm. Cooper (Marion, O. records, Vol. 1, p. 269). Marion Co. was created from the so-called Delaware District, and Morrow Co. from Marion. See Map.

Daniel md., 1st., his second cousin, Elizabeth Jackson, Nov. 4 1824. (County records, Mt. Vernon, O.). He md., 2nd., a widow, Harriet (? Camrier) Allen, Oct. 28 1873 (Morrison, Ill. records). Harriet died, March 8 1883, and was buried beside her first husband at Morrison, Ill. She had no children.

Elizabeth Jackson, born, Oct. 28 1805, near Rockaway, N. J., was the daughter of David and Prudence (Hatheway) Jackson, and a granddaughter of Benjamin and Abigail (Mitchell) Jackson, who moved from New Jersey to near Fredericktown, O. in 1814. There are three gravestones in the Jackson lot in the old cemetery at Fredericktown, O. One is in memory of Ziba Jackson (Died Sept. 27 1848, Aged 71 Y. 7 M. 25 D.), to Phebe (Died July 11 1836, Aged 54 Y. 4 M. 24 D.) and to Susannah Jackson (Died Mar. 9 1886, Aged 93 Y. 6 M. 17 D.). There is a headstone for Ziba with the same inscription, and a footstone with his initials. A second stone reads: "Benjamin Jackson, New Jersey, Sergt.-Hall's Co. Eastern Bn., June 6 1842." A third stone is marked: "Daniel Jackson, New Jersey, PVT.-Hall's Co. Eastern Bn. April 9 1836." A metal marker on Daniel's grave has written on it: "S A R 1775, Daniel Jackson 1753-1836." In Belleville cemetery, near Mansfield, O., there is a tombstone carrying these inscriptions: "Benjamin Jackson, Died, June 6 1842, Age 91 years 3 months; Abigail, wife of Benjamin Jackson, Died Nov. 1 1843, Age 88 yrs. 10 mos. 23 days." Benjamin Jackson was the son of Joseph and Mary who moved from near Flushing, L. I. to Rockaway, N. J. in 1732 (Rockaway Records, J. Percy Crayon, 1902), and great^3 grandson of Robert and Agnes (Washburn) Jackson of Hempstead, L. I. Abigail Mitchell, daughter of Nathaniel and Abigail (Harris) Mitchell, was a sister of Hannah who married John Young (1750-1826).

Daniel and Elizabeth Young had twelve children, the last five of whom were born on the old homestead near Morrison, Ill. They also raised Frederick Young Robertson, son of their daughter Emily who died when Frederick was 10 days old. F. Y. Robertson was for many years a Vice President of the "United States Mining, Smelting and Refining Co." Grateful for his grandparents care, he provided for the perpetual care of their burial lot.

The will (1885) of Daniel B. Young, on file at Morrison, Ill., names 10 children, 3 grandsons, and 1 granddaughter. Children of Daniel and Elizabeth (Mrs. Sylvia A. (Young) Hutchinson).

104. i. Emily, b. Oct. 22 1825
105. ii. Abigail, b. Apr. 14 1827
106. iii. Charity Ann, b. Feb. 25 1829
107. iv. Harriet, b. Dec. 30 1830
108. v. Jacob Clark, b. Aug. 22 1832
109. vi. Lucy, b. May 18 1834
110. vii. Tryphena, b. Apr. 27 1836
111. viii. Aaron Nelson, b. Apr. 3 1838
112. ix. Jackson Beers, b. Nov. 17 1839
113. x. John Mitchell, b. Feb. 22 1842
114. xi. Sylvia Ann, b. Dec. 12 1845
xii. Emaline Amelia, b. Dec. 3 1847, d. Feb. 1 1848, Morrison, Ill.

43 CHARITY ANN YOUNG

born, June 21 1802, Sussex Co., N. J., died, Sept. 5 1855, and was buried in Grove Hill cemetery, Morrison, Ill. where her husband also lies at rest. She md. in Knox Co., Ohio, Jan. 16 1823, her 2nd cousin, Aaron Case Jackson (b. Oct. 29 1800, Morris Co., N. J., d. June 19 1879; Morrison, Ill., Cemetery records).

Aaron C. Jackson was the son of Ziba and Phebe (Lyon) Jackson whose tombstone in the old cemetery at Fredericktown, O., has inscribed upon it: "Ziba Jackson, Died, Sept. 27 1848, Aged 71 Y. 7 M. 25 D." and "Phoebe Jackson, Died, July 11 1836, Aged 54 Y. 4 M. 24 D." On the south side of this stone is engraved: "Susanna Jackson, Died, Mar. 9 1886, Aged 93 Y. 6 M. 17 D." Ziba Jackson was a brother of David whose daughter Elizabeth married D. B. Young (Rec. 42), brother of Charity. Aaron was the great^5 grandson of Robert (and Agnes Washburn) Jackson who settled at Hempstead, L. I. in 1643. (Mrs. C. C. Spooner, Marquette, Mich., granddaughter of Aaron). Aaron was the brother of Nathaniel Mitchell Jackson (1803-1891) who md. Emily Allen, daughter of Jobe and Elizabeth (Jackson) Allen. (Elizabeth was the daughter of Benj. and Abigail Mitchell Jackson). He was also a brother of Benjamin Jackson (b. 1807) who md. Azuba Ann Talmage of near Mt. Gilead, O.

Aaron moved his family from Ohio to what is now Mt. Pleasant Township, Whiteside Co., Ill. about 1839. In this year he was commissioned a Justice and as such he md. Harriet Young (Rec. 104) and Dr. Elbert Pinney. He was elected to the State legislature for 2 years in 1842, was a member of the Constitutional Convention in 1847, was elected in 1852 Supervisor of the township, and was Postmaster at Morrison, Ill. during the administration of President Lincoln (Hist. of Whiteside, Co., Ill. Chas. Bent, 1877).

Phebe Lyon Jackson, mother of Aaron, was the daughter of Abraham and Phebe (Bobbett) Lyon. Capt. (of Cavalry) Abraham Lyon or his father came from Glamis Castle, Scotland, whence came Lady Elizabeth Bowes-Lyon, present Queen Elizabeth (Mrs. C. C. Spooner).

The names of the children of Aaron and Charity with their birth dates are shown in Bent's, Hist. of Whiteside County, Ill. The names also appear in the settlement of the estate of Jacob Young, Mt. Gilead, O.

i. Daniel Beers, b. Oct. 31 1823, was drowned July 8 1837.
ii. Flavius Josephus, b. Aug. 22 1826.
115. iii. Susan L., b. Feb. 13 1828.
iv. John Young, b. Sept. 14 1829, md. Cordelia Huntley, Dec. 17 1857.

v. Tryphena, b. June 15 1831, md. Mr. Vennum (? John Newton, b. Apr. 4 1826, son of John and Phebe (Jackson) Lewis Vennum. J. N. Venum lived a time in Grundy Co., Ia.

vi. Elizabeth, b. May 27, 1833, md. 1st. Mr. Rugg, 2nd. Mr. Summers.

vii. Phebe L., b. Sept. 2 1835, md. Mr. Lane.

116. viii. Silas Mitchell, b. Oct. 22 1837.

ix. Amanda, b. Dec. 8 1840, md. Mr. Lewis.

x. LaFayette J., b. Feb. 23 1843, d. July 22 1875, Grand Rapids, Mich.

44 NATHANIEL MITCHELL YOUNG

born, Aug. 19 1807, in Wayne Township, Knox County, O., died there, Oct. 11 1883, as his tombstone in Forest Cemetery, at Fredericktown, O., tells us. He became a prosperous farmer and was content to spend his life on land that his father bought in 1805 and which then was covered by a virgin forest. He was a neighbor of his uncle with the same name (Rec. 14). His will dated March 26 1860, gave his property to his wife with instructions that she give stated amounts of money to his children.

Nathaniel md., Aug. 19 1834, Belinda Shur (b. May 26 1814, d. 1904), near Fredericktown, O. She was the daughter of Jacob (b. Feb. 27 1776, d. Nov. 25 1844) and Margaret (Porter) Shur (b. Nov. 6 1785, d. Nov. 27 1876). Jacob and Margaret Shur had 11 children: John, b. July 16 1804, d. Nov. 6 1885; William, b. Sept. 17 1806, d. March 1877; Eliza, b. Jan. 13 1809; Maria, b. Feb. 5 1811; Belinda; Sarah P., b. June 20 1818; Phebe Ann, b. July 23 1820; Cyrus P., b. Oct. 22 1822; Jacob J., Nov. 8 1824; Samuel Porter, b. Dec. 18 1826; and Milton M. Shur, b. March 16 1831. Eliza md. a Mr. Weider. Maria md. Mr. Beers. Sarah md. Mr. Barttell. Margaret Porter had brothers and sisters: Sarah, b. Apr. 26 1784; Mary, b. Nov. 3 1787; John, b. Aug. 27 1789; William, b. Aug. 10 1791; Samuel, b. Oct. 20 1793; Thomas and Alexander, b. Jan. 13 1796; and Joseph Porter, b. March 8 1798. N. M. and Belinda Young had three children.

117. i. Margaret Shur, b. Jan. 26 1835.

ii. Jacob, b. Aug. 1836, fell in the Battle of Grand Coteau, La., Nov. 23 1863, and was buried at Fredericktown, O. His mother went to the battle field and brought the body of her Sergeant son home for burial.

118. iii. Abigail, b. March 18 1840.

FAMILY RELATIONSHIPS IN RECORD #45

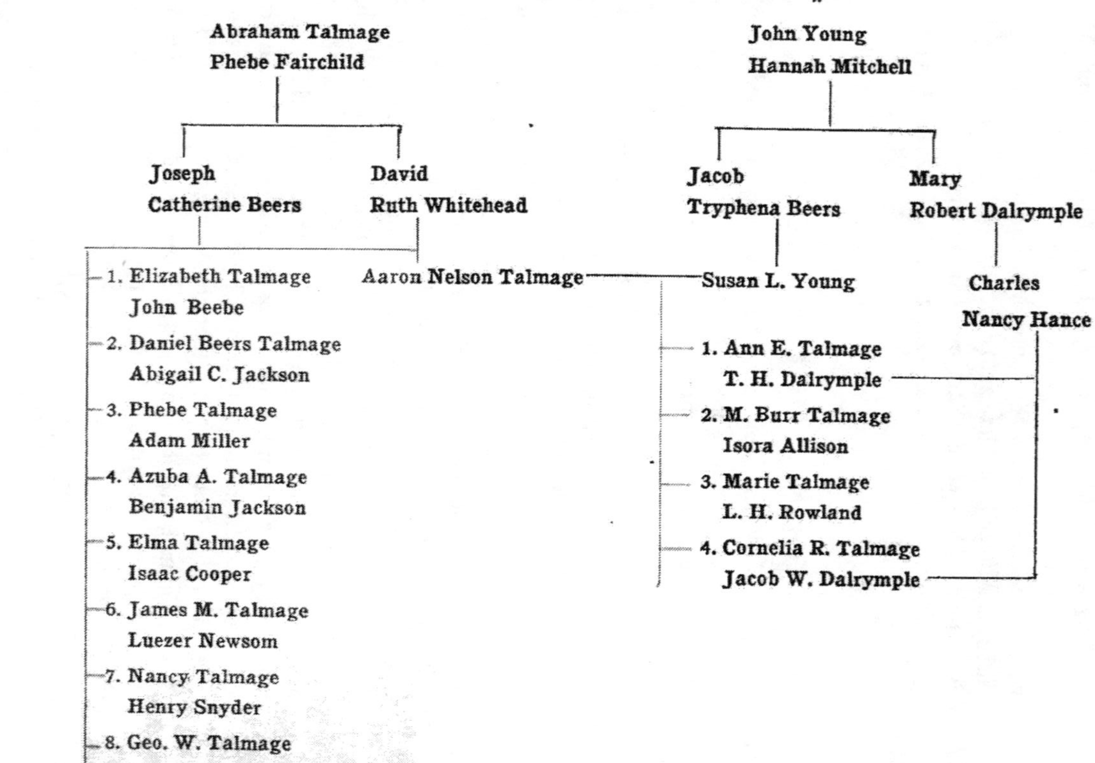

Abraham Talmage
Phebe Fairchild
Joseph
Catherine Beers
David
Ruth Whitehead
1. Elizabeth Talmage
John Beebe
2. Daniel Beers Talmage
Abigail C. Jackson
3. Phebe Talmage
Adam Miller
4. Azuba A. Talmage
Benjamin Jackson
5. Elma Talmage
Isaac Cooper
6. James M. Talmage
Luezer Newsom
7. Nancy Talmage
Henry Snyder
8. Geo. W. Talmage
9. Andrew J. Talmage
Aaron Nelson Talmage
John Young
Hannah Mitchell
Jacob
Tryphena Beers
Mary
Robert Dalrymple
Susan L. Young
Charles
Nancy Hance
1. Ann E. Talmage
T. H. Dalrymple
2. M. Burr Talmage
Isora Allison
3. Marie Talmage
L. H. Rowland
4. Cornelia R. Talmage
Jacob W. Dalrymple

45 SUSAN L. YOUNG

born, Nov. 27 1810, near Fredericktown, O., died, in 1893, at nearby Mt. Gilead (originally Whitstone, Township 13, Range 21, District of Wooster) and was buried there in the old cemetery from which later her body and that of her husband were moved to Rivercliff Cemetery, at Mt. Gilead, O. In 1824, Jacob Young, Susan's father, bought land where the town of Mt. Gilead now stands and Whitstone was called Youngstown. Jacob sold some town lots to Charles and Chloe (Cook) Webster, natives of Litchfield, Conn. A son of Charles, M. G. Webster, (b. 1804) md. Maria Newsom whose sister Luezer md. J. M. Talmage. The Young-Talmage-Webster family relationship is reflected in a release claim dated June 25 1834 on a lot in Mt. Gilead which was recorded at Marion, O. (Morrow County had not been created.) Nath. Talmage and Daniel B. Young released claim to Roswell P. Webster, Sarah and George Webster. The marriage record, in old Knox County, O., of Susan to Aaron Nelson Talmage (1807-1846, Gravestone dates) has not been found, nor have the birth dates of their children been kept. The County records at Mt. Gilead (Jan. 2 1843, Vol. 14, p. 554) show that Aaron N. Talmage and Susan L., his wife, and John H. Young (his brother-in-law) and Phebe Ann (Lyon), his wife, of Morrow County sold land for the site of the Constitutional Church of Mt. Gilead. Mr. Talmage and John Young received this land for a nominal sum from Judge Jacob Young before Morrow Co. was created and by an unusual "Agreement" between the parties concerned. The Agreement was both a sale and a series of legacies.

Aaron N. Talmage was one of three children (the other two: David Smith, b. 1814, md. Susan Snyder, and Marie, md. Elias Cooper who died 1868, Age 80 yrs, 2 mos. 12 days, bur. Wayne Cemetery, Fredericktown, O.) of David (b. Aug. 18 1784) and Ruth (Whitehead) Talmage. David was a son of Abraham Talmage (b. Feb. 16 1736, a soldier of the Revolution who came to Ohio from N. J. in 1816) and his second wife Phebe (Fairchild) Talmage (b. May 19 1750, md. 1768). Two brothers of David Talmage were: John, b. June 23 1786, d. Jan. 2 1867, md. Rhoda Gardner; and Joseph, b. Oct. 17 1780, d. Sept. 4 1837, md. Catherine Beers, 1804, sister of Tryphena Young (Rec. 15). See page 62.

The children of Joseph and Catherine Talmage: Elizabeth, b. Jan. 5 1805, md. Sept. 29 1820, John Beebe (b. Oct. 17 1790); Daniel Beers, b. Apr. 11 1807, md. Feb. 18 1830, Abigail C. Jackson (b. Oct. 4 1810) daughter of Ziba, both bur. Salem cemetery, Knox Co. O.; Phebe F., b. 1809, md. Adam Miller, Oct. 13 1835; Azuba Ann, b. Sept. 29 1810, md. May 24 1827, Benjamin Jackson, son of Ziba and Phebe Lyon Jackson; Elma, b. 1812, md. Oct. 11 1840, Isaac Cooper, both bur. in old

Presbyterian cemetery, Mt. Gilead, O.; George W., b. 1815, d. 1815; James M., b. 1816, md. Luezer Newsom, Sept. 20 1840; Nancy C., b. 1820, md. Henry Snyder, 1839; and Andrew J., b. 1827, d. 1830.

Aaron and Susan Talmage had 4 children (N. A. Talmage, Mt. Gilead, O).

i. Ann Elizabeth, md. T. H. Dalrymple, son of Charles (b. June 8 1795, d. Feb. 22 1874) and Nancy Hance (b. July 10 1800), and grandson of Robert and Mary (Young) Dalrymple (Rec. 16). Ann was the granddaughter of Jacob Young, brother of Mary Young Dalrymple. T. H. and Ann Dalrymple were buried in Rivercliff cemetery, Mt. Gilead, O.

ii. Marmaduke Burr, b. July 27 1841, d. July 15 1934, at Mt. Gilead, O. and was buried there in Rivercliff Cemetery. He md. Isora Allison and they had seven children: Iva, Anna, Josephine, Edith, Helen, Irma, and Nelson Allison Talmage, b. July 21 1892, md. Nov. 28 1917, Ruth Loose, at Mt. Gilead, O. where Mr. Talmage is in the Insurance business.

iii. Marie, md. Lewis H. Rowland.

iv. Cornelia R., md. Jacob W. Dalrymple, brother of Thomas H. who md. her sister Ann Elizabeth.

46 JOHN H. YOUNG

farmer, land dealer, harness maker, born, Feb. 12 1813, near Fredericktown, O., died, Oct. 3 1894, at Clinton, Ia., and was buried beside his wife in Grove Hill cemetery, Morrison, Ill. The gravestone of his wife reads: "Mrs. J. H. Young, Died July 29 1890, Age 69 yrs. 10 mos. 25 days." Some 60 odd land deals by John are recorded at Mt. Gilead, O. where his father settled in 1824 with his family. John's earlier land deals are recorded at Marion O. John married, Dec. 16 1838, in Knox Co., O., Phebe Ann Lyon (Rec. Mt. Vernon, O.). Phebe was the daughter of Simeon (b. Aug. 22 1767, d. Jan. 22 1846, bur. in the Salem M. E. churchyard, near Fredericktown, O.) and Hannah (Searing) Lyon (1772-1858). She was one of 12 children: Mehitable, Abigail, Perninah, Benjamin (b. Feb. 4 1802, md. in 1828 Margaret M. Jackson), Elizabeth, Jane, Asher Newton, William, Caroline, Mary, Phebe, and Daniel Lyon. Our source of information is Mrs. Maude (Lyon) Mullin, daughter of Marion, b. 1842, d. 1933, and Amanda (Dickey) Lyon (1852-1928, buried Forest

FAMILY RELATIONSHIPS IN RECORD #46

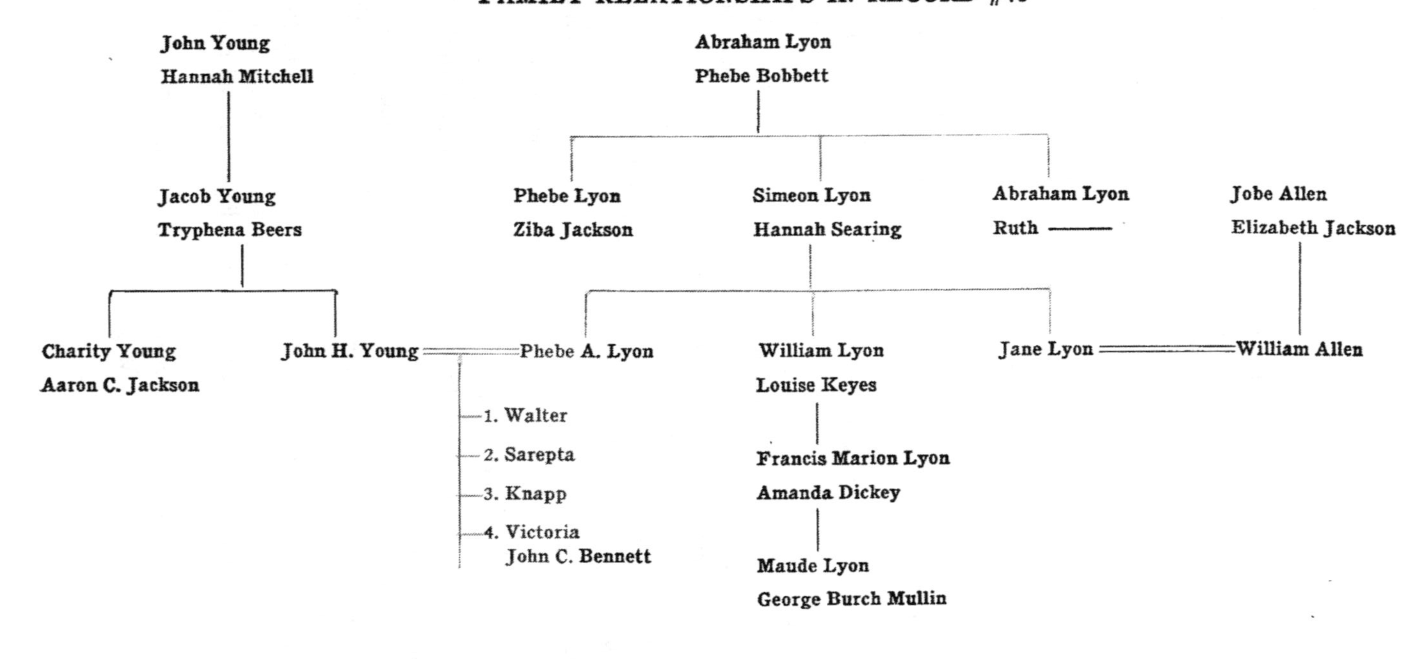

cemetery, Fredericktown, O.), and granddaughter of William (b. Aug. 14 1811, Wayne township, Knox Co., O., d. 1893) and Louise (Keyes) Lyon (b. 1814, d. 1903, buried Forest cemetery, Fredericktown). Maude Lyon, b. Oct. 27 1875, md. Sept. 26 1906, at Fredericktown, O., where she is living, 1947, George Burch Mullin (1876-1940). She has two children: Lyonel Burch (b. Aug. 20 1914, md. June 11 1932, Sarah Kathlyn Trott, and has 2 children, Lyonel Nichols, b. Apr. 9 1933, and John Michael Mullin, b. Nov. 17 1940) and Leah Marion Mullin, b. Sept. 19 1909. Jane Lyon perhaps married William Allen, son of Jobe and Elizabeth Jackson Allen. See page 65.

Abraham and Simeon Lyon joined N. M. Young in Knox Co., O. in 1804. Simeon who registered his "earmarks" at Mendham, N. J. in 1798 was the son of Abraham and Phebe (Bobbett) Lyon. (Mrs. Ella B. (Jackson) Spooner, Marquette, Mich.). Phebe (1782-1836) who md. Ziba Jackson was a daughter of Abraham and Phebe Lyon, a sister of Simeon, and a cousin of A. C. Jackson who md. Charity Young, sister of John H. Young.

Daniel Lyon (perhaps he whom the "Lyon Memorial" makes a son of Simeon) and his wife Hannah were original members, 1830, of the Salem M.E. Church, near Fredericktown, O. Buried in Salem cemetery are: the Rev. Ephraim Lyon (d. Apr. 8 1846, Age 68 yrs.), his wife Eunice (d. Jan. 24 1881, Age 97 yrs. 5 mos. 12 days), Ruth Lyon (1827-1908), Abraham Lyon (1816-1890), and Byram Lyon d. 1888.

Benjamin Lyon, with Elizabeth (Mitchell) Kent, sister of Hannah Young and Abigail Jackson, witnessed, May 1 1794, in Morris County, N. J., an "Agreement" between John Young and Nathaniel Shotwell, which was recorded in 1814 at Mt. Vernon, O. Elizabeth Kent with her husband joined the "Jersey Settlement" in Ohio in 1826. Their son, John Kent, b. 1816, settled in Union Grove, Ill. in 1839 (Bent's, "Hist. of Whiteside Co., Ill.").

The earliest alliance of the Lyon and Young families is one shown in the will, 1774, of John Young where Jean (Young) is called the wife of Asher Lyon.

Mrs. Maude Mullin has a letter written, Jan. 16 1881, by Phebe Lyon Young to her brother William Lyon, of Fredericktown. The letter describes the family life of John and Phebe in Clinton, Ia. and names three of their children.

i. Walter, lived at one time in Memphis, Tenn.

ii. Sarepta, died, May 11 1848, age 3 yrs. Buried, Mt. Gilead, O.

iii. Knapp, lived in Chicago, Ill.

iv. Victoria, md. John C. Bennett, at Clinton, Ia. Major Bennett served during the Civil War in the 10th Reg. Iowa Vol. Infantry (Adj. General, Des Moines, Ia.). Both are buried at Morrison, Ill.

47 ELIZABETH YOUNG

born, Sept. 19 1815, in the Jersey Settlement, near Fredericktown, O., md. there Sept. 15 1836, her 2nd. cousin, Silas Mitchell, son of William (b. July 14 1765, Morris Co., N. J., d. Aug. 10 1848, and was bur. at Mt. Vernon, O.) and Phebe Southard Mitchell (b. Aug. 20 1769, N. J., d. Feb. 24 1861, at Mt. Vernon, O. (See Records 6, 18, 39. Silas d. May 1 1889, Age 85. Elizabeth d. July 26 1898 (Gravestone dates, Mound View cemetery, Mt. Vernon, O.). They had no children. "Lizzie" Green, a cousin of Martha Young, Rec. 65, who lived with Mr. and Mrs. Young, inherited their property which included a set of dishes used by the Mitchell family near Morristown, N. J. when they entertained Generals Washington and La Fayette in their home. Mrs. Lena Mitchell (Vincent) Welker, Howard, O., supplied our data from the Bible of her grandfather William Mitchell, jr. (b. July 15 1811, Knox Co., O., md. Lucy Brown, May 23 1833). Several of the Mitchell family were buried in Troy cemetery, Lexington, O., one of God's acres no longer cared for because not used. Mrs. Welker is the daughter of Rollin Calkin Mitchell, b. Apr. 7 1847.

48 AARON PITNEY YOUNG

born, Feb. 17 1824, near Fredericktown, O., died, May 17 1906, at Morrison, Ill. where he and his wife were buried in Grove Hill cemetery (Gravestone dates). Aaron received his middle name from his maternal grandmother, Azuba Pitney Beers (Rec. 15 and 42). Elizabeth Pitney, sister of Azuba, md. a Mr. Baldwin (Will of Nath. Pitney, 1763, N. J. Archives). The first volume of land records at Mt. Gilead, O. shows that Aaron sold his farm, in Range 21, Morrow Co., O., to his brother-in-law Silas Mitchell, Sept. 14 1848. Aaron was the first school teacher in Whiteside Co., Ill. and was Collector for Mt. Pleasant township in the county 1873-4 (Bent's, Hist. of Whiteside Co., Ill.). The record of Aaron's marriage to Lydia A. Boyer (d. Feb. 29 1916, Age 82) appears in the records of Whiteside Co. but no date is shown. She probably was the daughter of Henry Boyer who settled in Whiteside Co. before 1840. Aaron and Lydia had two children whose gravestones at Morrison, Ill. give the dates following.

i. Jacob Burr (? Borr), died, Oct. 1 1861, Age 7.

ii. Edward Grant, died Nov. 10 1882, Age 18 yrs. 3 mos.

49 JAMES LOGAN YOUNG

born, Sept. 18 1808, in Morris County, N. J., died March 4 1882, near Wilmington, Ill. and was buried in Rock Creek Cemetery, Washington, D. C. He was brought in infancy to Richland County, O. by his parents. He taught school in Richland Co. before moving to Wilmington, Ill. where he was a Justice of the Peace for many years. He married at Mansfield, O., May 25 1836, Harriet Ayers (Mansfield, O. records), b. June 26 1815, at Burgettstown, Pa., d. Feb. 24 1881, at Wilmington, Ill. and buried there. Amongst the records at Joliet, Ill. referring to James is the following which also concerns record #50. "William Young and Maria, his wife, of Will Co., Ill., on Oct. 26 1864, gave a mortgage to George Young (Rec. 32) of Wayne County, O. for $600.00, which was paid in 1868 and witnessed to by James L. Young, Notary." Four children. (Mrs. E. E. Corwin, Highland, Calif.).

i. John Ramsey, b. Feb. 20 1837, at Wilmington, Ill., d. May 19 1920, at Washington, D. C. and was buried beside his wife in Rock Creek Cemetery, Washington, D. C. He was with the Paymaster's Department of the U. S. Army during the Civil War, and later, Clerk of the Supreme Court of the Dist. of Columbia until his death. He md. at Wilmington, Ill., Aug. 11 1862, Mary A. Massey who d. May 1 1912. They raised a foster daughter Julia Holderby Young who is living, 1946, in Baltimore, Md.

ii. Abigail, b. Sept. 20 1840, Wilmington, Ill., d. there Nov. 22 1840.

iii. Evelyn, b. May 28 1844, at Wilmington, Ill., md. there, Sept. 19 1866, John R. Stagg, who died and was buried in Mountain View Cemetery, San Bernardino, Calif. One child, Caroline Augusta Stagg, b. July 25 1868.

iv. Elizabeth, b. Nov. 30 1851, Wilmington, Ill., md. George B. Curtis, of Chicago, Ill.

v. Sarah Caroline, changed her name to Caroline S., b. Aug. 28 1853, Wilmington, Ill. is living, Nov. 1946, at the ripe old age of 93, with her daughter, Helena, and son-in-law, E. E. Corwin, at Highland, Calif. She md. at Wilmington, Ill., Sept. 25 1873, Charles Lewis Frazer, b. Dec. 19 1851, d. Nov. 13 1926, and was buried in Mt. View Cemetery, San Bernardino, Calif. Mr. and Mrs. Frazer had four children: (1) Guy Logan, b. Oct. 5 1874, at Ritchie, Ill., md. in Aug. 1909, Lola Argo, at Tacoma, Wash. He d. Aug. 24 1916, bur. San Bernardino, Calif. (2) Wm. Priest, b. March 2 1876, at Riverton, Ia., md. June 13 1905, Bertha Binkley, at Highland, Calif. (3) Charles Young, b. Jan. 28 (? 1879), Shenandoah, Ia., d. in infancy. (4) Helena Louise Frazer, b. Dec. 6 1881, Shenandoah, Ia., furnished most of this data. She md. Nov. 18 1911, Edwin Eugene Corwin, at Highland, Calif. where Mr. Corwin is Chief Clerk to the Division Engineer for the Santa Fé Ry. Mrs. Corwin has been Staff writer of the San Bernardino "Sun" since 1906. One child, Caroline Frazer Corwin, b. Oct. 27 1914, who is a professional musician (organist at St. Paul's Lutheran Church, Long Beach, Calif.) and expert accountant in the same city.

50 WILLIAM YOUNG

died, March 17 1864, age 54 years, and was buried in Oakwood Cemetery, at DeKalb, Ill. (Gravestone record). A nearby stone marks the grave of his son John who died April 4 18—, age 10 months. Mr. Young married Mary Lacey (b. 1814, N. Y. State, according to the 1860 U. S. Census for Sycamore, Ill). Three children: Edwin, b. 1844, William, b. 1846, and John. William is perhaps referred to in Rec. 49. The following item in the records at Joliet, Ill. seems to relate to some kin of our subject: "Feb. 11 1869, Charles Dickenson and wife, Agnes, of Peotone, Ill. sold to Lacey Young 120 acres of land in Range 12."

51 MARY ANN YOUNG

born, Feb. 20 1812, Richland Co., O., died, March 26 1864, Age 52 yrs. 1 mo. 24 days (Gravestone, Fairview cemetery, Troy Township, Richland Co., O.). She married, in Richland Co., O., Marcus Day, b. March 7 1808. No death date on his stone but under his birth date is inscribed: "Martha J., His wife, b. Aug. 15 1822, d. May 5 1889." Marcus probably remarried after the death of Mary. He was the son of Joseph (d. Jan. 11 1854, Age 74 yrs. 2 mos. 17 days, bur. Fairview cemetery above) and

Elinor (Thomas) Day (b. June 17 1788). Four children of Joseph and Elinor Day married into our Young family. The Days came to Ohio from Hagerstown, Pa. Some of the family are buried in Bellville cemetery, near Mansfield, O. where also rest many of the Jersey Settlement (LaFevers, Hathaways, Schooleys, Bonars, Teeters and Jacksons). Fred D. Young, of Rochester, Minn. gave us the names of the children of Marcus and Mary Day from the family Bible of Aaron Young (Rec. 18).

i. Sarah Ann, d. Nov. 5 1855, Age 24.
ii. John Thomas
iii. Joseph M., md. Mattie Stewart in Richland Co., O.
iv. Ellzy Harrison
v. William L., md. Jemina Garver.
vi. Cyrus
vii. Joshua Martin
viii. Elizabeth

52 SARAH YOUNG

born, June 8 1817, Richland Co., O., died April 8 1892, at DeKalb, Ill. and was buried there in Oakwood cemetery where her husband also lies. She married, in Ohio, William Harrison Day (b. Feb. 2 1817, d. Dec. 20 1900), a brother of Marcus who married her sister Mary. The children of John Young (Rec. 17) settled in and near DeKalb, Ill. William and Sarah had no children.

53 ELLZY PIERSON YOUNG

born, July 20 1819, Richland County, O., died, May 14 1874, at DeKalb, Ill. and was buried there in Oakwood cemetery, near his two wives, his sisters, his brother and his father. (Gravestone dates). With his brothers and sisters and their families, Ellzy went to Illinois when the land was being opened to settlers. Ellzy settled in Sycamore where he was in the banking business for some years. Upon retirement he moved to DeKalb. He married, 1st., Caroline Waldo Waterman whose gravestone at DeKalb reads: "Wife of Ellzy P. Young, Died July 3 1852, Age 28 yrs." Ellzy married, 2nd., Alida L. Ellwood, whose gravestone has written upon it: "Wife of Ellzey P. Young, Daughter of Abram and Sarah Ellwood, Born Jan. 31 1838, Died June 5 1889." Two children by his second wife died in infancy: Abbie, Jan. 6 1863, Age 4, and Kittie, Sept. 25 1864, Age 9 mos. (Gravestones). Ellzy and Caroline had two children, a son died in infancy, and Mary

Elizabeth, whose gravestone reads: "Mary E., Wife of Wm. Reed and daughter of E. P. and C. W. Young, Died Aug. 28 1868, Age 20 yrs. 9 days."

54 ELIZABETH YOUNG

born, Aug. 17 1813, Richland Co. O., died, Aug. 1 1892, Worth Co. Mo., where she was buried. She md. Apr. 18 1833, in Richland Co. O., John Logan, (b. July 11 1809, d. Apr. 28 1894, Worth Co. Mo.), son of Sgt. John Logan who served under Capt. Jacob Young in the War of 1812, and brother of Elizabeth and Mary Logan who md., respectively, John Young, jr. and James Harris, all of Richland Co. O. John and Elizabeth, with their three sons and their families, moved to Missouri in 1865 and settled about 5 miles from Grant City where they were leaders in church and community life. They had three children (Family Bible of Elizabeth Y. Logan, owned by Estella E. Stevenson, Savannah, Mo.).

119. i. William, b. March 13 1834
120. ii. Alvan, b. Sept. 14 1835
121. iii. Thomas Harvey, b. June 25 1837

55 WILLIAM MITCHELL YOUNG

born, March 14 1815, Richland County, O., d. July 9 1891, at Spring Green, Wis. where he and his wife were buried (Gravestone dates). He married Nov. 28 1839, in Ohio, Elizabeth A. Day, b. July 5 1820, d. July 3 1911 (Mansfield, O. Mar. Record). William became a homesteader in Sauk County, Wis. in 1849. The four children were all born in Richland Co., O. (Vernice J. Avery, Roscoe, Ill.)

122. i. Elizabeth Mary, b. Feb. 18 1843
ii. Lewis D., b. Dec. 6 1845, d. Feb. 17 1869, bur. Harrisburg, Wis.
123. iii. Sarah A., b. June 4 1848
124. iv. John Aaron, b. Aug. 28 1852

56 PHEBE YOUNG

born, April 10 1817, Richland Co., O., d. in 1870, Sauk County, Wis. and was buried with her husband in the cemetery at Spring Green, Wis. She married in Richland Co., O., Henry (Arthur) Dickerson, descendant of the Rockaway, N. J. family of that name. The family emigrated with relatives in 1849 to Wisconsin. Amongst those who left Ohio to settle in Sauk Co., Wis. were: William E. Pierson, and John Young; Joe and Henry Bear; Samuel Davis; the Bonham brothers; Jacob and Wm. Keifer; John, Solomon and Adam Cramer; and Smith Love ("Hist. of Sauk County, Wis.," Harry E. Cole). Three children.

i. Clarissa Amanda, md. in Sauk County, Wis., Frank Bitney and moved to near Atkinson, Nebr.

ii. William, b. in Sauk Co., Wis., md. in Nebr. Evaline Davis.

iii. Thomas, lived in Sauk Co., Wis.

57 HANNAH YOUNG

born, May 8 1819, Richland Co., O., d. April 18 1914, at Spring Green, Wis. where she and her husband were buried. She married, Feb. 21 1839, near Mansfield, O., Samuel Davis, b. Feb. 20 1815, d. July 30, 1864, (Gravestone record). He was the son of Samuel and Elizabeth (Cumberland) Davis. The family joined their relatives in Wisconsin in Oct. 1853. The first five of their seven children were born near Mansfield, O. (W. H. Davis, Glendale, Calif.)

i. Mary E., b. June 17 1840, d. 1881, md. April 13 1857, Stephen Mitchell Harris.

125. ii. John Logan, b. Aug. 2 1842

iii. Aaron Young, b. Jan. 9 1845, d. Jan. 5 1895, buried, Harrisburg, Wis. He md., Dec. 25 1867, Samantha Page.

iv. Elmore, b. June 24 1850, d. May 30 1932. He md. in Missouri, Adaline Roberts. A son Curts Davis lives in Grant City, Mo.

126. v. William Henry, b. May 5 1853

vi. Silas L., b. June 4 1857, d. March 13 1896.

127. vii. Tacy Arabelle, b. Aug. 17 1859

58 PIERSON YOUNG

born, June 11 1821, near Mansfield, O., died, Feb. 27 1897, age 75 yrs. 8 mos. 16 days, and was buried at Harrisburg, Wis. (Gravestone record) He became a homesteader in Troy township, Sauk Co., Wis. in 1849. He married, Feb. 25 1844, Julia Ann Cramer (Mansfield, O. records). Julia died, July 28 1894, age 69 yrs. 6 mos. 9 days (Gravestone rec., Harrisburg, Wis.). Three children.

128. i. Susan Ruhamah, b. Feb. 16 1845
129. ii. Mary Catherine, b. Feb. 5 1847
iii. Phebe, b. Aug. 11 1849, d. 1858, Harrisburg, Wis.

59 ABIGAIL C. YOUNG

born, Apr. 12 1824, near Mansfield, O., died July 25 1915, at Spring Green, Wis. She married twice, first in Richland Co., O., Aug. 5 1848, John Bear. The family moved with relatives to Wisconsin where Mr. Bear died, Dec. 21 1862, age 38 yrs. 8 mos. 2 days and was buried at Harrisburg. Abigail married, second, Wm. Claridge who died, April 23 1898, age 82 yrs. and was buried at Spring Green, Wis. John and Abigail Bear had three children, born in Sauk Co., Wis. Two of the children died in infancy during an epidemic and were buried at Harrisburg: John Logan, born Apr. 23 1849, and Benjamin, b. Sept. 25 1851, both died Dec. 24 1852. The third child Harvey A. Bear, b. Jan. 16 1857, md. Ida Wolf. They lived at one time near Rockford, Ill. Harvey and Ida had three children: Pearl md. a Mr. Godfrey, George W. and John L. Bear.

60 JOHN YOUNG

born, July 22 1826, Troy Township, Richland Co., O., died Nov. 1 1905, at Baraboo, Wis. where he was buried beside his wife. (Gravestone dates). He moved his family in 1853 to Troy Township, Sauk County, Wis. and was a homesteader on a farm adjoining that of his brother Aaron. The journey to the land of the Winnebago Indians and rattlesnakes, as one of the party wrote, took 25 days by wagon. From his first threshing from a 14 acre lot, Mr. Young gathered 273 bushels of wheat. He was as active in education and community affairs as he was on his farm. For a time he was in business in Reedsburg, Wis. In 1873, he was elected to the State Assembly, and in 1879, he was Sheriff of Sauk County. In 1902, Mr. and Mrs. Young celebrated at Baraboo their golden anniversary. Amongst the guests were Mrs. Young's brother, Cyrus Day, of Bellville, O., and her two sisters, Mrs. Jane Henry, of White Mound Wis. and Mrs. Elizabeth Lockhart of Waterloo Ind., the only surviving children of a family of 12 children.

John Young md. Jan. 8 1852 Amanda L. Day, b. Jan. 30 1831, on a farm located near the one on which her husband was born in Richland Co., O. She died, Apr. 23 1923, at Baraboo, Wis. The Days came to Ohio from Morris County, N. J. with a stopover at Hagerstown, Pa. Amanda was the daughter of Joseph and Elinor (Thomas) Day who rest in Fairview cemetery, Richland Co., O. John and Amanda had seven children (F. D. Young, Rochester, Minn.).

130. i. Alvin Logan, b. March 22 1853
131. ii. Benjamin Day, b. July 18 1855
iii. Elizabeth E., b. March 8 1857, d. July 20 1866
iv. Charles E., b. Aug. 4 1860, Sauk Co., Wis., died, Jan. 24 1898 at Madison, Wis. and was buried at Baraboo, Wis. He md. July 3 1882 Mary A. Carrell, in Sauk County.
v. Orra Belle, b. Aug. 31 1865, is living 1945 at Baraboo, Wis. She md. Jan. 25 1883, at Baraboo, Lorenzo J. Ferris, a decorator, who died Sept. 6 1941. There was one child: Mary Ferris, b. Aug. 30 1883, d. July 13 1925, at Baraboo, Mary md. Edward Boehm at Baraboo, Wis.
vi. Sarah Elnora, b. Oct. 6 1870, md. Nov. 2 1887, Emery Steel, at Baraboo, Wis.
vii. Jesse Edith, b. Oct. 2 1875, was drowned in the Baraboo river, Nov. 30 1879.

61 DAVID BONAR YOUNG

born, March 26 1821, near Fredericktown, O., died, Apr. 14 1915, at Albert Lea, Minn. in the home of his daughter, Mrs. Geo. A. King with whom he had lived since 1910. He was buried in Button cemetery near Gotham, Wis. He grew to manhood in the home of his grandparents, John and Hannah Young, and after marrying bought a farm in Richland Co., O. When his near relatives moved to Wisconsin, he followed them and settled near his brother, Aaron, on Honey Creek, Sauk County where he farmed until going to his daughter. The compiler visited Mrs. King in Albert Lea and is indebted to her for much information about the family which was told to her by her father and recorded in his Bible.

David md. three times: first, Jan. 1 1846, in Knox Co., O., Louise Merrihew, b. Aug. 29 1828, d. Sept. 25 1861; second, he md. Apr. 29 1862, Louisa Jane Gardner, at Madison, Wis. She was born, Feb. 5 1835, d. June 25 1863; David md., third, July 25 1865, at Sextonville, Wis., a widow, Henrietta Kennedy (Bennett) Martin, b. May 15 1832, at Dumfries, Scotland, d. Aug. 6 1921, at Albert Lea, Minn.

Children of David and Louise Merrihew Young.

132. i. Sarah Jane ("Kitty"), b. Feb. 24 1848
ii. John Milton, b. May 2 1851, d. May 6 1869, in the home of Smith Love, an uncle, in Sauk Co., Wis.

iii. Laura Edith, b. March 28 1853, md. Dr. Nat M. Smith and lived in Chase, Kan. where both died. They had one child who died at the age of two.

133 iv. Mary Elizabeth ("Minnie"), b. March 16 1855

134. v. Martha Ellen, b. Oct. 24 1858

vi. Francis William, b. July 19 1861, md. and lived in Iowa. No children.

Children of David and Henrietta Young.

i. Anna Belle, b. Nov. 25 1866

135. ii. David Mitchell, b. March 3 1868

136. iii. Margaret Ann, b. Dec. 15 1878

62 ELIZABETH YOUNG

born, Sept. 4 1822, near Fredericktown, O., died in July 1887, at Winterset, Ia. (Elisabeth W. Bowman, Denver, Colo.). She married, Dec. 5 1843, Dr. William Lewis Leonard (Polk Med. Directory, 1900). The family lived in Cheviot, O. and after the Civil War in Winterset, Ia. where both were buried. Both served during the Civil War, Dr. Leonard as surgeon and his wife as nurse in a Field Hospital. No children.

63 MARY YOUNG

born, Sept. 26 1828, near Fredericktown, O., died, Feb. 11 1857, and buried near her brother, David, in Button cemetery, Gotham, Wis. (Mrs. G. A. King, Albert Lea, Minn.). She married, Jan. 1 1850, at Fredericktown, O., Richard Struble. They had two children: Elizabeth, who became a school teacher; and Belle who married a clergyman. After the death of Mary in Wisconsin, Mr. Struble returned to Ohio and married again.

64 ISABEL YOUNG

born, Aug. 26 1830, near Fredericktown, O., died, Nov. 14 1851. She married in Knox County, O., Walden Potter. Isabel's death at the age of 21 probably accounts for the lack of data about the family. Walden is the family name of Martha Young's husband (Rec. 65).

65 MARTHA YOUNG

born, Sept. 4 1835, near Fredericktown, O., died, Feb. 21 1925, in the home of her daughter, Matilda, at Dayton, O. and was buried in Spring

Grove cemetery, Cincinnati, O. She married, July 3 1859, at Cheviot (now Westwood), O. where her sister Elizabeth was living at the time, John Morgan Walden, b. Feb. 11 1831, at Lebanon, O., and died, Jan. 21 1914, at Daytonia, Fla. He was buried at Cincinnati, O. At the time of his marriage, Mr. Walden was a Methodist minister in charge at North Bend, O. In 1884, he was elected a Bishop in the Methodist Church, an office which he held until he retired in 1904. He was admitted to the Cincinnati Conference in 1858, the year of his marriage. Bishop Walden in his earlier career was Editor of the "Independent Press," at Fairfield, Ill., and later of the "Free State," at Quindora, Kan. He was Superintendent of Public Instruction of Kansas when he was admitted to the Cincinnati Conference (N. Y. Christian Advocate, Jan. 29 1914). The children of Bishop and Mrs. Walden (Mary G. Royal, Dayton, O. and Elisabeth W. Bowman, Denver, Colo.).

i. Leonard, b. 1859, died 1932. He was for a time City Physician of Cincinnati, O.

137. ii. Mary, b. July 17 1862

138. iii. Matilda, b. Aug. 1 1864

iv. Elisha C., b. Nov. 24 1871, d. Oct. 19 1909. He md. Dec. 23 1901, Bessie L. Simms who after the death of Elisha, md. 2nd., Ben L. Hendricks, at Racine, Wis. No children.

v. Elizabeth Bonar, b. June 25 1876, at Madisonville, O., d. July 17 1900, at Denver, Colo. and was buried in Spring Grove cemetery, Cincinnati, O.

The Bonar and Walden Families

supplied by Miss Elisabeth Walden Bowman from the records of her mother Mary Walden Bowman (Rec. 134).

Barnet Bonar, b. March 8 1764, d. May 22 1844, md. Jan. 5 1791, Isabel Glen, b. 1768, d. Apr. 18 1856. They moved to Knox County, O. from Washington County, Pa. in 1812, and settled near Fredericktown, O. They had 10 children: David, b. 1793; Anne, b. 1795; Martha, b. 1797; Sarah, b. 1799, md. E. P. Young, record 20; Mathew, b. 1800; John, b. 1803; William, b. 1808; Isabel, b. 1809; Margaret, b. 1812; Josiah, b. 1805.

William Walden, father of Benjamin, moved from Virginia to Kentucky, from where Benjamin moved to Ohio and married Hannah Cooly. Benjamin and Hannah had 6 children: Sarah, b. 1792; James, b. 1794; Ebenezer, b. 1798; Elisha, b. 1799; Jessie, b. 1801, md. Matilda Morgan,

March 22 1829; and William, b. 1809. Jessie and Matilda Walden were the parents of Bishop J. M. Walden, husband of Martha Young, daughter of E. P. Young.

The family ties of the Bonar, Walden and Potter families have not been discovered but they are evident in the names of Walden Potter who md. Isabel Young (Rec. 64), and of Mathew Bonar Potter who md. Abigail Young.

66 ROBERT EARLE YOUNG

born, Aug. 5 1830, on his father's farm near Chester, N. J., died there in 1888 and was buried in nearby Mt. Pleasant cemetery (Gravestone dates). He learned the blacksmith's trade from Bryant Stout and worked for some years in Columbia, S. C. returning to Chester after the Civil War. He married Mary Ann Smith (1826-1911), daughter of David, of Mendham, N. J. Both were baptized in the 1st Presbyterian Church at Morristown, N. J., as were his parents and sisters, Sarah and Ruth. Robert is mentioned in the wills of his father and his brother Napoleon. Seven children (Mrs. W. E. Young, Chester, N. J.).

139. i. William Earle, b. Jan. 12 1852
140. ii. Rosetta, b. Nov. 5 1853
iii. Robert Earle, jr. b. Chester, N. J., md. Margaret Anderson
141. iv. Sarah Ann, b. March 20 1864
v. Mary L., died in infancy
142. vi. Douglas, b. 1866
143. vii. Lafayette Stout

67 RUTH ANN YOUNG

born, Aug. 30 1835, near Chester, N. J., baptized at Mendham, N. J., died, Feb. 2 1914, at Henry, Ill. and was buried there. She married, Aug. 19 1854, at Chester, the stepson of her mother, William Nichols Stout, b. July 14 1829, at Chester, d. April 23, 1903, and was buried in Sugar Grove cemetery, Marshall Co., Ill. The family went to Illinois in 1855. William was the son of Thomas Bryant and Deborah (Terr) Stout. After the death of Deborah, Thomas married the widow of Elias B. Young, mother of Ruth. One branch of the Stout family settled in Adams County, O. near Morgan Young, jr. and gave its name to Stout's Run. Warren Bryant Stout, of So. Orange, N. J., supplied the names of the children of William and Ruth.

i. Thomas Napoleon, b. Apr. 12 1855. Lived in Whitefield, Marshall Co., Ill.
ii. Louisa, md. Mr. Webber
iii. Lottie E., b. Jan. 31 1860, d. Nov. 13 1909. She md. and had 3 children.
iv. Walter Maxwell, b. March 13 1879
v. Bruce Frederick, b. July 9 1877. Lived in Wyoming, Ill.
vi. Charles Able, b. Dec. 5 1881. Lived in Wapakoneta, O.

68 CHARLES WESLEY YOUNG

born, Dec. 15 1840, Pennfield, N. Y., died, Nov. 19 1914, and was buried at Shipshewanna, Ind. He was taken by his parents to Lagrange County, Ind. about 1845 and spent most of his life there where he had a farm. He married, Sept. 21 1874, Sophia Ann Kimler, at Howe, Ind. Descendants of Charles live in Shipshewanna but they have not supplied data about themselves. Children of Charles and Sophia Young. (Mrs. Diantha Lilly, Sturgis, Mich.).

i. Niles W. Young, b. Dec. 31 1875, Lagrange County, Ind.
ii. A daughter, married Wesley Reifsnider, and lives at Shipshewanna, Ind.
iii. Edith, b. June 10 1880, d. Feb. 11 1889.
iv. A daughter, b. Sept. 9 1882, Middlebury, Ind. Married Frank Schrock.
v. Charles Alfred, b. Feb. 16 1885. The family lived in 1942 in Millersburg, Ind. There were two children: Charles Warner and James Byron Young. James lives in Goshen, Ind. and has three children. The names of two are known: Byron and Kay Young.
vi. Della, b. April 3 1887, So. Milford, Ind. married Milo E. Zook and lives in Sturgis, Mich. She has one child Frances.
vii. Winzel, b. Sept. 11 1891, d. 1940.

69 MARY ABIGAIL YOUNG

born, June 19 1842, Lagrange County, Ind., died and was buried at Sturgis, Mich. She married, Sept. 1873, at Sturgis, Mich., John Kennedy of Pennfield, N. Y., from where the two families came to Indiana. There was one child and she supplied the family data.

144. i. Gertrude, b. Nov. 26 1874

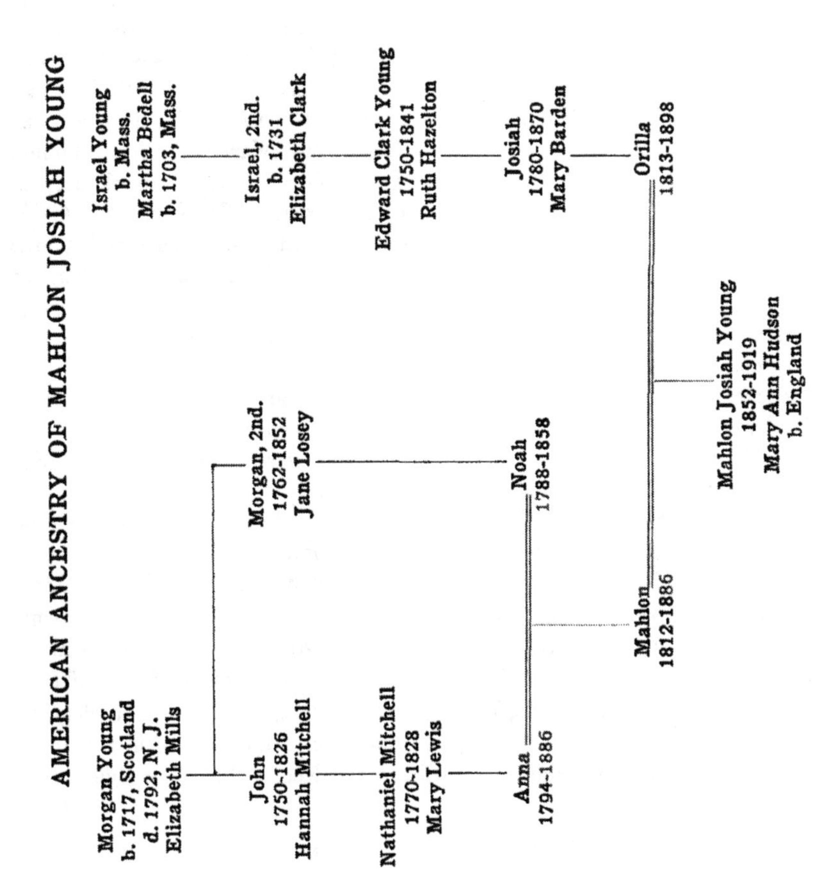
AMERICAN ANCESTRY OF MAHLON JOSIAH YOUNG
Morgan Young
b. 1717, Scotland
d. 1792, N. J.
Elizabeth Mills
John
1750-1826
Hannah Mitchell
Morgan, 2nd.
1762-1852
Jane Losey
Nathaniel Mitchell
1770-1828
Mary Lewis
Anna
1794-1886
Noah
1788-1858
Mahlon
1812-1886
Israel Young
b. Mass.
Martha Bedell
b. 1703, Mass.
Israel, 2nd.
b. 1731
Elizabeth Clark
Edward Clark Young
1750-1841
Ruth Hazelton
Josiah
1780-1870
Mary Barden
Orilla
1813-1898
Mahlon Josiah Young
1852-1919
Mary Ann Hudson
b. England

70 ALFRED DAYTON YOUNG

born, March 27 1862, Shipshewanna, Ind., was killed in a train accident, Feb. 23 1917, at Leonidas, Mich. where he and his wife were buried. He married, May 16 1883, Sara Belle Bachelder,(b. May 18 1860, Lockfort, N. Y., d. May 24 1908, Leonidas) at Centerville, Mich. One child,

145. i. Rheuama, b. April 24 1884

71 MAHLON YOUNG

born, March 12 1812, on his father's farm about 2 miles east of Fredericktown, O., died, Dec. 18 1886, and was buried at Collins, O. where he lived after retirement. (Norwalk, O. records). Mahlon followed the example set by his father and married a Young but Miss Young was of no kin. Mahlon married, Sept. 12 1837, at Cook's Corner, now North Monroeville, O., Aurila (Orilla), (b. May 7 1813, at Rochester, Vt., died, Feb. 23 1898, at Collins, O.), daughter of Josiah and Mary (Barden) Young. (Norwalk, O. rec. Vol. 1, Old Series, and Gravestone). An obituary in the Norwalk, O. "Chronical," Feb. 24 1898, reads: "In Nov. 1836 Orilla Young's parents, Josiah and Mary, with their family of 4 boys and 5 girls set out on an exploring expedition intending to find a home in the then far West. Their route was from Rochester, Vt. to Whitehall, N. Y., to Albany, thence by the Erie Canal to Buffalo. From there sailing in the schooner Virginia on Lake Erie to Huron, O. from which point they drove to North Monroeville, in Ridgefield township, Huron Co., arriving there on a Saturday evening. On looking around for a place to spend the night, they met Mr. Young; although bearing the same name, they were of no kin. Mr. Young provided accommodations. Finding this a desirable location, the father purchased a farm adjoining that of Noah Young, and about a year later Orilla married Mahlon, the son, at the home of the bride. The ceremony was performed by Squire Daniel Sherman, uncle of General John Sherman. In 1840, they purchased a home and moved to East Townsend and in 1860, they moved to Collins, O." Mahlon bought his farm at Townsend, Feb. 13 1834. It was on the main road from Monroeville to Sandusky (Norwalk, O. rec. Vol. 13). The compiler had the privilege in his boyhood days of seeing his great grandmother Anna Young in the home of his grandparents Mahlon and Orilla. See Rec. 298. The children of Mahlon and Orilla Young:

146. i. Sylvia Chapin, b. Jan. 19 1839

147. ii. Noah, b. Nov. 24 1840

iii. John Beebe, b. Sept. 4 1842, Townsend, O., was drowned,

July 18 1865, in the Ocmulgee river, at Macon, Ga. when on his way home after service in Co. F., 3rd Ohio Cavalry during the Civil War. He did not marry. His aunt Hannah md. John Beebe, and hence his given names. Roswell R. Beebe (? son of John) md. Oct. 14 1841, Mary Young.

iv. Mary Ann, b. April 10 1846, Townsend O. died, April 18 1924, at Sandusky, O. She md. Sept. 28 1882, Oran Mullen, a railway agent. They lived many years at Las Vegas, Nev. No children.

148. v. Martha Ellen, b. Sept. 26 1848

149. vi. Mahlon Josiah, b. March 22 1852

150. vii. Orilla, b. Sept. 4 1854

72 ELIZABETH B. YOUNG

died, Feb. 7 1861, and was buried in the old cemetery at New Haven, O. Her gravestone is so defaced that her age at the time of death cannot be read. She married, in 1832, Hezekiel Hough, b. June 18 1811, d. Feb. 21 1872 (Gravestone dates). After the death of Elizabeth, Hezekiel married her sister, Jane Boardman, a widow. Hezekiel and Elizabeth had one child.

151. i. Norman, b. Aug. 25 1833

73 NATHANIEL MITCHELL YOUNG

born about 1814 near Fredericktown, O., died at Howe, Ind. where he was buried. He married, 1st., Catherine Tindall (Tyndall), May 19 1836, at Norwalk, O. (Marriage records, Norwalk). The couple separated and Nathaniel married, 2nd., Sylvia Chapin. Nathaniel had one child by his first marriage and three by his second. Catherine T. Young md. second, Oct. 31 1846, W. Seymour Abbott, in Lagrange Co., Ind.

152. i. Susan A., b. 1837

ii. Nathaniel Mitchell, jr., son of N. M. and S. Young, died, Sept. 8 1841, age 13 days, and was buried in the cemetery at No. Monroeville, O. (Gravestone record)

iii. James Lewis, "son of N. M. and S. Young, died Jan. 19 1843" (Gravestone in No. Monroeville cemetery).

153. iv. George W., b. July 9 1845

74 PARSONS EBEN YOUNG

born, May 9 1817, Troy township, Richland, O., died, June 19 1851, age 33 yrs. 1 mo. 10 days. (Gravestone record, cemetery at No. Monroeville, O.) His name on the gravestone is spelled "Parson" but the Bible records of his wife, now owned by C. W. Connoran, Winterset, Ia., show Parsons. Noah Parsons was a neighbor of Noah Young, father of our subject, and also a relative by marriage. Noah Parsons, son of Samuel, married Ann Sharp, and died in Huron County, O., according to the family records of Charles W. D. Parsons (1872-1945), whose wife, living in Sparta, N. J., has the family genealogy. Parsons married, Dec. 25 1840, at Oxford, Erie County, O., Sarah Emily Andress, b. Oct. 28 1823, Wilington, Essex County, N. Y., died near Lehigh, Ia., Jan. 6 1900. Sarah moved in 1856, with her children, by covered wagon, to Winterset, Ia. to be near her sister, Mrs. Achsa Andress Tyron. In April 1858, Sarah married Henry Cox, at Union, Madison County, Ia. There were no children by the second marriage. Children of Parsons and Sarah Young.

i. Henry Lucien, b. Aug. 23 1842, near Monroeville, O., d. Aug. 17 1864, at St. Charles, Ark. from a fever contracted while serving in Company H, 23rd Iowa Infantry. He enlisted March 16 1864, age 22. He did not marry.

154. ii. Josephine, b. Oct. 29 1843

155. iii. Eugene Morgan, b. Nov. 3 1846

156. iv. Irene Elvira, b. Sept. 4 1849

157. v. Ebenezer Parsons, b. Nov. 11 1851

75 MORGAN YOUNG

born, March 9 1819, Lexington, Richland County, O., named for his immigrant ancestor, died, Sept. 24 1884, at Ripley, Huron County, O., and was buried in the old cemetery at New Haven, O. His Will, probated Nov. 7 1884, at Norwalk, gives the names of his wife and his seven living children. He was a farmer. He married, Nov. 29 1846, Amelia House, of Perkins township, Huron County, O. (Marriage record, Norwalk, O.). Amelia was born, April 20 1823, Huron County, O., and died there, Nov. 15 1911. There were eight children, all born in New Haven Township, Huron Co., O.

158. i. Lucy Ann, b. Oct. 5 1847

ii. Louisa M., b. Oct. 22 1850, died, Jan. 28 1941, at Windsor, O. She married, Feb. 7 1872, Robert A. Maynard. There was one child, Edith, b. Dec. 1 1872. She did not marry. After the death of her mother, Edith lived with her uncle Julius in Cleveland, O.

159. iii. Mehitable Amelia, b. Dec. 17 1852

iv. Julius Noah, b. Nov. 7 1854, married Hattie Pinney Shriner who died Jan. 2 1943. He died in Cleveland, O., Nov. 4 1943. Buried, Norwalk, O.

v. Albert Morgan, b. March 10 1857, died, Aug. 5 1942, at West Palm Beach, Fla. where he had lived since his retirement in 1913 from the shoe business in Shelby, O. He was buried in Shelby. He married, Oct. 9 1878, Elva R. Houfstatter, sister of Carrie who married Edwin, brother of Albert Young. No children.

vi. Clara, b. June 5 1861, died, Sept. 6 1863, and was buried in the old cemetery at New Haven, O. (Gravestone record).

160. vii. Edna Leona, b. Jan. 19 1864, twin of Edwin L., is living, Jan. 1945, with her son John E. Young, in Toledo, O.

viii. Edwin Leonard, b. Jan. 19 1864

76 JAMES LEWIS YOUNG

For his baptismal name and the spelling of Lewis, see record 14. He was born, Sept. 26 1820, near Monroeville, O., died, March 30 1910, at Chicago Junction, now Willard, O., and was buried in the old cemetery at New Haven O., as were his two wives. He was a farmer. He married, Sept. 30 1850, at Monroeville, Julia A. Warren who died, July 22 1866, age 41 yrs. 5 mos. 11 days (Gravestone date). Julia was a sister of Martha (d. July 27 1853, age 57 yrs. 9 mos. 10 days) Warren who married Gardner Young, son of Josiah and Mary (Barden) Young who brought their family to Monroeville from Rochester, Vt. Josiah was of no kin to our subject. Mary, sister of Julia Warren, married Brig. General Leonard F. Ross, Ohio regiment, Civil War. Julia A. was the daughter of John and Hannah (Austin) Warren who also came to Ohio from Rochester, Vt. James married, 2nd., Nov. 22 1868, Sarah E. Jennings, b. Dec. 27 1836, d. Jan. 29 1910, at New Haven, O. ("Firelands Pioneer," Norwalk, O., 1907-1915). James and Sarah had one child, Ella M. Young (Bible records of J. L. Young).

i. Edward Warren, died March 9 1854, age 1 yr. 6 mos.

162. ii. James Lewis, jr., b. March 1 1856

iii. Frances A., died Oct. 29 1857, age 1 yr. 9 mos.

163. iv. Rose Louise, b. Jan. 24 1858

164. v. Frederick A., b. May 17 1860

vi. Hattie Eliza, b. Nov. 25 1862, is living, 1945, at Willard, O. in the old home of her parents. She md. Elmer W. Severance, a lawyer (b. Aug. 16 1861, d. Sept. 24 1913) at Willard. One child: Florence J. Severance, b. May 11 1892, d. Nov. 2 1892.

vii. Nathaniel Mitchell d. July 18 1866, in infancy.

165. viii. Ella M., b. Jan. 25 1870

77 MARY ANN YOUNG

born, March 8 1822, in Richland County, O., was taken by her parents to North Monroeville, O. in her early youth. She died, Feb. 9 1902, at Perkins, O. and was buried there. The U. S. Government in 1941 took over this cemetery and neighboring property for war purposes and moved the bodies to Bogart cemetery, near Sandusky, O. The family homesteads (bought at the close of the War of 1812 from the Rev. Mr. Beattie who purchased the land from the Firelands Co. and lived on until 1941) had to be vacated. Perkins township was named after the Hon. Elias Perkins of New London, Conn. Julius House and Wm. R. Beebe bought land in Perkins about 1815. Mr. House and family with some 15 other families from Connecticut settled at Perkins and laid out a street which they called Yankee St. Records left by the pioneers describe the prairies as covered with thick grass so tall that a man on a horse could tie the grass over the top of his head. Deer were common and would come into the yards and lick the salt barrels. It was not uncommon to get 400 bushels of potatoes to the acre. It took six yoke of oxen to plow through the grass. Our clothing was homemade. We raised the flax, dressed, spun and wove it into cloth. ("Reminiscences," by Truman B. Taylor, at the 1864 Meeting of the Firelands Hist. Soc., Perkins, O.).

Mary Young married, Dec. 25 1841, Lindsey House (b. Mar. 23 1810, at E. Glastonbury, Conn., d. June 21 1898) son of Julius and Percy (Taylor) House, pioneer settlers in Erie Co., O. Lindsey and Mary celebrated at Perkins, Dec. 25 1891, their golden wedding anniversary. They had nine children, all born on the old homestead.

166. i. Althea Jane, b. Oct. 28 1843

ii. Laura Ann, b. Sept. 29 1845, md. John Newell DeWitt who d. Apr. 7 1893(?son of Isaac and Martha Young DeWitt, both of whom are buried in Riverside cemetery,

Monroeville, O.). John and Laura had one child, Lloyd Winter DeWitt, b. Dec. 8 1872, d. 1944, at Toledo, O. He md. Elizabeth Mooney and they had one daughter, Faye Dorothy DeWitt.

iii. Julius, b. July 22 1848, md. Mary Gannon. Both are buried in Bogart cemetery, near Sandusky, O. They had 3 children: Lindsey, Elon and Willard. Lindsey John House md. 1st., Mattie Howard, and 2nd., Doris ———. Elon G. House md. Laura Dely, and had a daughter, Elizabeth who md. Dec. 15 1943, Robert Lynn. Elon md. 2nd. Rose ——— and lives in Cleveland, O. Willard Arden House md. Rhoda ——— and lives in Akron, O. They have one child, Mary Jane House.

167 iv. Harriet Adelaide, b. March 22 1851

168. v. Elmina Mehitable, b. April 30 1852

vi. Marian, b. Jan. 25 1855, d. Apr. 29 1941, near Sandusky, O. She md. George B. Parker, brother of Jennie, 1st. wife of Lewis W. House. Marian had one child, Leroy J. Parker who md. Ada Steen and had 4 children: Glen, Steen, Paul and Janet Parker. Paul Parker md. Maribel, daughter of Harry E. and Helma (Heinzer) Storrs.

vii. Isabel, b. Feb. 26 1857, d. March 1857, at Perkins, O.

viii. Lewis Watson, b. March 23 1859, lived, in 1941, at Perkins, O. He md., 1st. Jennie Parker, at Perkins, O. They had 3 children, two of whom Elva and Albert died in infancy; the third, Ada House md. Byron Woolson and lives at Berlin Heights, O. Lewis md. 2nd. Dolly Vader. They had 8 children: Guy Watson; Ethel Adelaide, md. Claude Minor and lives in Sandusky, O.; Byron Lewis; Anabel, lives in Cleveland, O.; Rachel, md. a Rev. Mr. Thompson and lived in Youngstown, O.; Alta, md. Harold Groves, lives in Sandusky, O.; Dorothy Lois; and Faye Evelyn House (Mrs. Bertha C. (Geo.) Anderson, Los Angeles, Calif.).

169. ix. Rose Viola, b. March 28 1862

78 JANE N. YOUNG

married, July 4 1853, Samuel H. Boardman. Both are said to have been buried in the old cemetery at New Haven, O. They had one child. Benjamin Noah Boardman who was a clergyman and at one time lived in Columbus, O. He md. Mary Reeder and they had 4 children: Robert, Inez, Olive and Ruth Boardman. Jane married, 2nd. the widower of her sister Elizabeth, Hezekiah Hough. No children. (Mrs. Geo. Anderson, Los Angeles, Calif.).

79 CHILON H. YOUNG

born, July 31 1830, in New Haven township, Huron Co., O., died, Aug. 14 1871, and was buried in Houghstatter cemetery, Ripley township, about one mile from Delphi, O. He served during the Civil War in Co. M., 1st Reg., Ohio Heavy Artillery, and was discharged Oct. 25 1864. He was a farmer and carpenter. He married, Oct. 8 1856, Lucy Ann Case (Rec., Norwalk, O.), b. 1839, d. 1911, and was buried in Edwards (Ripley township) cemetery, in the Blackmore lot. Three children.

170. i. Frank Case, b. Nov. 28 1858
171. ii. Ella L., b. June 11 1861
172. iii. James Lewis, b. Aug. 18 1865

80 NOAH YOUNG

born, July 19 1817, near West Union, O., died, Sept. 13 1865, at Humbolt, Ill., where he was buried. The family, accompanied by several allied families, moved in 1863 from Adams County, Ohio to Coles County, Ill. where descendants now live on the original homesteads. Noah married, Aug. 23 1838, at West Union, Susannah Storer, b. April 11 1816, d. Oct. 15 1879, at West Union, and was buried there in Stone Chapel cemetery. She returned to Ohio after the death of Noah. Susannah was a daughter of Ezekiel (b. 1765, N. J., d. 1813, Washington County, Pa.) and Susannah ———, d. 1857, and was buried at New Concord, O. (Elbert Storer, Jacksonville, Fla.). Wilson Storer, brother of Susannah, married near West Union, O., Jane McKown, a daughter of Robert and Jane (McGarah) McKown, widow of John Young (Record #31). Lucinda Storer, sister of Susannah, married Amos Young. This marriage united the Daniel Young family of West Union, O. to that of Morgan Young of the same place. Amos was a son of Thomas and Mary (Finley) Young and a grandson of Daniel who served from New Jersey in the Revolution and later moved to Adams County, O. ("History of Adams County, O.," Evans & Stiver). Noah and Susannah Young had nine children, from one of whom, Nancy Belle, the compiler personally secured much of this data.

173. i. Elizabeth, b. Aug. 14 1839

ii. Jane, b. 1841, d. Dec. 26 1917, in New York City, where her only child, Rose E. Johnson, not married, is a nurse in 1941. Jane married Allen Johnson, at West Union, O.

iii. Margaret Ann, b. June 18 1843, West Union, O., died in 1928 and was buried at Humboldt, Ill. She married James Daugherty at West Union. There were two children, Stella, who married George Gowdy, no children, and Stewart who married Bertha Rogers and had four children. They live near Arcola, Ill.

iv. William, b. Oct. 15 1845, died sometime before 1857 when his sister, Nancy, was born.

v. David Storer, b. Oct. 29 1847, d. Nov. 23 1858, West Union, O.

174. vi. Levi Barker, b. Dec. 2 1850

vii. Harriett Sophrona, b. Sept. 9 1852, West Union, O., died about 1930 in Kansas where she was buried. She married, March 28 1877, Thomas J. Moats, at West Union. One of their four children, Ethel, married J. D. Wright and lives in Kansas City, Mo.

175. viii. Louella Frances, b. Oct. 2 1855

176. ix. Nancy Belle, b. Dec. 20 1857, died, April 5 1945, at Clarksville, Ia.

81 JOHN G. YOUNG

born, May 28 1822, near West Union, O., died there and was buried in Foster cemetery, with his wife. "Ivory," as John was familiarly called, moved his family in 1878 from his farm at Black's Ripple, Ohio Brush Creek, Adams County, O., to Iona, Jewell County, Kansas but returned to near West Union, O. the next year. The Rev. Andrew Losey Young, West Union, who lived in the family until he was 14 years old, accompanied them to Kansas in their schooner wagon. He says the trip took over six weeks. John married, near West Union, Sarah Belle Young, born, July 21 1829, West Union, died in 1885.

Sarah B. Young, daughter of John and Mary (McKenzie) Young, and granddaughter of Daniel Young, by her marriage united two pioneer Young families in Adams County, O. Presumptive evidence indicates that Daniel Young, a soldier of the Revolution in New Jersey ("History of Adams County, Ohio," Evans & Stiver) was a son of Thomas and Thankful

(Robarts) Young, of Pequannock, N. J., and a first cousin of Morgan Young, near whom he settled in Adams County, O. Proof of this relationship is impossible because of the incomplete records in New Jersey and Ohio. Daniel Young, son of Thomas, of Pequannock, N. J., was born in 1757 according to H. D. Vail ("N. Y. Gen. & Biog. Record, 1878) but this is an obvious error in view of the date given for the birth of his brother Morgan. Daniel, of West Union, when he married, Aug. 23 1825, Dorcas Coonrod, widow of John, for his second wife, said that he was 64 years old ("The Village Register," Aug. 25 1825, W. U., Ohio). John Coonrod and family were neighbors of Daniel and Morgan Young in Fallowfield township, Washington Co., Pa. in 1790 (Census report). John and Sarah had 7 children (Joseph A. Young, West Union, O.).

i. Elijah, twin of Coleman, died young.
ii. Coleman, died young.
iii. Robert Grafton, md. but had no children.
177. iv. William Newton, b. May 10 1861
v. Joseph Andrew, b. May 7 1863, West Union, O., married Leah Radar. They live, 1946, in West Union. No children.
vi. Margaret, md. John Grooms and moved to Kansas.
178. vii. Nancy Jane, b. near West Union, O., d. there in 1865.

82 JOHN YOUNG

was a telegrapher who lived with his family in the early 1880's in Moline, Ill. He married Mary McManus. There were three children. The names of two are known: Cyrus, a telegrapher, and Alfred, a baker. (Mrs. Jessie Robbins Dryer, Joliet, Ill.)

83 JANE YOUNG

born, Dec. 16 1825, Adams County, O., died in 1850, in Lagrange County, Ind. where she was buried. She married in Lagrange County, Ind. Jacob Roop (b. 1817, Pa.) who after her death moved to Oregon. One child. (W. P. Roop, near Woodbury, N. J.)

179 i. Christian Young Roop, b. Aug. 21 1850

84 CHARLES EDWARD YOUNG

born, 1830, near Sandusky, O., died about 1906, at Sabetha, Kansas where he was buried. He was a Veterinarian. He enlisted, July 30 1862, at

Wilton, Ill., for service in the Civil War and was mustered-in, Aug. 30 1862, at Joliet, Ill., as a private in Company H, 100th Ill. Infantry, and was transferred to the Invalid Corps, Sept. 1 1863. He moved from Wilton, Ill. to Sabetha, Kan. in 1876 (Military & Naval Dept., Springfield, Ill.). Charles married three times, first, Mary Jane Drown, b. March 8 1840, in Vermont, d. July 11 1871, at Wilton Center, Will County, Ill., age 31 yr. 4 mos. 23 days (Gravestone record). He married, 2nd., Martha Schoup, at Peotone, Ill. There were no children by this marriage. He married, 3rd., Lilly Linch, a widow, at Sabetha, Kan. There were five daughters by this marriage but no record of them has been found. Charles and Mary had six children, all of whom were raised by relatives after the death of their mother. (Mrs. Hazel Young Bell, New Cambria, Kan.)

180. i. Ida May, b. March 12 1859

181. ii. Charles Edward, jr. b. Sept. 18 1861

iii. Walker, twin of Charles E., b. Sept. 18 1861, Wilton Center, Ill., died in 1923 at Ottawa, Kan. He married twice and there were two children by his first wife: Clarence, a Veterinarian, who died in 1894 at Fort Worth, Texas, where he was a Meat Inspector, and Mabel, who married Albert Chester, at Ottawa, Kan.

182. iv. Melvin, b. May 20 1866

183. v. Emma Jane, b. March 20 1868

184. vi. Mary Etta, b. Jan. 28 1870

85 MORGAN YOUNG

born in 1832, at Sandusky, O., he left his parents home in Lagrange, Ind., where he had been living for five years, in 1849 to join the Gold Rush to California. He was pensioned for service in the Civil War and died, according to Miss Sarah J. Pepper, of Chicago, Ill., at Lower Lake, Calif. No record of his pension can be found. The Census report for 1870 shows a C. M. Young (born in 1842 in Illinois, where Morgan's father was living at this date) living in the Cyote Valley, Calif. with his wife and two sons: Wirt H., b. 1868, and Baxter, age one year.

86 JAMES H. YOUNG

Minister of the United Brethern Church, born, Feb. 28 1834, near Sandusky, O. spent 3 years in the Ottbein Home at Lebanon, O., and many years as Pastor at Van Meter, Ia. where he died and was buried. He married Augusta Morrell (Mrs. Wm. Green, Des Moines, Ia.). Four children.

185. i. Isaac F.
ii. Minnie
iii. Nora, md. ——— Cloud.
iv. Prudence, md. Timothy Lawson. She lives in Des Moines, Ia.

87 SARAH ANN YOUNG

called Sally, was born, July 3 1838, in Lagrange County, Ind., and died, June 27 1913, at Manhattan, Ill. where she was buried. She married, first, Dec. 24 1857, near Lagrange, Ind., James Gawthrop (died Jan. 22 1863 while serving in the Army), son of Christina Miller Gawthrop, the second wife of Losey Young. Elizabeth Gawthrop, sister of James, married Benjamin Young, unidentified, and moved to Kansas and later to near Carthage, Mo. Benjamin Young may have been related to John Davis Young who settled near Carthage about 1867 (See "Thomas Young," Laura Y. Pinney). Sarah Young married, second, Dec. 6 1864, William Pepper (born Dec. 27 1825, died Oct. 30 1911) in Will County, Ill. There were three children by the first husband and five by the second, one of whom died in infancy in 1875.

i. Loretta L., b. Nov. 4 1858, md. John Harrison.
ii. Laura Llewella, b. Dec. 11 1860, md. Charles Cockle. A. son, Wesley Cockle, lived in Sutherland, Nebr.
186. iii. Elizabeth L., b. March 25 1863
187. iv. Mary L. Pepper, b. Sept 4 1866
v. Clara D., b. July 18 1867, Will County, Ill., md. Daniel Keefer. She died, Oct. 6 1937, at Joliet, Ill. There were two children: Irene, md. William Sallman, and lived in Joliet, and Glen who married Edith Lindgren, and lived in Joliet.
188. vi. William A., Aug. 27 1871
vii. Sarah Jane Pepper, b. Oct. 7 1876, in Will County, Ill. is a retired Public School teacher living, 1945, in Chicago, Ill.

88 SUSAN FRANCES YOUNG

born, Oct. 18 1842, Lagrange County, Ind., died, April 21 1921, Manhattan, Ill. and was buried at Wilton Center, Ill. She taught several years at Mud Creek School, Will County, Ill. Susan married, Feb. 12 1866, John Robbins and they took over her father's farm near Manhattan, Ill. John Robbins, b. Oct. 29 1835, died Dec. 2 1907, was the son of Edward M. (b. May 30 1805, Northumberland County, Pa., died Nov. 5 1886) and Elizabeth (Hurd) Robbins (b. Clark County, O.). (Family Bible of Edward M. Robbins, Wilton Center, Ill.) There were three children.

189. i. Jessie, b. June 1 1868

ii. Bessie, b. April 9 1870, Wilton Center, Ill. md. William Mackender, and lives, 1943, with her daughter in Chicago Heights, Ill. Two children: the daughter with whom Mrs. Mackender lives, Gladys ———, and John who is married and has one child.

190. iii. Edward Moses, b. Aug. 25 1872

89 MARY JANE YOUNG

born, Feb. 22 1826, in Adams County, O., died in 1909, at Chicago, Ill. and was buried there. A certificate to teach in the Erie Co., O. public schools was granted to her in Sept. 1843 and she taught this year in the Sandusky schools. She married, 1st., at Sandusky in 1844, Franklin Potter who died in 1850. She married in 1856 for her second husband Herman Marshall Loomis and they lived in Chicago until her death. Letters from Mrs. Loomis to her nephew Delevan Young and to her niece Mrs. Almond J. Young of Conway, Kan. as late as 1907 furnished the writer with much material about the children and grandchildren of Morgan Young, jr. Mr. and Mrs. Potter had two children. No children by the second marriage.

i. Byron Young, "printer, age 18 years, birthplace, Sandusky, O., was enrolled July 9 1861 at Ann Arbor, Mich; was mustered into service July 13 1861, at Ann Arbor, in Co. E., 1st Mich. Infantry and was killed in action Aug. 30 1862 at Bull Run" (War Department, Washington, D. C.).

ii. Albert Henry, born in 1847 at Chicago, Ill., md. there. No children.

90 JOHN LOSEY YOUNG

born, July 14 1828, Erie Co., O., died and was buried at Cincinnati, O. He married, Oct. 11 1848, at Sandusky, O., Maria L. Francesco (Sandusky records). She died, Oct. 28 1901, age 72 yrs. and was buried in Oakland cemetery, Sandusky, O. (Gravestone rec.). One child, Merritt Young, who married but had no children. He was for many years treasurer for Barnum and Bailey's Circus. On their annual visits to Sandusky the circus owners placed flowers on his grave.

91 HENRY WASHINGTON YOUNG

born, March 4 1836, in Erie County, O., died, May 22 1896, near Howe, Ind. and was buried there beside his wife in Riverside cemetery. He married, in Lagrange County, Ind., Celestia Jennet Griffith, b. Aug. 2 1841, d. June 25 1889. (Delevan Young, Lagrange, Ind.). Six children.

191. i. Almond John, b. Aug. 18 1862

ii. Harry Jewell, b. July 30 1864, in Lagrange Co., Ind. is living there in 1945. He md., Dec. 25 1891, Isora Shermerhorn, d. Feb. 17, 1946. They celebrated their Golden Wedding Anniversary in their home in 1941. No children.

192. iii. Delevan, b. June 9 1868

193. iv. Eliza Lenure, b. June 21 1870

194. v. Benjamin, b. June 16 1879

vi. Bessie Edith, b. March 27 1889, near Howe, Ind. md. Oct. 18 1916, George F. Westfall, Postman, of Edwardsburg, Mich. He died, Sept. 24 1942, at Cassopolis, Mich. Three children (Mrs. Westfall, Cassopolis, Mich.): James Milan, b. June 9 1917, at Edwardsburg, Mich., Lieut. U. S. Navy 1942; Celestia Elizabeth, b. Nov. 9 1919, at Cassopolis, Mich., md. Oct. 24 1942, Bernard Fitzgerald, at Newport News, Va.; and Robert Thomas Westfall, b. July 5 1925, serving 1943 in the U. S. Army.

92 ELIZABETH YOUNG

first child of Losey and Christina Myers Young, born, Oct. 18 1827, in Adams Co., O., died, Apr. 27 1874, age 46 yrs. 6 mos. 8 days (Gravestone in Pretty Prairie cemetery, Lagrange Co., Ind.). She married, May 21 1848, Daniel Miller (born in Highland Co., O.), in Greenfield township, Lagrange Co., Ind. They had 11 children. After the death of Elizabeth, Daniel married again. (Mrs. Diantha Lilly, Sturgis, Mich.).

i. Selina Jane, b. 1849, d. 1938 and was bur. in Pretty Prairie cemetery, Lagrange, Ind. She md., Nov. 26 1872, Charles Stroud who bought a farm from Losey Young in Lagrange

County. Mr. Stroud died Dec. 7 1941. One child, Mary Beatrice Stroud, died at the age of nine.

ii. Manfred, b. Oct. 19 1851, md. Clara Patchin and lived in Kansas. They had seven children.

iii. Henry, md. Mary Moore and moved to Kansas.

iv. Samantha, died in infancy.

v. Diantha, b. Aug. 6 1857, d. Dec. 2 1943, and was buried in Pretty Prairie cemetery, Lagrange Co., Ind. She md., Oct. 22 1876, Carlton Lilly, in Lagrange County. No children.

vi. Carlton Losey, b. March 9 1859, d. July 30 1894, and was bur. in Peotone cemetery, Viola, Kan. He md. June 5 1881, Lodema Snyder. Three children, of whom one is Mrs. (Dr.) Freeman, of Goshen, Ind.

vii. Daniel, jr., b. April 19 1861. He md. Alta Carpenter. One child, Clarence Miller.

viii. Mary, b. June 6 1863, md. Elmer Diggins, of Kendallville, Ind. Two children: Marshall and Elmer Diggins.

ix. Almon N., b. Dec. 16 1865, d. Aug. 9 1945, at Viola, Kan. He md. Apr. 28 1897 Myrtle J. Graham, at Viola. Three children: (1) Almon Eugene, b. Sept. 22 1899, md. Jan. 11 1922, Ruth Ann Lewis, at Eldorado, Kan. One child, Norma G., b. Jan. 30 1924, at Witchita, Kan. where the family lives; (2) Dale Graham, b. Oct. 16 1902, Viola, md. June 8 1930, Pauline A. Wheeler, at Custer, Okla. One child, Dicky Dale, b. Nov. 28 1934, at Marion, Kan. Family lives in Wichita; (3) Alene, b. June 27 1907, Viola, md. June 2 1934, Clarence Porter, at Galena, Mo. Two children: Walter Almon, b. May 16 1939, and Charles Clayton Porter, b. Apr. 2 1943, at Viola, Kan. where the family lives.

x. Delos, b. Feb. 11 1867, md. Betty Plank. Two children: Harold and Ruth Miller. Ruth md. a Mr. White.

xi. Charles, b. June 6 1873, md. Ella Spaid and lives at Shelby, Mont. Three children.

93 NEWTON YOUNG

farmer, born, Feb. 7 1848, Lagrange Co., Ill., died, Dec. 6 1905, at Nampa, Idaho. He bought, Aug. 21 1872, from his parents, a farm of 160 acres near

Peotone, Will Co., Ill. (Joliet records). He went to Kansas with his father, and, on Oct. 4 1877, he married Jennie Stoner, at Wichita, Kan. The family moved to Nampa, Idaho, in 1901. The families of Newton and his half-sister Caroline Atfield lived near each other in Wichita. Four children, who supply the record.

195. i. Helen, b. July 20 1878

196. ii. Albert Homer, b. June 10 1880

197. iii. William Otis, b. July 28 1882

198. iv. Cora Stella, b. July 31 1884

94 CAROLINE YOUNG

only child of Losey Young and his second wife Christina (Miller) Gawthrop, born, Aug. 8 1852, at Howe, Ind., died, July 31 1940, in the home of her daughter Mrs. A. H. Warner, at Wichita, Kan. and was buried in Peotone cemetery, Viola, Kan. She married, March 7 1876, Job Atfield, at Wichita, Kan. Thirteen children.

i. Amy, d. in infancy.

ii. Nellie Maude, b. Sept. 21 1877, at Viola, Kan., d. Mar. 28 1942, at Anthony, Kan. She had her father's family Bible and gave the writer much data from it. She md. Mar. 7 1900, Horace Elmer Walton, at Viola. They moved to Wakita, Okla. where Mr. Walton farmed. Five children: Harold and Leonard, living at Wakita; Kenneth, Wilmington, Calif.; Willis, Long Beach, Calif.; and Bernice, who md. Jay Sneed and lives at Bay City, Mich.

iii. Claude, d. in infancy.

iv. Hannah Mable, b. Jan. 16, Peotone, Kan., md. Dec. 25 1908, Josiah Stake. She is living, 1947, at Lebanon, Mo. Three children: (1) Myron Wallace, b. May 16 1907, Wichita, Kan., md. Mar. 11 1925, Gladys May Hough, at Phillipsburg, Mo. They have four children, Patty Joan, b. June 7 1927, Lebanon, Mo., Dotty Jean, b. Nov. 11 1929, Lebanon, Thomas Myron, b. Aug. 23 1933, Springfield, Mo., and Caroline Sue Stake, b. May 7 1939, Lebanon, Mo. (2) Savilla Ann, b. Apr. 20 1912, Holton, Kan., md. Francis Bernard King, July 23 1940, at Buffalo, Mo. One child, Savilla Ann King, b. Sept. 12 1946, Lebanon, Mo. (3) Charles Lester, b. Jan. 13 1919, at Shenandoah, Ia., md. Dec. 5 1937, Verna Aislee Johnson, at Springfield, Mo. Three children: Joe Doran, b. August 25 1939, Lebanon, Mo., Charles David, b. Oct. 9 1941, and Becky Jean, b. Sept. 9 1943, Lebanon, Mo.

v. Etta Viola, b. Apr. 12 1883, Peotone, Kan., md. July 14 1903, Herbert M. Hinckley. Three children; Jobe Delos, b. Nov. 14 1904, is married and has two children, 1947; Guss Newton, b. Nov. 20 1910, is married and has one child, and three stepchildren; Donald M., b. Sept. 5 1921, is married and has one child.

vi. Lena Pearl, b. Aug. 22 1884, Peotone, Kan., md. June 8 1904, Neil Corcoran, d. Nov. 20 1904. She re-married, Aug. 23 1927, Joseph Michael Graley and lives at Lebanon, Mo.

vii. Lora Christina, b. Nov. 10 1887, Peotone, Kan., md. Aug. 23 1927, William Randolph Kane.

viii. Florence Irene, b. Aug. 11 1890, Peotone, Kan., md. Feb. 3 1914, John Richmond Butler, d. Feb. 9 1933.

ix. Alda May, b. Apr. 6 1892, Peotone, Kan., md. May 20 1912, Clement Harry Thompson.

x. Alva Raymond, b. Dec. 24 1894, Viola, Kan., md. Aug. 20 1921, Esther Fern Clark. Three children: Alva Raymond, b. June 7 1922, Wichita, Kan., md. May 11 1946, Jenot Adelaide Melee; Betty Fern, b. July 18 1930, Independance, Mo., and Billy Eugene Atfield, b. Aug. 20 1932.

xi. Locey Clyde, b. Sept. 2 1895, Viola, Kan., md. Nov. 19 1937, Grace Olive Sanders.

xii. Lester Charles, died in infancy.

xiii. Emma Marie, b. Aug. 11 1899, Viola, Kan., md. June 4 1922, at Wichita, Kan., Adolph Henry Warner. Three children: Adolph H., b. Dec. 7 1923, d. Dec. 12 1928, Wichita, Kan.; Norma Jean, b. June 5 1929, Wichita, Kan.; and Imogene Warner, b. Sept. 9 1930. The family lives in Oakland, Calif.

95 WILLIAM IRA YOUNG

born, Oct. 1 1830, near Allamuchy, N. J., died, Oct. 15 1920, at Andover, N. J., and was buried in the family lot at Newton, N. J. His will is on file at Newton, N. J. He was interested in genealogy and had his line back to his immigrant ancestor engraved on the family monument. He inherited the family story from William Young (Rec. 3) and to preserve it, had it published in the Gen. Column of the Newark Evening News (#5742). In his earlier life, William was a successful farmer in Sussex County, N. J. where he was active in promoting the welfare of the county. Later he moved to New York and engaged in the produce commission business in which he was eminently prosperous. He sold his farm in Andover township, March 13 1866, to his father (Newton records). He married Mary Burch (b. March 17 1833, d. June 12 1919) daughter of John and Nancy (Cromwell) Burch. Caroline, sister of Mary Burch Young, md. 1st Robert Porter Leland, and 2nd. ——— Wintermute. One child.

199. i. Willard Burch, b. 1856

96 AMANDA YOUNG

married James Britton Slater and they had two children, Isabelle and George A. Slater. Isabelle md. Jacob A. Wolfe and lived in Huntsville, N. J. They had one child, "Dolly," who md. Roy C. Van Sycle. Roy and Dolly had one child, John R. Van Sycle who md. Cecile Johnson. George A. Slater md. and had two children, William and Alvin, both live in Denver, Colo. William has a daughter, Helen Slater, and Alvin has eight children: Wesley, Roy, Dorothy, Norman, Virginia, Mildred, Delma and George Slater (Mrs. Milton L. Hunt, Andover, N. J.).

97 CHARLES MUNSON YOUNG

married twice. The name of his first wife is not known. He married for his second wife, Amanda, daughter of Samuel Young, in Sussex County, N. J. Charles had one child by his first wife. Charles was buried at Hackettstown, N. J.

i. Charles Munson, jr., b. Nov. 30 1864, d. Dec. 6 1926, at Waverly, N. Y. where he was buried. He was a dairy farmer. He md., Nov. 25 1903, Margaret MacGregor, at Waverly. No children (Mrs. C. M. Young, Waverly, N. Y.).

98 SARAH YOUNG

born, 1836, died, 1904, buried at Newton, N. J. (Gravestone rec.). She married, in 1854, Aaron Coursen Hazen (b. 1825, d. 1914) son of Joseph

Kerr (1796-1885) and Phebe (Primrose) Hazen (1799-1885). Six children.

200. i. Silas Lewis, b. Jan. 9 1856

201. ii. William Livingston, b. May 4 1861

iii. Sarah Emma, b. 1857, d. 1878 (Gravestone, Newton, N. J.)

iv. Joseph Kerr

v. Aaron C. jr., lives in Summit, N. J.

vi. Anna Belle, buried Newton, N. J.

99 ANNA YOUNG

married Henry B. Duncan, son of William and Catherine (Benson) Duncan who were married in 1823. Henry's brother, Livingston W. Duncan, married Julia Hibler Young, sister of Anna. The Duncan brothers owned a woolen mill at Franklin, now Nutley, N. J. Henry and Anna had four children (W. L. Duncan, Caldwell, N. J.).

i. William, died in infancy.

ii. Millie, md. 1883, T. C. Jackson. They had two children: Elizabeth L. and Charles L. Jackson. Millie md. 2nd. E. A. Mayhew in N. J.

iii. William Livingston, md. 1st. in 1918 Jessie Russ. After her death, he md. 2nd. in 1924 C. E. Darrass. He lives in Caldwell, N. J. No children.

iv. Julia, died in infancy.

100 LEWIS STUYVESANT YOUNG

was born in 1862 and died in 1941 (Gravestone rec. at Newton, N. J.). He married in Fredon township, Sussex County, N. J., Christine Greer, daughter of George (b. 1822, Newton, N. J.) and Margaret A. (Hibler) Greer, daughter of Adam (b. July 9 1801) and Elizabeth (Young) Hibler. Elizabeth Young was the daughter of John Young(s) of Andover township, Sussex County, N. J. (Snell's, Hist, of Sussex County, N. J.). Margaret J. Greer, sister of Christine, married Daniel Losey, of Morristown, N. J. Lewis and Christine had one child.

i. George Greer b. Oct. 12 1889, d. 1946, at Newton, N. J. where he was a Notary and Justice of the Peace. He md. in Oct. 1918, at Baltimore, Md., Susie Frances Phlegar, of

Roanoke, Va. Two children: Francis Theodore, b. Sept. 11 1922, at Newton, N. J., md. Nov. 21 1940, Flora May Drake, of Sparta, N. J. and has a son, Theodore Edmund, b. Feb. 21 1944, at Sparta; and Lewis Stuyvesant Young who is serving as rear gunner with the Air Forces in Italy in 1945. Francis is in training with the Air Force.

101 WILLIAM MITCHELL YOUNG

generally called "Mitch" was born, May 21 1830, on a farm about 3 miles west of Fredericktown, O., and died, April 1 1910, age 79 yrs. 11 mos. and was buried in Mound View cemetery, Mt. Vernon, O., Mr. Young was in the jewelry business for many years. He served in the Civil War in Company A, 96th O.V.I. He married, Oct. 14 1852, Roxanna Ward (1833-1922) at Mt. Vernon, O. Five children, all born at Mt. Vernon, O.

i. Carrie Cornelia, b. 1854, d. Nov. 13 1861
ii. James Lewis, b. 1859, d. Mar. 23 1864
iii. Minerva E., b. Dec. 31 1861, d. June 18 1924. She married, at Mt. Vernon, George Beaton. No children.
iv. Clarence Ward, b. 1863, d. March 5 1905
v. Carl Dwight, b. Sept. 15 1865, lives, 1945, at Delaware, O. He was associated with his father in the Jewelry business and carried on the business after the death of his father until he retired and moved to Delaware. Mr. Young supplied this family information from the Bible of his grandfather James Lewis Young, and from data collected by Mrs. Beaton, his sister. Her records state without the source being given that Morgan Young, immigrant ancestor, arrived in America from Scotland, Oct. 11 1722, aged 9 years. Carl married, Oct. 24 1900, Elsa Harris, at Mt. Vernon, O. One child, Mary Roxanna, called "Marox," b. Aug. 13 1904, at Mt. Vernon. She is living with her parents at Delaware, O. Marox md. June 11 1927, Whitney Cline Dunton, and has a daughter, Roxanna Dunton, b. July 10 1928, at Mt. Vernon.

102 ANN BEEBE

born, April 1 1829, near Norwalk, O., died, Dec. 16 1903. She married, June 28 1853, Charles Elliot Pennewell, b. Jan. 11 1829, at Sandusky, O., died in 1904 at Cleveland, O. Judge Pennewell was admitted to the bar of Ohio in 1851 and practiced his profession at Norwalk until 1875 when he moved his family to Cleveland. He was elected to the common pleas bench at Norwalk in 1869.

103 HENRY USTICK, JR.

born, April 30 1826, at Mt. Gilead, O., died, May 2 1907, at Chicago, Ill., and was buried at Morrison Ill. He married Susan McMullen at Savanna, Ill. Seven children. (M. C. Ustick of Lyons, Nebr. supplied the family data from the "Register of the Ustick Family," privately printed at Dubuque, Ia., 1894, by Wm. W. Ustick).

i. Sarah E., b. June 28 1849, married N. F. Pettitt, at Morrison, Ill. A son, Dr. H. L. Pettitt, lives in Morrison, Ill.

ii. Emily Abigail, b. July 6 1851, died and was buried at Morrison, Ill. She married, Nov. 5 1875, Lorin E. Tuttle, a son of Henry of Windham, N. Y. Two children: Ivy May, b. Oct. 2 1878, at Morrison, Ill., married, July 26 1900, Louis O. Woods, and lives in Morrison; and Mary Belle Tuttle, b. Nov. 19 1884, at Morrison, Ill. where she married Fred O. Jamison. They live in Morrison.

iii. Edward Payson, b. April 30 1853

iv. John William, b. April 13 1856

v. Lillie D., b. May 27 1858, married David Wink.

vi. Anna Belle, b. Nov. 12 1865

vii. Mitchell C., b. July 8 1869, at Morrison, Ill., lives 1945 at Lyons, Nebr. He married in 1906 Isadora Libby at Pasadena, Calif. No children.

104 EMILY YOUNG

born, Oct. 22 1825, at Mt. Gilead, O., died, May 13 1858, and was buried at Morrison, Ill. She married at Unionville, Ill., Aug. 7 1842, John Alexander Robertson, b. Aug. 5 1812, at Cambridge, N. Y., d. Dec. 5 1875, at Morrison, Ill. Mr. Robertson went to Illinois in 1836 on a trip of investigation, returned to his native state, and then in 1838, in company with Henry Ustick of Washington County, Pa., he went back to Whiteside County, Ill. to become one of the founders and proprietors of Unionville. He built a sawmill and hotel and soon became outstanding for his fine business ability and esteemed by the entire community. He retired from business in 1870 and resided with his daughter, Mrs. D. S. Spafford, at Morrison, Ill. In his retirement, he used to tell how while looking after his lumber business he would shoot deer which came to cross Rock Creek, near which his mill was located.

Mr. Robertson, like his wife, was of Scotch origin. He was the son of Adam (b. Jan. 19 1781, at Ancram, Jedburg, Scotland) and Katherine (Kennedy) Robertson. His grandparents, John Robertson and Christina Porteous, were married in Scotland about 1775 and came to settle at Cambridge, N. Y. in 1783-84. John was the son of Thomas (Presenter, at one time, in the Presbyterian Church, at Ancram) and Janet (Christie) Robertson. The children of John and Emily Robertson were all born in Whiteside County, Ill. (J. P. Robertson, Washington, D. C.).

202. i. Eliza Ann, b. Jan. 15 1844

203. ii. Andrew J., b. Nov. 26 1845

iii. Lewis, b. Feb. 16 1848, d. June 20 1927, at Los Angeles, Calif. He md. Feb. 6 1873, at Kewanee, Ill., Hannah S. Williams, d. Apr. 23 1893. One child, John Alexander Robertson, b. Aug. 12 1886, at Exeter, Nebr., is living, 1946, in Los Angeles, Calif. with his wife, née Mabel Cleveland, whom he md. March 10 1910, at Hermosa Beach, Calif.

iv. Beers Young, b. Feb. 24 1850, d. July 31 1855.

v. LeRoy, b. Aug. 7 1852, md. in 1898, Ethyl Garnett. A son, Garnett R. Robertson, lived in Lafayette, Calif. LeRoy went to Calif. about 1891 and became associated with the Bank of Calif. at Fruitvale. Earlier he was in the cattle business with his brother Andrew in Wyoming. From here he went to Kearney, Nebr. and was associated with Frederick Y. Robertson in the banking business. He died at Oakland, Calif., 1922.

204. vi. Ida May, b. April 9 1855

vii. Frederick Young, b. May 3 1858, at Morrison, Ill., d. July 12 1938, in the Doctor's Hospital, N. Y., and was buried at Morrison, Ill. His mother died shortly after his birth and he was raised in the home of his grandparents, Daniel B. and Elizabeth Young. He was, at the time of his death, Vice-President and Gen'l. Manager of the U. S. Smelting, Refining and Mining Co. and lived in Connecticut. He md. Oct. 14 1879, Eva Anderson, b. Oct. 1 1860, d. in 1939.

105 ABIGAIL YOUNG

born, April 14 1827, at Young's Mill, near Fredericktown, O., died, Aug. 26 1863, at Wethersfield, Ill. where she and her husband were buried. She married, Oct. 20 1847, at Morrison, Ill., Matthew Bonar Potter (b. Dec. 16 1821, in Coshocton County, O., died, Dec. 21 1891, son of David). David Potter and Daniel B. Young had adjoining farms in Ohio, and they moved their families in 1838 to Illinois where again they were neighbors. The children of the two families grew up and went to school together, and in time two sons of David married two daughters of Daniel. John P. Potter married Charity Ann, sister of Abigail Young. The Potters and the Youngs were amongst the first settlers in Whiteside County, Ill. Matthew and John Potter, sons of David and Elizabeth (Cosner) Potter (md. 1821), and grandsons of Philo and Mary (Hixenbaugh) Potter, built the first house in Kewanee, Ill. This house is now the Chapter House of the local D.A.R. It has on it a bronze tablet that reads: "This house was built in 1850 by Matthew and John Potter and was the only one standing on the town site when the village of Kewanee was laid out May 1 1854. It was a gift from the Masonic fraternity to the Chapter and was moved from the original site on North Main Street to the present location June 23 1903." When the C. B. & Q. Ry. bisected their farm, the Potter boys bought farms in nearby Wethersfield township. Matthew and Abigail Potter had four children, all born in Wethersfield, now Kewanee, Ill.

i. James Warren, b. March 19 1849, d. Oct. 1890, and was buried at Kansas City, Mo. He married, May 15 1878, Mamie Austin, at Kansas City.

ii. Lucy Caroline, b. Oct. 23 1851, d. May 27 1854.

205. iii. Matthew Henry, b. Dec. 27 1855

206. iv. Carrie E., b. Feb. 20 1858 - Died - 1947

106 CHARITY ANN YOUNG

born, Feb. 25 1829, at Young's Mill, Knox Co., O. (near Fredericktown), died, Dec. 5 1896, at Kewanee, Ill. where she and her husband were buried. She was taken by her parents in 1837 to Union Grove, Whiteside Co., Ill. She married, March 27 1849, at Lafayette, Stark Co., Ill., John P. Potter, brother of Matthew (Rec. 105), whom she had known from childhood, their father's farms having joined in Ohio. After living a few months in Wethersfield, they moved into Kewanee, Ill. John Potter, b. March 26 1823, in Knox (now Coshocton) Co., O., died, Oct. 23 1898, at Kewanee. Alvina was born in Wethersfield, the other children in Kewanee (Noble E. Potter, Kewanee, Ill.).

207. i. Alvina E., b. Jan. 18 1850

ii. Emily Rosalie, b. Jan. 21 1853, d. Aug. 1 1901, bur. at Kewanee, Ill. Not marry.

iii. Bessie Young, b. Apr. 26 1855, died in Jan. 1939, at Rapid City, S. D. where she was buried. She md. in 1885, at Sioux Falls, S. D., Herbert Green. They had one child, John Benjamin Green, b. in May 1887, md. and lived in Deadwood, S. D.

iv. Lucy Jacobs, b. in Oct. 1857, d. Oct. 9 1858, bur. at Kewanee, Ill.

208 v. Noble Elbert, b. Nov. 21 1859

vi. Daniel Beers, b. Feb. 24 1866, d. the same day.

vii. Charity Ann, b. Oct. 30 1869, d. Oct. 7 1870.

107 HARRIET YOUNG

born, Dec. 30 1830, at Mt. Gilead, O., died, May 29 1920, at Duarte, Calif. She was taken by her parents in 1838 to Whiteside County, Ill. where she grew to womanhood and married, March 29 1920, Dr. Elbert Pinney (b. Jan. 29 1824, in Penn., d. March 14 1914, at Duarte and was buried in Live Oak cemetery, Monrovia, Calif.), at Morrison, Ill. They were married by Aaron C. Jackson, J. P., husband of Charity Young, sister of Harriet. They celebrated their golden wedding anniversary in 1899. Elbert Pinney was educated in Meadville, Pa. and there began his study of medicine which he completed at Starling Medical College, Columbus, O. He practiced a short time in Wethersfield, Ill. and then took graduate work at Miami College, Cincinnati, O. After a few years practice in Kewanee, Ill., he moved his family in 1856 to White Rock, Texas. He served as a Surgeon in the Confederate Army. In 1868, he settled in Preston, Jaspar County, Mo. where he opened a general merchandise and drug store, in addition to practicing medicine and running his farm. At one time he was President of the First National Bank and of the Farmers and Merchants Bank of Carthage, Mo. In 1886 he gave up the practice of medicine and moved his family to an orange grove farm in the San Gabriel Valley, Duarte, Calif. and gave his full time to fruit growing (Grace Pinney Johnson, San Francisco, Calif.). Dr. and Mrs. Pinney had eleven children.

i. Elbert Clark, b. Apr. 21 1850, Kewanee, Ill., d. Dec. 5 1865, and was buried at Huntsville, Texas.

209. ii. Henry Beers, b. Dec. 28 1851

iii. John Lewis, b. March 20 1854, Kewanee, Ill., died, March 7 1935, Monrovia, Calif. He married, 1st., in 1877 Rose Waring, at Preston, Mo. In June 1882, he married, 2nd., Ludia Brown. To them was born a son, Elbert, who died Apr. 1889, aged 5 years. He married, 3rd, July 4 1889, Olga Miller, and they moved to Monrovia, Calif. John and Olga Pinney had two children: John Lewis, jr. born, Sept. 14 1903, Long Beach, Calif. who married and has a daughter; and Thelma Lucile, b. May 7 1904, Long Beach, married but has no children.

210. iv. Emily May, b. March 29 1856

v. Ida, b. Sept. 1 1858, at Greenville, Texas, d. Sept. 28 1870. Twin of Ada.

vi. Ada, b. Sept. 1 1858, d. Dec. 12 1865.

211. vii. Nettie Olive, b. Aug. 29 1861

212. viii. Lulu Bessie, b. June 29 1864

ix. Charity Virginia, b. Nov. 26 1866, Greenville, Texas, died Nov. 21 1933, Monrovia, Calif. She married, Oct. 29 1890, Leo M. Valentine, at Monrovia. Three children: Leo Clive, b. July 10 1894, d. Nov. 29 1913; Klea Carma, b. Dec. 19 1895, d. in 1940, md. Jan. 28 1918, Chester O. Finch, no children; and Edwin Merle Valentine, b. Oct. 15 1903, d. April 28 1906.

x. Joel Warren, b. April 25 1869, at Preston, Mo., d. 1935. He married, Jan. 12 1922, Maude Everet, at Los Angeles. One child: Ruth Adrian Pinney, b. Sept. 20 1922, is now living in Los Angeles, Calif.

xi. Elbert, jr., b. Sept. 29 1872, Preston, Mo. is unmarried and living in Duarte, Calif.

108 JACOB CLARK YOUNG

born, Aug. 27 1832, at Mt. Gilead, O., died, Dec. 16 1918, at Los Angeles, Calif. in the home of his daughter Cora with whom he spent the last 23 years of his life. He and his wife were buried in Fair Haven cemetery, Santa Ana, Calif. He was taken when about 4 years old by his parents to Whiteside Co., Ill. where he married, Nov. 4 1858, Amelia D. Harris, b. Aug. 25 1836, d. May 12 1897, daughter of John and Betsy (Folke) Harris, of N. Y. State. The family moved from Morrison, Ill. about 1875 to Jasper Co., Mo. From farming, Mr. Young tried prospecting in the region of Pikes Peak, Colo., and shortly after the death of his wife, he moved to California. There were six children, the last, unnamed, died the day of his birth, March 12 1881 (Mrs. Charles L. Logan, Los Angeles, Calif).

213. i. Emily Amelia, b. Sept. 11 1859

214. ii. Cora Paulina, b. Aug. 11 1863

iii. Gertrude, b. Jan. 13 1867, at Morrison, Ill., d. Feb. 25 1895, bur. Santa Ana, Calif. She was a public school teacher and did not marry.

215. iv. Roy Jackson, b. April 26 1870

216. v. Stella Evelyn, b. Oct. 5 1874

109 LUCY YOUNG

born, May 18 1834, at Mt. Gilead, O., died in Kansas City, Mo. where she and her husband were buried in Forest Hill cemetery. She was married by the Rev. L. L. Lansing, at Morrison, Ill., Aug. 20 1857, to the Rev. John Wesley Jacobs, b. Sept. 6 1823, at Watertown, N. Y., d. Jan. 26 1895. Mr. Jacobs was licensed as a Minister in the Methodist Church at the age of 18 years, and when 33, he was elder of the Niagra, N. Y. District. He was later in charge of the City Missions in Chicago, Ill. Because of ill health, he gave up regular pastoral work and moved to Jasper Co., Mo. where he farmed, raised stock and preached occasionally. In 1870 he moved to Carthage and later to Kansas City in order to better educate his children. Five children (Bible of Lucy Y. Jacobs, from Mrs. E. J. Pickens, Sarcoxie, Mo.).

217. i. Ernest Beers, b. July 20 1858

ii. Jay Wesley, b. Feb. 26 1860, at Mt. Pleasant, Ill., died May 4 1910, and was buried at Kansas City, Mo. He md. Apr. 26 1900, Ellen May Chase, at Carthage, Mo. Two children: Eliza May, b. Oct. 30 1901, Kansas City, Mo., d. in Nov. 1901; and Helen Merle Jacobs, b. Nov. 12 1903, Kansas City, md. Apr. 30 1924, Henry Izard, at Mobile, Ala. They have two children.

218. iii. Bessie May, b. July 29 1867

219. iv. Bertha Delight, b. Aug. 9 1872

v. "Baby" Jacobs, b. Dec. 28 1873, d. May 22 1874, at Carthage, Mo.

110 TRYPHENA YOUNG

born, April 27 1836, at Mt. Gilead, O., died, May 2 1914, and was buried beside her husband in Rose Hill cemetery, Chicago, Ill. She was a Charter member of the Chicago Woman's Club. She married, at Unionville, Ill., Jan. 13 1859, Willis F. Johnson, born, March 4 1834, at Big Stream Point, on Seneca Lake, N. Y., died March 26 1910, at Chicago, Ill. Mr. Johnson, at the age of 10 years, was taken by his parents to Palatine, Whiteside County, Ill. He completed his schooling by graduating from Waukegan Academy in 1885, and then entered the grain and lumber business of S. H. McCrea & Co. of which he soon became a partner. The firm was a member of the Chicago Board of Trade and when increased business called for his presence in Chicago, Mr. Johnson, in 1873, moved his family there to continue his activities until he retired in 1906. The partnership of McCrea & Co. was dissolved in 1883, Mr. Johnson then taking over the Morrison branch and placing it in charge of his brother-in-law, Aaron N. Young and establishing a new firm of W. F. Johnson & Co. in Chicago. Later Mr. Young joined Mr. Johnson in Chicago and the Morrison branch of the business was placed in the hands of Matthew Potter (Record #203). The unusual respect and esteem in which Mr. Johnson was held by his friends and colleagues in business is illustrated by the exceptional honor paid him on his 70th and 75th birthdays by his fellow members of the Board of Trade when they stopped all business procedure, called him on the floor and presented him with American Beauty Roses, one for each year of his life. Mr. Johnson shunned the urging of his friends to assume public office but delighted in helping needy boys and girls secure a good education and fit themselves for these duties. Geniality, uprightness and generosity were his outstanding characteristics. Mr. and Mrs. Johnson had two children. (Miss Anna B. Johnson, Chicago, Ill.).

i. Wealthy May, born, Nov. 30 1859, in Whiteside County, Ill., is living, 1945, in Chicago. She married, Oct. 7 1885, James William Ferry, at Chicago, Ill. Mr. Ferry was born, March 1852, died, March 21 1897, and was buried in Graceland cemetery, Chicago. He was a nephew and namesake of William Ferry who founded and endowed "Ferry Hall" school for girls at Lake Forest, Ill. He also assisted in founding and was the first President of the old Commercial Bank of Chicago, which later consolidated with the Continental Bank, predecessor of the Continental National Bank and Trust Company. Mr. and Mrs. Johnson had no children.

ii. Anna Blanche, was born, March 5 1869, in Whiteside

County, Ill., and is living with her sister in Chicago, Ill. Miss Johnson for some years was an active member of the Chicago Women's Club of which her mother was one of the first members. She also was President of the Young Fortnightly Club for three terms refusing a fourth to make room for new blood.

111 AARON NELSON YOUNG

born, April 3 1838, near Morrison, Ill., died, Dec. 6 1918, at Evanston, Ill. and was buried in Rosehill Cemetery, Chicago, Ill. Mr. Young, after a short business career at Morrison, Ill., became a member of the brokerage firm of S. H. McCrea & Co. of Chicago, and moved his family there. Later, the family made their home in Evanston where Mr. Young was a Trustee of Northwestern University, a Member of the Board of Education, and, for several years, its President. An "Appreciation" and a "Tribute" to Mr. Young are appended to this record. They are witnesses to the pionering interests, personal worth and social sense which he inherited from his father and grandfather. What Mr. Young inherited, he cultivated, and then, in life and in death, handed down to his beloved young people. The substantial scholarship fund that Mr. Young gave to Northwestern University for the use of needy students was in memory of his two sons, Albert and Paul, who died while students at Yale and Northwestern Universities, respectively. Mr. Young married, March 26 1867, at Sterling, Ill., Anna Maria Corell, born, March 5 1843, in New York State, died, April 6 1930, in the home of her son, Senator Sanborn Young, at Los Gatos, Calif. She was the daughter of Joseph and Maria (Sanborn) Corell, and a niece of William A. Sanborn, born, Jan. 13 1832, at Perrysburgh, Cattaraugus County, N. Y., and moved to Sterling, Ill. in 1852. Joseph and Maria Corell were married, May 29 1839, and lived many years in Portland, N. Y. before moving to Brockton in the same State. Joseph was born Dec. 21 1814 and died in the summer of 1895. His wife died July 4 1850. Their children were: Fanny Jane, b. Feb. 26 1840; Anna Maria, b. March 5 1843; Worthy Joseph, b. Feb. 26 1845, d. Nov. 20 1848; and Worthy A. Corell, b. Sept. 9 1848. Aaron and Anna Young had six children (The Hon. Sanborn Young, Los Gatos, Calif.).

i. Albert Joseph, b. Dec. 19 1867, d. June 14 1886, at Yale University, New Haven, Conn.

220. ii. Ruth, b. Oct. 10 1869

221. iii. Sanborn, b. March 2 1873

iv. Paul, b. Aug. 7 1876, at Evanston, Ill., d. there, while a student at Northwestern University, April 3 1896.

222. v. Helen, b. Sept. 2 1879

vi. Ralph Blaisdel, b. June 27 1881, is married and lives at Mill Valley, Calif. No children.

A TRIBUTE

to Aaron N. Young that the Board of Directors of the Evanston, Ill. Club unanimously ordered spread upon its records:

"The passing away of Aaron N. Young, Jan. 6 1918, has produced a profound and general sorrow among the members of the Evanston Club. Although one of the earlier and older members, Mr. Young was always youthful in spirits, a congenial companion and a sincere friend. He was devoted to the Club and took a leading part in all its activities. He loved its atmosphere and its work; In its games of diversion, he was a genuine sportsman, keen of enjoyment and always a generous and considerate opponent. He loved life and chose the best of it, in its seriousness and in its play. In return his associates loved him with an affection inspired by his generous, kindly and chivalrous nature.

In the passing of Mr. Young the City of Evanston also loses a leader among that class of high minded men who did so much to establish its splendid reputation and make it so attractive in its pioneer days. With his memory will always be associated the vision of a neighborhood of segregated homes and spacious grounds; the days of unselfish community service in the interest of the schools, the village, the city, the town and everything else that was worth while. He did much and asked nothing in reward. It is with a sense of doing honor to one who deserves the highest honor that the Board of Directors unanimously unite in ordering this tribute spread upon the records."

AN APPRECIATION

by

The Board of Trustees of Northwestern University upon the establishment of "The Bert and Paul Young School Fund" made possible by the bequest of $200,000.00 of Mr. Aaron N. Young:

"Mr. Young's great interest in the cause of education was almost proverbial and his special interest in the affairs of the University through many years had been evidenced in many ways and in part by his acceptance of membership on the Board of University Trustees. He had always been recognized as a friend of the Institution, had sympathized with its purposes, and had been classed among its active and efficient supporters. The cause of education was very near and dear to his heart. He ranked education as the most important and fundamental guarantee of a free and independent government. His fellow citizens had long been aware of his special interest in the development of our public school facilities, and had for many successive years availed themselves of his services on the various educational boards of the city. The splendid bequest referred to, and which was made for the purpose of assisting young men who would otherwise be unable to acquire special training for a life's work, is in entire harmony with his personal history and efforts. It will constitute a permanent beneficence. In all the years to come it will aid the persevering and industrious student, and will link together the memory of an honored citizen and a continuing benefaction. Most sincerely do we deplore the great loss which the whole community has sustained in his departure. We earnestly unite in the admiration of his genuine, sterling qualities, as a citizen, and remember with gratitude and appreciation his personal support and generous gift to the University." Signed by the Committee.

112 JACKSON BEERS YOUNG

born, Nov. 17 1839, at Union Grove, near Morrison, Ill., died Feb. 9 1924, and was buried at Oakland, Calif. He was a graduate, 1867, of the Law School of the University of Michigan. He practiced law successfully for about 8 years at Fairbury, Ill., removed to Sioux Falls, S. D. in 1877 where he organized the First National Bank, of which he was President until Nov. 1886 when he resigned and moved to Pasadena, Calif. He invested the earnings of a life time in real estate in Pasadena and lost all in the speculation. He married, first, Oct. 2 1865, at Ann Arbor, Mich., Lydia Lavinia Lyman, b. March 7 1838, d. June 26 1901, buried at Oak Park, Ill., daughter of Reuben L. (b. Russville, N. Y.) and Mary (Kimball) Lyman. There were four children. (Mrs. Mary Y. Oastler, Greenwich, Conn.). He married, second, May 3 1905, Rilla V. Paul (b. Geneseo, Ill.), in Calif. Mrs. Young lives in Oakland, Calif. No children.

i. Nelson Lyman, b. March 22 1867, at Ann Arbor, Mich., is living, a bachelor, in San Jose, Calif. He graduated from Northwestern University and is a member of the bar of Illinois, of Oregon, and of California.

223. ii. Homer Jackson, b. April 5 1869

224. iii. Mary Lyman, b. June 7 1872

225. iv. Harold Albert, b. Sept. 3 1878

113 JOHN MITCHELL YOUNG

born, Feb. 22 1842, at Union Grove, Ill., died, Aug. 1 1891, and was buried at Albany, Ill. He served in the U. S. Army during the Civil War. He married, March 25 1866, at Union Grove, Martha Mitchell who died, Oct. 15 1929, at Riverside, Calif. In 1877, the family lived in Miller County, Mo. Three children (Mrs. George L. Hutchinson, Monrovia, Calif.).

226. i. Willis Beers, b. Jan. 1 1867
227. ii. Lulu Elizabeth, b. May 18 1871
228. iii. John Brady, b. May 11 1875

114 SYLVIA ANN YOUNG

born, Dec. 12 1845, in the village of Unionville, Union Grove Township, Whiteside Co., Ill., died at Monrovia, Calif., Nov. 11 1944, one month before her 99th birthday. This compilation is deeply indebted to Sylvia for much early family history. It was she who first wrote the writer that her sister, Tryphena, visited their relatives in Ohio and brought back to Illinois an old family Bible that "was printed in the days when the f's and the s's looked alike," and in which, amongst other things, it was written that "Morgan Young arrived in America from the north of Scotland, Oct. 11, 1722 at the age of nine years." The old Bible has been lost but the notation was incorporated in the typewritten "Genealogy of the Daniel B. Young Family," compiled from their family records by children of D. B. Young in 1899. Sylvia married, Jan. 7 1867, at Unionville, Ill., George L. Hutchinson. They lived, in 1877, in Colorado and from there moved to California. Mr. Hutchinson, born, Dec. 19 1844, at Unionville, Ill., died, June 5 1904, and was buried at Monrovia, Calif. One child Milford Leland Hutchinson, born, Aug. 11 1867, at Wheatland Center, Clinton Co., Ia., died, Dec. 8 1894, at Monrovia. He married in Nov. 1890 Christian Lee who died in 1902. No children.

115 SUSAN L. JACKSON

born, Feb. 13 1828, near Fredericktown, O., was taken in 1838 by her parents to Whiteside County, Ill. where there was a gathering of the Jackson and Young clans, and where she married, Feb. 20 1845, John Vennum, born, Sept. 16 1818, near Mt. Vernon, O., son of Phebe (Jackson) Lewis Vennum, sister of Susan's grandfather Jackson. Charity Ann (Young) Jackson, mother of Susan, was both sister and sister-in-law of Daniel B.

Young. John Vennum was one of three who laid out Unionville, Ill. in 1841.

Phebe Jackson Lewis Vennum, born, June 23 1874, in Morris County, N. J., died at the age of 104 yrs. 11 mos. and 26 days in the home of her son Edward in Whiteside Co., Ill. She was the daughter of Major Benjamin and Abigail Mitchell Jackson, residents of Rockaway, N. J. She married, 1st., Feb. 25 1802, Isaac Lewis, d. between 1805 and 1811, son of Isaac (Will dated Jan. 26 1812, Morristown, N. J.) and Sarah Jackson, and grandson of Edward and Sarah (Morris) Lewis (Rec. 14). They had two sons: James L. Lewis, b. Jan. 25 1803, and Benjamin Jackson Lewis, b. July 4 1805, in N. J., d. March 27 1891, at Detroit, Mich. Her husband having died, Phebe, in company with her parents in 1814, moved to Knox County, O. where in 1817 she married for her second husband John Vennum, of Washington Co., Pa. He died, Feb. 12 1858, age 72 yrs. Mrs. Vennum, after the death of John, lived with her son Edward and his family (Miss Anna B. Johnson, Chicago, Ill.). Edward and Susan Vennum had seven children (Miss Ann Potter, Morristown, Ill.).

- i. Albert B., b. Dec. 12 1845, md. Nov. 28 1882, Laura Schaub.
- ii. Phebe A., b. Jan. 25 1848, md. Apr. 10 1866, P. S. Bannister.
- iii. Andrew J., b. Dec. 11, 1849, md. Oct. 11 1881, Rhoda Gallentine, d. Jan. 23 1874. One child known: Susan Vennum, md. Joseph R. Jahraus, and lived at Laguna Beach, Calif. She died Feb. 18 1931.
- iv. Columbus C., b. Oct. 31 1851, md. July 1 1880, Florence Twining. He died about 1940. Four children: Ethel V., md. ——— Craig, and lives in Phoenix, Ariz.; Stella, md. W. V. Steutville, and lives in South Sioux City, Nebr.; Fern, md. P. J. Roelfsema and lives in Piedmont, Calif.; and Ruby Vennum md. J. T. Latimer and lives in Glendale, Calif.
- v. Edwin P., b. Oct. 26 1853, md. Feb. 12 1880, Linder Reemer.
- vi. Abbie T., b. July 3 1856, d. Dec. 18 1873.
- vii. John G., b. Dec. 6 1864

116 SILAS MITCHELL JACKSON

born, Oct. 23 1837, near Mt. Vernon, O., died, June 27 1927, in Colorado. He was a babe in arms when his parents moved to Whiteside County, Ill.

Aaron Nelson Young
Record 111.

Sanborn Young
Record 221.

Ruth Comfort Mitchell
(Mrs. Sanborn Young)
Record 221.

William Ira Young, Mollie Burch Young,
Willard Young
Record 95.

Belinda Shur Young, Abigail Young Semple, Jennie B. Semple Macfadden, William Semple Macfadden
Record 118.

David Bonar Young
Margaret Young King
Records 61 and 136

William Pepper
Sally Young Pepper
Record 87

Newton Young
Record 93

James Lewis Young
Record 158

Mahlon Josiah Young
Record 149

Ezra Sankfield Young
Record 280

Log Cabin of
Alexander Young, Washington, Iowa
"Thomas Young" p. 27
Record 209

MAHLON AND ORILLA YOUNG
In retirement at Collins, Ohio. Record 71

SYLVIA YOUNG HUTCHINSON
Record 114

JOHN MITCHELL YOUNG
Record 113
Was in the posse which surrounded and killed John Wilkes Booth

His middle name takes us back to Rockaway, N. J. where the Jacksons, Mitchells and Youngs were intimate neighbors. The paternal grandparents of Silas were Ziba and Phebe (Lyon) Jackson. Phebe Lyon was the daughter of Capt. Abraham and Phebe (Bobbett) Lyon. (Mrs. Ella B. Spooner, Marquette, Mich.). Capt. Lyon was a descendant of the Lyons of Glamis Castle, Scotland, whence came Lady Elizabeth Bowes-Lyon, the present Queen Elizabeth of Great Britain. See Record #6. Silas married, June 17 1879, at Norborne, Mo., Rachel Moriah Brown, daughter of Manthano and Sarah Lawrence (Hamilton) Brown. Sarah was the third wife of Manthano. Silas and Rachel Brown had two children. ("The Brown Family History," Mrs. Ella B. Spooner, 1929).

i. Ella Brown, b. Dec. 3 1880, Denver, Colo., married, June 26 1902, at Salida, Colo., Charles C. Spooner, in 1943, professor in the Mathematical Department, North State College, Marquette, Mich. No children.

ii. Lawrence Louise, b. Feb. 28 1890, Salida, Colo., married, Oct. 13 1911, Everett H. Fisher, at Canon City, Colo. where the family is living. Two children: Lawrence Everett, b. July 19 1912, and Rachel Ada Fisher, b. May 26 1917.

117 MARGARET SHUR YOUNG

born, Jan. 26 1835, at Fredericktown, O., died, Sept. 22 1892, age 57 yrs. 7 mos. and was buried in Forest Cemetery, Fredericktown (Gravestone rec.). She married, Sept. 4 1855, at Fredericktown, Daniel Struble (b. 1828 in Sussex Co., N. J., d. Sept. 18 1912, age 83 yrs. 11 mos. 18 days, at Fredericktown. Mr. Struble was brought to Ohio by his parents, John D. and Mary (Hadley) Struble whose other children were: Rebecca, Headley, Daniel and Wm. J., born in N. J., and John S., Charles S., Oscar, David W., and Edwin Dallas Struble, born near Fredericktown, O. John D. Struble engaged in different enterprises and was a successful businessman. His son Daniel continued the business and added banking to his activities. Daniel and Margaret had two children (Mrs. Wm. C. Macfadden, Fargo, N. D.).

i. Mary Blanche, b. March 3 1857, Fredericktown, died there, Oct. 9 1894. She md. Nov. 6 1880, Frank R. Moore. No children.

ii. Ralph Young, d. May 13 1929, age 52 yrs. 5 mos. 10 days, and was buried at Fredericktown, O. He md. Helen

Wells who, after the death of Ralph, md. 2nd., Dale Workman. Mrs. Workman died, Apr. 8 1947, at Fredericktown. Ralph and Helen Young had two children: Margaret, b. 1910, d. March 6 1947, at Mt. Vernon, O. She md. 1st., Ralph Fox, and 2nd., Dr. W. Kennett Claypool, a Chiropodist, of Mt. Vernon; and Mary Young, md. 1st., Don Henry, and 2nd., Harold W. Anderson. Mrs. Anderson lives in Fredericktown and has two children: David S. Henry and Helen Wells Anderson.

118 ABIGAIL YOUNG

"Abbie," born, March 18 1840, at Fredericktown, O., died there, Aug. 31 1933, and was buried in Forest cemetery, beside her husband (Gravestone rec.). She married, Sept. 29 1859, Dr. Wm. F. Semple (1840-1923), a dentist who practiced his profession in Mt. Vernon, O. Three children.

i. George Borr, b. June 28 1861, d. June 8 1862.
229. ii. Jennie Bell, b. March 16 1863
230. iii. Carl Young, b. April 5 1873

119 WILLIAM LOGAN

born, March 13 1834, near Mansfield, O., died in Sauk County, Wis. He married, in Richland Co., O., Emma Coe, descendant of a N. J. family. With his parents and his brothers' families he moved in 1865 to Worth Co.., Mo. After a short stay here, William went to Wisconsin to join his mother's brothers. Three children (Miss Estella Stevenson, Savannah, Mo.).

i. Mary, b. in Richland Co., O., md. there Wm. Henry Davis, a second cousin (Rec. 126).
ii. Lorenzo
iii. Jennie, born in Sauk Co., Wis.

120 ALVAN LOGAN

born, Sept, 14 1835, near Mansfield, O., died, Feb. 14 1904, at Grant City, Mo. He married, in 1859, in Richland County, O., Mary Elizabeth Moon, b. July 28 1837, at Mansfield, O., d. April 17 1909, at Grant City, Mo., daughter of John and Elizabeth (McCune) Moon. He served during the Civil War in Company B., 163rd Ohio Volunteers National Guard, and after the war moved to Grant City, Mo. where he was a farmer and stock raiser, especially interested in fine horses. He helped in establishing the first Methodist Church in Grant City. Four children (Miss Estelle Stevenson, Savannah, Mo.).

231. i. Alice Catherine, b. Feb. 11 1861
ii. John Alvan, b. Dec. 1863 in Ohio, d. 1865 in Mo.
232. iii. Lucretia, b. Sept. 14 1867
iv. Elizabeth Young, b. Aug. 17 1870, lives in Grant City, Mo.

121 THOMAS HARVEY LOGAN

born, June 25 1837, in Richland Co., O., married twice. No record of his second marriage or his death has been found. He married, first, Mary Ann Simpson in Ohio and they went with his parents to Missouri in 1865. Mary died in 1900 and was buried in Grant City, Mo. They had one child Fanny Logan, born about 1862. She married Temp Godfrey. They had two children: Ray who died in infancy, and Clara who married William Bell. Mr. Logan moved his family to Colorado about 1900. A daughter of Wm. and Clara Bell, Mrs. George Cross, lives in Colorado Springs, Colo. (Miss Estelle Stevenson, Savannah, Mo.).

122 ELIZABETH MARY YOUNG

born, Feb. 18 1843, near Mansfield, O., died, Jan. 8 1876, age 32 yrs. 10 mos. 20 days, and was buried in Harrisburg cemetery, Sauk County, Wis., as was her husband. (Gravestone record). She married Timothy Frank Colby, a farmer, in Sauk County, Wis., Sept. 24 1860. He died Jan. 27 1918. Seven children (Bible of Elizabeth M. Colby, owned by Miss Vernice Avery, Roscoe, Ill.).

i. Alva E., b. July 6 1861, d. Jan. 21 1888.
ii. Sarah I., b. June 4 1864, d. Jan. 30 1866.
233. iii. William Lloyd, b. Apr. 4 1866
iv. John M. b. Oct. 25 1868
234. v. Susan E. b. Sept. 25 1870
vi. Mertie, died, Jan. 6 1869, an infant.
vii. Elmer, b. Feb. 8 1875

123 SARAH ASENATH YOUNG

born, June 4 1848, near Mansfield, O., died, Aug. 29 1929, at Eugene, Ore. where she and her husband were buried. She married, June 24 1868, in Sauk County, Wis., Daniel M. Baker, born, March 22 1842, died, Oct. 14 1937. Shortly after their marriage, Mr. and Mrs. Baker moved to Brooklin, Ia. where their eight children were born (Dr. L. L. Baker, Eugene, Ore.).

i. Mary Isabel, b. Apr. 22 1869, d. in 1880, bur. Brooklin, Ia.

ii. John Lincoln, b. Aug. 24 1871, d. in 1880, bur. Brooklin, Ia.

iii. Ira A., b. Sept. 17 1873, d. Jan. 4 1839, at Eugene, Ore. He md. and one of his five children was Dr. Perry A. Baker of Eugene, Ore.

iv. Walter G., b. Aug. 28 1877, md. and lived in Salem, Ore. Two children: Ray and Frank Baker.

v. Lawren W., b. March 21 1880, md. Ida A. Kuntz, at Brooklin, Ia. One child: Lee E. Baker, b. July 11 1903, at Brooklin, Ia., md. and has a son, Robert Constant Baker, b. March 12 1934, at Kansas City, Mo. L. E. Baker is practicing law at Lake Village, Ark.

235. vi. Lloyd Lewis, b. Dec. 9 1884

236. vii. Pearl Elizabeth, b. July 19 1887

viii. Ray D., b. March 23 1890, died the same day at Brooklin, Ia.

124 JOHN AARON YOUNG

born, Aug. 28 1852, on a farm near Spring Green, Wis. where his parents became homesteaders in 1849, moving there from Richland County, O. He died, Dec. 15 1922, and was buried in the cemetery at Spring Green. He married, Nov. 6 1872, Sarah Palmer, born, Jan. 18 1851, died, Jan. 25 1936. One child: Ajah Earl, who furnished our data on the family.

237. i. Ajah Earl, b. Sept. 21 1873

125 JOHN LOGAN DAVIS

farmer near Spring Green, Wis. where his children were born. He was born, Aug. 2 1842, in Richland Co., O., died, Dec. 24 1881, and was buried at Harrisburg, Wis. He md. Nov. 13 1867, his cousin, Susan R. Young, at Spring Green. Two children. (Mrs. H. C. Schaefer, Baraboo, Wis.).

i. George Edwin, b. Dec. 21 1868, d. Jan. 24 1892, at Spring Green, Wis. He did not marry.

238. ii. Elmarine, b. Sept. 15 1873

126 WILLIAM HENRY DAVIS

"Hank," his friends called him, was born, May 5 1853, near Mansfield, O. He died, Sept. 1 1942, at Glendale, Calif. in the home of his sister Mrs. Tacy Roberts with whom he lived after retiring from the grocery business in St. Joe and Grant City Mo. He married, 1st., a second cousin, Mary Logan, in Ohio. They lived in Missouri and during the hardships of the Civil War, they separated. He married, 2nd., Minnie Smith, at Rulo, Nebr. She died, April 1 1923, and was buried at Alboy, Nebr. No children.

127 TACY ARABELLE DAVIS

born, Aug. 17 1859, in Sauk County, Wis., is living in Glendale, Calif. in 1946. She married, March 16 1880, at Spring Green, Wis., James William Roberts, b. Oct. 1 1856, d. Oct. 18 1940, and was buried in Forest Lawn cemetery, Glendale. Six children (O. A. Roberts, Glendale, Calif.).

i. Flora Francis, b. March 26 1881, at Samborn, Ia., md. and lived at Sioux City, Ia., d. Feb. 26 1937, at Glendale, Calif.

ii. Jewell Horace, b. Oct. 5 1883, at Samborn, Ia., md., at Missouri Valley, Ia. and lives in Salt Lake City, Utah.

iii. Roy Ray, b. June 20 1887, md. 2nd., Dec. 25 1937, at Winchester, Mass. and lives in Glendale, Calif.

iv. Lloyd Silas, b. May 23 1893, md. June 15 1915, at Hartley, Ia. and lives in Glendale.

v. Beatrice Vivian, b. Feb. 4 1897, md. Oct. 5 1918, at Denver, Colo. and lives in Stamford, Conn.

vi. Otis Albert, b. March 12 1899, at Samborn, Ia., a veteran of the first world war, is single and lives with his mother in Glendale, Calif.

128 SUSAN RUHAMAH YOUNG

born, Feb. 16 1845, in Richland Co., O., died, Nov. 13 1923, in Sauk Co., Wis, and was buried at Harrisburg, Wis. She married her cousin James Logan Davis, Oct. 20 1867. (Rec. 125).

129 MARY CATHERINE YOUNG

born, Feb. 5 1847, near Mansfield, O., died, Dec. 10 1942, age 95 yrs. 10 mos. 25 days, in the home of her daughter Mrs. Henry Meng, at Prairie du Sac, Wis. Her parents moved to Wisconsin when she was two years old, one year before Wisconsin came into the Union. The family settled on a farm near Harrisburg where Roland Schaefer now lives, 1946. She married, Nov. 27, 1872, John Adolf Sorg (b. July 7 1847, d. Jan. 17 1927) in Sauk Co., Wis. They lived on the Young homestead in Troy township until 1913 when they retired to Spring Green, Wis. When Mrs. Sorg died, she had 8 grandchildren and 18 great grandchildren. She was buried at Harrisburg, Wis. Three children, one of whom died in infancy, Jan. 29 1875.

239. i. Lucy Belle, b. April 7 1876

240. ii. John Edwin, b. Feb. 8 1882

130 ALVIN LOGAN YOUNG

born, March 22 1853, near Mansfield, O. (the year that his parents moved to Wisconsin), d. June 7 1937, in the home of his son Fred at Rochester, Minn., and was buried at Baraboo, Wis. He was in the grocery business in Atchinson County, Mo., Griswold, Ia., and Baraboo, Wis. He married, at Franklin, Wis., Georgia Frederica, daughter of Dr. and Mrs. Richard Douglas, who came to Wisconsin from Goodrich, Ontario, where Mrs. Young was born in 1851. Three children (F. D. Young, Rochester, Minn.).

i. Florence Pauline, b. July 29 1881, at Baraboo, Wis., d. Aug. 13 1883, bur. Harrisburg, Wis.

241. ii. Fred Douglas, b. Aug. 29 1885

iii. Edwin Haswell, b. Feb. 14 1890, d. July 17 1914.

131 BENJAMIN DAY YOUNG

born, July 18 1855, in Sauk County, Wis., died, March 1 1933, and was buried at Harrisburg, Wis. He married, first, in Sauk Co., Wis., Nov. 2 1876, Susan Elizabeth Bonham (d. July 21 1884, age 30 yrs. 3 mos. 29 days. Gravestone record, Harrisburg, Wis.). She was the daughter of the Rev. George and R. E. Bonham. Two children (Mrs. Eva P. Edwards, Prairie du Sac, Wis.).

242 i. Eva Pearl, b. May 24 1878

ii. Jesse Leone

132 SARAH JANE YOUNG

born, Feb. 24 1848, near Mansfield, O., died in Nov. 1926 in the home of her son, Roy L. Taylor, at Long Beach, Calif. where she went in 1912. She married, March 27 1872, Allen Wheeler Taylor, in Illinois. They lived some years in Sauk County, Wis. and then moved to Emmettsburg, Ia. where Mr. Taylor was in business with his brother Charles. In 1884, the family moved to a farm near Spence, Ia. where Mr. Taylor died in 1903. He was the son of James A and Phebe (Harris) Taylor. One child. (Roy L. Taylor, Long Beach, Calif).

243. i. Roy L., b. July 6 1880

133 MARY ELIZABETH YOUNG

born, March 16 1855, in Richland County, Wis., died, Jan. 27 1932, at Winterset, Ia. where she went in 1869 to join relatives. She married, Aug. 14 1872, William Martin Travis (b. Dec. 28 1852, at Brookville, Wis., d. Sept. 20 1928, Winterset), at Peru, Ia. They celebrated their golden wedding anniversary in 1922. Ten children. (Mrs. Laura Travis Hollen, Winterset, Ia.).

i. Ernest Walden, b. Sept. 26 1873, d. Feb. 5 1931. He md. March 15 1905 Grace Catherine Campbell. Six children: Glenn, b. June 3 1907; Mary, b. June 17 1909; Ruth, b. Nov. 19 1914; Ralph, b. July 20 1917, d. Dec. 7 1923; Eloise, b. June 4 1921; and Ernest, b. March 17 1926.

ii. Bertha, b. Feb. 20 1875, md. John Cox, and lives, a widow, at Blue Lake, Calif. Three children: Grace, b. May 15 1898; Lois, b. July 8 1902; and Walter Cox, b. Oct. 26 1907.

iii. Carrie, b. Mar. 24 1877, md. J. W. Keller and lives at Des Moines, Ia. Five children: Everett, b. Mar. 3 1899; Arthur, b. Apr. 25 1901; Laura, b. Apr. 1 1905; Virginia, b. July 24 1909; and Gertrude Keller, b. July 6 1913.

iv. Lena Louisa, b. Mar. 14 1879, d. Mar. 23 1900. One child, Lena Louisa (b. Sept. 19 1899, Winterset, Ia.), md. Dec. 24 1921, James R. Sawyer. Mr. and Mrs. Sawyer have 4 children: Doris Kathleen, b. Aug. 11 1923, attended Ia. State Coll. at Ames; Phyllis Jane, b. Nov. 14 1925, is a student at State Coll., Ames, Ia.; Barbara Drake, b.

May 29 1928; and Phillip James Sawyer, b. Mar. 5 1931, Winterset, Ia.

v. Mae, b. Jan. 10 1882, d. Mar. 6 1941. She md. Harry B. Wise. Seven children: Morris, b. May 23 1909; Ruth, b. Mar. 5 1911; Gerald, b. Sept. 30 1912; Merrill, b. Jan. 29 1915; Dorothy, twin of Merrill; Margaret, b. May 30 1918; and Adelaide Wise, b. Aug. 21 1921.

vi. Adelaide, b. Jan. 22 1884, md. Harvey Preston, and is living, a widow, at Belvidere, N. J. Three children: Helen, b. June 21 1906; Elmo, b. Dec. 16 1908; and Kenneth, b. Apr. 15 1911.

vii. Elizabeth, b. Aug. 31 1886, md. A. L. Pennebaker, and lives at Clearfield, Ia.

244. viii. Laura, b. July 11 1889, at Winterset, Ia.

ix. Nell, b. Mar. 23 1892, md. L. H. Sprinkle and lives near Farmington, Mich.

x. William David, b. Sept. 15 1894, d. Nov. 22 1936. He md. Oct. 23 1920, Alicia Higgins, of Newark, N. J., at Des Moines, Ia. He served in World War I. One child, Frank Travis, b. May 14 1923, served in World War II. Mrs. Travis lives at Asbury Park, N. J.

134 MARTHA ELLEN YOUNG

born, Oct. 24 1858, in Sauk County, Wis. lived some time in Winterset, Ia. She married Lewis W. Mitchell and lived at Amourdale, Kansas City, Mo. Five children.

i. Albert

ii. Nettie, md. John Hoffman.

iii. Ernest

iv. Edwin W.

v. Bessie

135 DAVID MITCHELL YOUNG

born, March 3 1868, in Sauk County, Wis., married, 1st., Oct. 14 1890, at Golden, Colo., Mary Emma Maughan (b. Nov. 5 1872, died Oct. 1918, at Oakland, Calif.) and they had three children. Mr. Young who is in the grocery business at Alameda, Calif. married, 2nd, in Aug. 1923, at

Oakland, Alice Bennett (b. Aug. 18 1868), a widow. (Mrs. G. A. King, Albert Lea, Minn.)

i. Robert Gordon Young, b. March 28 1893, at Golden, Colo., married, Navy Day 1930, Mrs. Ida Davidson, at Stockton, Calif. Mr. Young is in business with his father. No children.

ii. Maude Henrietta, b. Dec. 4 1901, at Youngstown, N. D., md. Feb. 11 1923, at San Jose, Calif., Harold G. Simmons, b. July 28 1902. They are living in Oakland, Calif. One child, Harold George Simmons, b. Nov. 6 1924, at Oakland, Calif.

iii. Clyde David, b. March 25 1907, at Youngstown, N. D., married, Jan. 14 1934, Barbara Carol Jesperson (b. Nov. 1 1913), at Oakland, Calif. Two children: David William, b. Dec. 29 1934, and Philip Gordon Young, b. June 8 1942, at Oakland.

136 MARGARET ANN YOUNG

born, Dec. 15 1878, in Sauk County, Wis., died, Dec. 27 1943, at Albert Lea, Minn. where she was buried in Graceland Cemetery beside her husband. She married, Dec. 15 1893, at Gotham, Wis., George A. King (d. Jan. 19 1931). The family moved to Albert Lea, Minn. in 1900 when Mr. King became road master for the Rock Island Railroad in that area. The compiler visited Mrs. King in 1942 and secured from her much family information which she had received from her father, David Bonar Young, 1821-1915. Mrs. King was an active member of the Daughters of the American Revolution. One child.

i. Hazel, b. Feb. 20 1895, at Albert Lea, Minn., md. Aug. 10 1915, at Albert Lea, Fred L. Martinson, who is business manager of the Albert Lea "Evening Tribune." They have one child: Donald G., b. Feb. 21 1916, at Albert Lea. Donald was with the Wilson Packing Company, at Wasau, Wis. before starting his service in the U. S. Air Forces in which he became a Captain in Italy. He married, Aug. 17 1946, at Albert Lea, Alice, daughter of Mr. and Mrs. Charles Sund.

137 MARY WALDEN

born, July 17 1862, at Winterset, Ia. (when her mother was visiting her sister and brother-in-law, Dr. and Mrs. W. L. Leonard) died, April 1926, at Denver, Colo., and was buried in Spring Grove Cemetery, Cincinnati, O., as was her husband. She married, Nov. 20 1884, at Covington, Ky., Samuel B. Bowman (b. Apr. 9 1856, at Williamsport, Pa., d. May 1 1939, at Denver, Colo.), son of Bishop and Mrs. Thomas Bowman of the Methodist Episcopal Church. One child. (Miss E. W. Bowman, Denver, Colo.)

i. Elisabeth Walden Bowman, music teacher, b. Feb. 8 1893, at Denver, Colo. is living in Denver.

138 MATILDA WALDEN

born, Aug. 1 1864, at Cincinnati, O., died, Oct. 6 1935, and was buried in Spring Grove Cemetery, Cincinnati, O. She graduated from Wesleyan College, Cincinnati, Ohio, in 1882, and married, June 7 1883, Stalin Olin Royal. Three children:

i. Mary Goode, b. Apr. 24 1885, at Cincinnati, O., is a teacher in the public schools at Dayton, O.

ii. Martha Elizabeth, b. in 1887, at Dayton, O., died in 1891.

iii. Marguerite, b. Oct. 17 1892, at Middleton, O., is living in Dayton, O. with her sister, and teaching in the public schools.

139 WILLIAM EARLE YOUNG

born, Jan. 12 1852, near Chester, N. J., died, Oct. 25 1928, and was buried in Pleasant Hill Cemetery, near Chester. He was a forge worker. He lived a few of his youthful years in Charleston, S. C., returning to Chester in 1865 with his father. He married, May 27 1872, near Chester, Jennie Stout (b. May 27 1857), daughter of Andrew Jackson and Mary Etta (Paltry) Stout. Mrs. Young has been living in Chester for over 85 years and has supplied invaluable data about her own and collateral lines. There were five children, one of whom, Edward George, died in infancy.

245. i. Charles Dunster, b. Aug. 5 1875

ii. Mary Rose, b. Aug. 2 1877, at Ralston, N. J., d. Jan. 8 1943, and was buried in Chester, N. J. She married, 1st., Charles L. Moore, and 2nd., Oscar Gardner. No children.

iii. Ada Stout, b. Nov. 16 1879, Ralston, N. J., is living with her family in Chester, N. J. She married, 1901, Charles Rhinehart, farmer, b. May 18 1876. Two children: Vera R., b. Oct. 31 1902, at Chester, is a school teacher. She married John Dayton Allen, a farmer, and lives near Mendham, N. J. John and Vera have one child, John D. jr., b. Aug. 13 1937; and, Reginal Young Rhinehart, b. Dec. 4 1905, at Chester, N. J.

246. iv. Pierson Chamberlain, b. Nov. 4 1883

140 ROSETTA YOUNG

born, Nov. 5 1853, Charleston, S. C., died, Aug. 8 1900, and was buried at Rockaway, N. J. She married, at Chester, N. J., John Riggott b. Oct. 3 1850, at Davenport, Ia., d. Sept. 28 1917, buried at Rockaway, N. J. Eight children, one of whom died at birth, Feb. 1879. (Mrs. E. Morris Sellers, Dover, N. J.).

i. Sarah Louise, b. Apr. 13 1874, Rockaway, N. J., d. there Apr. 10 1893.
ii. Minnie Claire, b. Dec. 15 1876, d. May 26 1932, at Rockaway. She married in 1901 W. W. Bingham at Rockaway.
iii. John Steven, b. Sept. 4 1880, d. Aug. 4 1881.
iv. Mabel Blossom, b. June 4 1883, has not married.
v. Hazel Kirke, b. June 5 1886, Rockaway, N. J., md. at Rockaway, W. K. Talmage.
247. vi. Marguerite Ferne, b. Sept. 21 1889
vii. Beatrice Pauline, b. March 29 1895

141 SARAH ANN YOUNG

born, March 20 1864, at Charleston, S. C., is living in Newark, N. J., 1944. She married Adelbert Marvin Benjamin. Three children. Lyman Harry; May Florence, md. a Mr. McGuire and lives in Newark, N. J.; and Ida Belle Benjamin.

142 DOUGLAS YOUNG

born, in 1866, near Chester, N. J., died, in 1920, and was buried at Chester. He married in New Jersey, Lydia H. Skellinger (b. 1868, d. 1922). Five children.

i. John Rickett, druggist, living in Morristown, N. J., was born, Aug. 8 1888, at Boonton, N. J. He married, March 1920, Helen Plaut, of Montclair, N. J. One child, Douglas, b. June 23 1923, at Newark, N. J.

ii. Florence Woodruff, b. Nov. 7 1890, Boonton, N. J., married, June 8 1918, Frank E. Montgomery, at N. Y. City. They live in Summit, N. J. No children.

iii. Raymond Pierre, b. Nov. 19 1892, Boonton, N. J., md. June 12 1912, Evelyn Smith, at Morristown, N. J. One child, Albert b. May 2 1913, Morristown. Raymond married, 2nd., April 1921, Blanche Plaut, at N. Y. City. Two children: Raymond Pierre, b. May 1922, Newark, N. J., and Etna Virginia, b. Sept. 1924. Raymond married, 3rd., Helen Marie Hahn of Sterling, N. J., at N. Y. City.

iv. William Earle, florist, Morristown, N. J., was born Oct. 7 1894, married, March 30 1926, Gladys Oakes, at Nutley, N. J. No children.

v. Margaret Anderson, b. March 8 1897, Boonton, N. J., married Walter Gunther (b. Feb. 23 1896) of the Gunther Corporation, Mendham, N. J. where the family lives. Lt. Col. Walter Gunther, in 1943, is serving in the U. S. Army. Two children; Walter Dudley, b. Aug. 12 1921, and Barbara Jean Gunther, b. Aug. 23 1925, at Mendham, N. J.

143 LAFAYETTE STOUT YOUNG

born, near Chester, N. J., died 1928, at E. Orange, N. J. He married, Nov. 14 1895, Anna Arndt, at Washington, N. J. Mrs. Young is living, 1944, in Newark, N. J. One child.

i. Lafayette Earle, b. 1901, at Morristown, N. J. He married Sadie Waters. Three children: Dorothy, b. 1920; Muriel, b. 1924, and Robert Young, b. 1926.

144 GERTRUDE KENNEDY

born, Nov. 26 1874, at Sturgis, Mich., is living in retirement with her husband and daughter, 1943, at Kissimee, Fla. She married, Feb. 22 1899, Walter Gospill a Y.M.C.A. Secretary, at Sturgis. Two children. (Mrs. Gospill)

i. Dorothy Waltrude, b. Sept. 30 1900, at Sturgis, Mich., lives with her parents.

ii. Donald Kennedy, b. March 19 1903, at Sturgis, Mich., md. Nov. 5 1923, Marion Littlefield, at Sturgis. The family lives in Jackson, Mich. where Mr. Gospill teaches in the public schools. Two children: Mary Elaine, b. Apr. 27 1925, at Sturgis, Mich., and John Bernard Gospill, b. Aug. 5 1926.

145 RHEUAMA YOUNG

born, Apr. 24 1884, at Leonidas, Mich., married, Apr. 24 1917, Earl Woodworth, at Leonidas. He died, July 11 1938, at Battle Creek, Mich., and was buried there. One child: Juelma Kate Woodworth, b. Feb. 13 1918, at Factoryville, Mich., married, July 5 1941, at Byram, O., Walter James Maul. The family is living in Kalamazoo, Mich. (Mrs. Woodworth, Kalamazoo, Mich.)

146 SYLVIA CHAPIN YOUNG

born, Jan. 19 1839, in Ridgefield Township, Huron County, O., named after the wife of N. M. Young (Record #73), died, Jan. 24 1928, and was buried at Norwalk, O. She married, March 5 1863, George W. Mead, at Norwalk, O. One child.

248. i. Roy, b. April 24 1877

147 NOAH YOUNG

born, Nov. 24 1840, at Townsend, O., died, July 3 1917, at Collins, O., where he and his first wife were buried. They lived in retirement after 1905. Noah married, 1st., Emma Jarrett, b. Feb. 19 1844, daughter of Elias and Sarah Siphlet Jarrett, pioneer settlers in Huron County, O. Four children. There were no children by the 2nd. marriage.

249. i. Sarah D. Young, b. Sept. 18 1864
250. ii. Rose Carrie, b. Aug. 7 1866
251. iii. George Elias, b. Oct. 3 1871
252. iv. Arthur Noah, b. Aug. 9 1881

148 MARTHA ELLEN YOUNG

born, Sept. 26 1848, at Townsend, Ohio, died, Apr. 20 1924, and was buried in Woodland Cemetery, Norwalk, O. She married, July 3 1884,

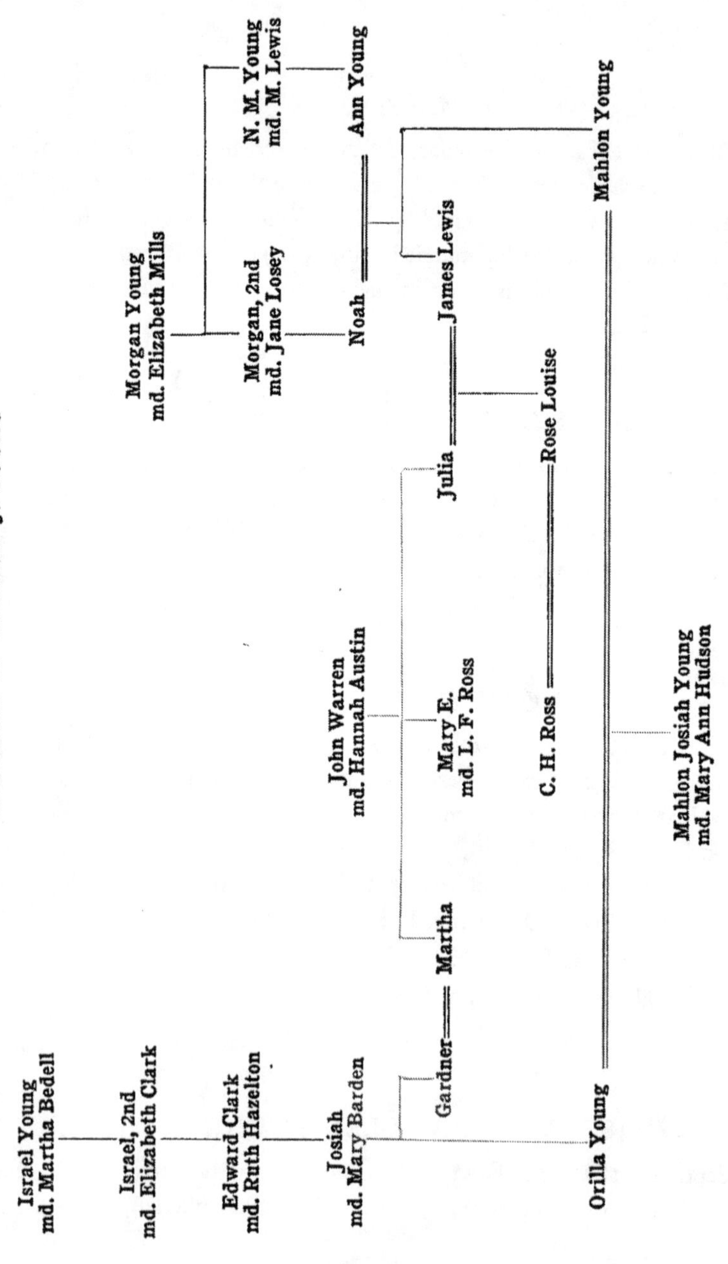
ANCESTRY OF MAHLON J. YOUNG
Israel Young
md. Martha Bedell
Israel, 2nd
md. Elizabeth Clark
Edward Clark
md. Ruth Hazelton
Josiah
md. Mary Barden
Gardner
Martha
Orilla Young
John Warren
md. Hannah Austin
Mary E.
md. L. F. Ross
C. H. Ross
Mahlon Josiah Young
md. Mary Ann Hudson
Julia
Rose Louise
Morgan Young
md. Elizabeth Mills
Morgan, 2nd
md. Jane Losey
Noah
James Lewis
N. M. Young
md. M. Lewis
Ann Young
Mahlon Young

at Norwalk, Alfred O. Noyes, who died Sept. 7 1923. Two children, twins, Orwell died in infancy.

253. i. Elver Alfred, b. Aug. 6 1885

149 MAHLON JOSIAH YOUNG

born, March 22 1851, at Townsend, Huron County, O., died, Feb. 27 1919, at Davenport, Ia., and was buried in Chippiannock cemetery, Rock Island, Ill. He was Commercial Agent for the C. B. & Q. Ry. at the time of his death. The family lived in Oberlin, O. before moving to Illinois in 1885. Mr. Young owned and managed a school of telegraphy in Oberlin in addition to being in charge of the railway station. He married, at Sandusky, O., Sept. 24 1874, Mary Ann Hudson, born, July 3 1850, at Epsom, Surrey, England, died, Jan. 10 1929, in the home of her nephew, Wm. Tomlinson Hudson, at Cleveland, O. while on a visit there. She was buried beside her husband. Mrs. Young was the daughter of William (d. Jan. 25 1879, at Venice, O.) and Mary (Lloyd) Hudson (d. Aug. 7 1876, at Sandusky, O., buried Oakland cemetery). Wm. Hudson was b. Jan. 31 1823, at Arundel, England, son of Henry (1794 d. May 31 1864, Epsom, Eng.) and Maria Marshall Hudson, and grandson of Richard and Jane Hotson. He md. Oct. 17 1847, Mary Lloyd, b. Feb. 21 1820, in Hertfordshire, Eng., in St. Pancras Church, Euston Road, London, England. He brought his family to America on the sailing ship *York Town* in 1853, taking six weeks for the voyage to Castle Garden and New York. A daughter, Eliza, died, April 22 1853, during the voyage, aged 10 months. Their other children were: William Henry, b. Aug. 3 1848, at Epsom; John Lloyd; and Alfred Hudson, b. Feb. 4 1855, Sandusky, O. William settled in Sandusky, O. and became active in the management of the local gas works and a bank. After retirement he moved to his vineyard and fruit orchards on the shores of Lake Erie at nearby Venice, O. Mahlon and Mary Young had five children.

254. i. Edward Hudson, b. July 13 1875

ii. Mary Orilla, b. Jan. 5 1877, at Oberlin, O., d. March 8 1901, at Rock Island, Ill. where she was a teacher in the High School. She studied at Leland Stanford University. She was buried in the Hudson lot, Oakland Cemetery, Sandusky, O.

iii. Mahlon Jay, b. Feb. 17 1880, at Oberlin, O., d. Feb. 27 1919, at Rock Island, Ill. He died the same day as his father and was buried beside him at Rock Island, Ill.

iv. Charles Gardner, b. March 7 1885, at Oberlin, O., d. Aug. 6 1885, and was buried at Sandusky, O.

v. Maude Ethel, b. Oct. 5 1887, at Rock Island, Ill. is living there in 1946. She studied at the Chicago Institute of Art but became interested in the organ and is now an Associate Member of the American Guild of Organists. She married, Sept. 3 1917, Harvey E. Sangren, at Davenport, Ia. No children.

150 ORILLA YOUNG

born, Sept. 4 1854, at Townsend, O., daughter of Mahlon and Orilla (Young) Young, died, Oct. 14 1930, and was buried at Cleveland, O. where the family lived. She married at Cleveland, Jan. 1 1887, Walter Lucas, a tailor, born in England. Two children, born at Cleveland.

i. Arthur b. Dec. 9 1887, was drowned at Annapolis, Md., May 17 1908, just after graduating at the U. S. Naval Academy.

ii. Walter. He md. and lived in Cleveland, O.

151 NORMAN HOUGH

born, Aug. 25 1833, died, Dec. 29 1899, near New Haven, Ohio, and was buried there, as was his wife, in the Old Cemetery. (Gravestone records). He married, July 4 18—, Theresa Davis, b. Sept. 17 1832, at Fairfield, O., died, March 21 1911, at New Haven, O. Four children (Mrs. Charles H. Underwood).

i. Emma, b. Aug. 14 1854, md. 1st., Aug. 11 18—, Upton W. Rank, who died Dec. 24 1925. She married, 2nd., Oct. 9 19—, John H. Dawson.

ii. William E., b. June 22 1855

iii. Edwin H., b. March 17 1857, d. Apr. 10 1940

255. iv. Elizabeth, b. Feb. 22 1859

152 SUSAN A. YOUNG

born, 1837, in Huron County, O., died, Nov. 20 1922, at Cleveland, O. and was buried beside her husband in Greenlawn Cemetery, Greenwich, O. She was raised by her grandparents, Noah and Ann Young. She married

William W. Waggoner, a farmer. Ten children, all born near Norwalk, O. (T. H. Waggoner).

i. Charles, md. Anna Healey. He was buried at Ripley, O. One of his children, Adeline, married G. C. Boor and lived at Greenwich, O.

ii. Ann, md. Frank Abbott, who farmed near No. Baltimore, O., where Ann is buried. One of the children was Charles, who lives in No. Baltimore. O.

iii. Harriett, md. Frank Mitchell. She was buried in Greenwich, O. Four children, all live in Greenwich: Carroll; Ruth, md. a Mr. Howard; Lucy, md. a Mr. Lindsay; and Melburn Mitchell.

iv. Frances, md. Jerome Robbins and lived in Traverse City, Mich. where she died. Three children: Albert and Vere, living in Traverse City, and Ethel who married a Mr. Packard and lives in Omaha, Nebr.

v. William, md. Minnie Rheineger, lived and died in No. Baltimore, O.

vi. Rose, md. Clay Keiser. She was buried at Ripley, O. Two children: Harold and Noel Keiser.

vii. George, md. Daisy Travis. They lived near Greenwich, O. and both are buried there.

viii. Thomas W., b. Feb. 10 1872, married, March 17 1892, Della Gibson, at Norwalk, O. They celebrated their golden wedding anniversary in 1942. Della was born, Sept. 22 1872, at Greenwich, O., only child of Edward and Camille Rickard Gibson. She died, March 16, 1943, and was buried at Fitchville, O. Three children: Golda, md. Albert E. Ruehe, a farmer, and lives at Milan, O.; Bessie, md. Ralph P. Spencer, and lives at Dillonville, O.; and Letha, md. Keith Roscoe, and lives in Norwalk, O.

ix. Myrtle, md. Orlie L. Jackson, and lives in Greenwich, O. No children.

x. Bessie, md. Fred Barnes. She is buried at Greenwich, O.

153 GEORGE YOUNG

born, July 9 1845, near Howe, Ind., died, Dec. 24 1919, at Sturgis, Mich. and was buried there. He was a harness maker. He married, at Sturgis, Electa Osbon. Three children (Mrs. E. C. Sturgis, Sturgis, Mich.).

i. Charles

ii. Ella

256. iii. Effie, b. July 11 1864

154 JOSEPHINE YOUNG

born, Oct. 29 1843, near Monroeville, O., died, Aug. 6 1932, at Seattle, Wash. and was buried there. She married, June 29 1859, Jeremiah H. Barker, at Winterset, Ia., where Mr. Barker was a pioneer jeweller. He was born in North Carolina. Five children, all born in Winterset, Ia. Bessie and William, the two youngest children, died and were buried at Winterset.

257. i. Ellis Luther, b. July 21 1863

ii. Bertine, b. Aug. 7 1870, is living 1946, in Zenith, Wash. She married, Oct. 31 1893, W. S. Snow, at Milwaukee, Wis. She has an adopted daughter, Iola Snow, b. Dec. 4 1907, at Salida, Colo., md. Sept. 2 1922, George W. Christensen, at Seattle. No children. Mrs. Snow is an active member of the D.A.R. and the Women's Club of Seattle, Wash.

iii. Wilma, b. Sept. 21 1873, md. Aug. 7 1894, T. E. Dean, at Chicago, Ill. She died, April 17 1946, at Seattle, Wash. There was one child, Leona Barker Dean, b. May 4 1902, d. Oct. 7 1930. Leona md. a Mr. Bonyer. One child, Robert Johnson Bonyer, b. July 11 1927, at Seattle.

155 EUGENE MORGAN YOUNG

was a farmer, born, Nov. 3 1846, in Oxford Township, Huron County, O., died, June 13 1926, at Willits, Calif. and was buried there. He served during the Civil War in Company H, 23rd Iowa Infantry. The family moved from O'Brien County, Ia., in 1885, to Mendocino County, Calif. He married, March 15 1866, Mary Margaret Compton, at Peru, Ia. Six children, all born at Shelton, Ia. (Clarence H. Young, Healdsburg, Calif. and Mrs. W. H. Ford, Willits, Calif.).

258. i. Clarence Henry, b. Jan. 31 1867

ii. Lewis Harmon, Physician, b. Sept. 13 1869, died, Oct. 13 1938, from an auto accident. He served in the Spanish-American War in Company C, 4th Iowa Cavalry. He married Janette Neil who is living in San Francisco, Calif. No children.

iii. Eva May, b. Feb. 1871, d. 1882, buried at Shelton, Ia.

iv. Fred Eugene, b. Oct. 20 1873, is living, single, near Willetts, Calif. where he raises cattle. He served in the Spanish-American War in Company C, 4th Iowa Cavalry.

259. v. Edith Laura, b. July 29 1878

260. vi. Grace Emily, b. July 4 1883

156 IRENE ELVIRA YOUNG

Public School teacher, born, Sept. 4 1849, near Monroeville, O., died, Aug. 16 1933, at Winterset, Ia. where she was buried. She was married, Nov. 9 1869, by the Rev. O. T. Conger, to Edward F. Connoran, pioneer Jeweler, in the home of her sister, Josephine Barker, at Winterset. Three children, born at Winterset. (C. W. Connoran).

261. i. Clifton Willis, b. June 22 1871

262. ii. Cora Daisy, b. June 3 1874

iii. Harry Edward, b. Dec. 25 1881, d. March 3 1896.

157 EBENEZER PARSONS YOUNG

His middle name is a variant of Pierson. He was a miner at Red Cliff, Colo., born, Nov. 11 1851, near Monroeville, O., died, Dec. 21 1826, at Denver, Colo. He married three times, first, Dec. 13 1874, at Lehigh, Ia., Augusta C. Simmons, b. April 21 1854, at Quincy, Mich., died, March 30 1893, at Orleans, Nebr. where she was buried. Two children: Elva Irene and Bessie J. Young. "Eben" md. 2nd., April 5 1894, Clara Simmons, sister of his first wife, at Chicago, Ill. She died, Dec. 5 1897, at Denver, Colo. He married for his third wife Fanny May Bovier, Aug. 1 1900, at Denver. One child, Eben P. (E. P. Young, Red Cliff, Colo.).

i. Elva Irene, b. Sept. 16 1876, at Burnside, Ia. is living at Long Beach, Calif. She md. Dec. 19 1894 at Orleans, Nebr., William S. Llewellyn who is working in the Calif. Shipyards during the war.

ii. Bessie Josephine, b. May 11 1878, at Burnside, Ia. md., first, Sept. 7 1898, Frederick Lee Brown, at Denver, Colo. He died, Apr. 24 1903, and Mrs. Brown married, second, Eugene Hyatt. Mrs. Hyatt is living with her sister.

263. iii. Eben Parsons, b. Nov. 28 1905

158 LUCY ANN YOUNG

born, Oct. 5 1847, in New Haven Township, Huron County, O., died, Apr. 16 1916, and was buried in Ripley Township Cemetery which was part of a tract of land taken over by the U. S. Government for war purposes in 1941. The bodies were moved to Bogart Cemetery, near Sandusky, O. Many living descendants of pioneer settlers on the land were compelled to seek new land and homes. Lucy married, Apr. 20 1880, Horace W. Barker, at Boughtonville, O. He was a kinsman of Jeremiah Barker, of Fredericktown, O., who married Josephine Young. One child.

264. i. Lee W. Barker, b. July 12 1882

159 MEHITABLE AMELIA YOUNG

born, Dec. 17 1852, in Huron County, O., died, in 1932, and was buried at Windsor, O. She married, Nov. 11 1875, William Wesley Howard, at Ripleyville, O. One child, Mildred, who supplies our family data.

i. Mildred, b. Aug. 9 1892, at Ripleyville (Delphi), O., married, Oct. 10, 1923, A. W. Clark, dairy farmer, at Windsor, O. Mrs. Clark was Postmaster at Windsor for 7 years. The family now lives in Middlefield, O. Two children: Arthur, b. July 12 1925, and Lee Calvin Clark, b. Aug. 9 1928, at Windsor, O.

160 EDNA LEONA YOUNG

born, Jan. 19 1864, twin of Edwin L., is living, 1945, with her son John in Toledo, O. She married, July 23 1881, Jerome Snyder, at Norwalk, O. He died, Feb. 24 1934, at Willard, O. Eight children: Jay; John Elbert; David; Jesse C.; Edith, md. Harry L. Smith, farmer, and lives in Attica, O.; Wayne; and J. Leland Snyder.

265. i. J. Leland, b. June 12 1901

161 EDWIN LEONARD YOUNG

born, Jan. 19 1864, near New Haven, O., twin of Edna, died, April 19 1942, at Cleveland, O. where he had been living with his son Arthur. Mr. Young started his career as a school teacher, later engaged in journalistic work in Norwalk, O., and from 1904 until 1933 was a leading executive of the Knights of the Maccabees. He was also vice-president and director of the Huron County Banking and Trust Co. of Norwalk. He was buried in Woodlawn Cemetery, Norwalk, O. He married, March 20 1884, Carrie M. Houfstatter who died March 27 1939. Two children, one of whom, Ethel, died in infancy.

266. i. Arthur F. Young, b. July 31 1889

162 JAMES LEWIS YOUNG

born, March 1 1854, near New Haven, O., died, July 22 1943, in the home of Mr. and Mrs. C. L. Green, at Mansfield, O. where he spent his last 11 years in retirement. He was buried in Woodlawn Cemetery, Norwalk, O. This compilation is widely indebted to James who lived his 89 years in close vicinity to Fredericktown, O. where his ancestors arrived in 1803 and started the "Jersey Colony in Ohio," and near where Josiah Young and his family arrived from Vermont in 1836. James was personally acquainted with many members of both of these two families who were of no kin but became allied by marriage, and he preserved invaluable records about them which are incorporated in this work together the records from his father's Bible. James attended Oberlin College and graduated from Baldwin-Wallace College at Berea, O. He taught and was Superintendent in the schools of New London, Greenwich and Fitchville, and ended his school career as Superintendent of the Townsend schools. For several years he was travelling salesman for a nursery. He married, Aug. 4 1875, Ursula Woodsworth (b. Oct. 23 1853, at New Haven, O., d. Feb. 5 1920) at Monroe, Mich. Ten children.

267. i. Hattie Mae, b. Aug. 13 1876

ii. Blanche Woodsworth, b. Apr. 21 1878, at New Haven, O., md. Horace W. Summers. Three children: (1) Verra Irene, b. Sept. 15 1897, md. Norman B. Niver, and lived near Willard, O. Four children: Donald D., b. Jan. 27 1923, served as gunner in U. S. Navy, World War II; James R., b. Aug. 14 1927; Ralph, b. Nov. 8 1932, and Richard Niver, b. March 6 1936. (2) Leona I. Summers, b. Nov. 18 1899, md. Harold W. Cooley, and lives in Elyria, O. Two children: William Robert, b. Feb. 7 1923, served in U. S. Navy, in So. Pacific Area in World War II. He md. Apr. 13 1943, Joan M. Rawson, at Elyria, O. and has a daughter Kristine Roberta Cooley, and Dorothy Cooley, b. Sept. 17 1931. (3) Evalyn, b. March 19 1903, at Elyria, O., md. Apr. 17 1929, at Norwalk, O., Lacey Vietch, a grocer. No children.

268. iii. Kent Warren, b. July 31 1879

269. iv. Alice Matilda, b. Sept. 13 1881

v. Lois Jeannette, b. Jan. 24 1883, at Fitchville, O., md. March 27 1910, Fred Adams Wilcox (d. Sept. 2 1933, bur. at La Porte, Ind.) at Norwalk, O. One child, Elaine Jeannette Wilcox, b. Feb. 6 1920, at La Porte, Ind. Mother and daughter live in Chicago, where Elaine is working and perfecting her musical education.

270. vi. Jennie Loida, b. July 30 1884

vii. James Zolomon, b. Jan. 1 1886, at New London, O. is a railroad engineer living in Toledo, O. He md. Aug. 28 1907, at Norwalk, O., Mabel E. Brant. Two children: Lois Elizabeth, b. Nov. 19 1908, at Norwalk, md. in Nov. 1933, Allan Hampton, at Toledo, O. where they live; and George Lewis Young, b. Nov. 20 1910, md. in June 1935, at Toledo, O. He served as Lt. in the U. S. Navy during World War II, with headquarters in Washington, D. C. Family lives in Arlington, Va. Two children.

271. viii. David Augustus, b. July 25 1888

272. ix. Mary Rosella, b. Aug. 15 1891

273. x. Gertrude Bernice, b. Oct. 18 1892

163 ROSE LOUISE YOUNG

born, Jan. 24 1858, near New Haven, O., died, Oct. 19 1945, in the home of her son, Frank F. and Mrs. Ross, at Fargo, N. D. where she was buried. She married, Jan. 7 1877, at New Haven, Charles H. Ross (d. April 22 1924, at Fargo, N. D.), son of a Civil War veteran, Iowa Service, Col. Leonard F. Ross and his first wife Catherine Mary Sims whose other children were Joseph, Emma, Adele and a son who died in his youth. Col. Ross married, in Ohio, for his second wife Mary Warren, daughter of John and Hannah (Austin) Warren, of Vermont and Ohio, and sister of Martha and Julia who married respectively Gardner Young, son of Josiah, and James Lewis Young, father of Rose Louise. These marriages formed a double alliance of the Warren family with two distinct Young families. Col. and Mary Warren Ross had four children: Willis W., living in Portland, Ore.; Ossian Myron, living in Yakima, Wash.; Frank F., d. 1937 at Hot Springs, S. D. and Cora Ross (d. 1928) who married Charles Clarke, a daughter of whom is Mrs. Betty Ross Clarke (R. F.) Jensen, of Los Angeles, Calif. Charles and Rose Ross had seven children.

i. Bertha, b. 1877, at Avon, Ill., d. 1805. She md. Clinton Pemberton. Three children: Helen, md. Jesse Broer, lives in Loron Hill, Ia.; Howard, d. 1937; and Rose L. Pemberton, Pasadena, Calif.

ii. Leonard James, b. Feb. 19 1880, at Avon, Ill., md. 1st., Ida A. Kirk, at Clements, Ia. Four children: Ralph C., Harold W., Floyd L., and Lena M. Ross. He md. 2nd., Martha Wall. Five children: Alma, Violet, Katheryn, Clifford and Elgene Ross.

iii. Frank Fulton, b. Dec. 18 1885, at Adele, Ia., md. Clesta Mills, at Adele. One child, Iris Ross.

274. iv. Donald Harvey, b. Jan. 1 1888

275. v. Bessie Elmina, b. June 4 1892

vi. Lewis Winans, b. April 1 1895, at Bromley, Ia., md. Stella Mooney in 1916. Seven children: Charles, Victor, Rex, Maxine, Lewis, jr., Frank F., and James Ross.

vii. Howard Warren, b. March 27 1898, at Bromley, Ia., md. in 1917 Igerna Parsons, at Marshalltown, Ia. Four children: Warren E., Bette, Louise E., and Robert H. Ross.

164 FREDERICK A. YOUNG

born, May 17 1860, near New Haven, O., died, Aug. 7 1938, at Hollywood, Calif. and was buried in Woodlawn cemetery, Norwalk, O. He married, in 1885, Lillian Bell, daughter of John and Chloe (Button) Kappel. Two children (Mrs. E. L. Bishop, Atlanta, Ga.).

i. Amy Marguerite, b. July 29 1888, at Norwalk, O., md. Sept. 27 1910, John R. Cox, at Norwalk, and is living in Los Angeles, Calif. One child, John Richard, jr., b. Apr. 14 1913, at Cleveland, O., known in Motion Pictures as "John Howard."

ii. Gladys Rose, b. July 25 1890, at Norwalk, O., md. Apr. 5 1915, at Washington, D. C., Everett L. Bishop, M.D., son of Wm. A. and Iola (Getchell) Bishop, of Norwalk, O. Dr. Bishop graduated from Davidson College, Davidson, N. C. in 1910, and from the medical department of the University of Maryland. He served in the Army Medical Corps in World War 1, and in the Navy Medical Corps as Captain in World War 2. He is now practicing in Atlanta, Ga. Three children:

(1) Everett Lassiter, jr., b. Aug. 5 1916, at Savannah, Ga. md. Oct. 5 1940, Irene Bucholtz. They live in Tuscaloosa, Ala. where Dr. Bishop is teaching in the U. of Alabama. He served as Lieut. in the Public Health Div. of the Army during the war. Three children: Michael Jay, b. Sept. 8 1941, at Iowa City, Ia.; Susan Ann, b. March 12 1943, at Savannah, Ga.; and Judith Ellen Bishop, b. July 22 1945, at Savannah, Ga.

(2) William Frederick, b. Oct. 18 1918, at Cleveland, O., md. Mary Linda Dawes in Feb. 1941 at Atlanta, Ga. where Mr. Bishop is working with an electrical equipment company. He was a Lt. Commander when he completed over 4 years service in World War II. He is a graduate of Emory University. Three children: Valerie Francis, b. March 23 1943, Charleston, S. C.; Patricia Lyn, b. Oct. 15 1944, Philadelphia, Pa.; and Steven David, b. Oct. 31 1945, Atlanta, Ga.

(3) Amy Louise, b. Sept. 13 1924, at New York, N. Y., md. C. Barry Henderson, in Feb. 1944, at Macon, Ga. and lives in Baldwin, Miss. where he is in the automobile business. He served as a Pilot of a B-17 during the war. One child, Anita Louise Henderson, b. Apr. 21 1945, Charleston, S. C.

165 ELLA M. YOUNG

only child of J. L. and Sarah (Jennings) Young, born, Jan. 25 1870, near New Haven, O., died, March 18 1908, and was buried at New Haven, O. She married W. Scott Clark. Five children, all born in New Haven, O.

i. Leona E., b. Aug. 18 1894, is teaching, 1943, in Cleveland, O.

ii. Walter Young, b. June 13 1902, is farming near New Haven, O.

iii. Haldon, b. May 1 1904, md., June 10 1925, Helen Stein, at Willard, O. Six children, one of whom died in infancy: Elizabeth, b. Apr. 30 1926, at Willard, O.; William, b. Jan. 13 1928, at New Haven, O.; Elmer Lee, b. Nov. 11 1928; Carolyn, March 1 1937; and Merilyn Clark, b. Dec. 18 1939.

iv. Helen Irene, b. Oct. 24 1906, md. James Seiple, at New Haven, O.

v. Ella Marie, b. March 3 1908, md. Warren Shrader, at Monroe, Mich. The family lives in Willard, O. Three children: Barbara, b. Jan. 21 1928, at Willard, O.; Donald Clark, b. July 14 1929, at Shelby, O.; and Linda Frances Shrader, b. Aug. 15 1938, at Willard, O.

166 ALTHEA JANE HOUSE

born, Oct. 28 1843, Erie County, O., died, June 1 1894, at Grand Rapids, Mich. She married Elon G. Stevens Wright who died in 1908 at Grand Rapids. Two children. (Mrs. Harry Laws).

i. Della Miranda, died, March 20 1945, at Grand Rapids, Mich. She md. Fred W. Fuller. Two children: Merle Reynolds, and Frederick Wright Fuller. Both are married.

ii. Althea Evelyn, b. Jan. 2 1869, md. Dec. 12 1887, at Grand Rapids, Mich., Frank Ansel Emorey who died March 24 1933, at Grand Rapids. Four children: (1) Elon Wright, b. Sept. 21 1888, md. Aug. 29 1908, Susie Buyze, at Grand Rapids. He died about 1916. (2) Claude Welton, b. Jan. 15 1892, md. Mary Vanderburg. (3) Ethel Viola, b. March 29 1899, at Grand Rapids, Mich., md. May 18 1920, Harry Laws, and has seven children: Edward J., b. Feb. 23 1922, at Otsego, Mich., md. Oct. 1940, at Kalamazoo, Mich., Lucille Williams, he served in World War II under Gen. Patton; Richard M. Laws, b. Nov. 5 1923, at Lansing, Mich., md. Hazel Machan, Feb. 14 1941, at Kalamazoo, Mich.; Richard A. Laws, b. Aug. 9 1924, at Allegan, Mich., served in World War II on U.S.S. Intrepid, md. Aug. 30 1946, Betty Jean Bersley, at Otsego, Mich.; Harry Junior Laws, b. Oct. 21 1928, at Lansing, Mich.; Bill Laws, b. Oct. 11 1930, at Lawton Mich.; Howard Laws, b. June 25 1933, at Ostego, Mich.; and Altha Mae Laws, b. April 10 1940, at Kalamazoo, Mich. (4) Howard Ansel Emorey.

167 HARRIET ADELAIDE HOUSE

born, March 22 1850, Erie County, O., died Jan. 21 1930, in the home of her daughter, Mrs. G. M. Anderson, at Pasadena, Calif. She married, as his second wife, Willard Curtiss, machinist, and lived in Kent, O., and Grand Rapids, Mich. Two children. (Mrs. G. M. Anderson).

i. Lindsey House, b. in March 1876, at Grand Rapids, Mich., d. there, March 29 1886.

ii. Bertha Florence, b. July 7 1874, at Grand Rapids, Mich., md. (1), June 24 1902, John W. Niemeyer. This marriage was dissolved and she md. (2) July 7 1915, at Los Angeles, Calif., Wm. F. Dugan who d. May 1916, at Pasadena. She md. (3), Nov. 20 1920, George M. Anderson, at Pasadena, Calif. No children.

168 ELMINA MEHITABLE HOUSE

born, April 30 1852, Erie County, O., died, Oct. 7 1926, was buried in the old Perkins cemetery, Erie County, O. She married, Dec. 7 1876, Arden Austin Storrs, b. Nov. 19 1851, d. Aug. 12 1921. Four children. (Mrs. R. T. Sour, Fremont, O.).

i. Edith Viola, b. May 20 1879, at Perkins, O., md. Ross T. Sour, music teacher, and lives in Fremont, O. No children.

276. ii. Maude Lucy, b. July 7 1881.

iii. Blanche Elsie, b. Jan. 1 1885, at Perkins, O., d. unmarried, Oct. 18 1910, at Perkins, O.

iv. Harrison Elisha, b. Nov. 23 1888, at Perkins, O., is a farmer. He lived on the old homestead until 1941 when the property was taken by the U. S. Government for war purposes. He md. Sept. 3 1914, Helma Heinzer, at Sandusky, O. and lives near Huron, O. Mrs. Storrs died May 6 1945 and was buried at Bogart, O. Three children: (1) Maribel, b. Apr. 20 1916, Perkins, O., md. Oct. 7 1937, Paul Parker, son of George B. and Marian (House) Parker, and lives near Huron, O. (2) Arthur, b. Nov. 3 1919, md. Aug. 28 1940, Genevieve Shrader, at Napoleon, O. and lives at Shinrock, O. (3) Austin, b. Feb. 7 1927, Perkins, O. is living on the old Storr farm near Huron, O.

169 ROSE VIOLA HOUSE

born, March 28 1862, in Erie county, O., married there Leonard Chauncey Hill, a farmer. She died, April 25 1946, in the home of her son Grant, near Bellevue, O. Five children (Mrs. L. C. Hill).

i. Hazen, md. Lena Arbite, lives near Clyde, O. Five children: Dorothy, md. Eddie Wilkin, lives at Sandusky, O.; Hazel, md. Alvin Orwig, lives near Clyde, O. with her two children, Carol and Nelson Orwig; Emily Rose lives near Clyde, O.; Alice, md. Alfred Brode and lives at Wellington, O. with her three children, Earl, Margery, and ——— Brode; and Lester Hill, Clyde, O.

ii. Lawrence, md. Ruth Tompkins and lives near Vickery, O. Five children: Ernest, md. Esther Hartley, lives Sandusky, O.; Paul; Robert; Marian, md. Alfred Lippis and has a daughter Ruth Ann who md. Paul Ging and lives at Monroeville, O.; and Blanche Hill who md. ———, and has two sons, James and Lawrence.

iii. Mildred, md. Eddie Prince and lives at Birmingham, O. Four children: Leona, Robert, Richard and Dolores Prince.

iv. Grant, b. July 22 1900, is farming near Bellevue, O. He md. Nellie Goodsite and has four children: Alfred R., b. Feb. 11 1922; Arlene Rose, b. Oct. 28 1923; Eloise J., b. Nov. 7 1926; and Leola Hill, b. Nov. 29 1928.

v. Theodore, md. Vera Lefevre and lives near Sandusky, O. Two children: Elnora and Rosemary Hill.

170 FRANK CASE YOUNG

farmer, born, Nov. 28 1858, at Delphi, O., died, Feb. 11 1940, and was buried in the mausoleum at Plymouth, O. He married, in Richmond Township, Huron County, O., Harriette Elizabeth Keesy who died, June 16 1943, aged 81 yrs. in the home of her daughter Mrs. Boyd A. Mitchell at New Haven, O. Two children.

277. i. Clyde Case, b. Oct. 24 1887

ii. Oleta R., b. Jan. 13 1894, at Tiffin, O., md. June 21 1923, Boyd A. Mitchell, a mail carrier, at Norwalk, O. and lives in New Haven, O. One child: Barbara Ann Mitchell, b. May 17 1927, at New Haven, is studying music at Oberlin Conservatory, Oberlin, O., 1945.

171 ELLA L. YOUNG

born, June 11 1861, at Fremont, O., is living in 1942 with her daughter Mrs. Fessenden. She married, 1882, at Delphi, O., William George Blackmore. He is dead. Three children.

i. Grace L., md. Huber D. Fessenden, a farmer, and lives at No. Fairfield, O. One child, Maxime, md., June 11 1939, Kenneth Westerman. She has a son James DeHart Westerman, b. Dec. 1 1942.

ii. Burton I., b. May 4 1886, in Darke Co., O., md. Dec. 3 1926, at Los Angeles, Calif., Helen Parsons, b. Apr. 27 1896, and lives in West Hollywood, Calif. Two children: Myra Lucille, b. Feb. 10 1928, and George R. Blackmore, b. Sept. 13 1932, at W. Hollywood.

iii. Lucille, b. March 12 1894, in Drake Co., O., md. at Delphi, O., Oct. 6 1917, Omar H. Frank who died, Apr. 23 1930, at Akron, O., where the family is living. Two children: Ellajean, b. May 31 1921, graduated in 1943 from Otterbein College, Westerville, O., and June Dorothy Frank, b. June 24 1923, at Akron, O. graduated in 1944 from Heidelberg College, Tiffin, O., md. June 9 1945, Milton J. Rood, at Akron.

172 JAMES LEWIS YOUNG

born, Aug. 18 1865, at Delphi, O., died, May 30 1941, in the home of his son Leland, at Shelby, O., and was buried in Edwards Grove Cemetery, near Greenwich, O. He married Ella Hufman, b. March 27 1872, d. Apr. 8 1933. Eight children. (Mrs. Elsie Mitchell, Lucas, O.)

i. Ralph, b. June 15 1889, did not marry, is buried in Edwards Grove cemetery, Greenwich, O.

ii. Ruth, b. Oct. 27 1891, at Plymouth, O., married, Sept. 20 1912, Blair Winck, at Mansfield, O. They live near Bucyrus, O. Four children: Elton Marion, b. Apr. 12 1913; Doris Vivian, b. May 6 1914, m. Fred Dicks, at Bucyrus, O.; Dueane Edward, b. Apr. 20 1925, and Stanley Dean Winck, b. Aug. 7 1927, at Bucyrus, O.

iii. Elsie, b. Feb. 17 1894, at Fitchville, O., married, Apr. 10 1912, George Mitchell, at Mansfield, O. and lives in Lucas, O. Eight children, all born in Lucas: James Lewis, b. Dec. 26 1913, d. Dec. 29 1913; Jacque Savon, b. Dec. 20 1914; Earl Woodrow, b. March 4 1917; George Theodore, b. Feb. 2 1919; and Helen Ione, b. Feb. 19 1922, mar. Albert Marsh, at Mansfield, O.; Virginia Maxime, b. Dec. 18 1924; Eloise Gladys, b. Feb. 21 1927; and Robert Leroy Mitchell, b. Dec. 6 1935.

iv. Glenn, b. Feb. 11 1897, d. Sept. 1 1905.

v. Gladys, b. Feb. 19 1900, at Delphi, O., mar. Jan. 28 1927, Newton Briner, at Monroe, Mich. She married, July 19 1918, Kark Kaylor, d. Oct. 19 1926, buried at Plymouth, O. Four children: James Kaylor, b. Jan. 16 1919, at Plymouth, O.; T. Marion Kaylor, b. Aug. 3 1923, Plymouth, O.; Nancy Lou Briner, b. Sept. 16 1928; and William Charles Briner, b. March 22 1932.

vi. Leland, b. Aug. 27 1902, at Delphi, O., married Bertha Barber, at Shelby, O. where they live. One child: Charles Larry, b. Oct. 1932.

vii. Stella, b. Oct. 9 1908, at Shelby, O., married, Dec. 24 1934, Marion Smith, at Newport, Ky. Two children: Mariella, b. Nov. 17 1935, and William L. Smith, b. June 23 1937.

viii. Orrie, b. 1905, is living 1942 in Shelby, O. Not married.

173 ELIZABETH YOUNG

first child of Noah and Susannah (Storer) Young, born, Aug. 4 1839, near West Union, O., died, Feb. 19 1926, at Humboldt, Coles County, Ill. where she was buried. She married, June 3 1857, at West Union, O., Andrew Jackson Piatt, son of John and Hester (Black) Piatt, and grandson of Benjamin and Mary Waddle Pyeatt. Mr. Piatt died March 16 1902. Of twelve children, all born in Adams County, O., four died in infancy. (E. Agnes Piatt, Bellevue, Ky.)

i. Oliver Byron, b. Oct. 11 1860, d. Nov. 24 1925, at Eaton, O. and was buried at Cincinnati, O. He married, Dec. 31 1902, Irene Shotwell whose forebears lived in N. J. She lives in Bellevue, Ky. No children.

ii. Elmer Norris, b. March 27 1866, d. June 9 1939, and was buried near Harrison, Ind. He md. Alnetta Minister who is living in Pleasant Ridge, Mich. She has a married daughter, Rosella, living in Seattle, Wash.

iii. Rosella, b. June 19 1868, married Carman Waring and lives in Hollywood, Calif. One child, Elmer Piatt Waring, b. Dec. 7 1925.

iv. Harry Kirker, m. Sept. 26 1920, Irene Danner, at Cincinnati, O. Two children: Harry K. jr., b. Feb. 26 1926, and John Carman Piatt, b. Dec. 25 1931. Both boys are in the U. S. Army in 1945. Family lives in Detroit, Mich.

v. Claudia Belle, m. John Schmieg and lives in Detroit, Mich. Three children, two of whom died in infancy, and Glen Melwood Schmieg, b. Aug. 25 1938.

vi. Ida May, b. Sept. 1 1869, d. June 5 1914. She md. Sept. 7 1893, John Ernst, at Bellevue, Ky. He is farming near Windsor, Ill. Two children: Ralph Gates, b. July 15 1895, md., Jan. 21 1919, Willey Dole, both were killed in an auto accident, March 22 1929, and were buried at Mattoon, Ill.; and Marian Ernst, b. June 1 1905.

vii. Vera Frances, b. Aug. 1 1875, md. Nov. 3 1904, John Rude who died at Bellevue, Ky. where Mrs. Rude is living in 1945.

viii. Enna Agnes, b. June 23 1881, not married, lives with her sister Mrs. Rude, Bellevue, Ky.

174 LEVI BARKER YOUNG

farmer, born, Dec. 2 1850, near West Union, O., was killed by a train in 1897 near Humboldt, Ill. where he was buried. He married, at West Union, Dec. 3 1874, Permelia Agnes Young, b. June 21 1850, died, Oct. 17 1941, at the age of 91 in the home of her son Charles at Humboldt where she spent the last 25 years of her life. Permelia was the youngest child of George and Elizabeth (McGarrah) Young, of West Union, O., and a granddaughter of Daniel Young and his first wife who were amongst the earliest settlers in Adams County, O. (C. B. Young, Humboldt, Ill.). Daniel Young, say Evans and Stiver in their "History of Adams County, O." was born in New Jersey in 1757, and was a soldier of the Revolution. "Daniel Young, age 65, married, Aug. 23 1825, for his second wife, Dorcas Coonrod, widow of John Coonrod." ("The Village Register," W. Union, O., Aug. 30 1925). The compiler believes, though he lacks proof, that Daniel was the son of Thomas and Thankful (Robarts) Young, of Pequannock, N. J. and a cousin of Morgan Young, jr. (Rec. 9) who reached Adams County, O. from Washington County, Pa. as did the Coonrod family. Three children.

278. i. Charles Brigham, b. Dec. 9 1875

ii. Julia Florence, b. March 22 1882, md. William Dreeson, a farmer, living near Humboldt, Ill. and later at Bay City, Mich. where Mrs. Dreeson died in 1942.

279. iii. Jessie Evelyn, b. Nov. 21 1886

175 LUELLA FRANCES YOUNG

born, Oct. 2 1855, near West Union, O., died, March 23 1941, and was buried at Humboldt, Ill. She married, Feb. 28 1886, Henry Williams, at Humboldt, Ill. where Mr. Williams farmed. Four children. (Walter Williams, Arcola, Ill.).

i. Ray, b. Jan. 21 1889, d. March 17 1903, at Humboldt, Ill.

ii. Dorothy, b. Aug. 9 1887, at Humboldt, Ill., md. Aug. 28 1915, Thomas Wenn, at Charleston, Ill. and lives in Galesburg, Ill. Three children: Everett Z., b. June 26 1916, at Humboldt, Ill. is serving in the U. S. Army in New Caledonia, 1944. He is married and has a home in Galesburg, Ill.; Edward J. Wenn, b. Dec. 18 1918, d. Feb. 2 1919, at Galesburg, Ill; and Chester F. Wenn, b. March 7 1923, is with the U. S. Army in Italy, 1944.

iii. Laura, b. June 26 1890, at Humboldt, Ill., md. Feb. 20 1913, B. T. McGuire, at Tuscola, Ill. She died, Jan. 11 1942, at Shelton, Wash. Six children: Sterling William, b. May 3 1914, md. and lives in Shelton, Wash., Eva Francis, b. Apr. 8 1917, d. Dec. 24 1920; Helen Belle, b. July 7 1918, d. March 17 1919; Mary Cecil, b. Jan. 3 1920, md. and lives in New York City; Bert Travis, b. Aug. 19 1924, is serving in the U. S. Army in 1945; and Walter Gene McGuire, b. Feb. 29 1928.

iv. Walter, b. Sept. 7 1893, is farming near Arcola, Ill. He married, Aug. 19 1915, Grace Hood (b. July 8 1897), at Charleston, Ill. Three children, all born at Humboldt, Ill. Mabel Irene, b. Nov. 6 1916, md. Glen Evans, at Humboldt, Ill.; Paul Albert, b. Apr. 24 1919; and Glenn Harold Williams, b. June 4 1921, is serving in the Signal Corps of the U.S.A. 1943.

176 NANCY BELLE YOUNG

kept family records and shared them with the compiler when he visited her in July 1943. She was born, Dec. 20 1857, near West Union, O. and died, April 5 1945, at Clarksville, Ia. where she was buried beside her husband, Samuel Minor Cooper, who died Sept. 5 1921. She married, in Stone Chapel, near West Union, Oct. 26 1876. One child.

i. Ola, b. Feb. 10 1884, at Clarksville, Ia. where his parents went in 1879 from Ohio. He married, June 2 1910, Anna Belle Serviss, b. July 25 1877, at Sherman, Texas, d. July 28 1931 and was buried at Morning Sun, Ia. She was the daughter of George Alpheus and Louisa Colvin Serviss. Ola lives in Clarksville where he practices the trade of an electrician. No children.

177 WILLIAM NEWTON YOUNG

farmer in Adams County, O. and for a brief time in Jewell County, Kan. was born, May 10 1861, near West Union, O., died, March 20 1931 and was buried in the I.O.O.F. cemetery at West Union. He married, May 22 1884, at West Union, Margaret (b. Apr. 12 1866), daughter of Wilson and Nancy (Copas) Grooms, both of whom were born in Adams County. Wilson was a Civil War veteran. The Newtons, who gave their name to the County Seat of Sussex Co., N. J., were neighbors of the Youngs before branches of each family emigrated to Ohio. W. N. Young was the son of John G. (Rec. 81) and Sarah B. (Young) Young (daughter of John and Mary (McKenzie) Young, of near West Union. Eight children (Judge E. S. Young, W. Union, O.).

280. i. Ezra Sankfield, b. March 18 1885

ii. Cary Alva, b. Jan. 28 1888, is a farmer living at West Union, O.

iii. Nancy Jane, b. Aug. 6 1890, at West Union, md. W. E. Wilmoth and lives at West Union, O.

iv. John Wilson, b. Sept. 16 1892, was killed in action in France, Oct. 9 1918.

v. Elijah Leroy, b. Dec. 14 1896, in Jewell County, Kan., lives at Wilmington, O.

vi. Harley Esto, b. Oct. 13 1901, at West Union, O., is farming near Wilmington, O. Two of his children are Marlow and Harold Young.

vii. Clarence Noble, b. Jan. 16 1904, at West Union, O. is farming near Wilmington, O.

viii. Oletha May, b. Sept. 10 1905, d. Nov. 27 1934, unmarried.

178 NANCY JANE YOUNG

daughter of John G. and Sarah Belle Young, died about 1875, near West Union, O. and was buried there. Her two sons were infants when she died and were raised by relatives in Adams County, O.

281. i. Andrew Losey Young, b. Feb. 17 1871
282. ii. John Arthur Young, b. Feb. 17 1873

179 CHRISTIAN YOUNG ROOP

born, Aug. 21 1850, near Lagrange, Ind., graduated at the University of Illinois in 1876, and died in 1929 at Holton, Kan. where he was buried. He married, in 1879, Lura Annabel Dickinson (1855-1938) at Lagrange, Ind. After the death of his parents, Mr. Roop lived with his uncle Joseph Roop who gave him his education. The family moved to Kansas in 1879 living in Holton and Salina until 1893 when they went to Santa Barbara, Calif., returning to Kansas City, Mo. in 1906. Two children, both born in Holton, Kan. (Com. W. P. Roop, Woodbury, N. J.).

i. Ethel Dickinson, b. March 19 1881, is living in Wenonah, N. J.
283. ii. Wendell Prescott, b. May 6 1887

180 IDA MAY YOUNG

born, May 12 1859, at Wilton Center, Ill. died in 1946 at Anadarko, Okla. She married, Aug. 3 1877, at Sabetha, Kan., Montville Law (d. Feb. 24 1924, at Anadarko, Okla). Seven children, all born in Anadarko, Okla.

i. Herbert, b. Sept. 15 1880, m. and lives in Ponca City, Okla.
ii. William Oliver, b. March 11 1882, m. Nov. 15 1902, Mary Justice, of Newkirk, Okla. He died in June 1942.
iii. Frank, b. Sept. 13 1885, d. March 14 1929, at Chicksa, Okla. where he md., Nov. 12 1912, Edith Hamilton.
iv. Cornie, b. Dec. 5 1887, m. Oct. 15 1906, Charles Hazen and lives in Anadarko, Okla.
v. Genevieve, b. March 3 1890, m. in 1908 Will Hurt and lives in Anadarko.
vi. Raymond, b. Nov. 24 1894, at Hiawatha, Kan., m. June 17 1929, Bessie Chapman, at Anadarko, Okla.
vii. Lonnetta, b. Sept. 29 1896, m. Jan. 1 1912, Ike C. Clark, and lives in Aanadarko.

181 CHARLES EDWARD YOUNG, JR.

Veterinarian, born Sept. 18 1861, at Wilton Center, Ill., twin of Walker, died, Sept. 14 1918, and was buried at Abilene, Kan. He was raised by Wm. and Sarah Pepper at Manhattan, Ill., lived for a time in Iowa, and went to Kansas in 1880. He married, Aug. 12 1888, H. May Lister, at Hays, Kansas. She died Dec. 9 1944. Ten children (Mrs. Hazel Y. Bell, New Cambria, Kan.).

i. Charles Henry, b. June 14 1889, Sabetha, Kan., d. June 1923, Ellis, Kan. He md. in Apr. 1913, Mabel Robinson at La Crosse, Kan.

ii. Bertha May, b. Sept. 16 1891, Sabetha, Kan., d. Mar. 21 1919, Plainville, Kan. She md. Terrence Hayworth at Junction City, Kan. Children: Charles Burton, Gladys Irene, Dayton E., Mary Alice, and Harold Hayworth.

iii. Edward, b. Mar. 21 1893, Detroit, Kan., d. Dec. 17 1896, Abilene, Kan.

iv. Otis Leroy, b. Dec. 6 1895, Detroit, Kan., d. Mar. 30 1945, Tacoma, Wash. Two children.

v. Edna, b. Feb. 20 1898, Abilene, Kan., md. June 1918, at Hays, Kan., E. B. Phillips, and lives at Oxford, Ohio. Children: Kenyon and Rosemary Phillips.

vi. Frank Allen, Dentist, practicing at Minneapolis, Kan., b. Dec. 16 1901, Abilene, Kan., md. Jan. 22 1927, Rachael Withers, at Kansas City, Mo. She was b. Sept. 9 1905, Cherryville, Kan. Four children: Florence Jane, b. Oct. 28 1928, Abilene, Kan.; George William, b. Apr. 22 1929, was drowned, July 21 1944, in Bennington State Lake, Kan.; Frank A. jr., b. Sept. 11 1932, Minneapolis, Kan.; and Franklin Phillip Young, twin of Frank, d. at birth.

vii. Clarence Edward, b. Apr. 24 1906, Abilene, Kan., md. and lives at Tacoma, Wash. He has a son and a daughter.

viii. Daniel Ward, Druggist, b. Apr. 24 1906, Abilene, Kan.. md. Lylia Breiki and lives at Tacoma, Wash. They have a son and a daughter.

ix. Hazel, b. Mar. 24 1910, Abilene, Kan., md. Jan. 28 1935, Edward J. Bell, at Salina, Kan. and lives at New Cambria, Kan. Two children: Philip Edward, b. Dec. 7 1935, and Susan Jewel Bell, b. Sept. 4 1941, at New Cambria.

x. Margaret Elizabeth, b. Mar. 18 1912, Abilene, Kan., md. 1934, Jess E. Reynolds and lives at Wichita, Kan. One child, Jeanine Reynolds.

182 MELVIN YOUNG

farmer, born, May 20 1866, at Wilton Center, Ill., died at Beattie, Kan. and was buried at Goff, Kan. He married, Nov. 27 1889, at Capioma, Kan., Minnie Shaffer, b. Apr. 6 1872, lives, 1943, at Frankfort, Kan. (Mrs. Hobart Reust, Frankfort, Kan.) Four children, all born at Goff, Kan.

i. Henry John, b. May 21 1891, md. Dorothy Conahan, at Seattle, Wash. where the family is living. One child, Frank John Young, b. Nov. 4 1928, at Auburn, Wash.

ii. Joseph Francis, farmer, b. March 13 1894, md. Dec. 5 1916, Elmie Miller, at Beattie, Kan. and lives near Westmoreland, Kan. Two children: DePhayne Ilene, b. July 26 1920, and Frances Young, b. Oct. 5 1926.

iii. Emmett Emerson, b. March 16 1898, md. Dec. 31 192–, Ruth Olive Dellenbach, at Beattie, Kan. and lives at Conoga Park, Calif. Two children: Dean Curtis, b. Oct. 6 1928, at Sabetha, Kan., and Edwin Ellis Young, b. July 23 1933, at Conoga Park.

iv. Edith, b. March 11 1905, md. March 24 1941, Hobart Reust, at Topeka, Kan., and lives in Frankfort, Kan.

183 EMMA JANE YOUNG

born, March 20 1868, at Wilton Center, Ill., after the death of her mother in 1871, lived with the family of her Uncle Losey Young until she was 16 years old and then moved to her sister Ida's home at Sabetha, Kan. Here she was married, Dec. 31 1890, to Elmer Stine, a farmer, who lived near York, Nebr. Mrs. Stine has been living in Caspar, Wyoming since the death of her husband, Dec. 16 1941. Five children, all born near Sabetha, Kan.

i. Harry Arnold, b. Jan. 4 1892, md. at Des Moines, Ia., Ida Anderson (b. March 25 1893, Omaha, Nebr.) and lives at Alameda, Calif. where he is with the Engund Terminals. Three children: Howard Arnold, jr., b. Aug. 9 1917, at Creston, Ia., d. in an auto accident, Apr. 29 1939, at Oakland, Calif.; Donald Arthur, b. Feb. 20 1919, at Omaha, Nebr., 1st Lieut. Pilot of a B-25 bomber, was taken prisoner in Africa and is held in Germany in 1944; and Robert Marion Stine, b. Sept. 8 1921, at Omaha, Nebr. is serving 1944 as a 1st Lieut. Pilot.

ii. George Elmer, Special Agent for the C. B. & Q. Ry. at Lincoln, Nebr., b. June 19 1896, md. at York, Nebr., Mabel Pearl Olson, b. March 3 1899, at Ontario, Ia. Five children: Marian Jane, b. Feb. 22 1920, at York, Nebr., md. June 23 1940, Malcolm LeRoy Wisdom, at Boise, Idaho, where he is Assistant Fire Chief at Gowan Air Base; Leah Louise, b. Oct. 9 1921, at York, Nebr., md., Nov. 27 1941, Harold Alvin Dougherty, at Lincoln, Nebr. He is a telegraph operator at Plattsmouth, Nebr.; Kenneth Neil, b. Oct. 14 1924, at York, Nebr. is a Navy Air Cadet at Mt. Vernon, Ia. in 1943; George Eugene, b. Sept. 24 1927, at Sheridan, Wyo., is in High School at Lincoln, Nebr.; and Ronald Larry Stine, b. Nov. 22 1938, at Lincoln, Nebr.

iii. Viola Margaret, b. June 14 1898, md. a Mr. Judkins and lives in Caspar, Wyo.

iv. Elsie May, b. May 13 1901, d. July 15 1910.

v. Charles Kenneth, b. June 28 1903, md. at York, Nebr., Nellie E. Phillips, b. Dec. 7 1909. He is a Special Agent of the C. B. & Q. Ry. at Keokuk, Ia. Two children: Leah L., b. July 2 1936, at St. Joseph, Mo., d. March 13 1937, and Dee Ann Stine, b. Feb. 16 1941, at Berwyn, Ill.

184 MARY ETTA YOUNG

youngest child of C. E. and Mary Drown Young, born, Jan. 28 1870, at Wilton Center, Ill., died, Apr. 29 1933, at Ellendale, N. D. She md. at Goodland, Ind., Feb. 18 1891, Clarke Edwin Pierce, b. June 24 1869, at Wilmington, Vt., d. May 6 1936, at Ellendale. After the death of her mother, Mary lived with a family named Lardner at Wilton, Ill. Nine children, of whom, Ethel died at the age of 10, Clark and Melvin, in infancy. (Mrs. E. W. Meier, Marengo, Ia.).

i. Rexford Vernon, b. Oct. 8 189–, married Hazel McMasters, at Ellendale, N. D. Two sons. Family lives at Long Beach, Calif.

ii. Raymond Ralph, b. March 1 189–, md. 1st. Anna Quatier. One son and one daughter. Md. 2nd, Anna Meyer. Three daughters. Lives at Ogilvie, Minn.

iii. Francis Milton, b. Sept. 5 1900, at Madison, N. D., md. Freda Riggs, at Ellendale, N. D. where he is living. Two boys and two girls.

iv. Ruth Mildred, b. Dec. 17 1902, at Madison, N. D., md. July 27 1924, Ernest W. Meier, at Wheatland, N. D. Three children: Kenneth Willard, b. May 6 1925, at Ellendale, N. D., md. July 27 1946, Ruth Freda Barnett, of Verndale, Minn.; Donald Eugene, b. March 5 1935, at Bussey, Ia.; and Patricia Ann Meier, b. March 18 1940, at Eddyville, Ia. The Rev. Mr. Meier is a Methodist clergyman serving in 1945 at Marengo, Ia.

v. Roy Linde, b. Dec. 13 190–, at Ellendale, N. D., md. in 1934 and has 2 sons and 1 daughter. Family lives in Inglewood, Calif.

vi. Grace Esther, b. Aug. 30 1908, is an adopted daughter, md. Gleason L. Stucker, and lives in Sioux Falls, S. D.

185 ISAAC F. YOUNG

son of the Rev. James H. and Augusta Young is said to have been living in California in 1942 but he has not been located. He bought land, April 18 1868, in Wilton Township, Wills County, Ill. (Records, Joliet, Ill.). On Feb. 28 1876, he bought the farm of Benjamin and Elizabeth Gawthrop Young in Range 11, Will County, Ill.

186 ELIZABETH L. GAWTHROP

born, March 25 1863, at Wallingford, Ill., died, Dec. 23 1943, at Des Moines, Ia., and was buried at Blue Hill, Nebr. beside her first husband. She married, 1st, March 1 1883, Thomas Fell, at Manhattan, Ill. Mr. Fell died, Dec. 30 1926, at Blue Hill, Nebr. Seven children. She married, 2nd, Aug. 3 1928, William Green, at Centralia, Wash. No children.

i. Myrtle, b. June 3 1885, at Manhattan, Ill., md. Wesley Cockle, a cousin, and lives in Sutherland, Nebr.

ii. Albert, b. Jan. 2 1887, at Manhattan, Ill., md. and lives in Ogallala, Nebr.

iii. Edna, b. Oct. 29 1890, at Manhattan, Ill., d. June 6 1912.

She md. a Mr. Byers and had one child, Bessie, b. Dec. 11 1809. Bessie was adopted as Bessie Fell by her grandmother, and is serving with the WAAC's in England, 1943.

iv. Florence, b. June 2 1893, d. Aug. 6 1893.

v. Marie, b. Sept. 9 1896, d. Dec. 9 1899.

vi. Inez, b. Oct. 28 1900, at Manhattan, Kan., md. May 9 1937, Arthur H. Ellis, at York, Nebr. She works for the "Register," at Des Moines, Ia.

vii. Olive Fell, b. Jan. 5 1902, at Blue Hill, Nebr., md. Harry Oberg, at Bladen, Nebr. One child, a son.

187 MARY L. PEPPER

born, Sept. 4 1866, in Will County, Ill., died in 1942, at Joliet, Ill. where she married, June 20 1895, Herbert A. Fraser, Public School teacher. Four children, all born in Joliet, Ill. (Mrs. H. A. Fraser, Joliet, Ill.)

i. Ruth Elizabeth, b. May 3 1896, md. Albert H. Brown, at Joilet, Ill. One child, Gale.

ii. Donald T., b. July 7 1898, md. Juliette Ferrell, and lives in Hammond, Ind. Two children: Mary Jane, and Sally Ruth Fraser.

iii. Robert S., b. May 30 1900, md. Jean Robbins, and lives in Fond du Lac, Wis. One child: Douglas Bruce Fraser.

iv. Helen L., b. Dec. 29 1902, md. Milo Hopkins, and lives in Montclair, N. J. Two children: Shirley L., and Richard Hopkins.

188 WILLIAM A. PEPPER

born, July 18 1871, in Will County, Ill., married, 1st., Abbie Patterson, and 2nd., Lena Armstrong. Mr. Pepper is with the Fluorescent Light Co., St. Charles, Ill. Two children by his first wife.

i. Genevieve Marguerite, md. Fred Dinoffria. One child, William Dinoffria.

ii. Lucille, md. Raymond Thomas. One child, Betty Lou Thomas.

189 JESSIE ROBBINS

born, June 1 1868, at Wilton Center, Ill., is living, 1942, in Joliet, Ill. She married, Jan. 11 1888, Henry Dryer in Will County Ill. Four children, all born in Will County, Ill.

i. Mabel, b. Aug. 18 1889, md. Fred Ingraham, and lives in New Lenox, Ill. Two children: Russell, b. May 31 1912, md. and has one child, Donald Ingraham, b. Jan. 21 1942; and Marian Ingraham, md. and has two children: Barbara Kay and Betty Lou ———.

ii. Roscoe Edward, b. June 12 1891, md. Feb. 21 1918, Elda Schoof, lives near Pieton, Ill. Three children: Dolores, Virgil and Verle (twin of Virgil) Dryer.

iii. Lucille, b. March 21 1894, md. in 1913 Sidney Benn, lives at Joliet, Ill. Three children: Thelma, md. Mr. Eberhardt and has six children; Kenneth; and Donald Benn.

iv. Burnell, b. May 14 1902, unmarried, lives with his mother.

190 EDWARD MOSES ROBBINS

farmed near Plainfield, Ill., son of pioneer homesteaders in Will County, Ill., born, Aug. 25 1872, at Wilton Center, Ill., died there, Oct. 2 1945. He married, Sept. 28 1904, Emma B. Berry, born Dec. 12 1874. Two children. (E. M. Robbins, Plainfield, Ill.).

i. Frances Jane, b. Aug. 26 1905, at Wilton Center, Ill., md. Sept. 9 1933, Harvey E. Brockway (b. Feb. 22 1896), at Plainfield, Ill. One child: Eileen Frances Brockway, b. Oct. 21 1943, at Elmhurst, Ill.

ii. Mildred Evelyn, b. July 11 1907, at Wilton Center, Ill., md. Sept. 4 1937, William C. Wilson (b. Nov. 14 1911, at Renville, Minn.), at Michigan City, Ind. Three children: Duanne Allen, b. Feb. 17 1939, d. Feb. 22 1939; Ronald Lee, b. Apr. 1 1940; and Carol Jane Wilson, b. Sept. 25 1942.

191 ALMON JOHN YOUNG

born, Aug. 18 1862, in Lagrange County, Ind., died, May 22 1889, during the diphtheria epidemic in Kansas. He was buried at Halstead, Kan. near where he farmed. He married, Feb. 10 1885, Josey Shirley in Kansas. Two children. (Mrs. Almo J. Dresher, McPherson, Kan.)

i. Edna Cecil, b. May 28 1886, near Halstead, Kan., d. Apr. 2 1889, a victim of the diptheria epidemic.

ii. Almo Josey, b. May 20 1889, at Conway, Kan., d. Apr. 20 1942, at McPherson, Kan. and was buried there. She married, Sept. 10 1911, Clifford H. Dresher, a teacher in McPherson. Two children: Bernice Gwendolwyn, b. July 16 1913, md. June 6 1937, Christian Johansen, at McPherson, Kan. Two children, Janis Kirsten Johansen, b. Sept. 15 1938, at McPherson and Lansing Kent Johansen, b. Nov. 20 1943. The family is living in Decatur, Ill.; and Doris Vivian Dresher, b. Apr. 18 1917, is Secretary to the President of McPherson College.

192 DELEVAN YVOUNG

farmer and furnace dealer, living near Lagrange, Ind., was born, June 9 1868, in Lagrange County, Ind. where his great grandfather Morgan Young, jr. was a pioneer settler. Delevan is President of the County Welfare Board, 1943, and active in all community affairs. The compiler is greatly indebted to him for family data which he received from his aunt, Mrs. Jane Young Loomis. Delevan married, Oct. 5 1892, at Wolcottville, Ind., Hattie R. Dickinson, b. April 7 1872, at Kendallville, Ind. They celebrated their Golden Wedding anniversary in the home of their daughter, Mrs. John McCoy, jr. near Lagrange, Ind. Six children, all born in Lagrange County, Ind.

i. Almond Paul, b. Dec. 27 1893, is now teaching in the Michigan College of Mines and Technology at Houghton. He married, July 28 1912, at Fort Wayne, Ind., Hazel Spore, b. Dec. 30 1891. Mr. Young spent six years teaching in the Methodist Mission Manual School, Baroda State, India, where his one child was born, Feb. 1 1926, Delevan Paul Young.

ii. Edna Lenora, b. Oct. 8 1895, md. Feb. 11 1916, Irvin W. Shultz, grain dealer, at Lagrange, Ind. The family lives in Howe, Ind. Seven children, all born in Howe. William Howard, b. Jan. 22 1918; Homer Irvin, b. Apr. 16 1923; Allen Ernest, b. Apr. 18 1925; Ralph Edward, b. Jan. 18 1927; Margarette Luella, b. Feb. 28 1929; Katherine Jeannette, b. Dec. 31 1931; Betty Jane, b. Dec. 26 1936.

iii. Mildred Isora, b. Aug. 13 1897, married, Sept. 27 1915, Paul E. Sherman, and lives in Howe, Ind. Four children, all born in Howe. Gilbert Delevan, b. Apr. 12 1916, is married and has two children, Martha Caroline, b. June 15

1938, and Joseph Paul Sherman, b. Apr. 4 1940; Harry Leroy, b. Sept. 9 1917; Keith Edward, b. Jan. 27 1922; and Mary Elizabeth Sherman, b. Apr. 9 1929.

iv. Mary Elizabeth, b. Aug. 4 1899, md. July 29 1934, John C. McCoy, jr., farmer, in the home of her parents, near Lagrange, where the families had gathered to celebrate their annual reunion, not knowing that a wedding was the special feature of the day. At the proper moment, the wedding invitations were passed around, and as Mary says, "no one had to dress specially or bring a wedding present, and everybody was there!" The pioneering spirit is still alive in the Young family. Five children; John Calvin, 3rd. b. June 25 1935; Harriet Rowena, b. Dec. 27 1936; Charles Arthur, b. June 20 1939; Maurice Earl, b. May 18 1941; and Henry Matthew McCoy, b. Dec. 10 1943, at Sturgis, Mich.

v. Delevan Samuel, b. Jan. 18 1905, d. Aug. 13 1909.

vi. John Dickinson, b. July 1 1909, md. Irma Garret, of Angola, Ind., at Lagrange, Ind. He is associated in business with his father. Two children: Rose Mary, b. Jan. 14 1940, and Linda Joe Young, b. Dec. 11 1943, at Lagrange.

193 ELIZA LENURE YOUNG

born, June 21 1870, near Howe, Ind., died, Oct. 4 1934. She married, Dec. 27 1891, William J. Schermerhorn, b. July 23 1868, died, Oct. 1930, and was buried at Cassopolis, Mich. Eight children, all born at South Bend, Ind. (Mrs. Geo. F. Westfall, Cassopolis, Mich.).

i. Henry James, b. Feb. 21 1893, died in July 1895.

ii. Carl Michael, b. Sept. 24 1894, d. May 25 1939, and was buried at Cassopolis, Mich. He md. in 1924, at Cassopolis, Elsie Parrish. Three children: Vada Marie, b. Oct. 16 1925; Carl Michael, b. in March 1928; and Rita Elnora Schermerhorn, b. in June 1930.

iii. Ernest William, b. March 16 1897, md. in 1925, Martha Muggler, of McPherson, Kan. Two children: Gail Marie, b. Oct. 5 1931, at Lansing, Mich. and Don Muggler Schermerhorn, b. June 27 1933.

iv. Sarah Josephine, b. Sept. 26 1898, md. in Dec. 1916, Victor F. Shank, of Cass County, Mich. Five children, all born at Cassopolis, Mich.: William Loren, b. Dec. 9 1917, is in the Air Service, 1941; Donnabella Marie, b. Aug. 16 1920; Edward Carl, b. Oct. 28 1921, is in the Marine Service, 1943; John Allen, b. May 20 1923, is in the Air Service, 1943; and Rowena Shank, b. April 15 1936. Donnabella Shank md. Dec. 10 1941, James E. Honeysette, and has two children: Jamie Ann, b. Feb. 12 1942, and Merna Marie Honeysette, b. Sept. 27 1943.

v. Albert J., b. Sept. 20 1900, d. Dec. 18 1946, md. June 9 1923, Beulah Spurgeon, of Dallas Center, Ia. He served in U. S. Army in Germany in World War II. Two children, born at Cassopolis, Mich., Neale, b. Dec. 21 1924, and Patricia Ann Schermerhorn, b. Feb. 11 1926.

vi. Asa Cyrus, b. Apr. 5 1905, md. in 1926, Martha Wagner, b. Aug. 4 1905, d. June 2 1945, at Cassopolis, Mich. Family lives in White Pigeon, Mich. One child: Stanley Hugh Schermerhorn, b. Oct. 31 1927, at Cassopolis.

vii. Leander, b. in 1908, died in infancy.

viii. Bennie, b. in 1909, died in infancy.

194 BENJAMIN YOUNG

born, June 16 1879, near Howe, Ind., died, Sept. 29 1940, at Kendallville, Ind. He married, in 1900, Maude Masters (b. Nov. 11 1878, d. April 1943), at Lagrange, Ind. Four children, all born in Kendallville, Ind. (H. J. Young, Kendallville, Ind.).

i. John Paul, b. July 27 1902, Electrician, md. first, in 1931, Ethel Mae Eshelman, and second, Mrs. Clara Bauer. They live in Kendallville. No children.

ii. Harry Jewell, Oil Distributor, b. Aug. 24 1904, md. Aug. 10 1929, Gertrude Eleanor Walker, at Kendallville, Ind. One child: Patricia Ann Young, b. Nov. 4 1936, at Kendallville.

iii. Dorothy Elizabeth, b. Jan. 4 1909, lives, unmarried, in Kendallville, Ind.

195 HELEN YOUNG

born, July 20 1878, at Viola, Kan., married, Nov. 17 1903, Edgar A. Moon, at Nampa, Idaho. The family lives in Twin Falls, Idaho where Mr. Moon has a furniture store. One child.

i. Ray b. Feb. 3 1913, at Twin Falls, Idaho, md. Jan. 17 1934, Ethel Mae Gross, at Nampa, Idaho.

196 ALBERT HOMER YOUNG

farmer, born, June 10 1880, at Viola, Kan., married in 1904, Samantha Groves, at Nampa, Idaho, where the family is living. Seven children, all born near Nampa. (A. H. Young, Nampa, Ia.)

i. Florence, b. Jan. 28 1906, married Earl E. Harris, and lives in Nampa, Idaho. Four children: Delbert P., b. July 21 1923; Earl Edward, jr., b. Dec. 9 1925; Willard E., b. May 27 1930; and Richard K., b. Nov. 9 1938.

ii. Edna, b. Aug. 16 1908, married Ervin John Doner, and lives in Huston, Idaho. Three children: Zolla Belle, b. Dec. 27 1927, d. 1937. Betty Jane, b. March 16 1932 and Harvey Ervin Doner, b. Dec. 6 1938.

iii. Fern I., b. Dec. 6 1911, married Arnold Clayton Covert and lives in Nampa, Idaho. Three children: Carol June, b. Oct. 23 1933; George Edward, b. Sept. 3 1939; and John Arnold Covert, b. March 23 1941.

iv. Homer Glen, b. April 20 1914, married Violet Margaret Richmond, and lives in Glendale, Calif. He is serving, 1943, in the U. S. Army. One son, born in April 1944, at Glendale.

v. Otis Alvin, b. Nov. 16 1916, married Clara Mary Meyers, at Nampa, Idaho where the family lives. Three children: Peggy Diane, b. Oct. 16 1938; Vickie Anne, b. May 29 1942; and Ronald Alvin Young, b. Feb. 7 1943, d. same day.

vi. Viola Alma, b. March 31 1919, married Clayton Ball Tollefson, at Nampa, Idaho, and lives there. One child: Jeffrey Lynn, b. July 30 1942.

vii. Jane Eileen, b. June 23 1923, married, May 21 1944, Robert Baldwin, at Nampa, Idaho. He is serving, 1944, in the U. S. Army.

197 WILLIAM OTIS YOUNG

farmer, born, July 28 1882, at Viola, Kan., died, Nov. 24 1919, at Twin Falls, Idaho, and was buried there. He married Mable Lammers, at

Waverly, Wis. She is living, 1944, with her son Roy. Three children.

i. Roy Otis, farmer, b. Oct. 4 1912, at Filer, Idaho, lives near Jerome, Idaho. Not married.

ii. Glenn Wilmer, b. Jan. 5 1915, at Filer, Idaho, is serving in the U. S. Army, 1944. He married, Sept. 20 1937, Elsie Johnson of Buhl, Idaho, at Twin Falls, Idaho. One child: Justine Marie, b. Nov. 20 1939, Twin Falls.

iii. Lulu Marie, b. Oct. 26 1909, at Nampa, Idaho, md. Nov. 29 1929, John R. Heck, at Twin Falls, where the family lives. One child: Ronald Eugene, b. Dec. 7 1940.

198 CORA STELLA YOUNG

born, July 31 1884, at Viola, Kan., married, Nov. 16 1909, Samuel M. Gross, at Caldwell, Idaho, and is living in Nampa, Idaho. Three children, all born in Nampa.

i. Claude David, farmer, living near Kuna, Idaho, b. July 12 1911, married, Apr. 12 1936, Violet Stewart, at Nampa, Idaho. Three children:

Gerald Dean, b. Feb. 6 1939; Larry Gene, b. July 4 1940; and Donald Elroy Gross, b. Sept. 23 1942.

ii. Dale Harry, farmer, living near Nampa, Idaho, b. Feb. 13 1916, md. Jan. 18 1941, Justine Ward, at Nampa. Two children: Carroll Josephine, b. Nov. 4 1941, and Linda Louise Gross, b. June 28 1944.

iii. Dorothy Mae, b. Feb. 10 1921, md. Sept. 30 1941, Harold Boyd, at Caldwell, Idaho, and is living at Bowmont, Idaho. One child: Ronald Leroy Boyd, b. Aug. 14 1942, at Nampa, Idaho.

199 WILLARD BURCH YOUNG

born, in 1856, in Sussex County, N. J., died, May 2 1922, and was buried at Newton, N. J. He was associated with his father in the commission business in New York City. He married Lillian Sargent Chambers (1858-1939). One child.

i. William Chambers, b. 1890, at New York City, md. first, Katherine Kay (b. March 31 1905, d. Jan. 4 1924, at Calais, Me.) daughter of Hugh and Katherine Morrison

Mooney, of Lubec, Me. No children. He married, second, Aug. 7 1930, Francina Mae Griffith (b. 1924, at Robbinston, Me.), at Calais. (City records, Calais, Me.)

200 SILAS LEWIS HAZEN

born, Jan. 9 1856, died, May 22 1910, and was buried at Newton, N. J. (Gravestone record). He married, in 1879, Emma Caroline Reed, b. 1856. Four children.

i. Harry W.

ii. Mabel Emma, b. Feb. 5 1882, at Newark, N. J., died, Dec. 28 1927, and was buried at Newton, N. J. She was a member of the D.A.R.

iii. Grace L., died March 1 1944 in N. Y. City where she was a registered nurse.

iv. Silas Arthur, is living in E. Orange, N. J.

201 WILLIAM LIVINGSTON HAZEN

Educator, born, May 4 1861, at Elizabeth, N. J., died, April 13 1944, at New York, N. Y., and was buried at Newton, N. J. He graduated with Phi Beta Kappa honors from Columbia University in 1883, and from the Columbia Law School in 1885. He was granted the honorary degree of Doctor of Laws by Manhattan College in 1893, and in the same year received the Columbia University Medal of Honor. Dr. Hazen founded in 1886, and for 58 years was Headmaster of the Barnard School for Boys, at Riversdale, N. Y. He was co-founder with Theodore E. Lyon of the Barnard School for Girls. He was cited for gallant action during the Spanish-American War. He married, Oct. 23 1889, Olive Starr, at Newark, N. J. They had one child.

i. Elizabeth Starr Hazen, b. March 27 1902, md. June 9 1928, at N. Y., Burritt Alden Cushman, and lives in New York, N. Y. Three children: Meredith, a dau., b. Dec. 22 1929; William Alden and Elizabeth Starr Cushman, twins, b. Sept. 8 1932. Mrs. Cushman has a keepsake in the form of an old pewter mug in which there is a card inscribed as follows: "George Washington drank from this cup, the day following the Battle of Brandywine, Sept. 11 1777, at the home of Arreka Jans, who gave the cup to her granddaughter, Sally Young, wife of Robert, son of William

Young, who gave it to her grandson, Robert Shaw, son of Hulda Young Shaw." See Record 3.

202 ANNA ELIZA ROBERTSON

born, Jan. 15 1844, in Union Grove Township, Whiteside County, Ill., died there, Dec. 11 1885, and was buried in Grove Hill cemetery, Morrison, Ill., beside her husband. She married at Morrison, Nov. 16 1865, Dwight S. Spafford, d. Feb. 9 1923, bur. Morrison, Ill. Four children (R. R. Spafford).

284. i. Frank Sumner, b. Aug. 23 1886

ii. J. Earle, b. June 19 1870, near Morrison, Ill., retired from the banking business in 1941 and lives at Los Angeles, Calif. He md. at Kearney, Nebr., June 27 1900, Nellie Donnell, b. March 15 1880, at Streator, Ill., d. Apr. 4 1945. No children.

iii. Rob Roy, b. Jan. 21 1874, Morrison, Ill., lives at Twin Falls, Idaho, where he is the Idaho representative of the Albert Dickinson Seed Co., of Chicago, Ill. He md. at Morrison, Ill., Jan. 5 1898, Lela M. Beuzeville, d. Dec. 1932. They have one child, Eloise Lela, b. Jan. 10 1899, at Morrison, md., 1st., Oct. 13 1920, Freeman C. Foss, at Boise, Idaho, and 2nd. Sept. 3 1929, Theodore Welker and lives at Twin Falls. Mr. Spafford md. 2nd., Feb. 13 1936, Jennie Swan, at Twin Falls, Idaho.

iv. Fred Dwight, b. Nov. 12 1885, is a salesman for Armour and Co., living in Janesville, Wis. He md. at Minneapolis, Minn., March 17 1918, Dollie P. Higgins, b. Sept. 25 1887. They have two adopted children: Lora Maxine, b. Apr. 7 1908, at Boise, Idaho, md. Dec. 7 1932, Russel Rebholz, at Madison, Wis. and lives at Stevens Point, Wis.; and Jack Propper Spafford, b. June 26 1910, md. Lucille Quicci, March 28 1940, at Canton, O.

203 ANDREW J. ROBERTSON

born, Nov. 26 1845, at Unionville, Ill., died, Dec. 10 1918, and was buried at Broken Bow, Nebr. He was engaged for some years in cattle raising with his brother LeRoy in Wyoming. Later he was in the banking business at Broken Bow, Nebr. where he was also Receiver, U. S. Land Office, 1892-

1896. He married, Jan. 8 1890, at Broken Bow, Dora May Reese, born, Feb. 17 1868, at Bellefontaine, O., died, July 9 1936. Five children (John P. Robertson, Washington, D. C.).

i. Emily Evelyn, b. Sept. 24 1890, at Minneapolis, Minn., d. July 6 1944, at Boise, Idaho.

ii. John Porteous, b. Oct. 8 1891, at Broken Bow, Nebr. was Receiver in the U. S. Land Office there from 1916 until 1920, and in the banking business from 1920 until 1926. He has been with the Department of Interior, Washington, D. C. since the death of Senator G. W. Norris whom he served for many years as private secretary. He owns his grandmother Young's Bible from which he has supplied much data for this compilation. He married, May 19 1920, at Washington, D. C., Hazel, daughter of Senator George William and Pluma Lashley Norris.

iii. Rob Roy, b. Oct. 20 1896, at Broken Bow, Nebr., md. Nov. 11 1926, at Grafton, Nebr., Ruth Hainey and lives in Ontario, Oregon. Two children: John Hainey, b. Apr. 26 1934, at Yakima, Wash., and Margaret Robertson, b. Nov. 27 1937, at Boise, Idaho.

iv. Frederick Reese, b. March 24 1906, at Broken Bow, Nebr., is in the U. S. Army, 1944, at Fort Warren, Wyo. His home is in Ontario, Oregon.

v. James Louis, b. Oct. 31 1907, at Broken Bow, Nebr., md. July 24 1928, Julia Jensen, at Omaha, Nebr. Mr. Robertson is Deputy Controller of the Currency, U. S. Treasury, Washington, D. C.

204 IDA MAY ROBERTSON

born, April 9 1855, near Morrison, Ill., died July 7 1936, and was buried at Morrison. She married James W. Boyd (b. Apr. 14 1858, d. Oct. 12 1942) at Morrison, Ill. One child. (J. W. Boyd, Kearney, Nebr.).

i. James W. Boyd, jr., b. July 15 1896, at Kearney, Nebr., lives in Kearney. He married, Feb. 20 19—, Henrietta Mattson, at Wahoo, Nebr. Four children: Bobette Rogers, b. March 25 1920; Ginger, b. Oct. 12 1927, sister of Don, b. Feb. 19 1928, are adopted children; and Billy Jim, b. May 26 1936, at Kearney, Nebr. Mr. Boyd is doing construction work in 1942 at Camp Carson, Colorado Springs, Colo.

205 MATTHEW HENRY POTTER

born, Dec. 27 1855, at Wethersfield, now Kewanee, Ill., died, Jan. 10 1943, and was buried at Morrison, Ill. He was engaged for many years in the coal, lumber and grain business at Morrison. He was also a Director of the First National Bank and a member of the Board of Education. He married, May 15 1884, at Morrison, Elizabeth, (b. May 2 1858, d. Nov. 26 1936) daughter of David J. and Ann Quackenbush of Morrison, Ill. Mr. and Mrs. Potter celebrated their golden wedding anniversary in 1934. Four children (Miss Ann Potter, Morrison, Ill.).

i. Albert M., b. July 19 1887, twin of Warren, is continuing his father's business in Morrison. He md. Oct. 25 1913, Lillian Paulson, at Morrison. They have three children: Albert M. jr., b. Apr. 22 1916, is in business in Clinton, Ia. He married, Oct. 4 1939, Portia Clarke, at Adel, Ia. Robert Henry, b. March 2 1918, is a Lt. in the U. S. N. R. 1942; James Warren, b. March 1 1925, at Clinton, Ia. is a freshman in college, 1942.

ii. Warren J., b. July 19 1887, at Morrison, Ill. is associated with his brother in business. He md. March 28 1914, Marion L. Smith, at Morrison. Five children: Elizabeth Ellen, b. Apr. 17 1915, d. May 19 1915, and was buried at Morrison, Ill.; Barbara Jean, b. May 21 1916, at Chicago, Ill., md. Jan. 1 1943, Beverley Page, at Morrison, and is living in Houston, Texas; Marjorie Louise, b. Feb. 5 1918, at Morrison, md. Dec. 25 1941, at Morrison, James D. Lea. Mr. Lea is the Texas Manager of Eastern Air Lines. One child: James D. Lea, jr., b. Oct. 1 1942, at Houston, Texas where the family is living; Polly Ann Potter, b. Oct. 20 1919, at Clinton, Ia., md. Jan. 1 1943, at Morrison, Ill., John Lea, 1st. Lt. U. S. Army Air Forces; and Nancy Jean Potter, b. July 17 1923, at Clinton, Ia., is a student at the Career Institute, Chicago, Ill.

iii. Matthew Bonar, b. Oct. 8 1890, md. Nov. 25 1916, at Sterling, Ill., Letitia Crawford (b. Aug. 14 1892, d. Sept. 16 1926). Two children: Virginia Ann, b. Jan. 30 1920, at Sterling, is a Registered Nurse serving in No. Africa with the Armed Forces; and Letitia Joan, b. Sept. 14 1926, at Clinton, Ia. is now attending Southern Seminary, Buena Vista, Va. Mr. Potter md. (2) Nov. 23 1929, at Galesburg, Ill., Maude Stephenson (b. July 28 1892, at Oneida, Ill.), a graduate of Knox College.

iv. Ann M., b. Dec. 27 1893, at Morrison, Ill., graduated at Northwestern University, Evanston, Ill. and became a member of the library staff of the University. After the death of her mother she managed the home for her father. She is now serving in the WAC at Heidelberg, Germany. We are indebted to Miss Potter for much data on her own and other branches of the Potter family.

206 CARRIE ELIZABETH POTTER

born, Feb. 20 1858, at Wethersfield, Ill., married there, Aug. 2 1881, Charles Otis, born, May 2 1855, son of Emmas and Mary E. Otis. The family lived at Topeka, Kan. where Mr. Otis died and was buried. Two children (Mrs. Grace Otis Smith, Salina, Kan.).

i. Helen, b. Sept. 12 1882, at Red Oak, Ia., d. Dec. 25 1937 and was buried at Girard, Kan. She md. at Topeka, Kan., F. W. Cole. One child: Helen Elizabeth Cole, b. Aug. 17 1912, at Girard, md. Earl Miller, at Kansas City, Kan. Earl and Helen have one child, Marcice Miller, b. Nov. 13 1938, at Salt Lake City, Utah.

ii. Grace, b. Sept. 18 1884, at Red Oak, Ia., md. Sept. 18 1907, Jay W. Smith, at Topeka, Kan. Two children: Adrian W., b. June 24 1908, at Topeka, is serving in the U. S. Army, 1943; and Charles Otis Smith, b. Apr. 21 1912, is serving in the U. S. Navy, 1946. He graduated at Kansas Wesleyan College, md. and has two children, Jay Ludes, b. Apr. 23 1939, and Susan Eleanor Smith, b. Jan. 26 1943, at Salina, Kan. where the family lives.

207 ALVINA ELIZABETH POTTER

born, Jan. 18 1850, in the old home at Kewanee, Ill., died about 1909, and was buried at Toulon, Stark County, Ill. She married, Dec. 3 1867, at Wethersfield, Ill., George S. Lawrence, b. June 9 1836, at Alamuchy, N. J. Two children. (Noble E. Potter, Kewanee, Ill.).

i. Abigail Young, b. Nov. 2 1868, at Kewanee, Ill., is living in Peoria, Ill. She md., Dec. 22 1890, at Toulon, Ill., J. Frank Ziegler, deceased. No children.

ii. Bessie, b. May 31 1870, at Toulon, Ill., md. at Toulon, Jan. 7 1896, Charles A. Foster, b. Feb. 22 1865, at Han-

LOIS MARRIED M. E. CAMPBELL. AUG. 7-1955 BOWIE, TEXAS
FRANCES MARRIED JAMES McCARTY, July 3 1955 - BOWIE TEXAS

over, N. H. They lived in Bowie, Texas. One child: Lawrence C. Foster, b. Sept. 26 1896, at Toulon, Ill., md. Seba Slaughter (b. June 21 1901, at Bowie, Texas, dau. of Geo. O. and Minnie L. Groves Slaughter) and has four daughters, all born in Bowie: Jane, b. Jan. 29 1931; Lois, b. Nov. 27 1933; Frances, b. Sept. 27 1936; and Virginia, b. Apr. 4 1938.

208 NOBLE POTTER - Died Nov. 7-'49.

born, Nov. 21 1859, at Wethersfield, Ill., is living hale and hearty, in Oct. 1946, with his daughter Mrs. S. L. Heaps in Kewanee, Ill. He was in the brick and tile business at Kewanee for many years, first with his father and later, alone. He married at Virginia, Ill., Oct. 20 1886, Emma L. Massey (b. May 9 1860, d. Nov. 10 1926, and was buried at Kewanee), daughter of Henderson Ellis and Martha (Marshall) Massey. One child.

6

7 - i. Charity Martha, b. July 19 1887, at Kewanee, Ill., md. at Kewanee, Feb. 21 1910, S. Leroy Heaps, a Civil Engineer, who until he took up war work was Surveyor of Henry County, Ill. One child: John Marshall Heaps, b. Aug. 18 1921, at Kewanee. After two years at the University of Ill. he enlisted for service in the Merchant Marine. He is Lt. in the Transportation Corps in 1946, at Manila, P. I.

209 HENRY BEERS PINNEY

Physician, born, Dec. 28 1851, at Kewanee, Ill., died, Aug. 10 1915, at San Francisco, Calif. He studied medicine with his father in Missouri, and later at the College of Physicians and Surgeons, Ann Arbor, Mich., and at Miami Medical College, Cincinnati, O. In 1875 he located at Joplin, Mo. and went from there in 1879 to Silver Cliff, Colo. where he practiced his profession and also engaged in the drug business. From 1880 until 1884 he practiced at Jaspar, Mo. and then moved to Chattanooga, Tenn. where, due to ill health, he gave up the practice of medicine and went into the real estate business. In 1900, after a year in Carthage, Mo., he moved his family to California and in 1901 settled in the real estate business in San Francisco, where he died. He married, at Carthage, Mo., May 6 1876, Laura Ann Young (b. Nov. 5 1849, at Washington, Ia., d. Dec. 21 1943, in the home of her daughter, at San Francisco) daughter of John Davis and Marie Eyestone Young. Mrs. Young is co-author of "The Pinney Family in America" and author of "Thomas Young," both works were privately published at San Francisco, Calif. Mrs. Young was of no kin, so far as is known, to her mother-in-law Harriet Young Pinney. However, further research may reveal a kinship. (Rec. 326) Both Young families are allied by marriage to the New Jersey Potters and intimately connected with the Kents. Members of the two families lived in Pennsylvania and in Adams County, Ohio, as well as in Missouri. One child.

285. i. Grace Maria Pinney, b. Aug. 26 1881

210 EMILY MAY PINNEY

born, March 29 1856, at Kewanee, Ill., died, March 5 1936, at Long Beach, Calif. She married, first, Dec. 25 1873, O. W. Rose at Preston, Mo. Six children. She married, second, Nov. 28 1888, David Jones Roberts, at Pacoima, Calif. Two children. Emily married, third, in Oct. 1908, A. J. Potter and lived at Long Beach, Calif.

i. Elbert Perry Rose, b. Nov. 10 1875, at Preston, Mo., is in the Real Estate business in Long Beach, Calif. He md. Sept. 26 1901, Elizabeth Pearl Wright.

ii. Olive May Rose, b. Feb. 14 1877, at Preston, Mo., md. March 9 1898, Edgar Lyle De Remer, Real Estate dealer, at San Fernando, Calif. Three children: Gladys Rose, b. Sept. 19 1899, d. May 14 1900; Edgar Merton, b. May 23 1903, md. Peggy ———, and has a daughter, Joan, b. Oct. 25 1927; and Kenneth Ross De Remer, b. March 6 1923.

iii. Winnie Blanche Rose, b. Dec. 18 1878, at Preston, Mo., md. Sept. 2 1896 Arthur Bland, at Pacoima, Calif. Two children: Dorothy Blanche, b. June 26 1903, at San Fernando, Calif. md. May 20 1920, Jimmie Hallihan; and Donald Arthur Bland, Sanitary Engineer, Long Beach, Calif., b. Jan. 21 1905, at San Fernando, md. Catherine Ward, 1926.

iv. Bruce Wellington Rose, b. Apr. 7 1882, in Kansas, d. Aug. 15 1886.

v. Jessie Pearl Rose, b. March 29 1884, at Westphalia, Kan., md. Milo Potter, at San Fernando, Calif. Two children: Lucille Rose, b. March 22 1903, md. Glenn Miller, and has a son Glenn; and Evelyn May Potter, b. Aug. 17 1904, at Los Angeles, Calif., md. Walter Smith, and has a daughter Barbara Jean, b. Sept. 1 1930.

vi. Carl Wellington Rose, b. Feb. 15 1886, at Westphalia, Kan., md. March 15 1910, Myrtle Tucker, at San Francisco, Calif. One child: Maxime.

vii. David Berwyn Roberts, Lawyer, son of David J. and Emily Roberts, b. Sept. 14 1890, md. Aug. 19 1914, Elizabeth Ruth Burke, and lives in El Centro, Calif. Two children: David B. jr., b. Oct. 7 1918, and Elinor Roberts.

viii. Roy Robert Roberts, b. Nov. 6 1895, d. Dec. 21 1914.

211 NETTIE OLIVE PINNEY

born, Aug. 29 1861, at White Rock, Texas, married, March 15 1879, Jewitt Allin, Real Estate Dealer, at Preston, Mo. They lived sometime in Chattanooga, Tenn. Mrs. Allin died, Oct. 24 1930, at Atlanta, Ga. Three children.

i. Thomas Carl, b. Oct. 18 1879, at Pilot Mountain, Tenn., md. March 27 1907, Sarah Dunk, at Chattanooga, Tenn. He died, Sept. 26 1923, at Jacksonville, Fla. where the family was living. Three children: Thomas Jewitt, b. March 7 1910, d. March 8 1910; Thomas Carl, b. May 7 1912, at Jacksonville, Fla. is an Executive in his uncle's laundries, in Jacksonville; and Dorothy Broadwell Allin, b. Jan. 5 1917.

ii. Lulu Ethel, b. in Jan. 1883, at Chattanooga, Tenn., md. Dec. 17 1907, Robert Russell. One child: Netta Gadsden, b. June 21 1909, at Atlanta, Ga. where the family is living.

iii. Jewitt, jr., Real Estate Dealer, b. Oct. 8 1884, at Chattanooga, Tenn., md. Dec. 10 1918, Lora Maude Churchill, at Spokane, Wash. They are living in Florida, 1942. Two children: Netta, b. Aug. 20 1920, and Jewitt, 3rd., b. March 6 1922, at Spokane, Wash.

212 LULU BESSIE PINNEY

born, June 29 1864, at Greenville, Texas, died, Jan. 22 1943, and was buried near her parents in Live Oak Cemetery, Los Angeles, Calif. She married, April 17 1889, Herschel E. Currey, M.D., at Pacoima, Calif. They lived in Baker, Ore. Two children.

i. Herschel Eugene, jr., Pharmacist, b. Aug. 28 1890, at Duarte, Calif., md. Dec. 19 1917, Gladys Heath, at Baker,

Ore. They are living in Portland, Ore. Two children: Eugene Elsworth, b. Sept. 10 1918, at Baker, Ore., md. May 5 1943, Marguerite Wichert, at Vancouver, Wash.; and Glenn Allison Currey, b. June 13 1923, at Portland, Ore.

ii. Pinney Alfred, Pharmacist, b. Nov. 1 1892, at Portland, Ore., md. June 10 1916, Edith Pearson, at Spokane, Wash. He operated his father's drug store in Baker, Ore. from 1919 until 1927 when the family moved to Los Angeles, Calif.

213 EMILY AMELIA YOUNG

born, Sept. 11 1859, at Morrison, Ill., is living, 1946, with her daughter and son-in-law in Los Angeles, Calif. She married at Morrison, Dec. 27 1882, James W. Henry, born, Sept. 26 1853, died, Nov. 27 1911, at Los Angeles. Mr. Henry was Vice Principal of the L. A. High School for 17 years prior to his death. He graduated, M.A. degree, from Dartmouth College, 1878. He was the son of Andrew Henry, several times a member of the Mass. Legislature, and Sarah (Claflin) Henry. Three children: Edith Henry, died in 1894, age 9 years, and a baby boy who died at birth.

iii. Mabel Gertrude, b. Oct. 30 1894, at Los Angeles, Calif., graduated from Leland Stanford University in 1915, md. at Los Angeles, Oct. 16 1921, Clifford Neal Amsden, graduate of Tufts College and now in charge of the Civil Service Department of Los Angeles County, Calif. He is a past Pres. of the Civil Service Assembly of the U. S. and Canada and is now on its Executive Board. Two children: Neal Franklin, b. Nov. 14 1927, is a student at the U. of So. California, and Emily Amsden, b. Nov. 10 1935, at Los Angeles, where the family is living.

214 CORA PAULINA YOUNG

born, Aug. 11 1863, at Morrison, Ill., married there, Feb. 23 1888, her childhood playmate Charles Lincoln Logan (died, July 23 1938, and was buried in Forest Lawn Memorial Park, Los Angeles, Calif.). They celebrated their golden wedding anniversary in 1938. Mr. Logan was the son of John Emmet and ——— (McCoy) Logan. His father at one time represented Whiteside County in the Assembly of Illinois. The family came to Morrison, Ill. from Elmira, N. Y. and moved to Los Angeles in 1890 where Charles was County Recorder for 31 years, after having been Deputy Recorder for 12 years. His brother, Dr. W. H. G. Logan, d. April 6 1943, was Dean of the Chicago Dental School. Two children.

i. Ruth, b. Feb. 16 1894, at Los Angeles, md. there Jan. 25 1917, William Holmes Harris, Electrical Engineer, and has one child, Marjorie Corinne Harris, b. July 28 1929.

ii. Stella, b. Oct. 6 1899, at Los Angeles, md. there, (1st), Sept. 12 1917, K. Omar Bolte, and (2nd), Jan. 9 1926, Alazo Schraeger. Two children: Charles Logan Schraeger, b. Jan. 7 1927, d. June 28 1943, and Robert Alan Schraeger, b. Sept. 21 1931, at Los Angeles, where the family is living.

215 ROY JACKSON YOUNG

born, April 26 1870, in Jaspar County, Mo., died, Jan. 16 1925, and was buried in Mt. View Cemetery, Oakland, Calif. He married, at Berkeley, Calif., July 26 1898, Flora May Robb, born Dec. 17 1872. Three children (Mrs. Flora M. Young, Berkeley, Calif.).

i. Robb Roy, Fruit Grower, living near Exeter, Calif., b. June 20 1899, at Merced, Calif., md. Aug. 17 1922, Hazel Pool, b. Jan. 12 1902, at Exeter. No children.

ii. Elizabeth Hope, b. March 20 1904, d. July 13 1907.

iii. Gladys Ruth, b. Aug. 15 1909, at Berkeley, Calif., md. there, July 9 1937, Grant Barton Youngs. They live in Greenville, Calif. where Mr. Youngs is a High School teacher. Two children: Susan Roy, b. Oct. 31 1939, and Grant Barton Youngs, b. Dec. 14 1941, at Berkeley, Calif.

216 STELLA EVALYN YOUNG

born, Oct. 5 1874, in Jaspar County, Mo., marrid, April 14 1904, at Los Angeles, Calif., Dr. Horace H. Henderson, Dentist (son of John Henderson, jr. and Elizabeth Geddie Johnstone), b. March 9 1874, at San Francisco, Calif., graduated 1901 from Univ. of Calif. Dental College. The family lives at Berkeley, Calif. Three children.

i. Evalyn Amelia, b. Dec. 15 1906, md. Orla St. Clair, Attorney, with offices in San Francisco and Washington, D. C. Lt. Col. St. Clair served in World War II in the Signal

Corps, U. S. Army, and received the Legion of Merit award.

ii. Horace Wheaton, b. June 8 1909, at Berkeley, Calif., md. May 8 1937, Margaret Wanzer, at Sacramento, Calif. He was Sgt. AAF in World War II, and is now an Exporter living in San Francisco, Calif.

iii. Margaret, b. Oct. 3 1913, is Office Manager, Radio Station, KROW, Oakland, Calif.

217 ERNEST BEERS JACOBS

born, July 20 1858, at Chicago, Ill., died Dec. 24 1927, at Carthage, Mo. where he and his wife were buried in the Mausoleum. Mr. Jacobs, for some years, was Cashier of the 1st National Bank of Carthage and Vice President of the 1st National Bank of Jaspar, Mo. He married, Nov. 12 1884, at Carthage, Carrie Farwell. Two children. (Family Bible of Lucy Young Jacobs).

i. Ernestine, b. Jan. 7 1894, at Carthage, Mo., md. (1) Oct. 8 1921, Wallace Bennett Cannon, b. Sept. 7 1894, Farmville, Va., d. in Sept. 1932, and was buried in Arlington National Cemetery. One child: Lura Virginia Cannon, b. June 14 1924, at Norfolk, Va. Ernestine md. (2), Oct. 11 1936, Greer Pickens, at Eaglecrest, Sarcoxie, Mo. where the family is living.

ii. Jay Wesley, b. Jan. 3 1898, at Carthage, Mo., a portrait painter, lives and has his studio on Long Island, N. Y. Unmarried.

218 BESSIE MAY JACOBS

born, July 29 1867, at Union Grove, Ill., died, March 28 1896, and was buried in Forest Hill Cemetery, Kansas City, Mo. She married at Kansas City, Mo., Nov. 8 1885, John H. Crandall, Court Reporter, son of William Crandall and Marian Nason. Three children.

i. Merle Chic, b. Nov. 15, 1886, at Kansas City, Mo., is living, a widow, in Webster Groves, Mo. She md. Richard Robertson and had three children: John Crandall, pilot of a B-29 in World War II, was killed, May 24 1944, in India; Elizabeth Knepp, md. Verde Blackwell, is a widow living at Glendale, Calif.; and Merle Chic Robertson, md.

Robert Eldred and lives at Webster Groves, Mo., where Mr. Eldred is regional superintendent of the Armour Packing Co.

ii. Helen Delight, b. May 27 1888, at Kansas City, Mo., md. there, May 11 1910, Leland Stanford Davis who has been in the insurance business in K. City for some 35 years. Two children: Leland S. jr., b. Sept. 5 1911, is associated in business with his father; and Doris Delight Davis, b. March 26 1914, graduated, a member of Phi Beta Kappa, at Sophia Newcomb College, N. O., La. She md. March 8 1941, Kiah E. Warden, at Kansas City, Mo.

iii. John Jay Crandall, b. March 3 1896, md. and lives in St. Louis Mo. where he is in the U. S. Postal Service. No children.

219 BERTHA DELIGHT JACOBS

born, Aug. 9 1872, at Carthage, Mo., died in the home of her daughter Lucile, Oct. 21 1937, at Evanston, Ill. She married, June 3 1891, Edward Grant Woodling, at Kansas City, Mo. Three children.

i. Lucile Delight, b. March 8 1892, at Cranford, N. J., is living in Evanston, Ill. Graduated at Wellesley College; md. Feb. 10 1917, at Cranford, Lambert Davis, Investment Broker, graduate of U. of Penn., b. July 13 1887, at Deadwood, S. D. One child, Marian Woodling, b. Jan. 18 1918, at Tacoma, Wash. Marian md. Oct. 1 1938, at Evanston, Ill., George C. Trippe and has three children: Gail Woodling, b. July 6 1941, at Evanston, Ill., and twin sons, William Lambert, and David Renfroe Trippe, b. Apr. 27 1945, at Evanston. Mr. Trippe is serving as 2nd Lt. with the U. S. Forces in the Philippines, 1945.

ii. Preston, b. Dec. 5 1901, Electrical Engineer, graduate of Mass. Inst. of Technology, lives at Riverside, Conn. He md. Oct. 6 1923, at Hingham, Mass., Dorothy Cynthia Richards. One child, Darthea Macgregor Woodling, b. Aug. 13 1928, at Summit, N. J.

iii. Edwina, b. Sept. 23 1904, at Cranford, N. J., lives at Stamford, Conn. She md. June 28 1924, at New York, Charles A. Plummer, b. March 19 1898. Four children:

Patricia Delight, b. Jan. 11 1927, at N. Y.; Dirk Arnold, b. Apr. 18 1930, at Stamford, Conn.; Roberta Edwina, b. Sept. 17 1935, d. Dec. 8 1935; and Woodling Plummer, b. Jan. 28 1937, d. Apr. 1 1937.

220 RUTH YOUNG

born, Oct. 10 1869, at Evanston, Ill., is living in 1946 in Chicago, Ill. She married at Evanston, Oct. 12 1893, John Alexander Orb, Banker, born, July 26 1854, at Westhofen, Germany, died, Nov. 21 1927, and was buried in Oakwood Cemetery, Chicago, Ill. Mrs. Orb, by her interest in the permanent preservation of the family records has ecouraged the compiler in his task and by her liberality has become a co-publisher of this work. Mr. and Mrs. Orb had three children.

286. i. Helen Ruth, b. Nov. 29 1894
287. ii. John Alexander, b. March 18 1898
288. iii. Katherine Sybil, b. Aug. 16 1901

221 SANBORN YOUNG

born, March 2 1873, at Chicago, Ill., was given the family name of his maternal grandmother as a Christian name. He is now engaged in ranching at Los Gatos, Calif. Mr. Young began his business career as a grain merchant in 1898 at Chicago. He was a member of the firm of Young and Nichols from 1899 until 1908. The firm name from 1908 until 1912 was Young and Company. In 1916, Mr. Young moved to California and in 1924 he was elected to the State Senate, of which he continued a member until 1939. Under appointment from President Hoover, he was a delegate in 1931 to the International Narcotic Conference at Geneva, Switzerland. He wrote "Drug Addiction in California" in 1926, and in 1936 another work on the same subject. He was chairman of the California State Narcotic Committee. Mr. Young is actively continuing a distinguishing characteristic of his pioneering grandparents in Ohio and of his parents in Illinois, that of the education of the young. He is also being of invaluable aid in the compilation of this work and is making a substantial donation towards its publication.

Mr. Young married, Oct. 3 1914, at Grand Canyon, Arizona, the nationally known authoress, Ruth Comfort Mitchell, daughter of John Samuel and Florence Standish (Mowatt) Mitchell. Mrs. Young has written, under her maiden name, many short stories, poems and some fourteen novels, amongst the best known being, "Of Human Kindness," and "A White Stone." She is a member of the National and International Business and Professional Women's Club and was a delegate to their International Congress at Vienna, in 1931. She belongs to the P.E.O. Sisterhood, Soroptomists, P.E.N. Club, Daughters of the American Revolution, Colonial Dames, is Honorary President of Camp Fire for Santa Clara County, and was State and National President of Pro America.

222 HELEN YOUNG

born, Sept. 2 1879, at Evanston, Ill., is living on Meadowhill Farm, Barrington, Ill. She is a co-publisher of this genealogy. She married, June 20 1904, at Evanston, Edward Keasley Hardy, born, July 25 1881, at Chicago, Ill. Mr. Hardy attended Yale (Sheffield) College in the class of 1904. For a time he was associated with the Diamond Rubber Co., Akron, O., and at present is Manager of the Ridgecroft Real Estate Co. He is also working on an improved real estate tax base which is receiving much support in Chicago and other large cities. Mr. and Mrs. Hardy have three children.

i. Edward K. jr., b. May 24 1905, at Akron, O., md. Oct. 27 1928, Mary Hall, at Los Gatos, Calif. They have four children: Edward K. III, b. Aug. 22 1933; John Radford, b. Sept. 11 1937; Margaret, b. June 8 1940; and Ruth Hall Hardy, b. July 26 1942.

ii. Faith, b. May 7 1913, at Evanston, Ill.

iii. Frances A. II, b. Nov. 26 1916, at Evanston, Ill., md. there, Feb. 3 1940, Lane Roby, and has two children: Laird Hardy, b. Oct. 23 1942, and Lynn Hardy Roby, b. June 8 1945.

223 HOMER JACKSON YOUNG

Salesman, born, April 5 1869, at Fairbury, Ill., died, May 18 1930, and was buried at Covington, Ky. He married at Kenosha, Wis., April 11 1911, Virginia Hughey, born, June 21 1885, at Covington, Ky., died Sept. 29 1944, at Cincinnati, O. Two children.

i. Jackson Lyman, born, June 13 1919, at Dayton, O., served his country in World War II as S/Sgt., Turret Gunner, B-24, U. S. Air Corps, and is now, 1946, a freshman at San José State College, in California. He is developing his fine voice.

ii. Robert Hughey, born, Nov. 7 1923, at Covington, Ky. served as Lt. in the U. S. Army in World War II. He was Co-Pilot of a B-25 until shot down by the enemy over the Brenner Pass, Feb. 6 1945, and captured. He received the Air Medal for his service. He was freed by Gen. Patton's Tank Forces, and is now a senior, with an honor scholarship, at Columbia University, New York.

224 MARY LYMAN YOUNG

born, June 7 1872, at Fairbury, Ill., lives in Greenwich, Conn. She spent her early life at Pasadena, California with her parents and received her education at Marlborough School, Los Angeles, Calif. She graduated in 1902 from the Wisconsin Conservatory of Music, and was church and concert contralto at Milwaukee, Wis. until she married, March 26 1913, the Rev. James Oastler, D.D. (born, July 19 1876, at Perry Sound, Canada, died, July 30 1943, at Greenwich, Conn.). Dr. Oastler served Calvary Presbyterian Church, Milwaukee, for 18 years, Greenwich Presbyterian Church from 1929 until 1933 and was Chaplain of Edgewood Park College until he retired in 1940. One child, adopted.

i. Barbara Mary, b. June 26 1918, at Milwaukee, Wis., md. Dec. 21 1944, Leon Edward Adams, Cpl. in the U. S. Air Corps, stationed at Mitchell Field, Long Island, N. Y.

225 HAROLD ALBERT YOUNG

born, Sept. 3 1878, at Sioux Falls, S. D. has been connected with the Los Angeles County Health Department for over 31 years and is at present Director of the Bureau of Sanitation. He lives in San Marino, Calif. During World War I, he was a Lt. in the U. S. Sanitation Corps. He married Cecilia Gately Munger, a widow, with one son, now John Allan Young who is in the mining business. Harold and Cecilia have a daughter.

i. Marjorie Lyman, b. July 16 1911, at Pasadena, Calif., graduated in 1935 at U. C. at Los Angeles, md. Aug. 31 1933, at Los Angeles, Merrill Worthington Lee, son of Arthur A. and Ethel Worthington Lee. They live at Bakersfield, Calif. Two children: Merrill W. jr., b. Dec. 16 1938, and Louise Charlotte Lee, b. July 14 1941, at Bakersfield.

226 WILLIS BEERS YOUNG

born, Jan. 1 1867, at Little Rock, Ark., is living in Olympia, Wash. He married, at Yakima, Wash., June 11 1889, Martha Thorp, born, May 22 1870, died, Oct. 10 1900, and was buried at Yakima. Two children, of whom one, Nelson, is deceased. (Mrs. J. B. Young, Olympia, Wash.).

i. John Burton, b. Aug. 20 1891, at Yakima, Wash. lives there and is Engineer at the Hotel Olympian. He md. Oct. 7 1910, at Yakima, Wash., Augusta D. Rohde. Two children: Gordon Owen, b. Dec. 26 1911, at Selah, Wash. is in the U. S. Navy, acting as Instructor in Radar, at Corpus Christi, Texas; and Graydon Burton, b. Dec. 24 1912, at Yakima, is Assistant Superintendent of the Olympia Canning Co. He md. Nov. 6 1942, Frances Wuerth, at Olympia, Wash. and has a son, Graydon, jr., b. May 9 1945.

227 LULU ELIZABETH YOUNG

born, May 18 1871, at Little Rock, Ark., died, Oct. 4 1940, at Riverside, Calif. where she was buried. She married at Hastings, Nebr., July 20 1891, James F. Clark, born, June 6 1858, died, Aug. 9 1937, at Riverside, Calif. Three children. (Mrs. Blanche Lynde, Riverside, Calif.).

i. Mattie E., b. May 30 1892, at Mt. Claire, Nebr., md. in Aug. 1915, Wilmot Long, at Santa Ana, Calif. where the family lives. One child: Wilmot Long, jr., b. July 17 1916.

289. ii. Blanche, b. Sept. 3 1893

290. iii. Fred Young, b. June 1 1896

228 JOHN BRADY YOUNG

born, May 11 1875, at Little Rock, Ark., is farming at Castlewood, S. D. He married, Dec. 30 1899, Maude R. Cory, born, Feb. 8 1878, in Devonshire, England. Two children, both born at Castlewood, S. D. (Mrs. J. B. Young).

i. Mattie Jane, b. May 30 1904, md. May 27 1931, Lester Hurlbut, farmer, at Watertown, S. D., and lives at Raymond, S. D. Two children: James Lester, b. June 28 1932, and Dean Roy Hurlbut, b. July 22 1933.

ii. Joyce Rowe, b. June 21 1909, graduated 1932 at Brookings (S. D.) College, md. Sept. 19 1936, Earl W. Meek, Lumberyard Manager, at Glidden, Ia. They live at Salem, S. D. One child: Donald Watson Meek, b. Feb. 4 1941, at Castlewood, S. D.

229 JENNIE BELL SEMPLE

born, March 16 1863, at Mt. Vernon, O., died, Jan. 22 1944, at Fargo, N. D. and was buried there. She graduated at Wellesley College, Wellesley, Mass. and at the Pratt Art Institute, New York. She married at Mt. Vernon, Sept. 26 1894, William C., son of Major William and Emma B. (Ward) Macfadden, and moved shortly after marriage to Fargo, N. D. where Mr. Macfadden engaged in the banking business. Three children (Mrs. W. C. Macfadden, Fargo, N. D.).

291. i. William Semple, b. Dec. 13 1895

292. ii. Margaret Louise, b. June 26 1899

iii. Ward, b. Oct. 13 1905, is, 1944, Lt. Commander, U. S. N. S. His home is in Chicago, Ill.

230 CARL YOUNG SEMPLE

born, April 5 1873, at Mt. Vernon, O., is living at Baxter Springs, Kan. He married, Aug. 26 1900, at Mt. Vernon, O., Florence Pope, b. June 29 1879. Two children.

i. Virginia Pope, b. Nov. 11 1909, at Mt. Vernon, O., lives at Baxter Springs, Kan. She md. 1st, June 8 1929, George R. Ireton who died in 1937. Two children: Carl R., b. June 9 1930, and Jo Ann Ireton, b. Nov. 20 1934. Virginia md. 2nd., Lawrence W. Jennings.

ii. Marian Ann, b. May 21 1913, lives in Oklahoma City, Okla. She md., June 26 1935, Richard T. Austin. Two children: Richard Thompson Austin, jr., b. Dec. 15 1940, and a son born in Aug. 1943, died in Nov. 1944.

231 ALICE CATHERINE LOGAN

born, Feb. 11 1861, near Mansfield, Ohio, died, Dec. 26 1935, at Savannah, Mo. where she was buried. She married, April 18 1882, at Grant City, Mo., William Holme Stevenson, born, March 20 1858, at Carlandville, Ill., died, April 26 1926, at Savannah, Mo. After some years as cashier of a bank in Grant City, he became a raiser of fancy stock and horses in Andrew County, Mo. Both he and his wife were active in community affairs, promoting especially schools and highways. Two children.

i. Clarence Logan, b. Nov. 11 1884, at Grant City, Mo., became a doctor of medicine and was finishing his training when he became ill and died, June 7 1911, at St. Louis, Mo.

ii. Estella Elizabeth, b. Oct. 13 1891, at Grant City, Mo., is living in Savannah, Mo. where she is City Collector. We are indebted to her for this family data.

232 LUCRETTIA LOGAN

born, Sept. 14 1867, at Grant City, Mo. is living there in 1944. She married, April 5 1893, Sherman Rybolt, born, May 23 1868, in Worth County, Mo., died in February 1939 and was buried at Grant City, Mo. Mr. Rybolt taught for several years and then turned to stock raising. Four children, all born at Grant City, Mo.

i. Myron Carson, b. April 15 1894, md. Dec. 22 1917, Helen Lamb, b. Jan. 4 1897, in Worth County, Mo., lives in Kansas City, Mo. One child: Stephen Ballard Rybolt, b. Oct. 29 1930.

ii. Dean Logan, b. Dec. 1904, md. April 23 1939, Anna Elnore Peters, b. Dec. 24 1912, at Bonner Springs, Kan., lives in Kansas City, Mo.

iii. Gaylord Alvan, b. July 29 1906, md. Dec. 22 1930, Katherine Ann Gale, at Chester, Ill., and lives in Lee's Summit, Kansas City, Mo. Two children: Ann Lou, b. Nov. 26 1932, and Gaylord A. jr., b. Jan. 31 1937.

iv. Bernice Esther, b. Jan. 4 1908, md. Glen McComas Warren, b. Jan. 23 1910, K. C., Mo. They live in Tulsa, Okla. Two children: John, b. Jan. 19 1941, at Kansas City, Mo., and Elizabeth Warren, b. 1942, at Tulsa, Okla.

233 WILLIAM LLOYD COLBY

farming since 1889 at Trout Run near Black River Falls, Wis., born, April 4 1866, at Spring Green, Wis. He married, Sept. 18 1889, Isabel Howstrawser, b. July 22 1871, at Black River Falls where she taught school, and was Postmistress in 1890. They celebrated their golden wedding anniversary in 1939. Four children, all born at Trout Run, Wis. (W. L. Colby, 1943).

i. Vivian Clara, b. May 7 1893, md. Harry Tabor, and lives in Madison, Wis. Two children: Norma Lu, b. 1921, and Ferne Tabor, b. 1925.

ii. Norma Merle, b. Aug. 19 1898, md. Louis Ziegler, and lives near Madison, Wis. Six children: Delores, b. 1924; Lyle Duane, b. 1926; Norman Colby, b. 1929; Kenneth Wayne, b. 1932; Robert, b. 1935, twin of Dick; and "Dick" Zeigler.

iii. Alva G., b. July 12 1902, is married and living in Minnesota, 1943. One child: Marilyn.

iv. Kenneth Wayne, b. May 1 1905, md. Marie ——, and lives in Pemberton, N. J. Three children: Doris May, William Lloyd, and Kenneth W. Colby, jr.

234 SUSAN ELIZABETH COLBY

born, Sept. 25 1870, in Harrisburg Township, Sauk County, Wis., died, March 21 1930. She married, March 31 1897, near Prairie du Sac, Wis., Fremont Avery. Two children. (Vernie J. Avery).

i. Velma, b. Nov. 25 1898, at West Point, near Lodi, Wis., md. June 30 1926, at Beloit, Wis., A. L. Patch, farmer and salesman, and lives near Roscoe, Ill.

ii. Vernice J., b. April 23 1901, near Lodi, Wis., is teaching in the Beloit, Wis. schools.

235 LLOYD LEWIS BAKER

born, Dec. 9 1884, at Brooklyn, Ia., graduated from Northwestern University Dental School, Evanston, Ill., in 1908, and has been practicing dentistry in Eugene, Ore. since 1912. He organized the Lane County Dental Society in 1913, was President of the American Society of Stomatologists in 1932 and 1933, Associate Editor of "American Dental Surgeon" 1925-29, and has written numerous professional articles for national and international magazines. He was vice-president of his church board for six years. Mr. Baker married, June 25 1913, Eva Violet Hyett, at Silverton, Ore. Three children, all born in Eugene, Ore.

i. Ruth Violet, b. Feb. 1 1915, md. Oct. 8 1938, John Warren Hockaday, at San Francisco, Calif. where the family is living. One child: Joanne Ruth Hockaday, b. April 26 1941.

ii. Dale Lewis, b. June 22 1920, is Sgt. in the U. S. Air Corps, stationed, 1944, at San Antonio, Texas.

iii. Mary Alice, b. June 25 1931, on the wedding anniversary of her parents, is living at home.

236 PEARL ELIZABETH BAKER

born, July 19 1887, at Brooklyn, Ia., married, Aug. 10 1915, Ralph Wayne Elliott, at Eugene, Ore. where Mr. Elliott had an implement store. The family now lives near Battle Ground, Wash. Three children, all born in Eugene. (Mrs. R. W. Elliott).

i. Waldo Ralph, b. Jan. 23 1917, is living in Los Angeles, Calif.

ii. Gordon Wayne, b. Nov. 6 1918, md. Jan. 23 1939, Lucille Nelson, at Vancouver, Wash. He is with the U. S. Forces in 1944.

iii. Ruth Winona, b. Nov. 4 1931, lives at home.

237 AJAH EARL YOUNG

born, Sept. 21 1873, in Sauk County, Wis., is station agent at Lone Rock, Wis. He married, Aug. 7 1898, Grace Davies, born Aug. 7 1877. Three children, all born at Spring Rock, Wis. (A. E. Young, Lone Rock, Wis.).

i. Dorothy Kathryn, b. July 4 1899, md. Ben Carpenter, and is living in Spring Green, Wis. Three children: Lyle, b. Nov. 6 1927; Paul, b. Feb. 2 1928; and Carol Carpenter, b. Dec. 18 1930.

ii. Gordon Davies, b. May 24 1903, md. Isabel MacDonald, and lives in Malden, Mass. Two children: Earl Robert, b. May 17 1926; and Claire Young, b. Aug. 3 1932.

iii. Roger Neal, b. Dec. 17 1906, md. Aug. 16 1910, Esther Bernice Froyen, and lives in Tacoma, Wash. where Mr. Young is associated with the Cascade Pole Co. One child: Ronald Earl Young, b. July 24 1939.

238 ELMARENE DAVIS

born, Sept. 15 1873, at Grant City, Mo., is living 1946, in Baraboo, Wis. She married, Sept. 15 1892, Henry C. Schaefer, (died Jan. 21 1940), at

Harrisburg, Wis. where all their children except Henry were born. (Mrs. H. C. Schaefer). Nine children.

i. Roland Ross, b. Aug. 16 1893, md. Aug. 18 1911, Meta Adam, at Black Hawk, Wis. and lives at Harrisburg, Wis. Three children: Caroline Elmarene, b. Apr. 13 1917; Doris Eileen, b. Dec. 4 1920, md. June 8 1944, Ernest Hosig, at Harrisburg, Wis., and Audrey Mae Schaefer, b. May 11 1926.

ii. Victor Reuben, b. Nov. 5 1895, md. Apr. 1 1924, Vida Eckhardt, at Viroqua, Wis. where the family lives.

iii. Samuel Davis, b. Feb. 13 1898, md. July 1 1920, Ruth Kimball, at Baraboo, Wis. where the family lives. Two children: Deane Russell, b. Jan. 9 1922, entered U. S. Army in Jan. 1943, discharged Feb. 1946 at Ft. Lewis, Wash., md. Aug. 8 1944, Louise Blide, at Hallock, Minn.; and Lloyd Samuel Schaefer, b. March 23 1928, at Baraboo, Wis.

iv. Myrtle Marie, b. Aug. 26 1900, md. Aug. 28 1920, Harry Giese, at Baraboo, Wis. and lives near Loganville, Wis. One child, Kenyon Ezra Giese, b. Dec. 21 1933.

v. Susan Genevieve, b. Apr. 25 1902, md. Feb. 22 1924, E. Walter Anderson, at Baraboo, Wis. and lives at Duluth, Minn. Two children: Donald Gordon, b. Jan. 15 1927, and Robert Davis Anderson, b. Apr. 2 1931.

vi. John Willis, b. May 29 1904, md. June 15 1936, Emma Gloff, at Neilsville, Wis. Two children: Alton Willis, b. June 17 1938, at So. Milwaukee, Wis. and Ronald Harlan Schaefer, b. Oct. 21 1944.

vii. Lorna May, b. March 20 1907, md. June 22 1929, Lawrence A. Rezash, at Baraboo, Wis. and is living at Green Bay, Wis. Five children: Lawrence Joseph, b. May 16 1930, twin of Robert Henry; Rodney Rogers, b. Oct. 1 1936; Susan Violet, b. March 30 1942; and Joseph Roland Rezash, b. July 24 1944.

viii. Edna Julia, b. Oct. 20 1909, md. Aug. 30, 1939, Alfred M. Reinhold, at Nashua, Ia. and is living at Atlanta, Ga. Three children: Dorothy Ann, b. July 12 1940; Richard Alfred, b. March 27 1943; and Karl Victor Reinhold, b. Apr. 1 1945, at Atlanta, Ga.

ix. Henry Ezra, b. Dec. 19 1913, at Baraboo, Wis., md.

Oct. 20 1936, Gertrude Walters, at Reedsburg, Wis. Mr. Schaefer has a shoe store at Baraboo, Wis. One child, Judith Elaine Schaefer, b. Feb. 23 1940.

238 LUCY BELLE SORG

born, April 7 1876, Sauk County, Wis., married, Oct. 6 1903, Henry J. Meng, born, Feb. 5 1875, and is living in Prairie du Sac, Wis. Two children.

i. Raymond I., b. Dec. 24 1906, md. June 10 1937, Lucille Steuber who died in 1941.

ii. Miles Ford, b. Aug. 15 1908, md. Aug. 15 1931, Pearl Danuser. Two children: Carl May, b. Dec. 12 1932, and Mary Ellen Meng, b. March 8 1937, at Prairie du Sac, Wis.

239 JOHN EDWIN SORG

born, Feb. 8 1882, in Sauk County, Wis., is living in Sauk City, Wis. He married in Troy Township, Sauk County, Wis., March 14 1906, Ida Justine Schubring. Six children, all born at Prairie du Sac, Wis.

i. Howard Lincoln, b. Feb. 12 1907, is farming in Sauk County, Wis. He md. Feb. 20 1926, Viola Alice Specher. Five children: Calvin Allen, b. March 18 1927; Joyce Ellen, b. Feb. 17 1928; John Elwyn, b. Nov. 18 1930; June Lorraine, b. June 15 1932 and Howard Frederick Sorg, b. May 17 1939.

ii. Evelyn Bernette, b. June 3 1909, md. May 22 1930, Alvin Hoppe, in Sauk County, Wis. where the family lives. Four children: Gordon Dale, b. Feb. 27 1931; Maurice, b. Feb. 26 1932; Bernetta May, b. Feb. 1 1937 and Joyanna Carol Hoppe, b. Oct. 27 1939.

iii. Arline Ellen, b. May 21 1912, md. Woodrow Vincent Nold who is serving in the U. S. Army as Captain in 1943. Family lives in Milwaukee, Wis. Two children: Woodrow Vincent, jr. born, June 15 1937, at Spring Grove, Minn. and Barbara Ellen Arline Nold, b. Dec. 2 1938, at Richland Center, Wis.

iv. Earl John, b. April 15 1915, md. Oct. 23 1937, in Sauk County, Wis., Merle Reible, b. Apr. 30 1915, and lives in Sauk City, Wis. Two children: Gary Lee, b. March 12 1939, and Darrell Early Sorg, b. Oct. 16 1941, at Sauk City, Wis.

v. Fern Winifred, b. Feb. 22 1918, in Sauk County, Wis., md. Feb. 14 1939, Sidney Enge in Sauk County where Mr. Enge farms. Three children: Dennis Leroy, b. Nov. 16 1939; Katy Marie, b. July 25 1941; and Robert Eugene Enge, b. Oct. 18 1942.

vi. Glen Edmund, b. April 4 1921, md. in 1942 Margaret Steinhorst, b. at Sheboygan, Wis. Family lives in Hermosa Beach, Calif. where Mr. Sorg is working in an airplane factory. One child: Leon Thomas Sorg, b. Feb. 1 1943, at Hermosa Beach, Calif.

241 FRED DOUGLAS YOUNG

born, Aug. 29 1885, at Baraboo, Wis. has been living in Rochester, Minn. since 1906. Fred inherited the family Bible of his grandfather Young which contains lengthy data on the Day, Douglas and Young families. This information is scattered in these records. Fred married, June 29 1918, Elsa B. Krause, b. Nov. 22 1897, at La Crosse, Wis., daughter of Ferdinand and Crescent Krause. Two children.

i. Douglas Frederick, b. Aug. 25 1921, at Rochester, Minn., is in the traffic office of the Mid-Continent Air Lines, at Rochester, after having served in the U. S. Naval Air Corps in World War II. He md. at Brainard, Minn., Betty Irene Linden, b. June 10 1921, at St. Charles, Minn. and has one child: Pamella Ann, b. June 20 1945, at Rochester, Minn.

ii. Roger William, b. Sept. 27 1931, at Rochester, Minn. is in Junior High School, 1946.

242 EVA PEARL YOUNG

born, May 24 1878, in Sauk County, Wis., married, Sept. 20 1909, in Sauk County, Howard Allison Edwards, born, Nov. 22 1878, at Chicago, Ill., died, April 27 1930, at Prairie du Sac, Wis. Two children.

i. Dorothy Jane, b. July 15 1912, near Magnolia, Rock County, Wis., md. Russell Glynn. One child: Joan Elizabeth Glynn, b. Apr. 27 1934, at Janesville, Wis.

ii. Grace Edith, b. Nov. 23 1913, at Evansville, Wis., md. Carl Thorsen and is living in Janesville, Wis. Two children: Carl Howard, b. Jan. 30 1935, and James Edward Thorsen, b. Sept. 21 1937, at Janesville.

243 ROY L. TAYLOR

born, July 6 1880, at Emmettsburg, Ia., spent his boyhood at Spencer, Ia. where the family moved in 1884. He is a building contractor living in Long Beach, Calif. where he went in 1912, after residing two years in Sacramento, Calif. He married, 1st., at Long Beach, in June 1921, Florence Martha Smith who died July 30 1933. He married, 2nd., at Long Beach, Esther (Ballard) Weed. Roy and Florence had one child.

i. Allan Waite, b. March 25 1923, at Long Beach, Calif., was killed in action, Dec. 22 1944, at Linnick, Germany, and was buried in the American Churchyard Cemetery, at Margraten, Holland. He was transferred on the day of his death to a Service Company, and made assistant to the Regimental Chaplain. Previous to this he saw service in Normandy, Belgium and Holland and was for weeks in the front lines at Aachen. He was awarded the Purple Heart.

244 LAURA TRAVIS

born, July 11 1889, at Winterset, Ia., married there, Aug. 19 1914, Norman E. Hollen, Assistant Cashier of the Union State Bank, at Winterset, where the family is living. Four children, all born at Winterset, Ia. (Mrs. N. E. Hollen).

i. Robert M., b. May 10 1918, md. Aug. 11 1946, Helen Martha Fils, at Creston, Ia. where they are living. He graduated, 1944, from Ia. State Vet. Coll., Ames, Ia. and is Federal Veterinarian for Southwestern Ia. He enlisted for service in World War II in 1942, served as 2nd Lt. in the Med. Adm. Corps, after a short service in the Army Air Corps.

ii. William Travis, b. Aug. 25 1922, md. June 8 1946, Doris Marie Berke, at Honolulu, Hawaii. Born at Portland, Ore., Mrs. Hollen served as surgical nurse in a civilian hospital at Honolulu. They live in Iowa City, Ia. where Mr. Hollen is completing his law studies that were interrupted by his enlistment in the navy in 1942. He saw service as Ensign in various capacities in the Pacific. He was commissioned Lt. (j.g.) in 1945 and discharged at Seattle in July 1946.

iii. Margaret Ann, b. Sept. 1 1931, twin of Marjorie.

iv. Marjorie Kay, b. Sept. 1 1931

245 CHARLES DUNSTER YOUNG

born, Aug. 5 1875, at Ralston, N. J., is living in retirement at New London, Conn. after many years of service in the engineering department of the New London Ship and Engine Co., of Groton, Conn. He was one of the group that went to Japan in 1904 to construct for Japan their first submarine of the Holland type. He married, Feb. 7 1906, at Elizabeth, N. J., Margaret Davenport (b. Jan. 4 1878), a descendant of the Rev. John Davenport, founder of New Haven, Conn., and daughter of William St. John and Adaleen (Taylor) Davenport. One child.

i. Elizabeth Davenport, b. Oct. 27 1917, at New London, Conn., graduated from Conn. College for Women; md. Feb. 5 1943, Lt. Wm. Robert Riedel, U.S.C.G., at Norfolk, Va. Two children: Robt. Bruce, b. Sept. 13 1943, and Margaret Ann Riedel, b. Dec. 21 1944, at New London, Conn.

246 PIERSON CHAMBERLAIN YOUNG

born, Nov. 4 1883, at Chester, N. J., is living in Maplewood, N. J. He was employed by the N. Y. Telephone Co. and the N. J. Bell Telephone Co. from 1904 until May 31 1944. Since June 1944 he has been with the U. S. Army, 2nd Service Command in New York as Telephone and Teletype Engineer. He married, Feb. 21 1910, Anna H. Dudley, daughter of Wm. James and Mary (Wylie) Dudley, at Newark, N. J. One child.

i. Marian Dudley, b. Jan. 10 1916, at Orange, N. J., md. at Somerville, N. J., Oct. 21 1939, Robert Elwood Lee, son of Wm. Joseph and Edna Wayne Lee. Mrs. Lee attended Cedar Crest College for Women, at Allentown, Pa. and Mr. Lee, N. Y. and Columbia Universities. He is presently on military leave from the Irving Trust Co., N. Y. He has served 3½ yrs. in the U. S. Navy, of which 23 months were as Chief Yeoman on the U.S.S. Cleveland.

247 MARGUERITE FERNE RIGGOTT

born, Sept. 21 1889, at Rockaway, N. J. married, at Newark, N. J., Oct. 2 1909, E. Morris Sellers, b. Aug. 6 1891, and is living at Dover, N. J. One child.

i. Kathryn Riggott, b. Nov. 16 1913, md. Kenneth George Sanders, School Teacher, and has one child: Robert Kenneth Sanders, b. Apr. 14 1941.

248 ROY MEAD

born, April 24 1877, at Norwalk, O., has spent his life there. He is a house decorator. He married, 1st., Oct. 29 1902 Jennie Fay McPherson, at Norwalk. One child, Fay. After the death of Jennie (Dec. 19 1916), Roy married at Norwalk, April 9 1932, Susie, daughter of Curtiss and Mary E. Lewis Nickols, of Townawanda, N. Y.

i. Fay Myrtle, b. Oct. 7 1904, at Norwalk, O., md. June 30 1930, Otto Blackert, at Norwalk, and has one child: Carol Sue Blackert, b. Sept. 11 1940, at Willard, O., where the family lives.

249 SARAH D. YOUNG

born, Sept. 18 1864, near Collins, O., died, Oct. 19 1923, in an auto accident near Collins where she was buried. She married, Dec. 14 1882, Lewis Krebs, fruit grower, at Collins, O. Two children.

i. Nellie, b. Sept. 25 1885, near Collins, O., md. Oct. 20 1934, James Moats, farmer and fruit grower, at Port Clinton, O. They live in East Townsend, O. No children.

ii. Blanche P., b. Dec. 19 1887, near Collins, O., md. April 14 1907, Charles Edwin Baker, at E. Townsend, O. They live at Amherst, O. Two children: Bonita P., b. Oct. 12 1909, at Lindsey, O., d. Nov. 29 1918, bur. at Collins, O., and Wilmot E. Baker, b. Nov. 15 1913, md. Geraldine Bond, Apr. 17 1934, at New Castle, Pa.

250 ROSE CARRIE YOUNG

born, Aug. 7 1866, near Collins, O., lives in Fremont, O. She married, Oct. 2 1890, at Fremont, Joseph Bates who died in 1936. Two children.

i. Verna May, b. May 3 1892, at Fremont, O., md. Sept. 24 1914, Ray Goebel, assistant superintendent of Oakwood Cemetery, Fremont, O. Three children: Richard Earl, b. May 6 1916, Mail Clerk, md. Sept. 30 1939, Esther Rearick, at Fremont, and has one child, Sharon Kay Goebel, b. Sept. 20 1940; Ruth Elizabeth Goebel, b. March 24 1921, is Secretary to the Board of Education, Fremont, O.; and Lynn Morgan Goebel, b. Apr. 10 1924, is a meat cutter at Fremont, O.

ii. Lester, b. July 2 1896, at Fremont, O., is practicing medicine there. Dr. Bates md. Nov. 28 1929, Pauline Jennings, at Clyde, O. They have two children: Thelma Jennine, b. Nov. 11 1930, and Caroline Sue Bates, b. Aug. 3 1935, at Fremont, O.

251 GEORGE ELIAS YOUNG

born, Oct. 3 1871, at Townsend, O., married, Dec. 10 1901, Rose Jane Isenberg, at Arch Springs, Pa. She was born June 18 1875, died, Aug. 7 1914, and was buried at Fremont, O. where Mr. Young is living. Two children.

i. Clarence Marshall, b. Sept. 6 1903, at Fremont, O., md. March 17 1929, Emma Dellia Little, at Ft. Wayne, Ind. and lives at Canton, O. where Mr. Young is with the Ohio Power Co. Four children: Edward Clarence, b. Aug. 29 1931, at Fremont, O.; Nancy Lee, b. Aug. 24 1932, at Fremont; Ray Arthur, b. Dec. 31 1936, at Newark, O. and Philip Dennis Young, b. Aug. 6 1939, at Canton, O.

252 ARTHUR NOAH YOUNG

born, Aug. 9 1881, at Collins, O. is living in Greeley, Colo. where he has been working for the Gas Co. for some 40 odd years. He married, Dec. 29 1903, at Albert Lea, Minn., Mary Lowe, born, Oct. 22 1878, at Albert Lea. Four children.

i. Leona Marian, b. Sept. 27 1904, at Collins, O., md. Dec. 9 1936, Herman A. Diekman, a carpenter, at Golden, Colo. They live in Greeley, Colo.

ii. Harold Arthur, b. Nov. 25 1907, at Greeley, Colo., md. Dec. 23, 1936, Mary Chrispen, at Greeley. They live in Denver where Mr. Young is engaged with Safety Stores.

iii. Hazel Alpha, b. Apr. 12 1910, at Greeley, Colo., md. Dec. 29 1938, Dan E. Schwalm, at Greeley where the family lives. He is a machinist. Three children: Beverly Jean, b. Jan. 6 1942, Jerry Arthur, b. March 20 1943, and Harold Paul Schwalm, b. Jan. 15 1946, at Greeley.

iv. William Paul, b. June 26 1914, at Greeley, Colo., md. June 17 1936, Emma Virginia Boston, at Littleton, Colo. and lives in Denver. One child, Carol Paulette Young, b. Aug. 1 1940, at Greeley.

253 ELVER ALFRED NOYES

born, Aug. 6 1885, at Norwalk, O., had a twin brother who died in infancy. Elver is a mechanic, living with his family in Lorain, O. He married, Sept. 3 1903, at Norwalk, Liddian M. Bailey who was born at Monroeville, O. in 1889. She is the daughter of James Everett and Lillian (Losey) Bailey who married, Oct. 26 1888, at Monroeville. Thomas E. Losey, (b. Oct. 28 1849, d. 1944, at Monroeville, O.), maternal grandfather of Mrs. Noyes, was the son of John Condit and Sally Ann (Cole) Losey, and the grandson of John and Sally (Munn) Losey, of New Jersey. T. E. Losey married, Feb. 22 1870, Mary Elizabeth Parsons, daughter of John. John Condit Losey, grandson of John, was born near Orange, N. J. in 1811. The mother of Sally A. Cole was a Miss Francisco before her marriage. The Parsons family were neighbors of Noah Young (Rec. 28), near Monroeville, O. Noah named a child, Parsons E. Young. Four children. (E. A. Noyes, and family Bible of T. E. Losey).

i. Gaynell Martha, b. Dec. 29 1909, at Lorain, O., md. Arthur Herner, farmer, and lives near Monroeville, O. Three children: James Frederick, b. Aug. 28 1932; John Gilbert, b. March 2 1936; and Russell Alan Herner, b. Oct. 13 1939.

ii. James Alfred, b. Sept. 18 1911, md. at Lorain, O., Margaret Linder, and lives at Lorain. Two children: James George, b. June 20 1941, and Judith Ortrude Noyes, b. June 15 1944.

iii. Lillian Frances, b. Apr. 25 1915, md. at Lorain, O., Otha N. Street. Two children: Philip Louis, b. June 5 1933, and Gaynell Patricia Street, b. June 25 1936, at Lorain, O.

iv. Mary Elizabeth, b. Apr. 23 1917, md. at Lorain, O. Richard Barnhart and lives in So. Amherst, O. Two children: Gerald R., b. July 21 1936, and Sharon L. Barnhart, b. July 10 1939.

254 EDWARD HUDSON YOUNG

compiler of this genealogy, was born in the home of his maternal grandparents, William and Mary Hudson, at Sandusky, O. After 24 years as a member of the Romance Language Department at Duke University, Durham, N. C., he retired from educational work begun in 1912 at Huron College, University of Western Ontario, London, Canada, where he was Dean of Residence and for one year Acting Principal during the sabbatical of Principal Waller. Prof. Young went to Huron College after two years study at the Sorbonne, Paris, France. Ordained deacon in the Episcopal Church at Middletown, Conn., he spent his diaconate studying institutional work in Grace Church, N. Y., from where he went to St. Andrews Church, Pittsburgh, Pa. and later to Christ Church, Pittsburgh, as Rector. He served as Hon. Capt. during World War I in Africa, France and England, and was attached to the Inter-allied Boundary Commission (French and Italian Armies), at Tetschen, Poland, for two years in post-war service. Mr. Young was an extensive traveller having made 35 trips to Europe and the near East. He married at New York, April 2 1902, Louise Ann Popham, of Welsh descent, daughter of William and Elizabeth (Daniels) Popham, of St. Thomas, Ontario. No children.

255 ELIZABETH HOUGH

born, Feb. 2 1859, died, Dec. 25 1940, at No. Fairfield, O. She married, Feb. 11 1890, Charles H. Underwood (died Oct. 23 1928), at N. Fairfield, O. Four children. (W. S. Underwood).

i. Norman C., b. Dec. 18 1890, lives in Greenwich, O.

ii. Adah E., b. Oct. 8 1892, md. a Mr. Palm and lives in Northfield, O.

iii. Wayne S., b. Sept. 18 1894, at New Haven, O., md. in 1920, Olive Cartwell (b. Dec. 24 1889, at Urbana, O.), at Gillette, Wyo. They moved to Calif. in 1921, where Mr. Underwood, a Building Contractor, is serving his country with the District Engineers at Beverly Hills. No children.

iv. Monroe E., b. Aug. 22 1896, md. and lives at Greenwich, O.

256 EFFIE MAY YOUNG

born, July 11 1864, at Sturgis, Mich., died there, Sept. 28 1943, and was buried in Oaklawn Cemetery. She married, Dec. 10 1884, Elmer Colonel Sturgis, grandson of Judge Sturgis who founded Sturgis, Mich. "Colonel" Sturgis, as he was commonly called and as his tombstone designates him, received his middle name when he was 12 years of age, while he was prospecting in the Black Hills of No. Dakota with his father. The father was enraptured by *the Colonel* of the moment, Davie Crockett, and told his son that he would give him a new rifle if he would take the title "colonel" as a middle name. The boy accepted and became Colonel Sturgis. He and his family were often asked in what war he got his rank. The answer, of course, was in terms of his two year covered wagon trip to the Black Hills, and his new rifle. Two children, one of whom died in infancy. (R. S. Kane, Sturgis, Mich.).

i. Gertrude Viola, b. Dec. 15 1892, at Sturgis, Mich., md. there in 1915, Francis Leo Kane. After the death of his wife, July 2 1927, Mr. Kane remarried, June 3 1935, Elsie Bernice Bradley Valyer, a widow, whose son, Donald Bradley, b. Nov. 26 1924, has been legally adopted. Donald Bradley Kane is enrolled at the U. of Mich. after having served with Gen'l. Patton's Army through the German campaign. Francis and Gertrude Kane had two children; Randall Sturgis, b. July 24 1918, md. June 1 1940, at Sturgis, Mich., Dorothy Muriel Janca, and they have one child, Randi Elizabeth Kane, b. May 10 1943, at Stockton, Calif.; and Norman David Kane, b. Dec. 19 1919, md. Elizabeth M. Storer, daughter of Wm. H. and Harriet E. Storer, at Cape Girardeau, Mo. They have one child Norman Dennis Kane, b. Sept. 17 1942, at Chicago, Ill. Randall Kane was commissioned and became an Army Pilot of a B-29, Nov. 25 1942. He was discharged in Jan. 1946 and is now studying Chemical Engineering at the U. of Michigan. Norman Kane, after 2½ yrs. service in the European theater of war, is associated with his father in the monument business at Sturgis.

257 ELLIS LUTHER BARKER

born, July 21 1863, at Winterset, Ia., died, Jan. 24 1937, at Rockford, S. D. He married, Sept. 7 1884, at Winterset, Jessie Fremont Adams, b.

July 3 1863, in N. Y. State, died, May 28 1939, at Rockford, S. D. Eight children.

293. i. Garnet, b. May 7 1886

294. ii. Hazel, b. Aug. 25 1888

iii. Milo Ellis, b. Nov. 8 1890, at Omaha, Nebr. died, May 5 1921, at Lead, N. D. He served in the U. S. Army in World War I.

iv. Guy Ross, b. Dec. 13 1893, at Alliance, Nebr., md. July 15 1928, Grace Mildred Miller, at Deadwood, S. D. and lives at Coeur d'Alene, Idaho. Five children: Junior Fred, b. Feb. 25 1929; Arlene Grace, b. July 17 1930; Lea Maxine, b. Apr. 13 1932; Milo Edward, b. Jan. 14 1937; and Shirley Mildred Barker, b. Jan. 31 1939.

v. Lyle Otis, b. Dec. 9 1896, at Winterset, Ia., md. Aug. 11 1921, Beatrice Walker, at Deadwood, S. D. He served in World War I. Seven children: Emily Elizabeth, b. Apr. 9 1922, at Deadwood, S. D.; Lyle Eugene, b. Nov. 6 1923; Barbara Bernice, b. Nov. 11 1925; Beverly Pauline, b. Oct. 5 1927; Peggy Ione, b. Sept. 14 1929; Beatrice Patricia, b. Sept. 13 1931; and Jessie Marie Barker, b. Oct. 26 1935.

vi. Bessie Mabel, b. March 4 1900, at Alliance, Nebr., md. Apr. 27 1921, Walter William Wolfe, at Rockford, S. D. Four children. Richard Thomas; b. Oct. 22 1924; Donald Walter, b. Feb. 3 1927; Ruth Helen, b. Feb. 10 1931; and Joan Marie Wolfe, b. Jan. 23 1940.

vii. Gladys Pearl, b. Apr. 16 1903, at Mystic, S. D., d. Feb. 7 1937, at Hill City, S. D. She md. June 15 1924, Ralph Moorhouse. Two children: Dale Adams, b. Apr. 22 1925, is serving in the Navy, 1942; and Theo Pearl Moorhouse, b. Jan. 19 1932, at Hill City, S. D.

viii. Roy Adams, b. Oct. 22 1905, at Mystic, S. D. is serving in the Navy, 1942.

258 CLARENCE HENRY YOUNG

born, Jan. 31 1867, at Sheldon, Ia., was 18 years old when the family moved to Willits, Mendocino County, Calif. In Iowa, he worked for a time for his uncle Eben P. Young. (Rec. 157.) He married at Willits, Oct. 8 1898, Sylvia Ida Sartain, born, Jan. 28 1884, and lives at Healdsburg, Calif. Two children. (C. H. Young).

i. Sylvia Myrtle, b. Nov. 20 1900, at Willits, Calif., md. (1) June 23 1920, Harshall McKee, and (2) July 6 1934, Conn Harrison, stock farmer, at Santa Rosa, Calif. One child, Lorraine Audry McKee, b. Apr. 24 1921, at Berkeley, Calif., md. Apr. 11 1941, Foy Bryant, at Reno, Nev. Mr. and Mrs. Bryant have one child, Steven Conway Bryant, b. Feb. 28 1942, at San Bruno, Calif.

ii. Janet Louise, b. June 5 1918, at San Francisco, Calif., md. June 25 1937, at Santa Rosa, Calif., Walter Minkler, Fireman, Mare Island. The family lives in Healdsburg, Calif. Two children: Deanna Louise, b. Apr. 1 1938, and David Richard Minkler, b. Feb. 6 1941, at Healdsburg.

259 EDITH LAURA YOUNG

born, July 29 1878, at Sheldon, Ia., married, Sept. 6 1896, William Henry Ford, at Willits, Calif. where the family is living. Seven children, all born at Willits.

i. Fred James, b. Sept. 18 1897, is a truck driver, living at Mina, Nev. He md. Aug. 22 1920, Maretta Lewis, and has three children: Madge June, b. June 22 1921, at Willits, Calif., md. June 24 1939, Everett Ayers, at Hawthorne, Nev. and lives at Flemington, Mo. One child, Billie Jean Ayers, b. May 25 1941, at Hawthorne, Nev.; Lloyd Ford, b. Sept. 7 1924, at Santa Rosa, Calif. is serving, 1942, in the U. S. Army; and Barbara Madine Ford, b. Apr. 14 1934, at Covele, Calif.

ii. Herman Webster, b. Aug. 5 1899, md. Feb. 19 1921, Evelyn May Simmerman, and lives at Willits, Calif. Three children, all born near Willits. Donald Andrew, b. June 5 1922; Eleanor May, b. March 28 1924, md. Lloyd Watson, lives at Willits; and Anna Maria Ford, b. Sept. 16 1925.

iii. Elvin Henry, b. May 2 1901, md. Aug. 21 1926, Leota Wannacott, at Willits, Calif. where they live. Five children: Doris Leota, b. July 29 1927; Vivian Lois, b. Aug. 14 1928; Mary Lou, b. Apr. 15 1930; Phyllis Joan, b. Apr. 12 1935; and Richard Elvin Ford, b. Oct. 7 1939.

iv. Franklin Arthur, b. Aug. 6 1905, md. Aug. 21 1937, Hazel Daisy Grande who died in 1939.

v. Theodore Claud, md. June 16 1927, Naomi Carmen Elliot. One child, Marian Ruth Ford, b. May 16 1928.

vi. Irma Edith, b. Aug. 28 1908, md. June 16 1927, William Edward Hinton. Three children: Eugene Edward, b. Dec. 15 1930; William Howard, b. Feb. 15 1937; and John Henry Hinton, b. Nov. 24 1942.

vii. Harold Elmer, b. Dec. 26 1919, is Pharmacist's Mate, U. S. Navy, 1942.

260 GRACE EMILY YOUNG

born, July 4 1883, at Sheldon, Ia., married, March 2 1902, Kearney LaCrete Brasket, at Willits, Calif. and lives at Stevenson, Calif. Seven children, all born in Humbolt County, Calif. (Mrs. K. L. Brasket).

i. Mary Cecilia, b. May 2 1906, md. Aug. 11 1923, Lloyd Mount Joy Sawyer and lives in Humbolt Co., Calif. Five children: Lucine Goldie, b. Apr. 11 1924; Lorin Ellis, b. Dec. 6 1927; Leland Marvin, b. Nov. 18 1928; Joy Estelle, b. Feb. 3 1930; and Dora Jane Sawyer, b. Nov. 21 1939.

ii. Alice Lucille, b. Sept. 20 1908, at Fortuna, Calif., md. June 24 1930, Leonard Monroe Whitlow, at Fortuna. Two children: Leonard Veldon, b. March 11 1931, and Ardis Elaine Whitlow, b. Aug. 27 1934.

iii. Arthur Eugene, b. July 30 1910, d. Sept. 30 1917.

iv. Kenneth LaCrete, b. Feb. 7 1917, at Fortuna, Calif.

v. Eva, b. Oct. 24 1919, d. Dec. 4 1919.

vi. Edith, twin of Eva, d. Oct. 25 1919, at Fortuna, Calif.

vii. Clyde Emile, b. Oct. 7 1920, at Fortuna, Calif.

261 CLIFTON WILLIS CONNORAN

Jeweller, for many years in Indianola, Ia., born, June 22 1871, at Winterset, Ia., where his father was a pioneer, has retired and is living in Los Angeles, Calif., 1946. He married, Jan. 12 1897, at Chicago, Ill., Glendora, daughter of Ephraim, III, and Lydia A. (Tremaine) Morrison, of Washington Court House, O. One child.

i. Irene Elizabeth, b. Apr. 3 1901, at Indianola, Ia., graduated, 1922, from Lombard College, from the U. of Wis.,

Ph.M. in 1926, and in 1936, from Simpson College, Indianola, Ia. She taught 5 years at State Teachers College, Dickinson, N. D. before marrying at Wibaux, Mont., June 22 1940, Clarence H. Plath who is with the Carnation Co., Los Angeles, Calif.

262 CORY DAISIE CONNORAN

born, June 23 1874, at Winterset, Ia., married there, June 23 1897, David Warren Smith, shoe merchant at Winterset for 25 years. Mr. and Mrs. Smith observed their Golden Wedding anniversary, June 22 1947, by entertaining their children, grandchildren and numerous guests. Mr. Smith was State Accountant for 6 years, County (Madison) Clerk for 6 years and Mayor of Winterset for 4 years. Two children, both born at Winterset, Ia.

i. Alden, b. May 7 1903, graduated from Simpson Coll., Indianola, Ia. and from Harvard University, and is now a partner in the firm of Price, Waterhouse Public Accountants, N. Y. He md. Dec. 1 1927, Bessie Lee Kelly, of Columbus, Ga. Two children: Betty Jane, b. Aug. 27 1931, at N. Y., and Clifton Harvey Smith, b. Nov. 23 1938, at White Plains, N. Y. The family lives at Scarsdale, N. Y.

ii. Clifton Warren, b. Aug. 27 1906, graduated from Simpson Coll., Indianola, Ia. and from State Coll., Ames, Ia. He also attended Iowa State University. He is now with the Bankers Life Insurance Co., Des Moines, Ia., lives, single, with his parents at Winterset, Ia.

263 EBEN PARSONS YOUNG, III

born, Nov. 28 1905, at Denver, Colo., was in the seed business there for over 20 years but is now living with his family in Red Cliff, Colo. He married, May 24 1926, Florence Lillian Ferguson, at Central City, Colo. One child (E. P. Young, Red Cliff, Colo.).

i. Fanniera Young, b. May 20 1927, at Denver, Colo.

264 LEE W. BARKER

farmer, born, July 12 1882, in Ripley Township, Huron County, O., married there, Nov. 14 1900, Olive M. McCullough. Two children.

i. Thelma Marie, b. July 19 1901, in Huron Co., O., md. Aug. 22 1938, Robert Slyh, at Lakeside, O. and lives in Columbus, O.

ii. Lois Evelyn, b. Aug. 22 1903, at Ripley, O., md. 1st. in Aug. 1926, David Gumbert, at Cleveland, O. One child, Norman Lee Gumbert, b. July 21 1928. Lois md. 2nd. March 10 1938, Edward Sharpless, at Greenwich, O. where they live.

265 J. LELAND SNYDER

Postmaster at Tiro, O. since 1936, was born, June 12 1901, at Boughtonville, O. He married at No. Fairfield, O., Sept. 25 1920, Lottie Myers, b. Feb. 24 1904, at Bloomville, O. Two children.

i. Robert E., b. Feb. 5 1922, at Plymouth, O. served as Sgt. in the U. S. Infantry, overseas, World War II.

ii. Marjorie I., b. Apr. 24 1926, at Tiro, O., clerks in the P. O. at Tiro, O. She md. Apr. 25 1943, Lewis A. Mayes, b. March 8 1925, at Nashville, Tenn. One child, Michael Lee Mayes, b. Jan. 26 1946, at Shelby, O.

266 ARTHUR FORAKER YOUNG

born, July 31 1889, at Norwalk, O., died, March 26 1943, at Lakewood, O. and was buried in Woodlawn Cemetery, Norwalk, O. At the time of his death he was a Vice-President of the National City Bank, Cleveland, O. He married, Feb. 24 1915, Gladys M. Kellum, at Norwalk, O. Three children.

i. Jeanne, b. Dec. 9 1915, at Cleveland, O., graduated at Duke University. In 1943, she is serving with the Red Cross in Australia. Previously she was secretary to the President of Western Reserve University, Cleveland, O.

ii. Arthur F. jr., b. Feb. 2 1918, at Cleveland, O., M.D., is serving in the Medical Corps of the U. S. Army. He md. May 31 1942, Helen Stewart, at Cleveland, O.

iii. Nancy, b. Oct. 4 1924, at Cleveland, O., attended Duke University and Flora Stone Mather College. She md. June 20 1945, Frederick Wilson Chockley, son of F. W. Chockley, of Lakewood, O.

267 HATTIE MAE YOUNG

born, Aug. 13 1876, at New Haven, O., married, 1st. Jugertha Belden MacPherson, (d. March 7 1922, at Navarre, O. and was buried at Norwalk, O.) at Norwalk, O. Six children. Hattie married, 2nd., April 27 1927, Frederick B. Wilhelm, at Massillon, O. No children.

i. Velma Blanche, b. May 3 1904, at Norwalk, O., md. Sept. 2 1924, Ralph W. Glick, at Wheeling, W. Va. and lives in Massillon, O. Two children: Janice Marie, b. Dec. 9 1946, and Ralph William Glick, jr. b. July 4 1929, at Massillon, O.

ter Wilhelm, at Massillon, O. Four children: Walter Jacob, jr., b. Dec. 11 1926; Richard Edward, b. Sept. 12 1931; Marilyn Suzanne, b. Jan. 17 1933; and Kathryn Mae Wilhelm, b. June 15 1935, at Massillon, O. where the family lives.

iii. Jeanette Dorothy, b. Dec. 17 1909, at Norwalk, O., md. June 12 1927, at Wheeling, W. Va., Peter Mochoskay who works for the Republic Steel Co. at Canton, O. Two children: Peter Louis, b. Nov. 25 1929, and Gloria Jean, b. Aug. 11 1931, at New Philadelphia, O.

iv. Olga Mae, b. Aug. 18 1912, at Navarre, O., md. Apr. 18 1928, Hale Null, at Canton, O. Two children: Shirley
ii. Mildred Ursula, b. Oct. 7 1906, md. Feb. 15 1924, Wal-
Mae, b. Apr. 25 1929, at Canton, and Richard Hale, b. July 24 1930, at Brewster, O. Olga md. 2nd., Feb. 11 1934, Ralph Bredenberg, at Massillon, O. Three children: Karl, b. Dec. 12 1937, at Massillon, O.; Rose Mary, b. June 9 1939, at Brookfield, O.; and Carol Jean Bredenberg, b. Dec. 13 1940, at No. Lawrence, O.

v. William David, b. March 2 1915, at Navarre, O., md. Jan. 16 1943, Sophia Stasko, at Bridgeport, Conn. where he works for the Remington Arms Co.

vi. Mary Kathryn, b. Jan. 12 1920, at Navarre, O., md. Apr. 29 1938, Eugene Cable, at Brewster, N. Y. They live in New Haven, Conn. Three children: Beverly Mae, b. Apr. 17 1939, at Bridgeport, Conn.; Ernest Sherman, b. Aug. 12 1940, at Bridgeport; and Betty Martha Cable, b. May 15 1942, at New Haven, Conn.

268 KENT WARREN YOUNG

born, July 31 1879, at Greenwich, O., married, Oct. 9 1899, at Hammond, Ind., Abbie June Payunk, b. June 22 1880, at Sheldon, Ia. lives with her daughter Helen, at Oakland, Calif. Mr. Young died, Jan. 8 1940, and was buried at Kansas City, Mo. Three children. (Mrs. K. W. Young)

i. Kent Warren, jr., b. May 2 1901, at Hammond, Ind., md. July 15 1922, Ethel Lorene Hawkins, at Kansas City, Mo. where he works for Swift & Co. Three children: Kent Warren, 3rd., b. Sept. 28 1928, d. Sept. 20 1928; Ronald Gordon, b. March 27 1932; and Norman Roger Young, b. July 15 1940, at Kansas City, Mo.

ii. Vesta Ursula, b. Oct. 16 1902, at Hammond, Ind., d. March 13 1903.

iii. Helene Christine, b. June 7 1905, at Hammond, Ind., md. Aug. 10 1931, Roy Vernon Rydbeck, at Liberty, Mo. One child, Robert Roy Rydbeck, b. May 26 1935, at Davenport, Ia. The family lives at Oakland, Calif. where Mr. Rydbeck is a ship inspector.

269 ALICE MATILDA YOUNG

born, Sept. 13 1881, at Greenwich, O., married, July 24 1902, at Norwalk, O., Martin Leo Sattig (b. Jan. 6 1881, d. March 28 1924, bur. in St. Paul's Cemetery, Norwalk, O.). Four children, first three born at Norwalk, O. (Mrs. C. W. Morrow).

i. Olive Lucile, b. Jan. 13 1904, md. Dec. 3 1938, Robert L. Henderson, High School Principal at Buchanan, O.

ii. Margaret Luella, b. July 27 1906, md. Dec. 19 1942, Richard L. Kelly, machinist, at Norwalk, O. and lives at New London, O.

iii. Willis Woodworth, b. Oct. 23 1908, md. Dec. 25 1936, H. Mary Clark, at Norwalk, O. He is now a member of the Norwalk Police Force, after having served in World War II. One child, David Bromley Sattig, b. July 21 1940.

iv. Louise Elizabeth, b. Feb. 16 1916, at Elyria, O., md. June 22 1938, Clifford W. Morrow, at Milan, O. Capt. Morrow served in the 37th Division of the U. S. Army, Pacific Area, from 1942 until 1944, and now lives near Milan, O.

270 JENNIE LOIDA YOUNG

born July 30 1884, at Fitchville, O., married, Jan. 14 1907, Albert Benjamin Fisher, at Monroe, Mich. The family lives in Lakewood, O. Three children.

i. C. Paul, b. Jan. 7 1909, at Norwalk, O., d. Sept. 21 1930, and was buried in Lakewood Park Cemetery, Rocky River, O.

ii. Wade Charles, b. Aug. 31 1912, at Cleveland, O., grad. at Oberlin College, Oberlin, O. in 1934, was accountant with the Curtiss Aircraft Co., at Buffalo, N. Y. before becoming Ensign and Gunnery Officer in the U. S. Navy, served in both the Atlantic and Pacific areas, and was Lt. j.g. at the close of the war. He md. Nov. 2 1935, at Batavia, N. Y., Helen E. Miner, a graduate of Oberlin Conservatory of Music. Now lives in Jamestown, N. Y.

iii. Albert B. jr., b. Aug. 2 1916, at Cleveland, O., grad. at Oberlin College, 1938, received his M.A. from Ohio State University. During World War II he served as Lt. in the U. S. Navy. He is now working for his Ph.D. in Business Administration at Ohio State University. He md. Dec. 26 1941, at Columbus, O., Evelyn McDonald, an Instructor and graduate student at Ohio State University.

271 DAVID AUGUSTUS YOUNG

born, July 25 1888, at New London, O., married, 1st., Hildegard Hansen, born, July 1 1885, at Kristianssand, Norway. One child. Mr. Young married, 2nd., Estelle Bergman, a widow. No children. Mr. Young is a member of the Chicago Police Force in the finger print department.

i. Gladys Louisa, b. July 15 1907, at Chicago, Ill., md. there, Aug. 4 1923, Edward Straubing who was in the Officers Training Camp, New London, Conn., 1943. Eight children, all born at Chicago, Ill.: Vernon Richard, b. Jan. 9 1925, d. Jan. 10 1925; Gloria, an adopted child; Ronald, b. Sept. 3 1926; Jack David, b. Oct. 26 1928; Lenora Violet, b. Apr. 22 1930; Joyce Constance, b. Feb. 18 1932; Eileen Helen, b. July 21 1936; and Vivian Hope Straubing, b. Apr. 2 1938.

272 MARY ROSELLA YOUNG

born, Aug. 15 1891, at Norwalk, O., married, March 8 1930, at Washington, Pa., Charles Lewis Green, Insurance Salesman, b. July 2 1896, at Berlinville, O., son of Oscar W. and Hannah (Hebblethwaite) Green. Mary was a teacher and principal of a grade school in Norwalk, O. before marriage. The family now lives at Mansfield, O. One child.

i. Charles L. jr., b. June 20 1932, at Mansfield, O., is showing unusual vocal and instrumental ability for his age while ranking high in his school work and Boy Scout activities.

273 GERTRUDE BERNICE YOUNG

born, Oct. 18 1892, at Norwalk, O., married there, Nov. 23 1911, Richard E. Frederici, Railway Ticket Agt. at the Terminal Station, Cleveland, O., born, March 8 1888, at Tiffin, O. The family lives at Lakewood, O. Three children, all born at Norwalk, O.

i. Wallace Gilbert, b. June 15 1912, is living in Mansfield, O. where he is with the Mansfield Tire and Rubber Co. He md. at Wellsburg, W. Va., Oct. 10 1935, Mary E. Wills, of Mansfield. Three children: Richard Wallace, b. May 19 1937; Barbara Ann, b. Dec. 31 1938; and Eileen Patricia Frederici, b. March 17 1941, at Mansfield, O.

ii. Ione Bernice, b. Oct. 24 1916, is working for the Cleveland Trust Co., Cleveland, O. She md. May 11 1946, Robert A. Wood, at Cleveland, O.

iii. Daniel Louis, b. Jan. 29 1922, is associated with the Cleveland (Ohio) Trust Co. He served during World War II in the U. S. Navy (Communications) at Washington, D. C. and at Pearl Harbor Headquarters. He md. Oct. 20 1942, at Washington, D. C., Lorraine Lucas, of Norwalk, O.

274 DONAL HARVEY ROSS

born, Jan. 1 1888, at Adel, Ia., was killed in an auto accident in 1936, and was buried at Fargo, N. D. He married, 1st., Alice Davis who died, July 3 1918, at Evanston, Wyo. and was buried at Wallsburg, Utah. Mr. Ross married, 2nd., at Fargo, N. D., Florence Williams, a widow. Donald and Alice had two children, both born at Evanston, Wyo.

i. Fern Louise, b. June 23 1918, graduated, 1940, at Brigham Young Univ., Provo, Utah, md. July 11 1941, Ray Fenn, at Logan, Utah. They live at Benson, Ariz.

ii. Faye Rose, b. June 23 1918, twin of Fern, grad. from B. Young Univ., 1940, and is teaching at Carsonville, Mich. 1943.

275 BESSIE EDMINA ROSS

born, June 4 1892, at Marshalltown, Ia., married, May 18 1915, at Clements, Ia., Theron L. Armstrong who owns a wholesale bakery at Fargo, N. D. where the family is living. Five children.

i. Dorothy Louise, b. March 8 1916, at Clements, Ia., md. July 1 1935, Robert Millar, at Fargo, N. D. where Mr. Millar is a salesman for the Fargo Glass and Paint Co. Two children: Terry Sue, b. Sept. 20 1939, and Sandra Louise, b. Feb. 5 1941, at Fargo, N. D.

ii. William Bennett, b. Dec. 20 1917, at Clements, Ia., grad. in Dec. 1942 at McGill Medical College, Montreal, Canada, and is serving his internship there. Dr. Armstrong md. Sept. 3 1942, Dorothy Arnold, at Fargo, N. D.

iii. Elgene Belle, b. Sept. 3 1922, at Fargo, N. D., is a student, 1943, at the State College, Fargo, N. D.

iv. Betty Sue, b. May 20 1928, at Fargo, N. D.

v. Peggy C., b. Jan. 31 1931, at Fargo, N. D.

276 MAUDE LUCY STORRS

born, July 27 1881, at Perkins, O., married there, Aug. 23 1910, Jesse C. Snyder, born, March 22 1880, at Port Clinton, O., son of Henry and Martha (Pfeil) Snyder. The family lives in Rochester, N. Y. where Mr. Snyder is sales engineer with the Stromberg, Carlson Mfg. Co. Three children (Mrs. J. C. Snyder).

i. Edward Harry, b. Oct. 14 1911, at Elyria, O., d. Sept. 10 1939, at Rochester, N. Y. and was buried there.

ii. Arden Henry, b. Jan. 15 1914, at Elyria, O., graduated, March 24 1943, from the Buffalo Medical College, and is practicing medicine in Holley, N. Y. He md. June 20 1942, Betty Jane, daughter of James Harold and Laura M. (Avery) Brinkerhoff, at Rochester, N. Y. One child, Arden Ray Snyder, b. June 11 1944, at Rochester, N. Y.

iii. Robert Ray, b. June 18 1923, at Rochester, N. Y., served about three years in the U. S. Army in World War II and was discharged Jan. 7 1946. He is now a student at Rochester Institute of Technology, living at home.

277 CLYDE C. YOUNG

born, Oct. 24 1887, at Delphi, O., married, May 31 1909, Lesta Runnion, at Plymouth, O. and is living in Willard, O. Three children.

i. Donna Belle, b. June 13 1910, near Shiloh, O., md. Apr. 15 1932, Lawrence McLaughlin, at North Fairfield, O. and lives in Willard, O. Two children: Gene Chalmers, b. Jan. 24 1933, and Larry Dean McLaughlin, b. May 27 1938.

ii. Elaine V., b. July 25 1912, near Shiloh, O., married Ronald W. Barr, at North Fairfield, O. He is serving in the U. S. A., 1942.

iii. Don C., b. Nov. 4 1917, near Shiloh, O., served in the U. S. Army in Australia, is in New Guinea, 1944. Before entering the army he was farming near Ripley, O.

278 CHARLES BRIGHAM YOUNG

born, Sept. 9 1875, near Humboldt, Ill., was in the grocery business there for many years, now is truck farming near Mattoon, Ill. He married, July 4 1905, Ola Kumre, at Effingham, Ill. Six children, all born near Humboldt, Ill.

i. Lona Agnes, b. May 21 1906, md. June 30 1933, Ralph Hall, and lives at Beloit, Wis.

ii. Phebe Helen, b. Apr. 13 1907, md. Sept. 4 1928, Emerson F. Lacy, and lives at Glen Ellyn, Ill.

iii. Rose May, b. May 27 1909, md. March 25 1940, Glen A. Hutton, and lives near Mattoon, Ill.

iv. Leslie Barker, b. May 20 1911, md. July 24 1932, Marion Niemeyer and lives near Humboldt, Ill. No children.

v. Jessie Evelyn, b. Sept. 23 1911, md. Oct. 26, 1935, Paul Ludke and lives at Wheaton, Ill.

vi. Maude Gertrude, b. March 5 1915, md. Max Munson, Aug. 28 1936 and lives at Humboldt, Ill.

279 JESSIE EVELYN YOUNG

born, Nov. 21 1886, at Humboldt, Ill., married, Sept. 12 1903, Charles Holmes, a farmer, at Tuscola, Ill. He was born, Sept. 14 1878, at North Lawrence, Ill. The family lives in Indianapolis, Ind. Five children. (Mrs. Charles Holmes).

i. Robert Levi, b. May 18 1907, md. March 21 1932, Nellie May McKenzie, at Terre Haute, Ind. where she died in July 1943. Three children: Dorothy May, b. Apr. 25 1933; Janet Louise, b. March 4 1938; and Dolores Ann Holmes, b. Sept. 12 1941, at Bloomington, Ill.

ii. Cecil Marvin, b. June 3 1909, md. Sept. 12 1935, Kathryn Henry, at Terre Haute, Ind.

iii. J. Kathryn, b. Apr. 5 1913, md. Apr. 18 1940, William Day, at Terre Haute, Ind. as her second husband. Kathryn had two children by her first marriage, Patricia Joan Day, b. Oct. 1 1931, and Mitzi Louise Day, b. May 13 1933.

iv. Hazel Eva Louise, b. March 4 1915, md. July 28 1937, Stanley Shake, at Terre Haute, Ind.

v. Lulu Margarette, b. Aug. 2 1917, md. in Sept. 1937, Walter Skierkowski, at Michigan City, Ind. Two children: Walter Holmes, b. June 26 1940, and Paul Charles Skierkowski, b. May 28 1942, at Michigan City, Ind.

280 EZRA SANKFIELD YOUNG

born, March 18 1885, near West Union, Adams County, O., was elected, without opposition in 1944, for his second term of six years, Judge of the Court of Common Pleas of his native county. He was elected prosecuting attorney of the county in 1928 and again in 1932 for two year periods. Between these periods, he served an unexpired term in the same office. Judge Young graduated from the Greenfield (Ohio) Business College, attended Ohio University, at Athens, O., and studied law under C. E. Robuck, at West Union before being admitted to the bar of Ohio. The family lives at Seaman, O., near where Judge Young owns a farm on which he raises pure bred Aberdeen Angus cattle and Hampshire sheep and does diversified farming. He married, April 28 1915, at Cincinniati, O., Anna Mabel Bloom, of Cherry Fork, O., daughter of Lewis and Mary (Downey) Bloom, of Adams County, O. Five children, all born at Seaman, O.

i. Harold Everett, b. Oct. 6 1916, is serving, 1945, as Sgt.

in 540 M.P. Bt., U. S. Army, in France. He md. May 3 1941, at Ironton, O., Roberta, daughter of the Rev. H. O. Stevens, of Georgetown, O.

ii. Vernon Lewis, b. Oct. 13 1919, graduated, 1942, in Law at Ohio Northern Univ. and is practicing law at West Union, O. He md. at Columbus, O., Apr. 9 1941, Eileen, dau. of Lewis and Eunice Humble, of Seaman, O. Three children: Robert Lewis, b. Feb. 1 1942, Loretta Lee Young, b. Nov. 7 1943, and Betty Jo, b. Mar. 10 1947.

iii. Mary G., b. Jan. 7 1921, is single and working for the Standard Oil Co., at Bakersfield, Calif.

iv. Ruth Margaret, b. Feb. 7 1923, md. at Dayton, O., June 30 1945, Cpl. Thomas C. Ferguson, son of Mr. and Mrs. Ralph Ferguson, of Dayton, O. Mr. Ferguson completed two years medical course before entering the armed forces and serving two years overseas. He is completing his studies at Ohio State Medical School, Columbus, O.

v. Anna LaJune, b. Oct. 15 1929, is a high school student, living at home, 1946.

281 ANDREW LOSEY YOUNG

born, Feb. 17 1871, at Greenbrier, Jefferson Township, Adams County, O. is living in retirement at West Union, O. He was reared by his maternal grandparents, John G. and Sarah (Young) Young, who took him in his youth by covered-wagon to Ionia, Jewell County, Kansas where the family remained one year and then returned to near West Union, O. Mr. Young returned to Kansas in 1894 and taught school there for some time. He served during the Spanish-American War in Co. L, 2nd U. S. Infantry. He was ordained in 1910 in the Christian Union Church. He married, (1), in 1899, Cora Fleming, at West Union, O. They had two children: Lloyd, b. Feb. 19 1900, d. Sept. 5 1901, and Homer, b. March 13 1904, d. May 19 1906. He married, (2), Nov. 13 1909, Mrs. Margaret (Wamsley) Weaver, a widow, whose father, the Rev. W. C. Wamsley, performed the ceremony at the bride's home in West Union, O. One child, Ralph G. Young. Andrew married, (3), Lydia A. Gorby, a widow, June 15 1939, at Dart, O. from whom he separated in 1940. His fourth marriage, Dec. 31 1942, to Nora E. (Young) Black, a widow, ended by a separation in 1944. (R. G. Young).

i. Ralph Gaston Younge, b. Apr. 10 1912, in Tiffin Township, Adams Co., O., added an "e" to his name to distinguish himself from three others in Adams Co. with the name Ralph Young. Mr. Younge is a Minister in the Methodist Church, serving at Bartlett, O. in 1943. He md. June 2 1937, Juanita Caplinger, at Otway, O. One child, Kay Elmora Younge, b. Feb. 19 1938, at Portsmouth, O.

282 JOHN ARTHUR YOUNG

born, Feb. 17 1873, in Adams County, O., is a retired railway employee, living with his family in Lansing, Ill. He married, Aug. 15 1898, Emma Augusta Wandrey, b. July 6 1879. The family lived many years in Kouts, Ind. Nine children, seven born in Kouts, Ind., and the last two in Lansing, Ill.

i. Hulda Augusta, b. Sept. 23 1899, md. June 14 1923, George Peterson, at Hammond, Ind. and lives in Lansing, Ill. Four children: Donald George, b. July 20 1925, at Calumet City, Ill., Gunman, U. S. A. F. was killed in an airplane crash, Apr. 24 1944, at Ardmore, Okla. and was buried at Lansing, Ill.; Darlene Mae, b. June 27 1927, at Calumet City, Ill.; Evelyn Jane, b. Oct. 31 1931, at Lansing, Ill.; and Howard Norman Peterson, b. Nov. 24 1936, at Lansing, Ill.

ii. William David, b. Oct. 23 1903, lives in Lansing, Ill.

iii. Stella Mae, b. Sept. 30 1905, md. Nov. 14 1925, Herman Schmidt, at Lansing, Ill. and is living in New Lenox, Ill. Four children, all born at Lansing: Lenora Jane, b. Aug. 26 1926; Raymond Melvin, b. March 6 1930; Ralph Herman, b. May 13 1935; and Ronald Roy Schmidt, b. Feb 10 1939.

iv. Clara Sophia, b. Jan. 8 1908, md. Apr. 20 1929, Melvin Vierk, at Lansing, Ill. where they live. Four children: Robert Eugene, Apr. 19 1933, at Hammond, Ind.; Shirley Ann, b. Oct. 25 1935, at Lansing, Ill.; James Leroy, b. Oct. 30 1937, at Hammond, Ind.; and Marilyn Ruth Vierk, b. July 10 1939.

v. Hattie Minnie, b. Apr. 3 1910, md. Dec. 4 1928, Peter Busch, at Lansing, Ill. and lives in Chicago, Ill.

vi. Leona Ione, b. May 26 1913, d. Sept. 12 1914, at Kouts, Ind.

vii. Kenneth Harold, b. July 6 1916, at Crownpoint, Ind., md. Nov. 30 1939, Vela Seevers, at Hammond, Ind. and lives in Lansing, Ill. Two children, Nancy Jane, b. May 6 1941, at Hammond, Ind., and Kenneth Richard Young, b. Oct. 28 1946.

viii. Arthur Franklin, b. Apr. 11 1921, md. Aug. 7 1943, Laura Moore, at Lansing, Ill. where they are living. He served in World War II. One child, Janice Arlene, b. Nov. 18 1946, at San Diego, Calif.

ix. Lorraine Dorothy, b. Apr. 6 1923, at Lansing, Ill. is living with her parents. She supplied the family data.

283 WENDELL PRESCOTT ROOP

Captain, 1944, U. S. N., serving abroad, born, May 6 1887, at Holton, Kan., married, June 2 1909, Naomi Crouch of Chico, Calif., at Oakland, Calif. The family home is at Anchorage Farm near Woodbury, N. J. Captain Roop inherited from his father some data about the family of Morgan Young, sr. which has been used in this compilation. Two children.

i. Frederick Crouch, Lt. j.g., U. S. N., b. Nov. 11 1914, at Berkeley, Calif., graduated at Princeton University, 1935, married, Sept. 12 1942, Helen Freudenberg, at Belleville, Ill. They are living near Pasadena, Calif. One child, Ellen Tryon Roop, b. Dec. 16 1944.

ii. Robert Wendell, Lt. U. S. N. R., 1944, b. June 11 1919, at San Francisco, Calif., graduated at Princeton University, 1939, married, May 10 1941, Katherine Booth of Burlington, Vt., at Damariscotta Mills, Maine.

284 FRANK SUMNER SPOFFORD

The three brothers of Frank spell the family name Spafford. Chas. Bent, in his "History of Whiteside County, Ill., 1877," writing about John A. Robertson (Rec. 104) says that when Mr. Robertson retired he lived with his daughter, Mrs. D. S. Spafford, at Morrison, Ill. Mr. Bent lived in Morrison and for many years was the editor of the local newspaper. Frank S. Spofford was born, Aug. 23 1866, at Morrison, Ill., died, March 12 1924, and was buried at Boise, Idaho. He married, June 11 1890, at Kearney, Nebr., Lillian Alice, daughter of Benjamin Holmes and Josephine (Hill) Goodell. Lillian was born, Aug. 20 1872, at Kearney, Nebr. Two children.

i. Helen Goodell, b. Nov. 15 1891, at Kearney, Nebr., md. May 6 1912, at Caldwell, Idaho, John Jay Mack, b. Dec. 25 1880, at Terre Haute, Ind., son of John Jay and Mary (Sullivan) Mack. Mr. Mack is an executive with Safeway Stores, and lives at Berkeley, Calif. One child: John Goodell Mack, b. March 6 1913, at Boise, Idaho, was educated in the public schools of Seattle, Wash. and San Francisco, Calif., the Montezuma School for Boys, at Los Gatos, Calif., and graduated from Leland Stanford Univ. in 1935. A Lt. in U. S. N. R., he served as Instructor in Recognition during World War II. He md. Nov. 13 1938, Helen M. Rodgers, at Dixon, Calif. and has one child, Stephen Barry Mack, b. May 29 1943, at Caldwell, Idaho. (J. J. Mack, Berkeley, Calif.).

ii. Benjamin Dwight, b. Feb. 18 1896, at Kearney, Nebr., served in the U. S. Army Air Corps, 1917-18, in all grades from private to 2nd. Lt., and as flying instructor and flight commander. He is again serving in World War II, as Major, in the Army Air Corps. He md. Jan. 5 1918, Lillian M. Estabrook, at Dayton, O. Two children: B. D. jr., b. June 19 1921, at Dayton, O., is a cadet, 1943, in the Army Air Corps, md. Nov. 19 1942, at Dayton, O. Janet Ann Jones, and has one child, Dee Ann Spofford; and John Sumner Spofford, b. Aug. 12 1930, at Dayton, O.

285 GRACE MARIA PINNEY

born, Aug. 26 1881, was the first child to be borne in Jasper, Mo. She married, July 12 1904, at Jasper, Arthur William Johnson who retired in 1940 from the grocery business which he had conducted for many years in San Francisco, Calif. where the family is living. Two children.

i. Arthur Beers, Chemical Engineer, b. Jan. 26 1906, at San Francisco, Calif., graduated from Leland Stanford University, 1927, received there, in 1930, his Ph.D. degree, works for the Standard Oil Co. and lives in Berkeley, Calif. He married, March 30, 1933, at Berkeley, Josephine Morrish, and they have one child, Kendrick Arthur Johnson, b. Sept. 1 1935.

ii. Frances Grace, b. July 2 1908, at San Francisco, Calif., md. Aug. 27 1929, Robert Cuthburtson Swain, a Chemical Engineer. Three children: Mary Frances, b. Jan. 16

1931, Robert Johnson, b. March 10 1934 at Palo Alto, Calif., and Nancy Elizabeth Swain, b. May 29 1936, at Plainfield, N. J.

286 HELEN RUTH ORB

born, Nov. 29 1894, at Chicago, Ill., is living, 1947, at Winnetka, Ill. She married, May 23 1925, at Chicago, Ill., Neil Booker Dawes, b. 1894, at Lincoln, Nebr., son of William Ruggles and Margaret (Booker) Dawes. Mr. Dawes is with the Federal Reserve Bank, Chicago, Ill. Mrs. Dawes is a gifted sculptor. They have two children, both born at Chicago.

i. Katherine Orb, b. July 29 1928

ii. William Neil, b. May 7 1933

287 JOHN ALEXANDER ORB

born, March 18 1898, at Chicago, Ill., died there, July 28 1920, and was buried in Oakwood Cemetery, Chicago, Ill. Mr. Orb served his country in World War I as a Lieutenant in the U. S. Army Air Corps. He married, March 25 1918, Rowena Walker, daughter of Quinn Franklin and Ann Rowena (Webb) Walker, at San Antonio, Texas. They had one child. Mrs. Orb, sometime after the death of Mr. Orb, married at San Antonio, William J. Monahan, who as Colonel in the Army Air Forces distinguished himself during World War II.

i. John Alexander, III, b. Feb. 9 1919, at Chicago, Ill., is Lt. Colonel, 1944, in the U. S. Army Air Corps, serving overseas. He md. Feb. 29 1942, Elizabeth Jane Nevins, daughter of Roger W. and Mrs. Nevins, at Tampa, Fla. They have two children: Linda Walker Orb, b. Nov. 3 1943, at Palm Beach, Fla., and Joan Alexandra Orb, b. Nov. 3 1945.

288 KATHERINE SYBIL ORB

born, Aug. 16 1901, at Glencoe, Ill., died, March 18 1926, and was buried in Oakwood Cemetery, Chicago, Ill. She was a gifted artist. She married, July 7 1920, at Waukegan, Ill., John Canfield, son of Frank Wheeler and Harriet (Winn) Canfield. Mr. F. W. Canfield was the inventor of the spark plug, at Onekama, Mich.

i. John Canfield, III, b. Jan. 30 1923, at Chicago, Ill.,

graduated from Riverside Military School, Augusta, Ga. and served as Lieutenant in the U. S. Air Service Command during World War II.

289 BLANCHE CLARK

born, Sept. 3 1893, at Mt. Claire, Nebr., is living at Riverside, Calif. where she married, June 4 1912, Anson D. Lynde, garage owner, born, May 21 1893, at Ischua, N. Y. Two children, both born at Long Beach, Calif.

i. Grace, b. July 25 1913, md. at Los Angeles, Calif., June 21 1939, Albert S. Bartscherer. They live at Whittier, Calif. Two children: James Sherwood, b. Dec. 4 1940, and Fred A. Bartscherer, b. March 13 1944.

ii. Lou Florence, b. July 8 1916, md. May 3 1937, Robert Norman Graham, at Yuma, Ariz. He served during World War II in the U. S. Navy. One child, Lynde Lou Graham, b. July 4 1940, at Los Angeles, Calif. where the family lives.

290 FRED YOUNG CLARK

born, June 1 1896, at Mt. Claire, Nebr., married, Oct. 20 1922, Katheryn McMullen, at San Francisco, Calif. The family lives at Long Beach, Calif. where Mr. Clark is in the button and hemstitching business. Two children.

i. Joyce Frances, b. Nov. 20 1923, at Long Beach, Calif. md. and is living there.

ii. William Roy, b. Sept. 30 1926, at Long Beach Calif. joined the U. S. Navy in Oct. 1944, and was reported killed in action, Apr. 1945, by a bomb explosion on the S.S. Franklin.

291 WILLIAM SEMPLE MACFADDEN

born, Dec. 13 1895, at Fargo, N. D., married, Sept. 14 1922, at Moorhead, Minn., Dorothy Elizabeth Sharp, born, Aug. 9 1898, at Moorhead, Minn., daughter of James H. and Philadelphia M. (Shuit) Sharp, and lives at Minneapolis, Minn. where he is associated with the brokerage firm of Piper, Jaffray and Hopwood. Four children, all born at Minneapolis, Minn.

i. Jane Christie, b. June 15 1923

ii. Dorothy Elizabeth, b. July 21 1926

iii. William Semple, b. Dec. 15 1928
iv. Mary Louise, b. Apr. 17 1931

292 MARGARET LOUISE MACFADDEN

born, June 26 1899, at Fargo, N. D., married, June 11 1931, at Fargo, N. D., Samuel L. Chesley, born, Nov. 7 1887, at Fargo, N. D., son of James Albee and Emma (Jones) Chesley. Mr. Chesley is in the lumber and fuel business at Fargo, N. D. Two children.

i. James Albee, II, b. April 24 1934
ii. William Samuel, b. Dec. 19 1939

293 GARNET BARKER

born, March 7 1886, at Winterset, Ia., is living at Red Bluff, Calif. She married, Sept. 2 1911, in Nemaha County, Nebr., John Walter Hacker, born March 28 1883. Nine children. (Mrs. J. W. Hacker.)

i. Lee Ford, b. June 15 1912, Ravenna, Nebr. md. Nov. 26 1937, Zelda Mae Evergart, and lives at Red Bluff, Calif. He served in the U. S. Air Corps in World War II.
ii. Vera Faye, b. Nov. 30 1913, Omaha, Nebr., md. Dec. 23 1938, Leslie Howard Swanson.
iii. George Elias, b. Mar. 18 1914, Omaha, Nebr., died there Jan. 5 1915.
iv. Guy Roy, b. May 12 1915, Omaha, Nebr., md. Nov. 5 1936, Marjorie Fields. He served 2 years in the U. S. Infantry, So. Pacific area, in World War II. Two children: Caroline Joyce, b. Aug. 16 1937, at Idaho Springs, Colo., and Gary Lee Hacker, b. July 9 1941. The family is living at Red Bluff, Calif.
v. Madge Ruth, b. Nov. 16 1918, Rockford, S. D., md. Mar. 27 1940, James Albert Davison. One child, Albert Lou Davison, b. July 29 1041, Red Bluff, Calif. The family lives at Igo, Calif.
vi. Neil Walter, b. Apr. 1 1920, Rockford, S. D., served in the U. S. Navy in World War II, md. Jan. 15 1946, Iola Fern Farrell and has a daughter, Curtis Lynn Hacker, b. Aug. 31 1946, at Red Bluff, Calif.
vii. William Clyde, b. July 9 1922, Mystic, S. D., served in

the U. S. Navy from 1941 until 1945, md. Jan. 20 1946, Imogene Ellen Richardson and lives at Red Bluff, Calif.

viii. Wilma Ione, b. Oct. 23 1924, Edgemont, S. D., md. Jan. 14 1942, Ross E. Sidebottom at Reno, Nev. One child, Sherry Lee Sidebottom, b. July 16 1946.

ix. Helen Pearl, b. Aug. 15 1926, Edgemont, S. D., md. May 29 1947, Collis E. Henderson, at Red Bluff, Calif. where they are living.

294 HAZEL BARKER

born, Aug. 25 1888, at Winterset, Ia., is living near Olympia, Wash. She married, Nov. 20 1909, Tallman Cairns Steere, a farmer. Six children.

i. Hazel Linnette, b. March 17 1911, at Lead, S. D., md. Sept. 20 1930, Carl J. Isaacson. Five children: Leo Carl, b. Nov. 16 1932, d. Dec. 26 1932; Carla Jeanne, b. Feb. 7 1934; Jo Lynn, b. Oct. 31 1935; William Isaac, b. June 18 1938; and Shirley Rae Isaacson, b. Aug. 17 1939.

ii. Leo Tallman, b. Oct. 18 1915, at Lead, S. D., md. Sept. 7 1940, Roseanne La Fond.

iii. Jessie Matilda, b. July 16 1918, at Mystic, S. D., md. Nov. 2 1940, Ford P. Mullen.

iv. Dorothy Evelyn, b. June 30 1920, at Mystic, S. D., md. May 17 1941, George K. Clishe. One child, Christine Carol Clishe, b. Dec. 24 1941.

v. Ellis Fred, b. June 30 1922, at Pactola, S. D., twin of Eleanor.

vi. Eleanor Jane, b. June 20 1922, at Pactola, S. D., md. July 27 1940, Kenneth G. Smith.

RELATIONSHIPS OF THE ISRAEL, MORGAN AND THOMAS YOUNG FAMILIES

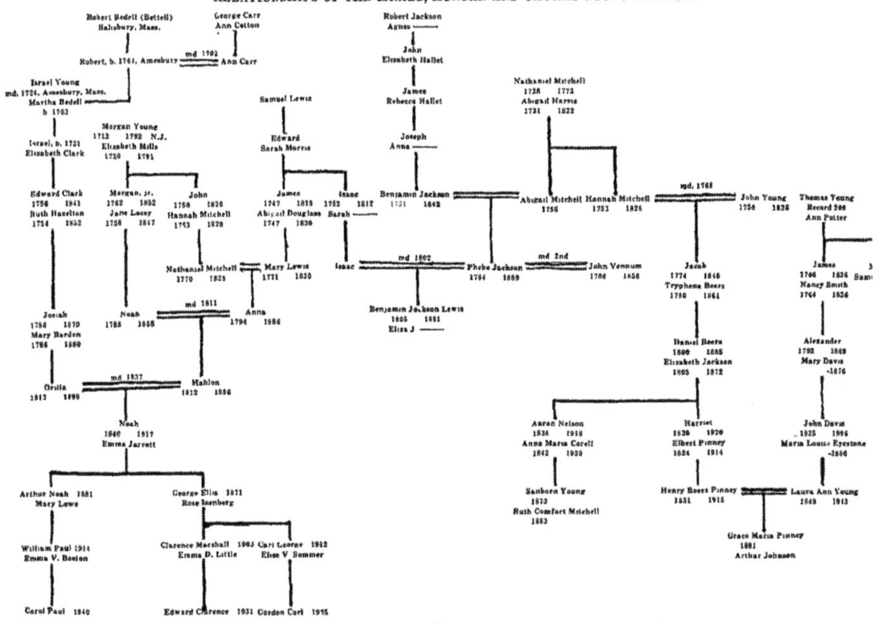

295 ISRAEL YOUNG

No record that identifies the parents of Israel Young is found. No record gives the place or date of his birth or of his death. The first record about him in this country is at Amesbury, Mass. which originally was a part of Salisbury, and for a time was known as Salisbury Newtown. In the records of the Mass. Bay Colony the name was spelled Emsbury. The "Vital Records of Amesbury, Mass. to 1849" (Topfield, Mass. Hist. Soc., 1913) show the marriage of Israel Young, Jan. 21 1724/5, to Martha Bettell (Bedell, Beatle, Bidle, Beetel), at Amesbury. It is possible that he was related to Israel and James Young who were residents of Exeter, N. H. in Nov. 1696, and to Israel, sr. and jr., Daniel and Jonathan Young who in 1710 enlisted from Exeter for military service (Chas. H. Bell, "Hist. of Exeter, Rockingham County, N. H.," 1888).

The Amesbury records give Nov. 10 1703 as the birth date of Martha Bedell, and the names of her parents as Robert (b. Jan. 5 1764, Salisbury, Mass.) and Anne (Carr) Bedell. The marriage of Robert and Anne Bedell took place at Amesbury, Nov. 11 1702. Anne Carr was the daughter of George, jr. (b. 1644) and Ann (Cotton) Carr (N. H. Hist Soc., Concord, N. H.). If these dates are authentic, as they seem to be, Major John Young, born 1714 at Haverhill, Mass. could not have been the son of our Israel and Martha Bedell Young as the typescript "Young Genealogy" of Guy Scoby Rix shows him to be. (N. H. Hist. Soc., Concord, N. H.)

Israel Young signed a Petition at Methuen, Mass. in 1741; he was a Surveyor of Roads in 1750; he and Richard Young are on the Tax List of Salem Province in 1754; Israel Young, sr. and jr. signed a Petition at Salem, N. H. in 1759; and in 1764, Israel Young had a pew in the church at Salem for which he paid 23 Pounds Sterling ("Hist. of Salem, N. H.," Edgar Gilbert, 1907). The Salem Church was in a parish of Methuen until the final boundary between Mass. and N. H. was established; its records begin in 1739.

What is shown about the children of Israel and Martha Bedell Young, unless otherwise noted, is from the Vital Records of Amesbury and Haverhill, Mass.

i. Mary, b. Aug. 20 1725, Amesbury; bapt. Salisbury, Nov. 19 1725. She apparently md. Sept. 28 1742, at Salem, Benoni Rowell (Church rec.)

ii. John, b. Nov. 8 1726, Amesbury

iii. Israel, b. Dec. 22 1728, Amesbury. Prob. died in infancy.

296. iv. Israel, b. Sept. 1 1731, Amesbury

v. Richard, b. May 26 1734, Haverhill

vi. Robert, b. Dec. 22 1736, Haverhill, bapt. Salisbury, Apr. 3 1737. A Robert and Elizabeth Young had 3 children, born in Salem: Hannah, b. 1761; John Dinsmore, b. 1763; and Janet, b. 1765 ("Hist. of Salem, N. H.," E. Gilbert)

vii. Joshua, b. Nov. 7 1739, Haverhill, bapt. Salisbury, Sept. 28 1740

viii. Martha, b. Jan. 7 1741/2, Haverhill. It is noted that a Martha Young, age 96, was living at Hancock, Addison County, Vt. in 1850 (U. S. Census). Ruth Hazelton Young, wife of E. Clark Young (son of Israel, jr.) died at Hancock, June 20 1852.

ix. Judith, b. May 13 1745, Salem (Gilbert, Hist. of Salem), bapt. Salem, May 30 1746 (Church rec.)

The typescript record of G. S. Rix adds:

x. Samuel, bapt. Oct. 2 1726, Salisbury

xi. Peter, prob. md. Ruth ———, and settled at Salem, N. H.

xii. Hezekiah, md. 1st, Nov. 23 1773, Judith Abbott, b. July 28 1755; md. 2nd, Apr. 15 1783, Mary Kimball, both of Concord, N. H.

296 ISRAEL YOUNG, JR.

Israel, son of Israel and Martha (Bedell) Young, born, Sept. 1 1731, at Amesbury, Mass. (V. R.), died at Manchester, N. H. (N. H. Hist. Soc., Concord, N. H.). He apparently married three times and is said to have had 23 sons and several daughters. He married, about 1754, Elizabeth Clark of Methuen, Mass. (V.R.). He and his father are on the Tax List of Haverhill, Mass. for 1754. He married Mary Harris in 1777 and they had a son, Joseph, born Dec. 25 1778. (Hist. of Salem, N. H., Edgar Gilbert.)

Elizabeth probably was the daughter of Edward Clark, jr. and Ruth Kelly (b. Jan. 15 1736/7, at Methuen, Mass. and d. June 18 175c (V. R.). She was the twin sister of Mehitable who md. Peter Merrill. Edward Clark, jr., in 1764, lived near Policy Pond, Salem, Mass. and owned a pew, as did his father, in the Salem Church. Edward, jr. was paid for work on the Meeting House in 1739 (Hist. of Salem, Mass., E. Gilbert). Mr. Gilbert says that John Ward and Edward Clark (?sr.) in 1659 drew lots in the "Uplands of Haverhill" or the 4th division of Salem. Haverhill, Mass. was the mother town of Salem, N. H., i.e. the earlier settlers of Salem were from Haverhill. (Hist. of Haverhill, Mass., Chase, 1861). Mr.

Gilbert, in his History of Salem, p. 239, shows, amongst the soldiers from Salem, *Ward* Clark Young (? *Edward* Clark Young) and James Young.

Ruth Kelly, daughter of Abiel Kelly, of Newbury and Methuen, Mass., and Rebecca Davis, was the granddaughter of John Kelly (b. 1642) and Lydia Ames, and the great gr. daughter of John Kelly (d. 1644) who came in 1635 to Newbury from England (N. H. Hist. Soc.).

Israel Young was living in Derryfield Town (now Manchester), Hillsborough County, N. H. in 1790 (U. S. Census). His family then consisted of 2 males over 16, and 9 males under 16 years, and 4 females whose ages are not shown. In the Census for 1800, James, Hugh and Israel Young are the 3rd, 4th, and 5th names listed at Derryfield. Jonathan Young is also here. The family of Israel in 1800 is composed of 4 males under 10, one between 10 and 16, one between 16 and 26 and one between 26 and 45, one female is under 10, two are between 10 and 16 and one between 26 and 45.

Of the many children of Israel five only have been found by the writer. The first four were children by Elizabeth Clark and the fifth by Mary Harris.

297. i. Edward Clark, often called "Clark Young," b. Oct. 10 1756, Salem, N. H. (Salem town rec.)

ii. James, b. 1758, lived at Derryfield, N. H. in 1790. Perhaps was the James, of Salem, Mass. who enlisted in 1777 in the Company of R. Dow, and who paid taxes in Salem in 1790. (Hist. of Salem, N. H., Gilbert)

iii. Elizabeth, b. Dec. 1 1760 (Gilbert)

iv. Levenne, b. April 1763 (Gilbert)

v. Joseph, b. Dec. 25 1778 (Gilbert)

297 EDWARD CLARK YOUNG

Clark Young is the abbreviated form of his name in several official documents including the U. S. Census of 1840 where he is listed as one of the living pension holders of the Revolutionary War. He was residing at Rochester, Vt. and his age was 87 years. An examination of his pension papers (W 18245) at the National Archives, Washington, D. C. proved him to be the writer's maternal great grandfather.

Edward Clark Young, son of Israel, jr. and Elizabeth Clark was born, Oct. 10 1756, at Salem, N. H. (Town rec. Vol. 2, p. 593). Edward confirms this date in his application for pension. He was baptized, Dec. 5 1756, in the Salem Church (Ch. rec.). He died, April 2 1841, at Rochester, Vt.

Home of
JOSIAH YOUNG, Rochester, Vt.
Record 298

GARDNER AND MARTHA WARREN YOUNG
Record 301

REUBEN A. YOUNG
Record 308

BENJAMIN DWIGHT SPOFFORD
Record 284.

John Alexander Orb, III
Record 287

John Canfield
Record 288

JACKSON LYMAN YOUNG
Record 223

ROBERT HUGHEY YOUNG
Record 223

John Goodell Mack
Record 284

John Marshall Heaps
Record 206

Albert B. Fisher, Jr., Wade C. Fisher
Record 270

Wm. Roy Clark
Record 290

Donald D. Niver
Record 162

Wm. Robert Cooley
Record 162

Allan Waite Taylor
Record 243

Edward Hudson Young
Compiler
Record 254.

(Pension papers). He married, Jan. 27 1780, at Salem, Rockingham County, N. H., Ruth Hazeltine (Hazelton) (Salem, N. H. Vital Rec.).

The records show that Edward Clark Young was granted a Revolutionary War pension, Jan. 25 1820, Vt. Agency, #16382. The last payment of pension was made at Burlington, Vt., March 16 1846, to Royal Flint (grandfather of a college classmate of the compiler!), as attorney for the pensioner. The same record shows that the pensioner had resided over 20 yrs. at Rochester, and had previously lived in Windsor, N. H. (Accounting Office, Washington, D. C.).

In a declaration for pension, April 10 1818, at Rochester, Vt., E. Clark Young stated that he was 62 yrs. of age, that he lived, in 1775, at Salem, N. H., and that he enlisted, May 10 1775 and served 8 months in Capt. Woodbury's Company, Col. Stark's N. H. Regiment; he was at the Battles of Lexington and Bunker Hill; he re-enlisted in Dec. 1775 and served one year in the same Company; he enlisted again in June 1777 and served a year in Capt. Barnett's Company, Col. Jackson's Regiment, and was at the Battle of Bemus Heights and Stillwater, and was at the taking of Burgoyne. He was granted a pension, Jan. 25 1820, Certif. #16382, at the rate of $8.00 per month, Vt. Agency. (Nat'l Archives, Washington, D. C.). Other service of the veteran is shown in the State Papers of N. H. (XVI Vol. 3, p. 257) where he is seen to have enlisted from New Salem, N. H., Aug. 31 1781, to serve at West Point, N. Y. He was discharged from this service, Dec. 21 1781 (Office of the Adj. General, Concord, N. H.). The files of Revolutionary War service in the Archives of Mass. show that Edward Clark Young, of New Salem (also given as of Haverhill, Salem, N. H. and Beverly, Mass.) served in various organizations, full details of which are given. It is here noted that he was 5 ft. 7 in. in stature; complexion and hair, light; eyes, blue. He arrived at Fishkill, N. Y. for service, July 4 1778.

The various Census Reports from 1790 to 1840 show some of the residences of Mr. Young and the make-up of his family. In 1790 he resided in Derryfield Town, Hillsborough Co., N. H. (now Manchester) and his family consisted of one male over 16, one under 16, and five females. In 1800, the family is in Windsor, N. H. and is composed of 2 males and 3 females under 10; 3 females between 10 and 16; one male and one female between 16 and 24; and one male and one female between 24 and 45. His son, Josiah and his family, were also in Windsor at this time. The family has not been identified in the Census of 1810. An Edward Young (and a Joseph) are listed at Stoddard, N. H. Josiah, son of E. C. Young, married at Stoddard in 1808. In 1820, Clark *Youngs* and wife lived at Rochester, Vt., as did also Josiah and his family. In 1840, Clark Young, Revolutionary

War Veteran, aged 87, lived with his wife, between 80 and 90 yrs. of age, at Rochester, Vt. Josiah immigrated with his family to Ohio in 1836.

The records of Salisbury, Mass. show that E. C. Young paid taxes there in 1785. He had property in Stoddard, N. H. in 1811 (Register, Keene, N. H.). He made a conveyance of property in Windsor, N. H. in 1811 (Register, Nashua, N. H.). He owned property in Windsor in 1815 (Town Clerk, Windsor, N. H.).

Ruth Hazelton Young, widow of Edward Clark Young, applied for a pension, July 19 1841, at Rochester, Vt. She stated that she was 87 yrs. old, that she married E. Clark Young, Feb. 27, about 64 yrs. ago; that their oldest son, Josiah, would be about 63 yrs. old, that a second child, a girl, was born in 1780; that neither she nor her husband had kept a record of their marriage date or the names of their children.

The General Accounting Office, Washington, D. C., says that Ruth was granted a pension of $40. per annum, June 24 1848, and that this was raised to $90. a year, Certificate #4631, Vt. Agency. This source adds that evidence was provided that Ruth Young died, June 20 1852, at Hancock, Addison Co., Vt. leaving the following known children: Mary, Sophia, Lydia, Edward and Phebe. Final payment of Ruth's pension was made Oct. 4 1852 at Montpelier, Vt. to E. Darling, as attorney for the administrator, Royal Flint.

Cora B. Young (Rec. 301) filled out an Application for Membership in the D.A.R. which is in the hands of the writer. She named in this Application seven children of E. Clark and Ruth Hazelton Young, and also the spouses of all except Edward and Phebe. The names of the remaining three children, indicated by the Census of 1800, have not been found.

298. i. Josiah, b. Feb. 27 1780, Salem, Mass. (Gravestone).

ii. Mary, md. Charles Meserve.

iii. Sophia, md. Charles Osgood.

iv. Lydia, md. Benjamin Dodge.

v. Edward, He perhaps was the Edward Young, b. 1797, at Stoddard, N. H., d. Nov. 1860, at Washington, N. H., md. March 13 1824, at Goshen, Rachel Tandy, native of Deerfield, d. June 1878. She joined the Baptist Church, Goshen, N. H. in 1823 (Goshen Bapt. Ch. rec.). The Church records and the Hist. of Washington, N. H. (1886) show the following children: (1) James T., b. Goshen, May 28 1830, lived at Washington, N. H.; (2) Sarah H., twin of James T., md. Geo. F. Jefts, Nov. 30 1847; (3) Hiram C., b. Goshen, Nov. 10 1831, md. Eleanor A.

Strickland, of Washington, Apr. 30 1859, was one of the proprietors of the Cresent Woolen mill. Children: Ida M., b. Washington, N. H., June 8 1860, md. Willie D. Brockway; Fred S., b. Oct. 28 1868, d. Feb. 4 1884; and Perley M., b. Dec. 5 1871, lives at Washington, N. H. (4) Lucius C., b. Jan. 10 1838, md. Apr. 17 1861, Angie H. Thompson, of Goshen, N. H. Four children: Irving E., b. Sept. 18 1863; Hattie M., b. Dec. 31 1868; George D., b. Aug. 23 1874; and Edwin A., b. Jan. 16 1881, at Washington, N. H. (5) Elvira, b. Mar. 13 1842, md. Amos Thompson. (6) Benjamin C., b. Mar. 30 1846, md. Addie M., dau. of Darius Y. Barnes, of Washington, N. H., Apr. 10 1876.

vi. Phebe, There are land transactions recorded at Rochester, Vt. by Phebe, after 1836, the year that Josiah took his family to Ohio. The Census reports for Rochester show her under her maiden name. The Census report for Hancock, Vt. in 1850 (where her mother died in 1852) lists a Martha Young, age 96, born in N. H., living with Frank and *Phebe* Hemenway. Was Martha a sister of Edward Clark Young?

vii. Margaretta, md. Jefferson Robbins.

298 JOSIAH YOUNG

is the only child mentioned by name by his parents in existing records of the family (Rec. 297). The fact that he was alive, in Ohio, apparently was unknown when the final payment of Revolutionary War pension was made to the heirs of his mother.

Josiah Young was born, Feb. 27 1780, at Salem, Mass. (now Salem, N. H., which was originally a part of Old Pentucket, and which became a part of Methuen, Mass. and remained so until the N.H. boundary line was settled. Methuen was part of Old Haverhill until 1825). He died, Sept. 18 1870, at North Monroeville, O. (earlier Cook's Corner) and was buried there. His death was caused by a fall down his cellar steps. He attended church the previous Sunday. His gravestone shows the above dates and also has the following inscriptions engraved upon it: "Mary, Wife of Josiah Young, born in Stoddard, N. H., Oct. 1 1785, died Feb. 10 1880"; on a second side of the stone, "Martha W., Wife of Gardner Young, Born in Rochester, Vt., Feb. 11 1822, Died, Oct. 13 1870," "Clara A. Young, died

March 5 1853, Age 2 yrs. 9 mos. 11 days," "Jennie Young, Died Feb. 10 1862"; on the third side, "Gardner Young, Born in Rochester, Vt., Dec. 23 1815, Emigrated to Ohio 1836, Died Nov. 18 1898," "Jessie F. Young, Died June 11 1927, Aged 69 yrs."; on the fourth side, "Sophronia Brown. Born Aug. 28 1818, Died Aug. 22 1898." There are seven headstones in the lot, inscribed: Father, Mother, Martha, Clara, Jessie, J. Y., and M. Y. The first five are on one side, the last two, on another side of the lot. After the death of Josiah, his wife Mary lived with her son John, in whose home near Monroeville, O., she died. (Mrs. Geo. Brown, of Cleveland, O. who who has the family Bible of Josiah).

The will of Josiah, made in 1867, executed at Norwalk, O., Oct. 1 1870, gave all his property to his wife, Mary. (Wills, Norwalk, O., Bk. 2). The will of Mary Barden Young, of Ridgefield Township, Huron County, O., dated, Dec. 22 1870, proved, Feb. 2 1888, at Norwalk, O., gave her household and personal goods to her five daughters, Orilla Young, Sophronia Patterson, Mary George, Martha DeWitt, and Ellen C. Mygatt, and her land, bounded by land once owned by Joseph Young (her deceased son) and by land now owned by Jonah Young (unidentified) to her seven children, Lorenzo, Orilla, Gardner, Sophronia, Mary George, Martha DeWitt, and John. Her son Reuben did not emigrate to Ohio and was probably dead. (Wills, Bk. 2, Norwalk, O.).

Josiah was living in 1790 with his parents in Derryfield Town (now Manchester), N. H. (Census). There are four deeds of land to Josiah Young and six deeds and mortgages from him recorded at Keene, N. H. between 1805 and 1811. In 1805, in a deed, Josiah gave his residence as Stoddard, Cheshire County, N. H. In 1810, he gave his residence as in nearby Goshen. (Registry, Keene, N. H.). The U. S. Census for 1810, in Goshen, Windsor Co., N. H., shows the family, consisting of himself, his wife, and one son. Josiah's father, Clark Young, was a resident of Stoddard in 1811 (Keene, N. H. rec.). The Edward and Joseph Young, shown in the same Census, of Stoddard, perhaps were relatives of Josiah. Philip Bardean, father-in-law of Josiah, was a resident of Stoddard, N. H. in 1810 (Census).

Family records state that Josiah went to Rochester, Vt. about 1812. This is confirmed by the land records at Rochester which show his first purchase there to have been from Thos. Bull, Oct. 30 1814. He increased his holdings, May 30 and 31, 1817, by two purchases totaling 67 acres from Ebenezer Sparhawk. On Feb. 29 1820, Josiah exchanged some land with David Warren (? related to John Warren, father-in-law of Gardner Young). On Nov. 7 1820, Josiah sold part of his land to Joseph Jefferson (Margaret Young, daughter of E. Clark Young married Jefferson Robbins).

The land held by Josiah in 1820 is in 1943 known as the Alexander and the Frank Hubbard places. Josiah bought, Apr. 24 1830, from Isaac McAllister, land that was formerly in Pittsfield, now known as the Perkins place. Reuben and Lorenzo, sons of Josiah, bought in 1830 land adjoining that of their father in Pittsfield. Josiah deeded, Jan. 1 1836, all his Pittsfield holdings to Lorenzo, and, on the same day, he deeded all his remaining property in Rochester to Larnard Atwood, receiving in exchange a mortgage for $2300.00 from Mr. Atwood, and one for $2250.00 from James M. Duinnell. On Sept. 9 1836, in preparation for his departure for Ohio, Josiah assigned these mortgages to Briggs and Tilden, local money lenders (Worth A. Shampney, Rochester, Vt.). There are land transactions recorded at Rochester later than 1836 by Phebe Young, sister of Josiah, who was caring for their parents. The land records at Brandon, Vt. indicate that Josiah, in 1812, made an effort to start his son Reuben in business. He bought farming land for Ruben but Reuben deeded the land back to his father the same year.

Josiah and his family, except Reuben who remained in Vermont, reached Cook's Corner, Huron County, O. in the evening and sought shelter for the night in a home which proved to be that of Noah Young (Rec. 28). When they introduced themselves, Noah replied to Josiah, "That is my name, a good name, Young." Josiah, pleased by his entertainment and the look of the land, halted his covered wagons and bought land near Noah from Luman Tracy, on the main road between Monroeville and Sandusky (Rec. Norwalk, O., Vol. 13, p. 512). In less than a year, Mahlon, son of Noah, and Orilla, daughter of Josiah, were married. They were of no kin. Two collateral lines of New Jersey Youngs were united to one from Massachusetts. Noah was a grandson and his wife was a granddaughter of Morgan Young (Rec. 2).

Josiah Young was married, May 15 1808, by the Rev. Dr. Isaac Robinson, at Stoddard, N. H., to Polly (Mary) Barden, born, Oct. 1 1786, at Stoddard, N. H. (Stoddard, N. H. rec., Bk. 1, p. 135. The date does not agree with that of the gravestone. The vital records of Stoddard show the following additional children of Philip and Phebe (Bassett) Barden: Eunice, b. Aug. 4 1782; d. May 13 1785; Lucy, b. July 31 1784; Esther, b. Oct. 26 1788; Susanna, b. Oct. 9 1790; Rebecca, b. July 28 1793; Lewis, b. Oct. 11 1798; and Achsa, daughter, b. Oct. 16 1802. Philip Barden and his wife, Mary, of Walpole, Mass., deeded in 1783, to their son, Phillip, of Walpole, land in Stoddard, N. H. (Stoddard, N. H. rec.).

Josiah and Mary Young had ten children and they adopted one, George A. Young. All except Reuben, were born at Rochester, Vt.

299. i. Reuben, b. Apr. 15 1809, near Stoddard, N. H.

300. ii. Lorenzo, b. in 1811
71. iii. Orilla, b. May 7 1813
301. iv. Gardner, b. Dec. 23 1815
302. v. Sophronia, b. Aug. 28 1818
vi. Mary, died, March 1 1888, at Bellevue, O. She married a Mr. George. Two children: Josephine, md. ——— Moore; and Josiah George.
303. vii. Martha W., b. Aug. 18 1823
304. viii. Joseph, b. July 31 1825
305. ix. Helen C., b. May 2 1831
306. x. John, b. May 20 1833/4
xi. George A., an adopted child whose name is inscribed on the "Memorial to Those Who Died in the War of the Rebellion," in the cemetery at No. Monroeville, O. George was killed by a boat explosion on the Mississippi river as he was returning, 1865, from war service.

299 REUBEN YOUNG

born, Apr. 15 1809, in or near Stoddard, N. H. (Rec. 298), married, July 9 1829, Hannah Augusta Austin, born, Apr. 5 1809, daughter of Nathan Austin, jr. (1769-1847), of Vermont (Fam. rec. of Mrs. H. J. Young). Reuben bought land in Pittsfield, now Rochester, Vt., in 1830, and in Brandon, Vt. in 1832, giving his residence as Brandon. He was a bootmaker, working in Boston, Mass., and coming home periodically for a visit. He returned in Dec. 1834 to Rochester and brought his wife a tray and set of pink luster china. On his return to Boston, he mysteriously disappeared. His wife moved to Worcester, Mass. where she worked to support her children and searched to find Reuben, a search which she never gave up. She secured a divorce, Feb. 23 1838, and married, March 29 1840, John Emerson, jr., of Rochester, Vt. (d. 1891), a widower with two sons. The U. S. Census for 1850 of Rochester shows Augusta Young, daughter of Reuben and Hannah, age 17, living in the home of John, jr. and Hannah Emerson. Hannah A. Austin was one of 22 children, seven of whom died within a period of two years (Letter of her son, R. A. Young, Nov. 3 1887, to his daughter Lottie): Nathan; Thomas; Samuel; Betsy; Polly, md. ——— Washburn; Melinda and Minerva Austin. Another sister of Hannah was Almira Austin Hall, and a brother was Francis B. Austin. Hannah was a niece of Hannah Austin (d. aged 65 yrs. 11 mos. 5 days, buried with her husband at No. Monroeville, O.) who married John

Warren, d. July 27 1853, aged 57 yrs. 9 mos. 10 days. Gardner Young, brother of Reuben, was guardian of the minor children of John and Hannah Warren (Norwalk, O. rec.). Reuben and Hannah Young had three children.

307. i. Henry Josiah, b. June 9 1831

308. ii. Reuben Augustus, b. Oct. 29 1832

iii. Hannah Augusta, b. Oct. 29 1832, twin of Reuben A., md. a Dr. Cheeseman and lived in June 1870 in Winona, Minn. where she died in early life. She was buried at Winona. No children.

300 LORENZO YOUNG

farmed in Vermont, Ohio and Michigan. He was born in 1811 near Goshen, N. H. where his father bought property that year and gave Goshen as his residence (Keene, N. H. rec.). He died in 1884 and was buried in Union Cemetery, Whiteford Center, Mich. He owned a farm in Vermont until 1841 (Rochester, Vt. rec.). His last purchase there was from his father, Jan. 1 1836 (Rec. 298). When he emigrated to Ohio he settled at Enterprise, in Huron County. He married, 1st., June 17 1835, at Tunbridge, Vt., Hannah Button (Burlington, Vt. rec.), the Rev. James Campbell performing the ceremony. Lorenzo gave his residence as Rochester, Vt. He married, 2nd., in Huron County, O., a widow, Lena (Mackey) Stanbury (1823-1890), of Sandusky, O. She had two children, Byron and Frances Stanbury (md. James Shelton). Mrs. Young was a sister of Judge Mackey of Sandusky, O. Lorenzo moved his family from Ohio to Whiteford Center, then called Bugtown because of its many fire-flies. Lorenzo and Hannah had one child, Lois. He and Lena had four children.

i. Lois, born in Vermont, was under 5 in 1840 (U. S. Census). She md. Mathew Northrup and they had three children: Justin, became a clergyman and spent his last days in Minneapolis, Minn.; Howard; and May, who md. Charles Baker and lived at Mankato, Minn. They had one child, Lois Baker.

309. ii. Ellen Mary, b. Apr. 19 1856

iii. Leota, b. 1858, d. 1925, md. ——— Collier. They lived at So. Whiteford, Mich. No children.

iv. Louis M.

310. v. James DeWitt, b. Feb. 14 1863

301 GARDNER YOUNG

filled with the pioneering spirit of his father became a prosperous farmer and a prominent figure in church, school and social activities in Huron County, Ohio. Born, Dec. 23 1815 at Rochester, Vt., he died, Nov. 18 1898, in his home at Monroeville, O. A Norwalk, O. newspaper reported that "a vast concourse attended the funeral service in his home, amongst those present being his son Henry, from Oxford, Kan., his son Albert, from Holyoke, Colo., and his brother-in-law James L. Young, from New Haven, O. The service was conducted by the Rev. E. T. Hagerman, of Norwalk, the Rev. Mr. Knapp, of Monroeville, and the Rev. B. J. Mills, of New London, O." On his gravestone in the cemetery at No. Monroeville, O., it is inscribed that he emigrated to Ohio in 1836 from Vermont (Rec. 298).

Gardner returned from Ridgefield, Huron Co., O. to Vermont to marry a companion of his youth to whom he had been engaged for ten years. He was married by the Rev. Daniel Warren (? related to his wife), at Rochester, Vt., Sept. 6 1847, to Martha Warren (Rochester, Vt. rec.). Martha, daughter of John (1795-1853 No. Monroeville, O.) and Hannah (Austin) Warren, born, Feb. 11 1822, at Rochester, Vt., was killed, Oct. 13 1870, when thrown from a buggy by a runaway horse near the DeWitt home in Monroeville, O. (Mrs. Geo. G. Brown, Gates Mill, O.). Martha's sister Julia married Col. Leonard F. Ross, in Ohio. A son of Col. Ross married Rose, daughter of James L. Young (Rec. 163), and made thereby a double alliance of the Warren-Young families. Gardner and Martha had eight children, all born at No. Monroeville, O.

i. Henry Josiah, b. Aug. 28 1848, d. Apr. 12 1932, at Los Angeles, Calif. and was buried (Space 9—Lot 2—Block 5) in Santa Ana, Calif. cemetery. He md. at Monroeville, O., Elizabeth Mary Lewis, b. March 2 1850, at Monroeville, died, Jan. 9 1916, at Tustin, Santa Ana, Calif. Their one child, Laura Lewis Young, b. Oct. 24 1884/5, died unmarried and was buried next to her father. Her headstone bears the dates, "1885-1916." She attended Southwestern College, Winfield, Kan. The family lived some years at Oxford, Kan. moving from there to Calif. about 1910 ("Lewisiana," Vol. 15, #773, N. Y. Pub. Libr.). What happened to Henry's substantial properties (and those of his brothers and sisters) is a sorry tale in the Courts of Southern Calif. In Henry's case, there was not enough left to erect a headstone to his memory!

ii. Clara A., b. July 20 1850, d. March 5 1853 (Rec. 298).

iii. Alice, b. 1854 (twin of Albert W.), d. Nov. 29 1932, at Toledo, O. where she was buried. She md. E. K. Fisher. Having no children of their own, they adopted Pearl, now Mrs. F. C. Munson, of Hattiesburg, Miss. Alice gave her mother's Bible to James D. Young, a cousin, but the records in it have been inaccessible to the writer.

iv. Albert Warren, twin of Alice, d. March 21 1906, at Holyoke, Colo. and was buried in Strong's Ridge Cemetery, near Bellevue, O. He md. Feb. 21 1899, Anna Seymour, of Bellevue (b. June 1 1854). There was a difference of 5 days in their ages (Mrs. Frank B. Seymour, Bellevue, O.). After the death of her husband, Mrs. Young returned to Bellevue where she died, Oct. 21 1933, and was buried beside Mr. Young.

v. Jennie, d. Feb. 10 1862 (Rec. 298). Twin of Jessie. Second set of twins.

vi. Jessie Fremont, b. 1858, d. June 11 1927, age 69 (Rec. 298). Twin of Jennie, a teacher, died unmarried. Jessie, like Henry and Alice, left considerable wealth. The settlement of her bequests was long delayed bcause James D. Young, a cousin, petitioned for Letters of Administration and for Probate of a Foreign will in the Court at Bakersfield, Calif.

vii. Cora B., b. Jan. 28 1860, d. Nov. 15 1939, at Los Angeles, Calif. where she went from Ohio in 1891, and where she taught in the Public Schools for many years before retirement. In Sept. 1939, the writer called on Cora and received valuable family records, elsewhere recorded in this work. He also was told how "she been tricked out of her property and her legal rights in her brother's (Charles S.) property." "An exceptional character and teacher," says W. R. Roalf, a former student, now Librarian of Duke Law School.

viii. Charles Sumner, born in 1868, died in Sept. 1925, at Gore, Okla. where he was buried until 1941 when his remains were removed to Forest Lawn Cemetery, Glendale, Calif. and placed beside those of his sister Cora. He did not marry. His will which disposed of a substantial fortune (some 70% interest in over 1400 acres of oil land in and around Bakersfield, Calif. included) was declared invalid because of having been made but a few days before his death and because more than one third was left to charity. For many years Mr. Young was interested in the welfare of our Indians and at the time of his last sickness was perfecting a "Clara Barton Sequoyah Foundation," to which he meant to leave most of his wealth and at the same time memorialize his long and intimate friendship with Clara Barton. (See "Clara H. Barton," Wm. E. Barton). Mr. Young's beloved Indians and his natural heirs received little when the legal wranglings were over (See Bakersfield, Calif. Court records).

Charles Sumner Young graduated from Ohio Wesleyan Univ. and received his Ph.D. degree at Johns Hopkins Univ., Baltimore, Md. He left Ohio to settle at Reno, Nev. where he began a literary, educational and political career which he continued while engaged in pioneering in the oil business in which he became an expert and a successful operator. He left Ohio in 1877 and became State Superintendent of Public Instruction of Nevada in 1883, a position he held until 1886. His activities in this office are recorded in the State's Journals. By wide travelling, study and his writings, Mr. Young became known for his efficiency. A result of this was his election, 1886-7, as President of the Nat'l. Education Soc. In 1887, he moved to Southern California where he became a pioneer expert in the development of the Kern river oil district. He spent some time in Mexico assisting in the development of the oil fields there. Later he turned to literature, writing, and in efforts to better the welfare of the Indians. The latter work took him often to Washington and the offices of the Department of the Interior. In 1915, he moved to Gore, Okla. where he ended an energetic and successful life. "On Memorial Day, 1917, Col. Charles Sumner Young, of Gore, Okla., gave an address on the life of Clara Barton in memorial hall, Oxford, Kan., under the auspices of the local G.A.R. post. His address was an eulogy surpassing anything ever heard in Oxford on a woman the town delights to honor" (Newspaper clipping).

302 SOPHRONIA YOUNG

born, Aug. 28 1818, at Rochester, Vt., died Aug. 23 1893, in the home of her son George, at Chicago, Ill. where she was on a visit to the World's Fair. The funeral service was held in the home of her brother Gardner at Cook's Corners, now No. Monroeville, Lyme township, Huron county, O. and the burial was in the nearby cemetery in her father's family lot. She married, Dec. 23 1837, at No. Monroeville, Joel P. Brown and spent most of her married life at Seneca, near Adrian, Mich. where Mr. Brown died in 1858. Seven children, the last five were born at Seneca.

i. Charles Exera, b. Oct. 28 1839, telegrapher, went to Nashville, Tenn. in 1863 to serve in Alabama and Tenn. as military telegrapher under Col. J. C. Van Duzer. After the war, he was railway agent at Osgood, Ind. for a few years and then embarked in the business of publishing trade circulars, city directories and railway gazeteers at Adrian and Saginaw, Mich. "The Telegraph Age," of Sept. 16 1908, gives a sketch of Mr. Brown's life together with a good picture of him. He md. ——— Ketchum. Six children, the names of two are known: Maude and Ada (md. ——— Whiteman) Brown.

ii. Martha Maria, b. Sept. 24 1842, at No. Monroeville, O., died, May 19 1910, at Adrian, Mich. where she md. May 19 1862, Thomas Hay, b. Dec. 22 1829, d. Jan. 18 1919, at Norwalk, O., buried Woodlawn cemetery. The family moved to Norwalk in 1865. Mr. Hay was an undertaker and is said to have conducted over 8000 funerals. Four children: Fred H., whose widow lives in Norwalk in 1942; William T., lived in Cleveland, O.; Charles, lived at Harrington, Kan.; and Maria who md. ——— Bates, and lived at Marshall, Mich.

iii. Henry, called Harry, b. Sept. 30 1844, at Seneca, Mich. was a newspaper man, d. at Chicago, Ill. in 1913, unmarried. He served in a Mich. regiment during the Civil War.

iv. Mary Elizabeth, b. Jan. 22 1846, md. Isaac Mosher at Adrian, Mich. Three children: (1) Eva Estella, b. Oct. 23 1864, md. Aug. 25 1887, James W. Bartley (d. Sept. 16 1937), at Adrian, Mich. She is living with her son, Wilfred Earl Bartley (b. Sept. 18 1894, Chicago, Ill., md. July 20 1921, Olive Marion Fleming, and has two children: Patricia Maria and Joyce Olive Bartley, b. Detroit, Mich.

where the family is living); (2) Ida May Mosher, b. Aug. 13 1866, md. Dec. 15 1887, Julius A. Barrett. She died Jan. 7 1936. Five children: Gordon W., d. 1939; Edna M.; Estella B.; Edward M. lives Clairton, Pa.; and Florence M. Barrett, b. Oct. 14 1899; (3) Arthur DeWitt Mosher, b. Nov. 13 1873, Adrian, Mich., md. Dec. 25 1899, Ora B. Husted, at Hudson, Mich. Two children: Geraldine E., b. Feb. 27 1901, at Cleveland, O. and Dorothy Belle Mosher, b. Nov. 25 1905, d. Jan. 18 1906.

v. Frank Garrison, b. Feb, 25 1849, md. and lived at So. Bend, Ind. where he was Western Union agent in 1875. No children.

vi. Angella Medina, b. Sept. [illegible] 1852, md. (1) Samuel Chatterton and had two children: Vernie and Daisy Chatterton who were living in Calif. in 1942; md. (2) Frank Mears and lived at Redondo, Calif.

vii. George Franklin, b. Feb. 14 1855, md. Nora Harless. He owned and was operating the Hotel Vendome, Chicago, Ill. in 1893. Five children, three of whom died in infancy: Minnie Layne and Lawrence Brown who live in Calif.

303 MARTHA W. YOUNG

born, Aug. 18 1823, Rochester, Vt., died, March 23 1906, at Monroeville, O. where she lived all her life. She married, Dec. 1840, Isaac DeWitt (Rec. 11), b. Sept. 17 1816, d. June 1 1902. Both were buried in Riverside Cemetery, Monroeville, O. They celebrated their golden wedding in 1890. Mrs. Young's mother was killed by a runaway in front of their home. Three children: Burton L., b. July 15 1852, d. July 2 1903; Ella M. DeWitt, d. 1867, age 25, md. James G. (? Fish) (Gravestone rec.), and Isaac DeWitt, jr. who was engaged in mining in the west.

304 JOSEPH YOUNG

born, July 21 1825, at Rochester, Vt., died, May 28 1868, due to a runaway accident, and was buried in the cemetery of Lyme Trinity Church, on the highway east of Bellevue, O. He was married by the Rev. Milton Rowley, of Norwalk, O., April 13 1850, to Emma (Fowler) Sawyer, daughter of Stephen Fowler (1786-1870), who came to America from London, Eng. in 1819. Emma, born, Aug. 10 1826, at Lyme, Conn., died, Oct. 2 1900. (Bible of Walter U. Young & gravestone rec.). Six children, all born near No. Monroeville, O. where Mr. Young farmed, and baptized in Lyme Church. After the death of Mr. Young, his wife lived with her two sons, Wilbur and Walter, at Forest, O. where her daughter, Mrs. Todd, also lived.

i. Emma Jane, b. Oct. 26 1852, d. Nov. 19 1889, bur. at Evanston, Ill., md. Dec. 31 1868, Franklin C. Todd, at Monroeville, O. Two children: Arthur and Eva Todd. Eva md. Sperry B. Pope and lived in Chicago, Ill.

ii. Alfred Eugene, b. Oct. 26 1852, d. Aug. 17 1877, bur. Lyme, O. cemetery.

iii. Ambrose Jay, b. Nov. 7 1854, d. Apr. 4 1941, bur. Forest, O. He md. Hannah Mary Mann of Gahannah, O. Three children: (1) Mabel, b. Apr. 30 1883, d. Apr. 18 1941, at Rochester, Minn. while under the care of the Mayo Clinic. She md. A. O. Bailey, as his second wife and lived at Chicago, Ill. where Mr. Bailey is chief engineer for the Chicago Bridge and Iron Works. One child; Betty Lou Bailey, b. Apr. 25 1929, at Chicago. (2) Emma Gertrude, b. Mar. 11 1891, md. Aug. 4 1920, Wm. E. Hougendobler and lives at Forest, O. Two children: Dorothy Evelyn, b. Oct. 11 1926, and Wm. Ambrose Hougendobler, b. Oct. 31 1929, at Forest, O. (3) Ethel Marie, b. Aug. 12 1895, md. Leo R. Jones, at Forest, O. where they live. One child: Thomas Allen Jones, b. Apr. 28 1932.

iv. Wilbur Joseph, b. Dec. 15 1859, d. Nov. 20 1911, at Toledo, O., bur. Upper Sandusky, O. as was his wife. He md. Oct. 22 1885, Clara Maxwell (d. March 1943), of Wyandot Co., O. Two children: J. Maxwell, b. 1886, is a Publisher's representative at Los Angeles, Calif. 1942, and Alfred W. Young, b. 1892, md. Helan Conlan and lives at Beverly Hills, Calif. Wilbur Young owned a grocery store at Forest, O. for some years.

v. Evaline Adelia, b. in Mar. 1861, d. Oct. 16 1865, bur. Lyme, O.

vi. Walter Ulysses, b. Nov. 18 1865, d. Apr. 23 1942, on his 80 acre farm, one mile east of Gratis, O. on the Germantown Pike. He graduated, 1890, from Ohio Wesleyan Univ., was a salesman at Toledo, O., and taught school some years before retiring to his farm. He md. June 16

1892, Orpah Mary Henkel, dau. of Dr. Henkel who practiced medicine some 40 yrs. at Farmersville, O. Mr. and Mrs. Young celebrated their 49th wedding anniversary in 1941. Three children: (1) Byron Walter, b. Apr. 7 1900, at St. Mary's, O., graduated from Ohio Univ., Athens, O., md. Feb. 7 1931, Olive G. Burdsall, at Cincinnati, O. and lives in Hamilton, O. where he is with the Nat'l Cash Register Co. Two children: Janet Ruth, b. Nov. 26 1931, and Marjorie Ann Young, b. Sept. 7 1933, at Hamilton, O. (2) Paul, b. in 1894, d. June 24 1918, at Gratis, O. and (3) Kathryn Eileen Young, d. in infancy, at St. Mary's, O.

305 HELEN CATHERINE YOUNG

called Ellen in the will of her mother (Rec. 298) was born, May 2 1831, at Rochester, Vt. The family moved to Cook's Corners, now No. Monroeville, O., in 1836, and here, Aug. 30 1855, Helen married Milton Mygatt (Rec. Norwalk, O.). She died, Feb. 5 1921, at Oakland, Calif. where her ashes rest in the columbarium of the Chapel of the Chimes. Mr. and Mrs. Mygatt moved from Ohio to Iowa City, Ia. where their only child, Lillian, was born. From Iowa, the family moved about 1860 to Virginia City, Nev. where Mr. Mygatt engaged in the mining business. He was secretary of the Keystone Mining Co. in 1863, and is listed as late as 1872 in the city directory as a miner. Mrs. Mygatt, in 1875, was a teacher in the school at Goldhill and was living with her daughter and son-in-law, William E. Sharon. She was living in the Palace Hotel, San Francisco, in 1906, at the time of the earthquake and fire. Milton Mygatt, of Scotch ancestry, son of Germain and Susan Mygatt, was born, Oct. 29 1831, and died Dec. 30 1914, at Redding, Calif. ("A Historical Notice of Joseph Mygatt," 1853, Frederick T. Mygatt, Brooklyn, N. Y.)

i. Lillian, born, Jan. 16 1858, at Iowa City, Ia., died, Sept. 4 1937, at Oakland, Calif. She md. Dec. 25 1876, at Virginia City, Nev., William Evan Sharon, b. March 22 1852, d. Jan. 22 1926, at Piedmont, Oakland, Calif. Mr. Sharon was the son of Smiley (b. 1826, Jefferson county, O.) and Sarah Ann (Hurford) Sharon, both of Quaker ancestry. He went from Wheeling, W. Va. to Nevada in 1872 and became superintendent of all the mines in the Goldhill district. In 1892, he became part owner of the Reno Evening Gazette ("Hist. of Nevada," 1904, Wren). He was a nephew and secretary of Nevada's (1875-1881) U. S. Senator William Sharon, b. 1821 in Jefferson county, O., d. 1885 in Calif. Senator Sharon went to Sacramento Calif. in 1849, moved to San Francisco, and later to Virginia City, Nev. where he was in charge of the Ralston Bank when he bought the Comstock and other mining properties. Wm. and Lillian Sharon had 8 children:

1. Claude Sumner, b. Nov. 1 1877, Va. City, Nevada, md. 1907, Ivy Evans, at San Francisco, Calif. He md. (2) Edith Logan.
2. Florence Emma, b. July 12 1879, md. (1) May 2 1902, Peter C. Allen, at Oakland, Calif.; (2nd) Ilia Jadovsky; (3rd) J. E. Johnston; (4th) Herbert H. Brown. She lives at Carmel, Calif. and has five married children and eight grandchildren.
3. Blanche Wilhemina, b. June 23 1881, Va. City, Nevada, md. at Piedmont, Calif., June 3 1902, Harry Farr. She died in 1924. One of their children is William Sharon Farr of Chevy Chase, Md. He md. Janet Sharon Johnston, dau. of Dr. Wm. B. and Janet (Newlands) Johnston, of San Francisco. Wm. S. and Mrs. Johnston have 4 children: Sharon, b. Aug. 12 1937, at Portsmouth, N. H.; Janet Marion, b. Jan. 3 1939, Washington, D. C.; Sheila Ladd, b. Aug. 29 1941, Washington, D. C.; and Gavin Malloy Farr, b. Dec. 6 1942, at Washington, D. C.
4. William Kirk, b. Dec. 29 1887, died at the age of 3.
5. Robert Alexander, b. Mar. 26 1890, at San Francisco, Calif., md. June 1 1915, Hazel Ingels, at Oakland, Calif. A son, William Willard Sharon, md. Ruth Ann, dau. of Mr. and Mrs. Joseph A. Yanish, of Hamden, Conn.
6. Ruth Carrie, b. Apr. 20 1892, Oakland, Calif. died in 1930. She md. March 26 1917, Alberto De Grassi and had 2 children.
7. Esther Lillian, b. Apr. 8 1895, Oakland, Calif., md. June 23 1918, Lucius Grinnel Norris, and lives at Oakland. Four children: Lucius Henry, b. 1919, d. 1934; Westrik, b. 1921; Elise Esther, b. 1923, d. 1928; and Sharon Norris, b. 1929.

8. Hurford Clarence, b. Apr. 17 1898, md. (1) in 1921 Narcissa Cerini who died in 1928 at Oakland, Calif. Two children: William Francis, b. 1925, and John Hurford Sharon, b. 1927. He md. (2) Evelyn Reyland in 1929 at Oakland.

306 JOHN YOUNG

born, May 20 1833, at Rochester, Vt., died, Feb. 10 1898, and was buried in the cemetery at No. Monroeville, O. He married, Dec. 17 1850, Catherine Loa Starr Clark, born 1833, at Wilkes-Barre, Pa., died, Oct. 31 1888. (Norwalk, O., rec. Vol. 3, Old Series). Three children.

i. Laura Belle, b. in June 1856, near Monroeville, O., d. in May, 1929, at St. Petersburg, Fla. She md. Dec. 16 1875, John T. Haskell (Norwalk, O. rec.).

ii. Grace Helen, b. July 19 1868, near Monroeville, O., md. in 1896, George G. Brown, at Berea, O. After retiring from business, Mr. Brown moved to St. Petersburg, Fla. where he died in 1941. Three children: Kathryn Jane, b. May 25 1897, md. ——— Gilmore; Edgar A., b. May 8 1899, md. and lives at Gates Mills, O.; and Florence E. Brown, b. Apr. 17 1907, md. E. W. Stage, and lives at Gates Mills, O.

iii. Clifford Edgar, b. May 17 1871, near Monroeville, O., md. and in 1941 was engaged in the plumbing business in New York, N. Y.

307 HENRY JOSIAH YOUNG

physician, born, June 9 1831, Rochester, Vt., served as surgeon in Wisconsin regiments during the Civil War, settled in Waseca, Minn. in 1867 (Minn. Hist. Society Biog., Vol. 14, 1912). Dr. Young was licensed to practice in Minn. by the Act of 1887. He graduated in 1854 from the Vermont Medical College, Woodstock, Vt. His address in 1900 was Thorsby, Ala. (Polk Med. Directory, 1893-6). He died, Apr. 23 1900, in the home of his son Carl at Lebanon, Ore. where he was buried. Henry and his brother, Reuben A., are listed as students in the catalogues of Springfield (Vt.) Wesleyan Seminary for the years 1851-53. Henry also began his study of medicine in 1851 at Springfield under Dr. E. A. Knight. He practiced for one year at Temple, N. H. and from there went to Sheboygan, Wis. where he practiced until commissioned with the rank of Major in 1852 in the 1st Wisconsin Cavalry. In 1864, because of poor health, he was assigned to the 47th Wis. Infantry at Sheboygan, Wis. At the end of the war he was given charge of the Gen'l. Hospital, at Tullahoma, Tenn., from where he returned to Sheboygan to practice until 1867, when he moved to Waseca, Minn. and conducted the Maplewood Dairy and Stock Farm (Hist. of Waseca, Minn.). He went to Thorsby, Ala. in 1897, and to Lebanon, Ore. in July 1899. He married, Jan. 14 1856, Lucia Holt Preston (1834-1908), at Pittsfield, now Rochester, Vt. She was the daughter of Lucius and Rebecca Holt Preston, and a sister of Lorietta who married Reuben A. Young, brother of Henry. Two children.

311. i. Carl Henry, b. Dec. 8 1860

ii. John Cadwell, b. Aug. 8 1864, at Sheboygan, Wis., d. Dec. 13 1891, at Knoxville, Tenn. where he conducted a Business School. He md. Dec. 30 1886, Alice L. Dye (d. 1901). One child, Helen Young, b. May 26 1889, at Knoxville, Tenn., d. Nov. 3 1908.

308 REUBEN AUGUSTUS YOUNG

born, Oct. 29 1832, at Brandon, Vt., according to a Baptismal Certificate dated Jan. 23 1918, at Reno, Nev. His father bought land in Brandon in 1832 (Rec. 299). He studied at Wesleyan Seminary (1851-53), Springfield, Vt., went to California via Cape Horn in 1854, and settled in Sheboygan Falls, Wis. in 1856, where he married, July 11 1858, Lorietta Preston, b. July 3 1838, at Pittsfield, Vt., died, Jan. 22 1905, at Willow Ranch, Modoc County, Calif. where the family moved in 1895. The family went in 1861 from Sheboygan Falls to Virginia City, Nev. by covered wagon. Mr. Young mined at Virginia City and in California. He became Editor of the Virginia City "Chronicle" and was active in politics. He was a member of the first State Legislature of Nevada, 1865, representing Storey County. He was one of the first aldermen of the city and an original member of the National Guard of Nevada. The family moved to San Francisco in 1882, and Mr. Young spent some months as a mechanical engineer on Douglas Island, Alaska, building the Treadwell Quartz Mill. After the death of his wife in 1905, he lived with his daughter Bertha at Highland Springs, Calif. for 11 years, and then 2 years with his daughter Lottie at Reno, Nev. where he died, Feb. 21 1918, and was buried in Mt. View cemetery (I.O.O.F. Sect.). Five children. A twin sister of Lottie died at birth. (Mrs. Ida M. Hays, Palo Alto, Calif.).

312. i. Lorietta Augusta, b. Nov. 9 1861

ii. Bertha Louise, b. Mar. 7 1871, at Silver City, Nev., d. Feb. 5 1932, at Kelseyville, Calif. She md. (1) Frank Tabor, who died in 1894, at San Francisco, and (2) Joseph W. Kingry, rancher, in 1897, at Lakeview, Ore.

iii. Elmer Augustus, b. in 1872, Silver City, Nev., d. 1919, at Willow Ranch, Calif. He did not marry.

iv. Mabel, b. Apr. 14 1884, at San Francisco, Calif., d. June 8 1906, buried Lakeview, Ore. She married John Duckworth, in 1904, at Lakeview. One child, Mabel Olive, a graduate nurse, b. May 17 1906, at Lakeview, Ore., md. Feb. 6 1936, Floyd Bernard McGrath, rancher, at Paget, Idaho, and lives at Cloverdale, Calif. Three children: John Bernard, b. Nov. 29 1936; Thomas Floyd, b. Aug. 11 1938, at Lakeview, Ore.; and Myra Joan McGrath, b. Jan. 10 1946, at Santa Rosa, Calif.

309 ELLA MARY YOUNG

born, April 19 1856, at Enterprise, Huron County, O., is living, July 1947, at Lambertville, Mich. She married, Feb. 22 1876, at Whiteford Center, Mich., William Henry Howenstine who died, in April 1921, at Lambertville. One child.

i. Ethel Lee, b. Aug. 15 1880, Lambertville, Mich., md. at Toledo, O., Aug. 20 1904, Daniel T. Knepper, Insurance Administrator, and lives at Lambertville. Three children: (1) William T., b. Sept. 1 1907, Detroit, Mich., md. June 8 1929, Elizabeth Reuter, at Toledo, O. where they live with their four children, David, b. Nov. 13 1936, Kay, b. Sept. 21 1940, Janet, b. Oct. 14 1932, and Wm., b. Oct. 7 1930; (2) Lorin M., b. March 20 1911, Detroit, Mich., served as M. Sgt. in the U. S. Army during World War II in the Pacific and is now with the Vet. Admin. at Detroit; (3) and Leota Knepper, b. Nov. 11 1913, Detroit, Mich., md. Sept. 7 1935, at Lambertville, Albert Sparks who was a radio operator in World War II and received the Bronze Star for merit in action in France. Mr. Sparks now works in the offices of the Packard Auto Co., Toledo, O.

310 JAMES DeWITT YOUNG

born, Feb. 14 1863, at Whiteford Center, Mich., died, Jan. 6 1929, at Detroit, Mich., where he was a superintendent at the Ford Motor Works. He married Georgia Lee Ostrander, b. April 1 1873, d. Nov. 13 1929, at Toledo, O. Four children.

i. Mildred Mackey, b. March 28 1892, at Toledo, O., md. June 23 1929, at Toledo, William Edward Hanna, an industrial engineer, and is living at Los Angeles, Calif.

ii. James DeWitt, b. Oct. 15 1895, md. Feb. 22 1920, Dorothy Elizabeth Webster (b. Feb. 22 1893), at Toledo, O. Three children: (1) James Harding, b. Mar. 4 1921, Toledo, md. Sept. 4 1942, Jane Caroline Loxley, and has one child, James Carter Young, b. Oct. 12 1944; (2) David Robert, b. May 2 1924, at Pontiac, Mich., is serving in the U. S. Army in 1947; (3) Alice Louise Young, b. Apr. 22 1927, Pontiac, Mich.

iii. George Lorenzo, b. Oct. 28 1898, at Toledo, O., d. in March 1901.

iv. Eliza Helen, b. Aug. 18 1902, is better known as "Welcome E."

311 CARL HENRY YOUNG

born, Dec. 8 1860, at Sheboygan Falls, Wis., died, Dec. 23 1938, at Waterville, Ore. (where he lived with his daughter Charlotte after the death of his wife) and was buried in the Odd Fellows cemetery about 8 miles from Eugene, Ore. He had a varied career. He began the study of pharmacy at Northfield, Minn. but changed to a business course which served him well when he helped his brother with the latter's business school in Knoxville, Tenn. and in his last years when he was secretary for the Scottish Rite at Eugene, Ore. He farmed some in both Minn. and Oregon, and for a time was a forest ranger in Oregon. He married, Dec. 13 1883, Mary Edith Blatchley (1863-1930), at Waseca, Minn. Four children.

i. Margie, b. July 6 1885, at Waseca, Minn., md. June 4 1908, Archie Odessa Knowles, and lives at Mapleton, Ore. Four children: (1) Carl Albert, b. Aug. 14 1909, md. twice: (a) Doris Kuyendall and had one child, Carl A. jr., b. Jan. 5 1931 (b) Frances Johnson Martin, a widow, and had 2 children: Katherine M., and Lorence Eric, b. Aug. 2 1945; (2) Mary Lillian, b. Oct. 5 1910, md. Donald

Charles Kingsley, and lives near Eugene, Ore. (3) Odessa Marian, b. Jan. 3 1913, md. Donald F. Johnson, lives near Mapleton, Ore. and has 3 children: Ann Jeanette, b. Dec. 20 1938; Shirley Marie, b. Mar. 26 1943; and David Calvin Johnson, b. Mar. 18 1946; and (4) Robert Silas Knowles, b. May 30 1919, lives with his parents.

ii. Charlotte, b. June 28 1888, at Waseca, Minn., md. Dec. 29 1909, Robert Sherman Huston (d. Dec. 30 1936), at Eugene, Ore. She is living with her daughter in Portland, Ore. One child, Norma, b. May 12 1911, graduated 1934 from the Univ. of Ore. with Phi Beta Kappa honors, md. Feb. 6 1937, A. Wilfred Frazee, an Engineer, associated with the Ore. Shipbuilding Co. at Portland, Ore. One child, Paul Sherman Frazee, b. Mar. 30 1941, at Portland, Ore.

iii. Mary Augusta, b. Jan. 7 1892, at Waseca, Minn., md. Jan. 19 1911, Edward Burgis Starr, and lives near West Cornwall, Conn. Eight children: Adelaide Emerson, b. Feb. 14 1912; Sherman Lay, b. Sept. 20 1913, d. Apr. 1 1933; Edward Preston, b. Jan. 8 1915; John, b. Mar. 30 1916; William Comfort, b. in Jan. 1918, d. Sept. 16 1918; Charlotte Hope, b. May 12 1922; Norman Winship, b. Aug. 21 1923; and Comfort Starr, b. July 21 1925.

iv. Reuben Carl, b. Aug. 22 1902, at Lebanon, Ore., md. June 19 1929, Olive, daughter of Prof. Percy Adams of Eugene, Ore. Mr. Young is Editor and Publisher of the Curry County "Reporter," Gold Beach, Ore. where he has a strawberry garden of some 20,000 plants. Three children: Richard Henry, b. Dec. 20 1932; Wilbur Leslie, b. Sept. 3 1935; and Margaret Ann Young, b. June 21 1937.

312 LORIETTE AUGUSTA YOUNG

"Lottie," born, Nov. 9 1861, shortly after the family's arrival at Virginia City, Nevada, from Wisconsin, died, Jan. 5 1920, at Reno, Nev. and was buried there beside her husband, in Mt. View cemetery. She was married, Oct. 6 1878, at Virginia City, by the Rev. O. W. Whitaker, to George Monroe Holmes, born, 1858, at Bangor, Maine, died 1919. Two children (Mrs. Ida Holmes Hays, Palo Alto, Calif.).

i. Ida May, b. July 30 1879, at Silver City, Nev., grad. A.B.

from Univ. of Nev., 1900, md. Mar. 6 1901, David Walker Hays, Irrigation Engineer (grad. B.S., same year, same University), at Virginia City, Nev. Three children: (1) Harford Holmes Hays, Accountant, b. Jan. 31 1902, at Carson City, Nev., grad. A.B. and A.M. (1926) from Stanford Univ., Palo Alto, Calif. and lives at Berkeley, Calif. He md. June 19 1936, Margaret Collins, at Lone Pine, Calif. Two children: Elizabeth Loretta, b. July 22 1937, at Fresno, Calif., and Ellen Margaret Hays, b. Apr. 22 1943, at Palo Alto, Calif. (2) Vida, teacher, b. Dec. 23 1903, Reno, Nev., lives at Palo Alto, Calif., md. Nov. 23 1926, William Henry Suffern, of Decatur, Ill. Both grad., 1926, Leland Stanford Univ. One child, William Henry, jr., b. Dec. 4 1929, at Decatur, Ill. (3) Alice Loretta, b. Aug. 7 1907, at Fallon, Nev., attended Cal. School of Fine Arts, San Francisco, md. Sept. 12 1929, Francis J. Scheid, Moving Picture Sound Engineer, at San Gabriel Mission, Calif. and lives in No. Hollywood, Calif. He served as Capt. in the U. S. Army Air Forces during World War II.

ii. Wallace Monroe, electrician, b. May 26 1885, Virginia City, Nev., d. Apr. 8 1946, at Stockton, Calif. He md. Nov. 19 1910, Genevieve Cavis, at Virginia City, Nev. Five children: (1) Walter Cavis, b. Sept. 4 1913, at Sparks, Nev., md. in June 1942, June Robinson, at Stockton, Calif. One child, James Wallace Holmes, b. Jan. 14 1944, at Stockton; (2) Ida Virginia, b. Nov. 17 1915, Sparks, Nev., md. Aug. 4 1934, Gordon Gerry North, at Reno, Nev. and lives at Antioch, Calif. One child: Jean Arlene North, b. Apr. 15 1936, Stockton, Calif. (3) Edwin Willard, b. Dec. 16 1917, at Mason, Nev., md. in 1939, Lila Fredabeth Crader (d. 1942). He served in World War II and is now a Petty Officer, U. S. Navy Submarine Service. (4) Miriam, b. Aug. 13 1919, at Stockton, Calif., md. Nov. 24 1938, Alfred Hensel, at Stockton. Two children: Judith Ellen, b. Oct. 3 1942, at Lodi, Calif., and Daniel Alfred Hensel, b. Dec. 29 1945. Family lives at Victor, Calif. (5) Robert Charles Holmes, b. Apr. 8 1924, Stockton, Calif., served at Lt. j.g. U. S. Naval Aviation Reserve, in the Pacific area, md. Apr. 13 1946, Nancy Lou Kaiser, and lives at Stockton, Calif.

313 ROBERT YOUNG

Robert Young, sr., of Morris County, N. J., was one of a family of eight children whose parents and birth dates are unknown. Three *Items* in the will of his brother John (Rec. #1) partially identify him. Our further identification of Robert is based on the fact that his family were Quakers and that our Young family was the sole Quaker family in N. J. with the name Young. The first *Item* in John Young's will makes Robert the father of James Young; another *Item* calls by name two other sons, Morgan and Robert Young, Records 314-316; and a third *Item* reads as if Robert may have had more than these three children: "I give and bequeath to each and every of the children of my brother Robert. . . ." No descendant of Robert has been found.

Robert Young, sr., in 1768, owned property adjoining that of John Losey, of "Mendom" (Morristown, N. J. record). This record read in the light of information contained in road surveys and maps at Morristown indicates to the compiler that our Robert Young was he who lived next to John Losey. The property of Robert Young adjoined that of a Mrs. Losey as shown on the map of J. B. Shields, published 1853. This property is mentioned in a report of road surveys at Morristown under Road A-55(1769): "This road began at an apple tree near Robert Young's dwelling (near Shongum Lake) and ended on a road that leads from Morgan Young's to Schooley's Mill. The earliest property Deed abutting the beginning point of this road is one from John Phillips to Silas and Daniel Young (H-70 (1799). Daniel Young received part of this land in Deed F-214(1802), in which John Phillips said that he bought the land from James Young." Silas and Daniel were sons of James Young, and James was the son of Robert Young. Unless there were two families with these same several names who were Quakers, the above Robert Young of the survey was our Robert Young. James Young, at the proving of the will of John Losey, sr., July 2 1765, witnessed as Quakers did, by affirmation, while Nathaniel Mitchell witnessed by oath. Jane Losey, daughter of John, sr., married Morgan Young, jr. (Rec. 9). The tax list of Mendham, Morris County, N. J. shows the names of Robert Young, sr. and Robert Young, jr. Their names appear in a sequence of our Youngs, suggesting that their properties adjoined. (State Lib., Trenton, N. J.)

The deed records at Morristown, N. J. show that Jonas and Phebe Phillips bought 230 acres of land from James Young, which they sold, May 14 1799, to Silas and Daniel Young, with James Young as witness, and also that Daniel sold his share of the land to Silas in 1802. The executors of Silas Young who left $200.00 to be used in erecting a stone fence around the yard of the Randolph (Quaker) Meeting House were Lewis

Loree and John Lewis Carrell. They sold the property of Silas, Oct. 6 1863, to John Mott. Record 317.

Family records give Mary as the first name of Robert Young's wife. Her family name is unknown. Robert and Mary may have been the parents of Jean, wife of Asher Lyon, legatee of John Young (Rec. 1), and of Sarah Young, Quakeress, who with Nathan Simcock and William Schooley witnessed the first Deed by which Robert Schooley sold to James Brotherton and Jacob Laing land at Mine Hill, in 1758, on which to build the Quaker Meeting House. ("Hist. of Dover," p. 425, Chas. D. Platt). Perhaps it was this Sarah Young who married, Dec. 2 1769, Isaac Hatheway. James and Robert Young witnessed, March 10 1786, the will of Isaac Hatheway. An effort to identify Elizabeth Young who married Robert Schooley, Feb. 17 1747, failed. The known children of Robert and Mary Young were:

314. i. James, b. July 8 1738
315. ii. Morgan
316. iii. Robert

314 JAMES YOUNG

was the first legatee of his uncle John Young (Rec. 1). A part of his record is shown under that of his parents, Record 313. He was born, July 8 1738, in Mendham township, Morris County, N. J. He married Sarah Benjamin, born, April 5 1742. They had 8 children.

i. Mary, b. Jan. 4 1765, d. 1771
ii. Kesea, b. Nov. 23 1766, md. John Knapp
iii. Johnathan, b. Aug. 17 1768, md. Rhoda ———
iv. Isaac, b. Nov. 1 1770
317. v. Silas, b. Feb. 20 1773
vi. Jacob, b. Mar. 21 1775, d. 1775
vii. Daniel, b. Mar. 13 1777
viii. Lewis, b. Apr. 8 1779

315 MORGAN YOUNG

is named in the will of his uncle John Young (Rec. 1) as the son of Robert and the brother of James and Robert Young, jr. Nothing more is definitely known about Morgan. Three of the four Morgan Youngs mentioned in the will of John Young are listed in the tax list for 1785 of Mendham, N. J. (State Lib., Trenton). These three are identified as: (1) Morgan, husband of Elizabeth Mills, Wagon-master during the Revolution; (2) Morgan, jr., husband of Jane Losey, private in the Revolution; and (3) Morgan, son of

Thomas Young, of Pequannock, N. J. Morgan, son of Robert, may have been he who is listed as a sergeant during the Revolution in the Office of the Adjutant General at Trenton, N. J. He received Depreciation pay, in May 1784, for service in the Morris County Militia with the Continental Troops.

A widespread exodus of the Youngs and allied families (Jackson, Losey, Carrel, Hatheway, Lyon, Bryant, Dalrymple etc.) from N. J. to Pennsylvania and Ohio began shortly after the Revolution. Morgan, son of Robert Young, may be he who appears on the tax list of Catawissa township, Northumberland County, Pa., in 1786 and 1787. The tax list shows him as having 30 acres in 1786, and 300 acres in 1787. (State Archives, Harrisburg, Pa.). His family in 1790 consisted of himself and wife, 1 son over 16, 1 son between 10 and 16, and 2 daughters. The U. S. Census for 1800 shows the family as living in Fishing Creek township, Northumberland County, Pa. No descendants are known.

Robert Young, Rec. 8, states in his application for a pension in 1829 that most of his relatives have gone to N. Y. State and Ohio. Morgan Young, jr., Hercules, John and Silas Young were in Washington County, Pa. when the first Census was taken, 1790. The latter three signed a Petition in Fallowfield township in 1784 (State Archives, P.R.P., Vol. 23, p. 65, Harrisburg, Pa.). Our subject does not appear in the 1810 census for Pennsylvania.

316 ROBERT YOUNG, JR.

son of Robert and Mary, married, Jan. 1 1767, Elizabeth Morris, according to the "Combined Register of the 1st Presbyterian Church, Morristown, N. J." The same record shows the baptisms of 3 of their children: An unnamed child, b. 1769; Hannah, b. June 2 1773; and Joseph born July 3 1775. No further record has been found.

This Robert Young may have been the Captain Robert Young, under whom Morgan, son of Thomas Young, of Pequannock, and James Young (Rec. 7) claim in their pension applications to have served during the Revolution.

317 SILAS YOUNG

Quaker, was born, Feb. 20 1773, in that part of Mendham which became Randolph township, Morris county, N. J. His will, dated, March 7 1862 (Bk. H, p. 353, Morristown, N. J.), leaves legacies to his wife Margaret, to his executors, and a sum of $200.00 to erect a stone wall around the Randolph Meeting House, on the outskirts of Dover, N. J. His executors,

Lewis Loree, of Mendham, and John L. Carrell, of Randolph, sold his land on the road from Shongum to Openeka Lake to John Mott by order of the Orphans Court, Oct. 6 1863 (Bk. O, 6, p. 118, Morristown, N. J.).

The U. S. census for 1850 of Randolph, Morris county, N. J. shows that household No. 300 was composed of Silas and Margaret Young, and John Mott. Dr. Frank J. Tone in his "Hist. of the Tone Family," Niagara Falls, N. Y., 1942, suggests that Margaret Tone, daughter of Thomas and Content (Hance) Tone, married Silas Young, in view of the fact that Margaret Young and John Mott, jr. were the executors of the will, dated, March 8 1825, proved, June 25 1825, of Content Hance Tone. Nancy Hance, b. 1800, md. 1821, Charles Dalrymple, son of Robert and Mary (Young) Dalrymple.

John Lewis Carrell was a grandson of Daniel Carrel (spelled Carral, in his will, and Carle, in his land deeds), who married Margaret Young, sister of Robert, Record 313. Charles S. Carrell, of Morristown, N. J., nephew of Eugene A. Carrell, (1852-1942) grandson of Daniel and Margaret Carrell, supplied the following story told by Eugene Carrell in 1932 and printed at that time in the Morristown "Daily Record":

EUGENE A. CARRELL

Tells Story Told Him by Silas Young Who Knew George Washington Personally

"Eugene A. Carrell remembers as a boy Silas Young of Shongum telling him of a personal experience with George Washington. At the time Young was about 8 years of age and faced a life which ended when he was in his nineties. (89 to be accurate). This story, never before published, is important as adding another sidelight on the character of the Father of his Country and also evidences that Shongum might still have had a Washington's Headquarters had not the house fallen into decay and been torn down. Stone from the foundation was used in the building of a gardener's house for Hubert M. Schott which burned in 1930 and other stones were used in edging the driveway and forming the rock garden at his Shongum place. Mr. Carrell on this Bicentennial year visited the site and has written of the episode as follows:

"The story that always gave Silas Young, of Shongum, much pleasure to tell his friends was of the time when he, as a little boy, slept with Washington. The writer remembering to have heard this story from Mr. Young now desires to give an account of the same and of the attending circumstances of the interesting event so that the incident may not entirely fade way from mind and memory.

"The writer in his boyhood days lived with his parents on a good sized farm in the central section of Randolph Township, Morris County. This farm was part of a large tract of land purchased by his ancestors in 1732 (Rec. 319), the Deed for the same being a large and very curious document of the "Defender of the Faith" style. In the early 1860's, my father, the late John L. Carrell, occasionally visited Silas Young, a friend and kinsman, who had requested that he do so that he might consult him as to the affairs of his farm which was situated at Shongum, in the Southeastern section of Randolph township. Mr. Young's farm was a large one which with his advancing years was causing him much concern in its management. Mr. Young was born in 1772 (?) and so was nearly if not quite 90 years of age in the early 1860's. Sometimes when my father went to see Mr. Young, I was allowed to accompany him. The great stone house in which Mr. Young lived, with its colonial type of construction, also the great stone fireplace and chimney was most interesting to me, besides seeing the people whom we met there. I shall never forget about it all. On one occasion which was, as I recall, a very hot afternoon in summer, I went with my father, and as we rode along, he talked with me about Mr. Young, who, he said, could remember George Washington and that he had when a little boy of about 8 years slept with him. As I kept asking my father questions, he finally told me that if Mr. Young seemed to be well enough, he would ask him to tell me the whole story, which pleased me greatly. When we reached Mr. Young's home, we entered the great door yard and found him sitting under the shade trees some of which were black walnut. We sat down and for some time he talked with my father about his farm affairs. When we were about to leave my father said to Mr. Young that he thought Eugene would enjoy very much hearing his Washington story. This seemed to please Mr. Young and he told me the story which was as follows:

"It was during the winter of 1779-80 when Washington's Army was encamped in and about Morristown and the General was occupying the Ford mansion as his headquarters. These were dark days for Washington and for his soldiers and for the American cause. There was little food, clothing, money which meant much suffering and hardship to be endured, and in which all were obliged to share. The situation was pitiful. It became necessary at once and all through the time that Washington and his Army remained in Morristown for the officers to go out into the countryside searching for food, clothing and whatever else could be found to sustain the encamped army.

In the northern section of Mendham, now Randolph, township there were found quite a number of families who were members of the Society of Friends who were thrifty folk with something to divide, and so they were often visited and much feed, hay and grain and other necessities were procured from them by the food searching parties. Upon such an errand General Washington, with the usual escort, set out from his headquarters on a lowery and threatening afternoon. When the company reached Nicky Brook, at Shongum, a great storm broke but the company kept pressing on and soon came to the farm house of Robert Young (Silas Young's father) who, when he saw the horsemen, went out and called to them to take the horses to the barn and for the men to come into the house until the storm had spent its fury. This the General and his staff gladly did. As the afternoon passed the storm increased in violence. When supper time came Mrs. Young prepared the best she had for her guests and invited them to partake of it with the family. After supper, as the storm continued, and they found broken limbs of trees on the road, Mr. Young advised General Washington not to think of going back to Morristown in such a storm and said that he and his company would be quite welcome to stay with them and they would care for them to the best of their ability.

After a pleasant evening by the fireside, talking about the war and its trials, bed time came and with it the problem of placing the visitors so that all would be comfortable. Notwithstanding the fact that Mr. Young's family was not a small one, this was accomplished. Mr. Young was reporting this fact to Washington and was showing him the room he was to occupy when they saw little Silas standing quite near, and his father said to him, "Why Silas, could you not find a place to sleep? Well, well, I must see to that," but before he could add anything, Washington seeing the situation, said to Mr. Young, "Let the little boy come with me." And so it came about that Silas Young could always tell that, when a boy of 8 years, he had slept with Washington. And how great was his pleasure all through his long life to be telling others of this event! When the morning came and the storm had subsided, and having breakfasted with Mr. and Mrs. Young, thanking them for all their kindness, Washington and his company returned to Morristown."

"As our country is celebrating this year the 200th anniversary of the birth of Washington and everything he ever said or did is being told and retold, it seemed to be an appropriate time to tell this story."

Signed: Eugene A. Carrell. Morristown, N. J., Aug. 4 1932.

The Morristown records make James Young (Rec. 314), from whom John Phillips bought land at Shongum, the father of Silas who died in 1862. Robert Young was the grandfather of Silas.

318 MARY YOUNG

Quakeress, was a sister of John (Rec. 1). John Young made a bequest "to each and every of the children of my sister Mary" and he mentioned by name one of her children, "John Miller, son of Adam Miller." Mary's marriage, Sept. 6 1746, to Adam Miller in the Quaker Meeting, at Woodbridge, N. J., together with the names and birth dates of their children, was transcribed by H. D. Vail from the Rahway-Plainfield Quaker records in the "N. Y. Genealogical & Biog. Record," July 1879, p. 142. The same records show the marriage, in 1747, of Elizabeth Young to Robert Schooley. No descendant of Adam and Mary Miller has been found.

		day	*month*	*year*
1. Conrad	born	2	4	1747
2. Catherine	"	3	11	1749
3. Anna	"	22	1	1751
4. John	"	20	12	1752
5. Robert	"	16	10	1754
6. Elizabeth	"	4	3	1757
7. James	"	12	10	1759
8. Margaret	"	21	7	1762
9. Conrad	"	29	5	1765
10. Thomas	"	5	12	1768

NOTES ON THE MILLER-YOUNG FAMILIES

Adam Miller was one of the administrators of the estate of John Young (Rec. 1), of Roxbury, N. J.

Conrad Miller, of Mt. Hope, Pequannock, N. J. was a bondsman, Dec. 25 1796, to the estate of Michel Rider, and helped with the Inventory (Wills, N. J. Archives).

Adam Miller, Sept. 19 1761, on behalf of the heirs of Thomas Hartshorn, sold to Thomas Young, 63 acres of land in Morris City, on Beaver Brook, a branch of the Rockaway river (Rec., Morristown, N. J.).

Members of the N. J. allied families, Miller, Young, Losey, Dunham, Denman, Beers, Pierson and Talmage, emigrated to the present sites of Mansfield, Mt. Vernon, and Mt. Gilead, Ohio, and were pioneering neighbors. Catherine Beers Talmage (Rec. 42) writes of a contemplated visit to Nancy (Losey) Miller, a great granddaughter of James Puff Losey, an administrator, with Adam Miller, of the estate of John Young. Jacob Miller, husband of Nancy, was the son of Abraham and Catherine (Denman) Miller. Daniel Miller married Elizabeth Young (Rec. 15). Silas Miller bought land from Jacob Young, June 13 1837 (Rec., Marion, O.).

319 MARGARET YOUNG

The parents of Margaret, her birth, marriage and death dates are unknown. John Young (Rec. 1) left legacies to "the children of my sister Margaret," and named without identifying five of the children: "I give the three daughters of Daniel Carryl, viz.—to Mary, to Peggy, and to Hannah five pounds each," and "I give to Daniel and to Hercules Carryl, sons of Daniel Carryl, to each of them, the sum of ten pounds." The spellings of the name Carrell in the various documents quoted are retained here. The memorial stone to Daniel and Margaret Carrell in the churchyard of the Friends Meeting House, Dover, N. J. was erected by their descendants, Eugene A. and Martin B. Carrell. The latter's widow, Mrs. Elizabeth Bryant Carrell is living, 1947, near Dover, N. J., on a part of the old Carrell homestead, and has aided much in completing this record.

"Daniel Carrell came to America from Northern Ireland in 1730, settling in Virginia. In 1732 he purchased land near Dover, N. J., where his descendants held the homestead in 1902. He married Margaret Young. Mary Carrell, born in 1753, was one of seven children. She married Moses Kerr. G.M." (Gen. Col. #2843, Newark Evening News, Sept. 18 1809). The initials G. M. are those of Gertrude Moodey, great granddaughter of Moses and Mary (Carrell) Kerr.

Mrs. Martin B. Carrell recently gave to her cousin, Charles S. Carrell, of Morristown, N. J., what seems to be the original deed of purchase by Daniel Carrell. Through the kindness of Mr. Carrell we are able to quote from the deed. It is dated "the first day of Dec. in the 10th year of the reign of George the Third, Anno 1770." By the deed, "Daniel Carle, of Mendom, in Morris County, in East Jersey, purchased from Samuel Smith, of Burlington, West Jersey, and Joseph Pemberton, of Philadelphia, Province of Pennsylvania, part of Lot 7 (Center Grove, N. J.), beginning at a white oak tree at a corner of Morgan Young's land . . . thence to a heap of stones being a corner of Morgan Young's land . . . thence to the white oak the place of beginning, containing 254 acres, being part of the land surveyed unto Joseph Kirkbride." Margaret Young was a sister of Morgan (Rec. 2). Her marriage to Daniel Carrell seems to have been a marriage of neighbors. In a "History of Morris County, N. J.," published, 1882, by W. W. Munsell, N. Y., under "Randolph Township," it is written that "a family by the name of Youngs, consisting of Robert, Mitchell, and John Youngs, settled on a farm west of the Carrell property where Lawrence Dalrymple now (1882) lives, but they left no descendants in the township." John Young(s) bought the property of his father Morgan, which the above deed shows adjoined the Carrell land. Mitchell Young was the son of John.

Robert Young probably was he with whom John and N. Mitchell Young quarreled (Rec. 4).

The will of Daniel Carral (Trenton, N .J., 648-N) dated, Oct. 8 1785, was proved, Jan. 17 1786, at Morristown, N. J., by the testimony of John and Hannah Young, and Letters of Administration were granted, Feb. 3 1786, to James Carrell. Nathan Simcock, John and Hannah Young were witnesses to the will. The executors were "my trusty friend John Brotherton and my son James." The Inventory appraised, Feb. 3 1786, by Hartshorn Fitz Randolph and Isaac Hance, was made up "the 13th day of the 1st month, 1786." Daniel does not mention his wife in his will. She probably was dead. He lists eight children: James, whom he calls his eldest son, is given the house in which Daniel is living, his loom and the tackling thereunto belonging, and a part of the plantation. The rest of his home plantation is bequeathed to his three sons, Thomas, Daniel, and Hercules Carrel. Thomas is to have that part of the plantation on which he is living, Daniel and Hercules to share the remaining part. Daniel leaves 5 shillings to his daughter Elizabeth. His moveable estate is to be sold, his debts paid, and the balance is to be equally divided between his daughters, Mary, Hannah, and Sarah. *Peggy* Carryl, called daughter of Daniel by her uncle John Young, does not appear under this name in the will of Daniel.

Daniel Carrell, Morgan Young and Nathan Simcock witnessed the will of Thomas Young, brother of John (Rec. 1) and Margaret Young Carrell.

Eugene A. Carrell, in a family letter dated June 3 1920, listed the children of Daniel and Margaret Carrell. He omitted Elizabeth and Hannah and added John to the list in the will of Daniel.

i. James, is called "my eldest son" in Daniel's will.

ii. Daniel, b. Aug. 30 1745, d. Oct. 19 1838, md. Jane Clutter, b. Mar. 13 1765, d. Feb. 22 1845, daughter of William and Mary (Niblack) Clutter. Daniel had ten children (Mrs. Ella E. Baird, Dover, N. J., daughter of D. Hudson Dalrymple and Sarah Jane Cooper). (1) Mary, 1874-1819, md. Jan. 12 1808, Daniel Dalrymple, b. 1783, d. Jan. 14 1860, brother of Robert who md. Mary Young (Rec. 16). Daniel and Mary had one child who lived beyond infancy, Solomon, b. Aug. 20 1810, d. Jan. 23 1895, md. Jane Smith (1818-1901). One child of Solomon and Jane was Daniel Hudson Dalrymple, b. Oct. 15 1842, d. Apr. 30 1918, md. Sarah Jane Cooper. (2) Sarah, (3) Margaret, (4) Ann, (5) William, (6) James B., b. 1797, md. Elizabeth Baker. One of their children was James H. Carrell, b. 1835, d. July 3 1900, md. Louise

Hulbert (Gravestone, Mt. Freedom, N. J.). A son of James and Louise was Martin Butterworth Carrell, b. Dec. 12 1860, d. 1933, md. Elizabeth M. Bryant, b. 1866, daughter of Dorastus Logan and Caroline (Snelling) Bryant. She is living, 1947, on a part of the old Carrell homestead. (7) Eliza, (8) Hannah, (9) Samuel D., (10) John Lewis Carrell, b. Mar. 27 1811, d. Apr. 16 1885, md. Nov. 25 1827, Emily Dalrymple (1819-1867), daughter of Henry and Harriet (Hoagland) Dalrymple. Their children: Charles Henry, b. June 19 1839, d. July 30 1862; James Willson, b. Aug. 27 1840, d. Mar. 9 1894, md. Dec. 23 1874, Ella Searing, a son of whom is Charles Searing Carrell, b. Sept. 2 1884, md. Oct. 19 1910, Mary Toms, and lives in Morristown, N. J. Charles and Mary had two sons, James S., b. Oct. 19 1911, and Stuart Toms Carrell, b. Apr. 2 1913, d. Sept. 13 1940; Alonzo; Laura Augusta; and Eugene Ayers Carrell, b. Dec. 6 1852, d. July 6 1942, md. June 23 1880, Hannah Adele Day, b. Apr. 13 1856, d. Nov. 29 1919.

iii. Thomas, Daniel, and Hercules Carrell were living in Fallowfield township, Washington county, Pa. in 1790 (U. S. Census). Thomas Carrell, William Young and Andrew Bryant witnessed, 1777, the will of Wm. Olliver, in Morris county, N. Y. Thomas died in 1825, and his wife Elizabeth Richey in 1834, says Mrs. J. I. Tod, a descendant, who lists their children: James, Daniel, Hannah, Thomas, John, Stephen, and Hercules Carrell. Thos. Carrell, jr. md. about 1805, in Pennsylvania, Hannah Kerr, a first cousin, daughter of Moses and Mary (Carrell) Kerr. Two of the children of Thomas and Hannah were: Eliza, who md. R. D. Cottrell and lived in Hillsdale, Mich., and Wm. Parkinson Carrel, who was born in Mentor, O. Wm. moved about 1847 to Royalton, O. where he md. Elizabeth Waite, an English girl. A son of Wm. and Elizabeth was Moses Gary Carrel, b. at Royalton, O., d. and was buried at Mentor, O. Moses md. Jennie Bailey, and lived in Reading, Mich. from where they moved to Hillsdale, Mich. Lou C. Carrel, daughter of Moses and Jennie, b. Aug. 11 1876, at Reading, Mich., md. Jonathan Ingersoll Tod, Sept. 16 1902, at Cleveland, O., is living, 1947, at Tampa, Fla. Mr. and Mrs. Tod have three children: Carrel

Ingersoll, b. Jan. 29 1905, at Avalon, Pa.; David, b. Aug. 9 1908, at Bellevue, Pa.; and Elizabeth (Tod) Johnson, b. July 1 1912.

iv. Hercules, b. 1773, d. Jan. 1 1886, md. Sarah Wheeler, d. 1824. He is said to have had 16 children, one of whom, James, md. June Todd, d. Jan. 13 1886. Hercules and his brother Thomas in 1812 witnessed a sale of property by Silas Young, husband of Hannah Carrel, their sister (Rec. Washington, Pa.).

v. Elizabeth, named in her father's will but not in that of John Young (Rec. 1).

vi. Mary, b. May 4 1753, d. July 29 1832, bur. Mentor, O. She md. Moses Kerr, b. Apr. 29 1763, d. Oct. 4 1834, and lived near Pittsburgh, Pa. before moving to Ohio. The records at Washington, Pa. show a sale of land in 1810 by Silas Young to Moses Carr (Kerr). Silas Young was a brother-in-law of Hannah Kerr who md. Thomas Carrell. Descendants of Thos. and Hannah Carrell spelled their name Carroll. Kerr's Mill, now Fredericktown, O. received its name from a member of this family. Moses and Mary Kerr had six children (Miss Antoinette P. Moodey, Plainfield, N. J.): (1) William, b. 1784, d. 1868, Mentor, O., md. Ann Moodey (1797-1859) in 1812. (2) Hannah, b. 1787, d. 1863, Lyons, O., md. Thomas Carrell, b. 1780, d. 1859, Willoughby, O., son of Thos. and Elizabeth (Richey) Carrell. Their children spelled the name Carroll. (3) Margaret, b. Apr. 6 1790, Washington county, Pa., d. Mar. 3 1873, Painesville, O., md. Apr. 6 1815, Robert Moodey. They celebrated their golden wedding anniversary, Apr. 6 1865, with some 70 relatives assisting, at Painesville. One of their children was Moses Kerr Moodey, b. Sept. 20 1820, d. May 6 1883, md. Hannah Maria Chapin. A son of Moses and Hannah is Herbert Lyman Moodey, b. Mar. 30 1860, at Brooklyn, N. Y., and living, 1947, at Plainfield, N. J. He md. July 12 1882, at Painesville, O., Helen Antoinette Paine, b. Sept. 22 1862, at Painesville, d. Apr. 8 1920, at Plainfield, N. J. A daughter of Herbert and Helen is Antoinette Paine Moodey, b. May 15 1884, at Minneapolis, Minn. She lives with her father. (4) Daniel 1791, d. Aug. 6 1871, Painesville, O., md. Catherine Cass (1791-1878). (5) Levi Jay, b. 1794,

d. May 7 1869, Painesville, O., md. Elma Lawrence, Oct. 5 1826. (6) Mary, b. 1797, d. 1879, Pittsburgh, Pa., md. July 3 1827, James Gray, b. 1780, d. 1857.

vii. Hannah, md. Silas Young who was living in 1797 in Fallowfield township, Washington county, Pa. from where the family moved to Geauger county, O. On Oct. 30 1810, Silas and Hannah Young, of Geauger county, O. sold to Moses Carr (Kerr) his property in Washington county, Pa. Rec. Bk. I-V, p. 241, Washington, Pa.). Hercules and Thomas Carrell were witnesses to this deed. The land was warranted to Silas Young, Jan. 16 1797.

viii. Sarah

320 ANNY YOUNG

sister of John (Rec. 1), who made her son, John Clark, jr. one of his legatees, joined the Newark (Kennett) Quaker Meeting, at Kennett Square, Chester county, Pa. in 1742, and the same year in this Meeting, married John Clark (Quaker rec., Philadelphia, Pa). When the family moved to N. J. is not known. Anny's brother, Hercules, transferred from the Newark Meeting to the Woodbridge Meeting, N. J. in 1749. A John Clark witnessed the will (made 1749, proved 1750) of John Chapman which disposed of land in Chester county, Pa. (Wills, N. J. Archives). The Chapmans and the Clarks may have moved to N. J. about the same time (Rec. 7 shows an alliance of the Youngs and Chapmans). John and Hannah Young (Rec. 6), on Apr. 1 1788, sold land in Hanover township, Morris county, N. J., that was adjacent to the land of John Clark (Deed Bk. A, p. 355, Morristown, N. J. John Young (wife, Hannah) was a nephew of Mrs. John Clark. John Young (Rec. 1) may have left a legacy to Nathaniel Doty because of a connection by marriage. Nathaniel Doty married, 1753, Abigail, daughter of Henry Clark, of Shongum and Rockaway. John Doughty (?Doty) was a witness to the will of John Young. These items are offered for someone's study.

No descendant of John and Anny Clark is known. Their son, John, may have been the elder of the Rockaway Church who died, July 26 1828, and whose six children are named by J. P. Crayon, in his "Rockaway Records," p. 223. The name of John's wife is not given.

321 HERCULES YOUNG

John Young, in his will (Rec. 1), twice bequeaths sums "to the children of my brother Hercules" but he does not name any of them. No descendant of Hercules has been identified.

Hercules Young joined the Newark (Kennett) Quaker Meeting, Kennett Square, Chester county, Pa., July 4 1742, and in this same Meeting, he married Feb. 1745, Sarah, daughter of James Phillips (? relatives of John Phillips, Rec. 313). Hercules and Sarah transferred to the Quaker Meeting at Woodbridge, N. J., Jan. 4 1749. Mary (Rec. 321), sister of Hercules, married in the Woodbridge Meeting in 1746. ("Newark Quaker Minutes, 1739-91, Ch. 12-F," Hist. Soc. of Pa., Philadelphia.) These marriage records of Hercules and his sister Anny contain the earliest authentic dates we have for our Young family. They suggest that our Young family were related to Morgan and Mary Young, of the Philadelphia Quaker Meeting, whose daughter, Mary, was born, Dec. 26 1690. ("Encyclopedia of Amer. Quaker Genealogy," Vol. 2, p. 329).

Hercules Young and Benj. Hart made an Inventory, March 7 1763, of the estate of Thomas Throckmorton, of Roxbury, N. J. William Young (Rec. 3) nephew of Hercules, married Miriam (Drake) Throckmorton, widow of Thomas.

Hercules was one of the earliest of our numerous kin who emigrated from New Jersey to Pennsylvania and Ohio. Hercules, John and Silas Young, in this order, signed, Nov. 5 1784, "A Petition of sundry inhabitants of the township of Fallowfield, in the county of Washington, Pa. to change the location of one Justice so that he would be more easily reached." (State Archives, Harrisburg, Pa., P.R.P. Vol. 23, p. 65). Silas Young, unidentified, married Hannah Carrell (Rec. 319). John Young (Rec. 6) was the son-in-law of Abigail (Harris) Mitchell, who with her brothers Thomas, George and John Harris, emigrated from N. J. in 1787 to Washington county, Pa. John and Silas Young are listed as heads of families in Washington county, Pa. in the U. S. Census of 1790, as also is Morgan Young, jr.

The following items copied from the records in the Recorder's office at Chillicothe, O. may refer to the family of Hercules. In 1800, before the State of Ohio was created, the record of N. M. Young's (Rec. 14) purchase in the Northwest Territory was filed at Chillicothe.

Item 1. Deed dated Nov. 1 1834. Jacob Young and Frances, his wife, of Highland County, Ohio, give a quit claim to Hercules Young, for certain land on Paint Creek, Ross County, Concord township, survey 3975.

Item 2. Deed dated Dec. 15 1834. Hercules Young and Margaret, his wife, sell to George Bargle, land situated on the north fork of Paint Creek, Concord township, Ross County, Ohio.

Item 3. Deed dated May 29 1852. Hercules Young and Margaret, his wife, sell to William W. Young, land in Concord township, Ross County, land granted to Thomas Patterson by the President, conveyed to John Cowley, conveyed to Jacob Young, on the north fork of Paint Creek, touching the land of H. Young and John Ferrel.

Item 4. Quit claim, dated June 17 1889, given to Andrew J. Timmons (Limmons), Executor of Hercules Young, for $1.00, on land in Concord township, Ross County, by the heirs of Hercules Young, deceased, by William W. Young and Sophia, of Westerville, Franklin County, by James and Eliza A. Young, of Westerville, by Nelson B. and Martha A. Young, of Fayette County, Ohio, by Isabella and Nancy E. Young, both single, of Frankfort, Ross County, Ohio.

322 THOMAS YOUNG

Yeoman, of Pequannock, Morris County, Province of East Jersey, is the last of the immigrant eight brothers and sisters of our Young family to be recorded in this work. Like his brothers and sisters he was a Quaker. This is an all important item in that it distinguishes the early members of our family from other Young families in colonial New Jersey. The will of Thomas Young (264N, Trenton, N. J.) which follows is abstracted in the "N. J. Archives." It was "affirmed," in Quaker fashion, March 6 1769, which places the death of Thomas between this date and the date of the will, Feb. 18 1769. His executors were his "Trusty friends," James Brotherton and Thomas Carol (Rec. 319), and his witnesses were, Daniel Carol, Morgin Young (Rec. 2) and Nathan Simcock. He probably was buried in an unmarked grave in the yard of the Randolph Friends Meeting House, near Dover, N. J. The record of his marriage, April 19 1743, to Thankfull Robarts, is recorded in the "Combined Register of the 1st. Presbyterian Church, Morristown, N. J."

The Will of Thomas Young

"I, Thomas Young, of Pequannock, in the County of Morris and the Province of East Jersey, Yeoman, being very sick of body but of sound and perfect mind and memory, praises be given to Almighty God therefor: do make and ordain this my last will and testament, in manner and form following (that is to say), First and principally, I recommend my soul to God that gave it and my body I commit to the earth to be buried in a decent and christian like manner at the discretion of my executors hereafter mentioned; and as touching the disposition of all such temporal estate as it hath pleased God to bestow upon me, I give, devise and dispose thereof in manner and form following, viz:—

First, I will and do order that all my just debts and funeral charges be fully paid and discharged ———

Item, It is my will and I do order that all my personal or moveable estate shall be sold as soon after my decease as it can conveniently be done, except one feather bed and bedding which I give to my loving wife Thankfull.

Item, I give, devise and bequeath to my son Arthur thirty acres of land off of the upper end of my house lot, and to his heirs and assigns forever.

Item, I give to my loving wife Thankfull all my house lot, to her only proper use and behoof so long as she remains my widow and in lieu of her dower and right of thirds and for the bringing up of my children until they are fit to put out to trades, and it is my will and desire that they should be put to trades when they are fit, and I do hereby authorize and impower my executors to allow so much out of my estate as shall be reasonable for the bringing up my children aforesaid more than what is already allowed. It is further my will and I do order that if my said wife marry after my decease that my executors shall sell the said home lot or if she remain my widow then the same to be sold after her decease and all my other lands wheresoever and whatsoever as soon after my decease as may be convenient for the advantage of my estate and the benefit of my children and the money my said land shall sell for to be put to interest for the use of my four sons, Thomas, Morgain, Daniel and David and paid to them in the following manner, viz: to my son Thomas, one fourth part, to my son Morgain, one fourth part, to my son Daniel, one fourth part, to my son David, one fourth part, to be paid to them severally and as they arrive to the age of one and twenty years, and I do hereby authorize and impower my executors to make, do and execute any Deed or Deeds, conveyance or conveyances for my lands aforesaid as fully and as absolutely as I myself might or could do were I alive and personally present.

Item, I give to my six daughters all the money my personal estate shall sell for which I would have put to interest or so much thereof as shall be left and remain after all my just debts and funeral charges are paid and discharged and paid to my said daughters in manner following, viz:

To my daughter Margaret one sixth part to be paid to her within one year after my decease, to my daughter Elizabeth one sixth part to be paid to her one year after my decease, to my daughter Phebe one sixth part to be paid to her when she arrives to the age of 18 years, to my daughter Thankfull one sixth part to be paid to her when she arrives to the age of 18 years, to my daughter Mary one sixth part to be paid to her when she arrives to the age of 18 years, to my daughter Hannah one sixth part to be paid to her when she arrives to the age of 18 years, and if any of my children should die under age or without issue, it is my will that such child's part be equally divided among the rest of my children, if a son amongst the sons and if a daughter, the daughters.

And lastly, I do make, ordain, constitute and appoint my trusty friends James Brotherton and Thomas Carol my executors of this my last will and testament, and I do hereby disannul all former and other wills by me heretofor made or expressed to be made, ratifying and allowing this and no other to be my last will and testament, in witness whereof I have hereunto set my hand and seal this eighteenth day of the month called February in the year of our Lord one thousand seven hundred and sixty nine.

Thomas Young
his mark

Signed, sealed, published, pronounced and declared by the testator to be his last will and testament in the presence of us—
Daniel Carol, his mark
Morgin Young
Nathan Simcock

Morris County, N. J. Morgan Young and Nathan Simcock two of the witnesses of the within will being [*duly sworn on the Holy Evangel of Almighty God*] two of the people called Quakers did severally declare and affirm that they saw Thomas Young the testator therein named sign and seal the same and heard him pronounce and declare the within testament to be his last will and testament, and at the doing thereof the said testator was of sound and disposing mind and memory as far as these affirmants know and as they verily believe and that Daniel Carol, the other subscribing evidence was present and signed his name as a witness together with these affirmants in the presence of the testator.

Morgin Young
Nathan Simcock

Affirmed the sixth day
of March An. Dom. 1769
before me,
Abraham Ogden, Surr.

The alteration from an oath to an affirmation being first made before the affirmation taken. Abraham Ogden, Surr.

Morris County, N. J. James Brotherton and Thomas Carol, two of the executors in the within testament named being two of the people called Quakers did severally declare and affirm that the within testament contains the true last will and testament of Thomas Young the testator therein named and so far as they know, and as they verily believe, and that they will well and truly perform the same by paying first the debts of the said deceased and then the legacies in the said testament specified so far as the goods, chattels and credits of the same deceased can thereunto extend and that they will make and exhibit into the Surrogative Office at Perth Amboy a true and perfect inventory of all and singular the goods, chattels and credits of the said deceased that have or shall come to their knowledge or possession or to the possession of any other person or persons for their use and render a just and true account when thereunto lawfully required.

Affirmed the seventh day of
March Anno Dom. 1769
before me.

Abraham Ogden, Surr.

James Brotherton
Thomas Carrel

Mr. Hugh D. Vail, transcribing from the Woodbridge-Rahway-Plainfield Quaker records in the "N. Y. Gen. & Biog. Record" (July 1878, p. 28), lists nine of the eleven children of Thomas and Thankfull and gives their birth dates. In this transcription the names of Hannah and David are omitted, and there is obviously an error in the birth date of Morgan or Daniel. Mr. Vail notes the fact that several members of the Mendham Quaker Meeting, a branch of the Woodbridge Meeting, came from Craigforth, Aberdeen County, Scotland. The children:

				day	*month*	*year*
323.	i.	Arthur,	b.	10	7	1744
	ii.	Margaret,	b.	15	4	1746
324.	iii.	Elizabeth,	b.	27	2	1748
	iv.	Phebe,	b.	19	9	1750
325.	v.	Thomas,	b.	13	11	1752
	vi.	Thankfull,	b.	26	4	1756
326.	vii.	Morgan,	b.	18	10	1758
327.	viii.	Daniel,	b.	20	2	1759
	ix.	Mary,	b.	16	5	1761
	x.	Hannah				
328.	xi.	David				

John Young, in his will (Rec. 1), speaks of Thomas as "my deceased brother" and leaves a legacy to each of his children. He names two of these nephews, "Thomas Young, son of Thomas Young," and "Morgan Young, son of Thomas Young."

Thomas Young, according to the records of the Proprietors of East New Jersey, Perth Amboy, made four purchases of land on the Rockaway river between 1751 and 1761. His first purchase, about six months after his brother John had bought on the Rockaway, was on the east side of the river, one mile below Jackson's forge. The second was at "Sucksunna" (Succasunna). The third purchase was made "at the request of the heirs of Thomas Hartshorn" from Adam Miller (Rec. 321), husband of Thomas' sister Mary. The last purchase was on the north side of the Rockaway river.

Mr. T. F. Chambers ("Early Germans, and Other Early Settlers in N. J., 1893, p. 579"), writing about the "Youngs of Draketown," lists the children of Thomas as they are given in Thomas' will, and expresses the belief that Daniel, son of Thomas, probably was he who left a will dated in 1786. See Record 327.

323 ARTHUR YOUNG

son of Thomas and Thankfull Young was born, July 10 1744, in Pequannock, Morris County, N. J. (Quaker rec.). There are good reasons for thinking that he wrote the will dated, April 15 1822, which was recorded at Newton, N. J., Sept. 4 1822. The language of the testator suggests that he was a Quaker or of Quaker origin. His executors are "my son Silas and my *trusty friend* David King of Morris County." The will begins "Arthur Young, now of Newton, Sussex County, N. J. but late of Morris County." The witnesses to the will were: James Iliff, Isaac Struble, and John Sickles. The name of Arthur's wife is not found. She perhaps died before he went to live with his son Silas. Arthur's legacies were: "to the children of my deceased son James"; "to my daughter Hannah Little (Elias)"; "to my daughter Elizabeth Lindley"; "to my granddaughter Elizabeth Bailess"; "to my son Silas"; "to the children of my deceased son Thomas." His farm of 96 acres near Dover, Morris County, is to be sold and "payment is to be made to Silas for my keep from the time that I came to live with him."

Arthur Young was amongst the Freeholders of Pequannock who pledged themselves to the Continental Congress in 1766. Like other Quakers of the area, he was a contributor to the building of the Rockaway Presbyterian Church. He sold, May 1st. 1815, property to Asa, son of Titus Berry (Rec., Morristown, N. J., Bk. II-102). The following children were named in his will:

329. i. James, died, according to his father's will, before 1822.

ii. Hannah, md. March 10 1797, Elias Little.

iii. Elizabeth, md. ——— Lindley.

iv. Silas, perhaps was he who wrote the will dated, July 29 1835, recorded, Nov. 9 1835, at Morristown, N. J. His wife was Mary P. Young, and three of their children were:

Harriet W., Arthur, and William. A witness to this will was Wm. A. Wood (Rec. 330).

v. Thomas, was dead in 1822. He md. and had children. A Thomas Young md. Sept. 22 1806, Susan Berry. (Essex Marriages," "Gen. Mag. of N. J.") Susan Young was named guardian of Malinda, Jane, Sarah and John Young, children of Thomas Young, Dec. 15 1815. (Morristown, N. J. record). Susan Berry was the name of the wife of James Young, Record 330.

324 ELIZABETH YOUNG

born, Feb. 27 1748, in Pequannock, Morris County, N. J., died May 12 1794. She married James Lum (b. June 7 1747, d. May 4 1805, son of Obadiah), a Revolutionary soldier in Capt. Josiah Hall's Co. of Denville, N. J. He witnessed a deed, Apr. 1 1788, of John Young, cousin of his wife (Rec. 6). The family lived at Franklin, N. J. They had nine children ("Lum Gen.," Edw. H. Lum, Chatham, N. J.). A great granddaughter, Caroline Hurd, md. Sept. 6 1843, William A. Wood, son of William and Susannah (Berry) (Young) Wood (Rec. 330). Children of James and Elizabeth Young Lum:

i. Margaret, 1768-1846
ii. Nancy, 1771-1813
iii. Daniel, 1772-1844
iv. John, 1775-1777
v. Hannah, 1777-1823
vi. Elizabeth, 1779-1855
vii. Squire, 1781-1854
viii. Irana, 1785-1862
ix. Dency, 1788-

325 THOMAS YOUNG, JR.

was born, Nov. 13 1752, in Pequannock, Morris County, N. J. (Rec. 323). He was a legatee of his uncle John (Rec. 1). He and his brother Arthur are on the tax list of Mendham, N. J. for 1780. Earlier they are listed in Pequannock. No descendants are known.

A THOMAS YOUNG OF ADAMS COUNTY, OHIO

arrived there about the same time as did Morgan Young (Rec. 9). He bought land about 4 miles west of West Union, O., in 1808, and is listed as a Resident-Proprietor of Adams Co. in 1810 (State Lib., Columbus, O.). He md. June 11 1808, at West Union, Rachel McIntire. John Young, of Seaman, O., (Rec. 328) supplied the names of their children: I. Thomas, II. Andrew, III. William, IV. Rachel, V. Jane, VI. Joseph.

I. Thomas, jr., of Eagle Creek, md. Cynthia Holmes and had 6 children: a. Angus, b. Newton, c. James, d. Nancy, b. Aug. 6 1848, md. ——— Riffle, and had a son Charles W. Riffle, e. Sarah, md. James Shell and had 8 children: Thos. Edgar, b. June 26 1876, d. Dec. 21 1944, md. Feb. 7 1912, Blanche Kleinknecht; Nannie, md. ——— Roush, of Wayne Township; Mary Isabel, b. Mar. 15 1879, d. Nov. 4 1944, md. a Mr. Ellis; William; Ira; Ray; George; and Sheridan Shell, f. Andrew Young, b. Apr. 11 1854, md. Elizabeth Ann Bell and had 12 children: (1) Nora, b. Feb. 26 1874; (2) Henry Newton, b. Mar. 1 1875; (3) Thomas, b. Dec. 22 1876, md. Dec. 18 1901, Ida Pearl Hook, at Manchester, O. and lives at Cherry Fork. They have 4 children, (a) Franklin Andrew, b. Nov. 5 1906, at Hickory Ridge, Brown Co., O., md. Rose Ellen Minzler, Sept. 5 1935, at Wilmington, O. (b) Esta Faye, b. June 26 1909, md. Feb. 9 1927, George Watters, at New Antioch, O. (c) Cora Mildred, b. June 28 1912, at Ripley, O., md. Glenn Howard, Sept. 5 1936, at Cincinnati, O., and (d) Raymond Carl Young, b. Oct. 3 1915, near West Union, O., md. Aug. 17 1935, Mary Ruth Minzler; (4) John; (5) Etta, b. Mar. 25 1881, md. a Mr. Dalrymple and lives at Gallipolis, O.; (6) Otto, b. Aug. 7 1882; (7) Bell, b. Jan. 11 1885; (8) William, b. Sept. 1 1887; (9) Leroy, b. Apr. 5 1889; (10) Dennie, b. July 27 1891; (11) Harley, b. Mar. 21 1895; and (12) Mae Young, b. May 25 1897. II. Andrew (1812-1852), of Youngsville, O., md. Elizabeth Ann Dryden and had 3 children: Mary Elizabeth, Thomas A., and James Wilson Young, b. May 30 1848, md. Oct. 10 1877, and had 5 children: Otto W.; Nelle, b. 1884, md. M. T. Kepperling; John Harvey, b. 1887; Elmer A. and Harvey B. Young, b. 1896. III. William, b. 1819, d. July 6 1892, at West Union, O., md. ——— Hemphill, d. Sept. 7 1870, and had one child, John, b. Nov. 13 1858, d. 1941, md. Mary Kendall. John and Mary K. Young had one child, the Rev. Hodson K. Young, living 1947, at Cincinnati, O. IV. Rachel, md. a Mr. Diboll and had a son Charles who lives at Wilmington, O. V. Jane md. and moved to Iowa. VI. Joseph was killed in the Civil War.

326 MORGAN YOUNG

identified as the son of Thomas, deceased, in the will of his uncle John (Rec. 1), was born in Oct. 1752 in Morris County, N. J. and was 80 years old when he applied, Nov. 19 1832, as a resident of Berkshire Township,

Delaware County, O., for a pension for service as a private in the Revolutionary war. (Pension Application, S-4-741). The Quaker record (Rec. 323) places his birth on "the 18th day, of the 10th month, in the year 1758," and the birth of Thomas in 1752. The Quaker record as transscribed is faulty. It omits two of Thomas' children, and is obviously wrong about the birth date of either Morgan or Daniel. Morgan died, Jan. 1 1844, in the 96th year of his age, according to the inscription on his tombstone in the cemetery at Galena, O. He was buried beside his wife, on whose gravestone is written: "In Memory of Elizabeth, Wife of Morgan Young, died Jan. 8 1839, in the 86th year of her age." The family name of Elizabeth is unknown. Morgan's name is spelled *Morgain* in his father's will, and also in some N. J. land deeds. His family name is variously written, Youngs, Yong and Yongs.

Morgan said in his pension application that he left New Jersey for Wyoming County, Pa. "about 20 years after the close of the war and lived in Wyoming County about 15 years before going to Delaware County, O." This description of his travels is confirmed by official records. The Census for 1840 of "Veterans of the Revolutionary War still Living" lists Morgan, age 89, living with his son, Andrew, in Sunbury Township, Delaware County, O. It is recorded in Deed Book, No. 1, at Morristown, N. J., that "Morgain Young, and Elizabeth, his wife, of Washington Township, sold, Oct. 8 1801, Hacklebarney Forge and the land around it, on Black river to L. Freeman." "Morgain Yongs, and Elizabeth his wife, of Kingston Township, Luzerne County, Pa. sold land May 1 1816, for $1500.00 to Jacob Frantz (Wilkes-Barre, Pa., Bk. 21, p. 327). This sale was not recorded until April 4 1821. On July 20 1816 Morgan Young, of Sunbury Township, bought from Samuel Heath for $700.00 land adjoining that sold the same day to Thomas Young, along the Walnut Creek. Thomas' deed of purchase has a note on it which reads: "the name Morgan Young was erased and Thomas Young inserted in lieu thereof before signing." (Delaware, O. rec.) Thomas was the son of Morgan and grandson of Thomas Young, of Pequannock, N. J.

Morgan, son of Thomas Young, could have been he who is listed in the tax reports for Catawissa Township, Northumberland County, Pa. for 1786, with 30 acres of land, and for 1787, with 300 acres, provided he had left N. J. earlier than he said he did. The compiler thinks this Northumberland Morgan may have been the son of Robert Young (Rec. 313). The census of 1790 for Northumberland shows the family of Morgan to have consisted of one boy over 16; one boy between 10 and 16; and two girls. The census of 1800 shows 1 male and 1 female over 45; one male and one female between 16 and 26, and places the family in Fishing Creek Township, Northumberland County.

When the census of 1810 was taken, the family of our subject was listed in the Kingston District of Luzerne County, Pa. where Morgan and Elizabeth went about 1801 (Pension papers). The family consisted of 1 male and 1 female over 26 years of age, two boys between 16 and 26, and one girl between 16 and 26. In 1820, Morgan and Elizabeth with two sons, Andrew and Elijah, were living in Sunbury Township, Delaware County, O. Thomas, a third son, was there also, listed in the census as the head of a family. Morgan and Elizabeth sold land, in equal parts, to their sons, Elijah and Andrew, Sept. 10 1822 (Delaware, O., Bk. 6, p. 166).

Morgan describes his war service with N. J. troops as follows: he was called out with the Militia in the Spring of 1776 to Elizabethtown where he enlisted for 5 months in Capt. Gaston's Company, Col. Munson's Regiment, and was in the battle of Long Island; during 1777 and 1778 he served 3 tours of one month each, one month under Capt. Carnes and Col. Frelinghuysen, one month under Capt. Samuel Morris, and one month under Capt. Wm. Young and General Wayne, and was in the battle of Elizabethtown. Morgan's record in the Office of the Adj. General at Trenton, N. J. shows that he served as a private in the Eastern Reserve Regiment, Morris County Militia, under Captains Zopher Carver, Joseph Morris and Robert Young, and was residing in Delaware County, O. in 1832. Morgan was granted a pension of $30. per annum. He was blind for many years due to his war service. Morgan and Elizabeth Young had four (perhaps 5) children, all born in New Jersey.

330. i. Thomas, b. 1785
331. ii. Andrew, b. 1790
332. iii. Elijah
iv. Daughter, see Rec. 332.

327 DANIEL YOUNG

son of Thomas and Thankfull was born in Pequannock Township, Morris County, N. J., Feb. 20 1759. (Friends, "Rahway, Plainfield Meeting Rec." R. S. 379 B. p. 29) This date or that of the birth of his brother, Morgan (Rec. 326) is wrong.

T. F. Chambers in his "Early Germans and Other Early Settlers in N. J., 1893," under the heading "The Youngs of Draketown," p. 579, lists the children of Thomas Young and says that Daniel was "probably he who left the will, dated Hanover, June 1 1786, of Budd's Lake (but may have been, Daniel, son of Stephen, son of Robert, the Scotsman, of Newark)." The compiler believes that Daniel moved from N. J. to Penn. and Ohio, as did his brother Morgan and several of his cousins, together with their allied families. He perhaps was Daniel Young, of Jefferson Township, Adams County, O., who was married for the second time, Aug. 23 1825, by Henry Young, J. P., to Dorcas Coonrod, widow of John. Daniel then gave his age as 64 ("The Village Register," Aug. 25 1825, West Union, O.). Evans and Stivers, in their "History of Adams County, O., 1900," say that "Daniel Young, paternal great grandfather of the Hon. John Brooks Young, was a soldier in a N. J. regiment during the Revolution. He was a pensioner, died in Adams County and was buried in Foster cemetery, Green Township." It was to Adams County that Morgan Young (Rec. 9) and the Coonrod family came from Washington County, Pa. No pension record for Daniel has been found but the N. J. files show a Daniel Young as having served during the Revolution. Mitchell ("Mitch") Morrison Young (1855-1942), of near West Union, O., told the writer that Daniel and Morgan Young were related but that he had forgotten the relationship. Mrs. Myrtle (Young) Osman, of Adams County, great granddaughter of Daniel, has family records which show that Thomas, son of Daniel, was born, Sept. 4 1783, in Pennsylvania. The name of Daniel's first wife is not known.

The only mention of Daniel in the records of Adams County, O. is in a Quit claim given by his son Samuel and the latter's wife Sarah to Daniel and his heirs, Apr. 1 1817. He was living in Jefferson Township in 1820 (U. S. Census). The children of Daniel and his first wife were supplied by Mitchell M. Young. The order of birth is uncertain.

333. i. Thomas W., b. Sept. 4 1783
334. ii. David
iii. Samuel, md. Sarah ——.
335. iv. John
336. v. William K., b. 1796
337. vi. George, b. Dec. 25 1799
vii. Hiram
viii. Polly
ix. Agnes
x. Rhoda

328 DAVID YOUNG

son of Thomas and Thankfull (Robarts) Young is named in his father's will, as also is his sister Hannah. Both children are omitted in the Quaker list of Thomas' children (Rec. 325). Nothing more is known about David.

A DAVID YOUNG OF ADAMS COUNTY, O.

whose parents are unidentified by his descendants may have been one of our

Young family. He is one of four with the name Young shown on an "Official List of Resident-Proprietors of Adams County, O. in 1810" (State Lib., Columbus, O.). Descendants of his son, James, say that David came to Ohio from Fincastle, Va. Fire in 1910 destroyed most of the vital statistics of Adams County but two books were saved and in one of these it is recorded that on Aug. 1 1801, David Young was married to Mary Morrison, at West Union, by Thomas Kirker, J.P. Our further record of David and Mary comes from the Deed Books at West Union; from the family Bible of James, their son; from an unsigned letter about family relationships written on the stationary of F. D. Bayless, Attorney, at West Union, O. (doubtless written by his second wife); and from data furnished by Marie Bayless, granddaughter of James Young. David Young served as Ensign in the War of 1812 in Capt. Morrison's company.

David bought, Jan. 30 1806, 178½ acres on Cherry Fork of Brush Creek, in Wayne Township, from James and Susannah January, and two days later, sold 60 acres to Samuel Paul who, on Apr. 12 1808, sold the land to Thomas Young, unidentified but probably he who married, June 11 1808, Rachel McIntire, and who was a Resident-Proprietor in 1810 (Rec. 325). John Young (1858-1941), of Seaman, O., grandson of Thomas and Rachel, told the writer that Thomas settled on Hill's Fork, about 4 miles west of West Union. David Young in 1810 was living on 118½ acres of land originally entered for David Jackson. On Feb. 21 1817, David and Mary sold part of their land, in common, to Robert (wife, Nancy) and James Young (wife, Sarah). On March 14 1833, David made three sales, seemingly to three sons, since the price was $1.00: to Joseph, land adjoining that he sold in 1817 to Robert, to James F. Young, and to David H. Young, jr., land adjoining that of Edward Young. Andrew Young witnessed these Deeds. There is a recording of part of David's will, lost in the fire, in the land books at West Union which shows that the will was made Aug. 20 1842 and that it ordered the sale after his death of land touching that of James F., of James D., and of John C. Young. David's last sale, Dec. 24 1842, was to John Young, of land touching that of David H. Young, jr. David died, Jan. 3 1843, and his wife, Polly, Sept. 22 1842. Four children of David and Mary are identified in the Bible of his son, James. Mitchell M. Young (1854-1942), of near West Union, says that Andrew and Robert Young were sons of David.

i. Jane, b. Apr. 25 1807, d. Aug. 13 1849, md. Aug. 23 1825, at W. U., Ohio, Samuel C. Wasson, b. Mar. 21 1804, d. Aug. 11 1849. Steward Wasson, bro. of Samuel, had a son James M. who md. Mary Jackson. Two children of Stewart, Samuel C. Wasson, 3rd., and Mrs. Chas. W. Purcell live in Winchester, O.

ii. James Finley, b. Feb. 7 1811, d. Dec. 24 1891, had a store in Youngsville, O. in 1840, md. (1) Aug. 9 1832, Ann Chapman who d. Oct. 7 1838. He md. (2) Jan. 11 1842, Eliza Hooper, d. June 29 1889, daughter of Mary Hooper Snelbacker, d. Apr. 5 1867, daughter of Daniel. James and Ann had 4 children: (1) John Chapman, b. July 16 1833, d. July 21 1833; (2) Andrew Peace, b. July 6 1834, d. July 20 1834; (3) Joseph S., b. Aug. 23 1835, d. Mar. 21 1909, md. Rachel ———, and lived in Monmouth, Ill. Joseph had 5 children: Mary and Helen, now living in Calif., Charles, Fanny, md. Mr. Parsons, and Bertha Young; (4) James Darius, b. July 9 1837, md. Jan. 9 1862, Mary Ann Phillips.

James and Eliza Young had 7 children: (1) Mary Ann, b. Nov. 16 1842, md. Edward Silcott; (2) Helen Maria, b. Jan. 28 1844, md. Nov. 22 1869, Franklin DeCamp Bayless, b. Feb. 2 1839, d. Feb. 2 1919, a lawyer, at West Union, O. He was the son of Elze and Jane DeCamp (dau. of David) Bayless who came to Ohio from Louden County, Va. Earlier the Bayless family lived in N. Y. and N. J. and there were allied by marriage with the Youngs. Helen is said to have been a cousin of John Brooks Young, great grandson of Daniel Young (Rec. 327). F. D. and Helen Bayless had 2 children, Marie DeCamp, b. Oct. 28 1877, and Beatrice Bayless; (3) William Thornton, b. May 29 1845, md. Miss Burwell and had two children, Lillie and Maude Young. (4) Samuel Marion, b. Jan. 16 1848, d. July 10 1848; (5) Esther (Hester), b. Sept. 20 1851, d. Dec. 12 1859; (6) David Fisher, b. Dec. 25 1854, d. Sept. 4 1859; and (7) Fannie Elnora Young, b. July 3 1861, md. 1st. July 3 1878, at Youngsville, John D. White, and lived at Georgetown, O. where 2 children were born: Wm. Chilton, b. Sept. 17 1879, and Jessie White, b. Mar. 3 1882, d. Jan. 4 1893. After the death of Mr. White, Fannie md. Oct. 8 1885, F. D. Bayless, widower of her sister Helen. One child, Gwendolyn Bayless, b. Nov. 6 1894.

iii. Mary Ann (Polly), d. Sept. 18 1847

iv. David H. jr., md. May 23 1832, Mary Sharp, of Scott Township. He had a store at Youngsville, O.

v. Joseph, was md. Mar. 14 1826, to Elizabeth (?Walker) by the Rev. Wm. Baldridge.
vi. Andrew
vii. Robert

329 JAMES YOUNG

began his will thus: "The will of James Young of Hardiston Township, Sussex County, N. J., son of Arthur of Morris County, Dec. 26 1803" (Rec. 323). The will was recorded at Newton, N. J., May 4 1804. James left his property to his wife Susanna "to be used for the proper education of my five youngest sons" whom he does not name. He does name "my eldest son, Barney." His executors were: "my wife and my *trusty friend* Thomas Dell." The witnesses: John P. Losey, Titus Berry and Peter Hoagland. James Young married Susannah (b. Apr. 8 1772), daughter of Titus and Hannah R. Berry (Mrs. Edith Livermore Sasse, Richmond Hill, N. Y.). The will of Titus Berry, of Pequannock, Morris County, N. J., drawn, Dec. 19 1828, probated, Dec. 22 1830, Morristown, N. J., left legacies "to my five grandchildren, children of my daughter Susan." The children of Susan are not named. One of the children of James was not a legatee of Mr. Berry. The six children:

i. Barney, called "my eldest son" by his father.
ii. Israel, lived in Jefferson Township in 1821.
iii. Arthur, jr., the Deed books at Morristown, N. J. (Bk. oo, Apr. 8 1819) show that "Arthur, jr., son of James Young, of Hardiston, N. J.," sold land that he inherited from his father to William Woods, with Thomas and Jesse Dell as witnesses to the deed. The *jr.* may have distinguished him from his grandfather. Arthur and Arthur, jr. contributed to the building of the Rockaway Presbyterian Church.
iv. Silas, of Jefferson Township, sold, Apr. 5 1919, to William Woods, the land "where James Young formerly lived and which James bequeathed to Silas" (Bk. oo-106, Morristown. N. J.). On March 12 1824, Silas Young and David King, executor of Arthur Young, late of Newton, Sussex County, sold to John Struble, jr., land in Pequannock, near Dover, N. J. The sale was witnessed by John and Thomas Dell (Bk. PP, 124, Morristown, N. J.).
v. James, lived in Bloomfield Township in 1821.
vi. Henry, lived in Jefferson Township, Morris Co., in 1821.

After the death of James, his widow Susannah Berry Young, md. Aug. 1

1808, William Woods who died, Oct. 8 1832, age 54. The children of Wm. and Susannah Woods spelled their name without an s.

i. Freeman Wood, b. Feb. 4 1809, d. Aug. 1891, md. Mary Burwell (1813-1899) daughter of Wm. and Susan (Halsey) Jackson, and granddaughter of Stephen and Mary (Burwell) Jackson. Mary Burwell, daughter of Adam, had a brother John who md. Catherine Losey, sister of Jane who md. Morgan Young (Rec. 9). Descendants of Freeman and Mary Wood are living in Berkeley, Calif.

ii. Maria Berry Wood, b. Nov. 4 1810, d. Feb. 14 1863, md. Dec. 7 1831, John Marshall Losey, b. Apr. 2 1805, d. Sept. 22 1857, son of John Puff Losey and Sarah Wood, sister of William who md. Susannah Berry Young. A daughter of John and Maria Losey, Ella Wood Losey, md. Raymond B. Livermore whose daughter, Edith Livermore, b. March 3 1872, d. Nov. 22 1945, at Richmond Hill, N. Y., md. Andreas A. Sasse. Mr. and Mrs. Sasse had three children: Andreas Raymond, Edith, and Hilmar Livermore Sasse.

iii. Harriet Wood, b. Oct. 7 1812, d. Feb. 25 1815.

iv. William A. Wood, b. May 25 1818, d. Jan. 15 1870, md. 1st., Sept. 6 1843, Carolina Hurd, daughter of John L. and Elizabeth Hurd (b. Apr. 12 1816, d. March 7 1861). William md. 2nd., Phebe A. Hurd, cousin of his first wife. Betsy Wood, daughter of Clement and Sarah (Canfield) Wood, md. James Lum Hurd, grandson of James and Elizabeth (Young) Hurd (Rec. 324).

330 THOMAS YOUNG

was born, in 1785, in Morris County, N. J. The date is fixed by the record on his gravestone in the cemetery at Galena, O., "Died, May 5 1832, Age 47." His wife, Charity Calhoun, "Died, June 11 1878, Age 89 years, 5 months, 7 days" and was buried beside her husband, on whose tombstone the record is written. Thomas came to Ohio with his father and they bought land on the same day, July 20 1816, in Sunbury Township, Delaware County, O., from Samuel Heath. One of the deed was first made out to Morgan and then "the name Morgan was erased and Thomas inserted in lieu thereof, before signing." The second deed was made out for Morgan for land adjoining that of Thomas. The U. S. Census, 1820, for Sunbury Township, lists Thomas, his wife, one daughter between 16 and 26, two sons and one daughter between 10 and 16 years of age. Three children were born after 1820 according to family records.

i. Elizabeth, md. Eliphalet (Eli) Bigelow. Two children: Sarah, md. Newton Garvin and had one son, Clifton Garvin; and Rose Bigelow, md. Perley Keyes and had three children: Orville, Lawrence and Lydia Keyes. Orville Keyes md. and had three children: Willis, Charles and Maude Keyes. Lydia Keyes md. Clarence Bidwell, a brother-in-law of Mrs. Annis F. Gore, of Galena, O., to whom we are indebted for this family record. Clarence and Lydia had one child, Joseph Orville Bidwell.

ii. Morgan, b. Jan. 12 1814. No record.

iii. Catherine Ann, b. in July 1816, md. and presumably was the mother of some of the unidentified heirs of her uncle Andrew Young (Rec. 331).

338. iv. Elijah, b. Nov. 30 1818

339. v. Mary (Polly), b. near Galena, O.

340. vi. Mehitabel (Esther), b. Feb. 20 1826

341. vii. Sarah Jane, b. July 7 1830

331 ANDREW YOUNG

was born in 1790 in Morris County, N. J. The birth date is fixed by the inscription on his gravestone in the cemetery at Galena, O. He died in 1851, age 61 years. He was living, in 1810, in the Kingston District of Luzerne County, Pa. He had a sister between 16 and 26 years of age in 1810 (U. S. Census, Luzerne County, Pa.) who has not been identified. She perhaps was Polly Carver who was living in Kingston, Pa., in 1851, when Andrew made his will, and to whom he left, after the death of his wife, two thirds of the estate. Andrew left his wife, Polly, "for life or until she remarries, the plantation of 50 acres on which we live." The following record at Delaware, O. may relate to Andrew and his wife: "March 20 1845, Andrew Young married Mary Williams." The list of Andrew's heirs indicates that he had no children. On March 4 1845, Andrew bought and sold a lot to Alpheus and Jane Bigelow. No wife signed the deed.

Andrew's will, filed at Delaware, O., "was produced Oct. 21 1851." The Executors were, Sammie Carver and George W. Wells. With the will, there is an accompanying paper which reads, "On Feb. 15 1854, Geo. W. Wells petitions for the sale of certain real estate, which was sold on March 18 1854, on behalf of the following respondents." It is noted that "Polly Nicholls owns in her own right a part of the real estate and that the sale is subject to her dower." This explains Andrew's disposition of only two-thirds of the estate. The respondents:

Polly and Charles Scovell
Polly Carver
Polly and Charles Nicholls
Hetty and Henry Sherman
Sarah J. Fuller
Elizabeth and Eliphaz Bigelow
Hugh Lorenzo Edwards
Elijah Edwards
Andrew Edwards
Sarah Leonard
Eli Edwards
Sally Lindenberg
Loretta Sharp
Louisa Sharp
William Landon
Jabeth Edwards
Norinda Edwards

The 1840 U. S. Census shows Morgan Young, age 89, living with his son, Andrew, in Sunbury, O. Morgan served in the Revolution under Capt. Zopher Carver. The U. S. Census of 1800 for Luzerne County, Pa. lists the following allied families of Andrew: Samuel Carver, Nathaniel Landon, John Leonard and Oliver Bigelow. Members of these families moved to Delaware County, O., as did Andrew Young. Benjamin and Mary Nichols of N. J. had a son Charles.

332 ELIJAH YOUNG

born in Morris County, N. J., was taken by his parents as a child to Wyoming County, Pa. and about 1816 to Delaware County, O. where he married Amy Larkin, born in N. Y. State, died, July 11 1872, age 74 yrs. 2 months, and 21 days (Gravestone rec., Teeter's Cemetery, near Fremont, Ind.). Elijah died in the home of his son Riley, in Camden Township, Hillsdale County, Mich., about 12 years after the death of his wife, and was buried beside her. Elijah and his brother, Andrew, bought in equal shares, on the same day, land from their parents in Sunbury Township, Delaware County, O. Elijah and Amy sold their land, in part, Aug. 8 1849, and the balance, April 17 1854 (Deed Bk. 6, Delaware, O.). About this date the family moved to near Richwood, O. Eight children.

342. i. Joseph L., b. Dec. 17 1826
ii. Nancy, md. ——— Hedges. She is buried in the cemetery at Richwood, O.
iii. Zeruah, b. 1830, d. June 23 1898, bur. Galena, O.
343. iv. Steven VanRensler, b. Oct. 26 1831
v. Robert Bruce, b. near Richwood, O. He md. and had 4 children: Mamie, md. Mr. Worth and lived in Cleveland, O.; Nettie; John; and Lillian Young.

vi. Hannah Jane (Rachael), said to have moved to Ind. with Riley.

344. vii. Morgan, b. Sept. 27 1837

345. viii. Riley Parker, b. Feb. 17 1840

333 THOMAS W. YOUNG

born, Sept. 4 1783, in Pennsylvania, died, Jan. 10 1867, near West Union, O. and was buried in Foster cemetery, Green Township, Adams County, O. He married, June 7 1807, Mary Finney, b. Feb. 11 1788, in Ireland, d. May 11 1868. Thomas and "Polly" sold land in Green township, June 14 1836, to their son Carson. The earliest Ohio census, 1820, places Thomas in Green, and his father and brother Samuel in Jefferson township. Ten children.

i. Carson, b. Dec. 7 1809, d. June 18 1884, md. July 12 1830, Esther Fleming. He farmed in Adams county, O. Eight children (Mrs. Clyde Osman, Winchester, O.). (1) William, a Civil War veteran, d. 1926, md. Sarah Richards d. 1933, a sister of Mary who md. Joseph, brother of William. Two children: Olive, md. ——— Wolf who died, June 1933, at West Union, O., and Nora Young, md. ——— Easter, and lived at Muncie, Ind. (2) Ann, md. Richard Hayslip, brother of Oliver. (3) Jane, md. Oliver Hayslip. (4) Alexander, md. Susan Hayslip, was a Civil War veteran. (5) Joseph, b. June 27 1847, Adams County, O., served in the Civil War, md. Mary Richards who died in 1916. Two children: Mark, b. 1872, lives, 1942, at Fremont, Ind., md. Nannie Abbott and had two children, Pearl and Milby Young, and Myrtle, b. Jan. 24 1878, md. in 1894 Clyde Osman, and lives at Winchester, O. Myrtle has one child Maude who md. F. H. Doyle, of Winchester, O. (6) Nancy, md. John Malone. (7) Martha, md. Abner Bentley, and (8) Thomas Young, md. Sarah McGary, and had a daughter Julia Young.

ii. Sarah, b. June 26 1810

346. iii. Daniel, b. Oct. 27 1813

347. iv. John, b. March 17 1816

v. Ann, b. Oct. 7 1818

348. vi. Thomas, b. June 25 1820

vii. Amos, b. July 8 1823, md. Lucinda Storer, b. Sept. 6 1820, sister of Susan who md. Noah Young, Rec. 31. He farmed at Stout's Run, Brush Creek, Adams Co., O. Seven children: Edward Smith, Annias Barker, George Washington, W. Wilson, Henry Milton, John, and David Young. Edward S. Young md. Almead Hudson (Hutson) and had a daughter Nora who md. Carl Dickson (Dixon). He md. 2nd., Harriet Wilson. Annias B. Young md. Ada Smith and had 3 children, one of whom, May, md. Wiley Young, son of Nelson and Isabel. (Mrs. Clay Fleming, Seaman, O.)

viii. William, b. Apr. 20 1825, d. Sept. 5 1866

349. ix. Foster, b. July 20 1826

x. Nelson, b. Dec. 18 1830, d. March 9 1886, md. his cousin, Isabel, daughter of William and Mahala (Moore) Young. Isabel md. 2nd. Absolum Bentley. Nelson had 7 children: (1) Meredith, md. 1st. Lizzie Nixon. They had a son Lawrence. Meredith md. 2nd. Rebecca Rogers and they had five children: Flora B., Floyd, Chester, Bessie and Ora Young. (a) Flora Belle md. Frank Stevenson of Lynx, O., and had 8 children: Alberta, Paul, Ione, Virginia, Margery, Martha, Franklin, jr. and Marie Stevenson. (b) Floyd, md. Viola May Young and had six children: Donna, Everett, Martin, Dalles, Beulah, and Floyd Young, jr. (c) Chester md. Edyth Osman and lived near Manchester, O. They had children, one of whom was Carl Young. (d) Bessie md. Richard Cox. Two of their children were Helen and Louise Cox. (e) Ora md. Ira Siberal. (2) Ann md. John Kinney. (3) Dora md. John Spires. (4) Mary, after the death of her sister, Dora, md. John Spires and had 5 children: Homer, Alva, Charles, Clara and Roby Spires. (5) Elhannon md. Rillie Russell and had 4 children: Jewitt Young md. Dora Cook; Albert N. md. Ocie Bayless and has a son Clyde A. Young serving, 1944, in the Army; Ethel md. Elza Rodgers; and Annie md. Clinton Easter. (6) Jane, died at age of 18 yrs. (7) Wylie md. Mary Armstrong at West Union, O. and moved from the neighborhood.

334 DAVID YOUNG

married at West Union, O., June 27 1820, Mary (Polly) Truitt. He was a farmer in Adams County, O. Four children.

350. i. Joseph

ii. George, did not marry, died in California.
351. iii. Rhoda
352. iv. Parker, born about 1827.

335 JOHN YOUNG

married at West Union, O., first, April 2 1821, Mary McKenzie. They had eight children. After the death of Mary, John married Catherine Black for his second wife. John farmed at Black Ripples, Scioto Brush Creek. (Rev. A. L. Young).

i. Jane, married William Fleming.
ii. Margaret, md. Newton Chandler. Lived at Brennen Landing, O.
iii. Rhoda, md. ——— Fleming and lived on her father's farm.
353. iv. Susan Belle, b. July 21 1829
v. Elizabeth, md. "Frought" Young, unidentified.
vi. Duncan, md. and had a large family. A grandson with his name was a clergyman. Lived in Highland County, O.
vii. William did not marry.
354. viii. Lafayette, b. July 23 1840

336 WILLIAM K. YOUNG

born in 1796, died in Adams County, O. and was buried in Foster Cemetery. He married, May 22 1820, Mahala Moore, born, Dec. 10 1800, died, June 1896, daughter of Hosea and Isabel (Burkett) Moore who bought Morgan Young's farm (Rec. 9). Isabel Moore died, Feb. 22 1851, age 85 years. Hosea is said to have been a brother of the Rev. Joseph Moore, b. June 9 1754, in N. J., md. Rebecca Foster, b. June 1 1755, daughter of Nathaniel, of N. J. William and Mahala had 7 children. (Mitchell M. Young).

i. Tresa (Tessy), was 26 years old in 1850 (U. S. Census), md. and had a son who md. Eva Storer, sister of Susan, and daughter of William Storer. Tessy md. 2nd., John Grooms.
ii. Mitchell, blind from the age of 24, inherited his father's farm which he gave to his nephew, Mitchell M. Young, with whom he lived the last years of his life.
355. iii. Patterson, b. Sept. 1826, Green Township, Adams Co.
iv. Isabel, Rec. 333.
356. v. Hosea Moore, b. Nov. 3 1830
vi. Nancy, md. John Liggett.

vii. Harriett, d. 1906, md. Patterson Malone (brother of Harriett who md. Lafayette Young, Rec. 354. Three children, Mahala, Moses and Fanny Malone.

337 GEORGE YOUNG

born, Dec. 25 1799, died, Dec. 15 1869, on his farm on Brush Creek, some 12 miles South-East of West Union, Adams County, O. He married, Aug. 10 1826, Betsy McGarey (West Union, O. records). Elizabeth McGarey (b. Apr. 6 1808, d. Feb. 18 1900) was the daughter of William and Margaret McGarrah (Rec. 31), and a sister of Jane who married John Young. Rec. 31. Eleven children. (Elizabeth F. Denning, Matoon, Ill.)

i. Washington, b. July 4 1827, d. in early youth.
ii. Sarah, b. Apr. 4 1829
iii. Jane, b. March 18 1831
iv. Susannah, b. Oct. 29 1833
357. v. Rhoda, b. Jan. 4 1836
358. vi. Henry, b. May 3 1838
vii. Margaret, b. Sept. 22 1840, d. May 7 1900, md. ——— Fleming.
viii. Elizabeth, b. Oct. 1 1843
359. ix. Mary Evaline, b. Sept. 22 1845
360. x. Addison Neblik, b. Sept. 19 1847
xi. Permelia Agnes, b. June 21 1850. Record 174.

338 ELIJAH YOUNG

son of Thomas and Charity Calhoun Young, sometimes called "2nd" to distinguish him from his uncle, was born, Nov. 30 1818, near Galena, O. He died at Galena Nov. 12 1884, age 66. He married, April 26 1843, Hulda Van Auken, of N. Y. State. (Rec., Delaware, O.). She was born, July 14 1822, died, Feb. 26 1894, age 71 years, 7 mos. 12 days, and was buried beside her husband (Gravestone rec.). By the purchase of Quit claims, Elijah came into possession of his father's land which he farmed until his death. Three children. (G. D. Neilson)

i. Thomas H., b. 1844, d. 1926, bur. Galena, O. Did not marry.
ii. Nathaniel Emery, b. Oct. 12 1846, d. May 2 1925, bur. Galena, O. He md. Feb. 23 1875, Juliana Gibson, in Delaware Co., O. Two children: Etta, b. Nov. 26 1879, d. Mar. 1936, bur. Galena, did not marry; and Georgia F.

Young, b. Nov. 5 1881, md. Dec. 27 1906, George Denny Neilson, graduate of Ohio Wesleyan University, now farming near Sunbury, O.

iii. Mary F., b. 1855, d. 1932, did not marry. (Gravestone, Galena, O.).

339 MARY YOUNG

called "Polly," was born in 1821 and died in 1932, at Galena, O. (Gravestone rec.). She married Chester Scovell. Three children: Jay, md. Ella Courter, both buried at Galena, O.; Anna Mary, b. Nov. 9 1851, d. June 2 1942, at Lancaster, O. and was buried in Forest Rose Cemetery, md. Nov. 17 1868, at Galena, James Perfect (son of Thomas, son of William and Elizabeth Day Perfect, of Virginia), had three children: Horace, died in infancy, Lacie E., b. Dec. 25 1873, lives in Lancaster, O., and Nellie Carmen Perfect, b. Feb. 9 1880. Nellie married, 1st., the Rev. I. D. Sleman and had one child, Helen Sleman. She married, 2nd., Earl Deputy. Emma Scoville, third child of Mary, b. Oct. 3 1853, at Lancaster, O., md. Jan. 18 1877, Clarence M. Sammis, at Galena, O. where both are buried. One child, Grace Sammis, md. Bertram Haverkamp and lives at Florissant, Mo. Chester Scovell md. 2nd., Sarah Young Fuller, sister of Mary. Rec. 341.

340 MEHITABEL YOUNG

called Hetty and sometimes Esther, was born, Feb. 20 1826, Sunbury township, Delaware county, O. She died there and was buried in nearby Berkshire cemetery. She married at Galena, O. Henry Sherman, born, Apr. 18 1825, died, May 13 1880, son of David Thompson (1794-1867) and Sarah (Cablas) Sherman. Four children:

i. Charles, lived in Chicago, Ill.

ii. Everett, md. Eunice Johnson.

iii. Emma, md. a Mr. Mosier.

iv. Lunette (Nettie), b. 1848, md. 1866, Newton Smith, son of John R. and Sarah (Martin) Smith, and had four children: Alton, lived and died in Kansas; George died in Kansas but was buried in Green Lawn cemetery, Columbus, O. His widow, Annie, lives in Renoldsburg, O.; Vernon, d. about 1900 and was buried at Berkshire, O.; Cora May Smith. Cora, b. May 18 1870, at Berkshire, O., died in Dec. 1943, at Columbus, O. She md. in 1892 Marshall A. Smith, son of Marshall A. and Elvira A. (Thrall) Smith and had 4 children: (1) Harold Albert, b. July 24 1894, at Sunbury, O., d. Aug. 30 1944, Columbus, O. He md. Dec. 5 1917, Elizabeth Welch, at Columbus, O. and had one child, Marshall A. Smith, b. Apr. 9 1920, who served as Lt. in the Army in World War II. Harold served as Lt. in the Air Corps in World War I. At the time of his death, Harold was President of the Smith Agricultural Chemical Co., Columbus, O. and was active in civic and fraternal affairs. (2) Hertha M., deceased, md. a Mr. Swartz. (3) Marjorie E. and (4) Adrienne L. Smith.

341 SARAH JANE YOUNG

born, July 7 1830, married, 1st. Ralph Fuller, in Delaware county, O. Three children: (1) Joseph, md. Mary Stark, and had five children, Leonard; Myrtle; Guy, d. 1913, age 30 yrs., md. Jessie Brumfield, and had one child, May Fuller; Mable md. Clyde McNeil, and had 4 children, all living in California, Fuller, Hugh, Jo Anne and Gloria McNeill; Florence, md. Raymond Hicks, and has two children living in Columbus, O., Dorothy and William Hicks. (2) George, md. Emma McCreary, and had 3 children: Maude md. John Mitchell; Goldie md. Harry Mantor; and Helen Fuller, md. Gilbert Toye. (3) Howard Fuller md. May 29 1881, Mary Sackett and had 4 children: Lucius, b. Apr. 14 1882, md. Larnetta Phillips; Annis, b. May 15 1884, md. Feb. 16 1908, Charles Gore, at Galena, O. He died Aug. 25 1925. One child, Mary Gore; Doris Fuller b. June 3 1896, md. Charles Bricker and has five children: David, Howard, Charles, Dayna and John Bricker; Von, b. June 28 1887, md. Ferne Walker and has 2 children, Howard and Floride Fuller. After the death of Ralph, Sarah md. 2nd. Chester Scovell, widower of her sister Mary.

342 JOSEPH L. YOUNG

born, Dec. 17 1826, near Galena, O., died, March 13 1891, at Sunbury, O. He married, Sept. 18 1850, at Galena, O., Rachel Van Auken who died Dec. 27 1877. In 1885, Joseph married, 2nd., a widow, Mrs. Sarah Ramsey Miller Orsbom (? Osbon), mother of his daughter-in-law, Louisa Jane Miller. Joseph and Rachel had six children.

i. Lutell, d. in childhood, bur. Galena, O.
361. ii. Howard, b. Jan. 1 1856
362. iii. Durell, b. Sept. 15 1858

iv. Emma, died in infancy.
v. Amy B., b. 1869, d. 1939, md. Benjamin Feasel.
363. vi. Clarissa M., b. May 31 1871

343 STEPHEN VANRENSLER YOUNG

born, Oct. 26 1831, near Galena, O., died in Union County, and was buried in Bethlehem Cemetery, Richwood, O. He went west in 1856 and mined in the Sierra Nevada mountains for a time. Returning to Ohio, he bought his father's farm near Richwood which he worked until 1904 when he moved into Richwood. He married Berthena Bellfield, an English girl. Three children:

364. i. Willis E., b. June 19 1864
365. ii. Lutell, b. Nov. 1 1867
iii. Daughter, b. 1870, d. at age of 3.

344 MORGAN YOUNG

born, Sept. 27 1837, near Galena, O., died, Oct. 23 1918, and was buried in Claibourne Cemetery, Richwood, O. He farmed near Richwood. He married, Aug. 26 1862, Elnora Finch, b. 1841, d. March 26 1910, at Richwood, O. He spent a few years mining in the west and returned with his brother Stephen. Eight children.

i. Frank, b. Feb. 13 1864, md. Laura Treese who died, Dec. 28 1943, and was buried near her husband in Price Cemetery, near Essex, O. He was a farmer. No children.
ii. Arthur, b. May 11 1866, d. in infancy
iii. Amy Marilla, b. Feb. 14 1868, d. Nov. 22 1868
iv. Idora, b. March 25 1870, d. in infancy
366. v. Edward D., b. Aug. 5 1871
vi. Vinnie, b. Jan. 10 1873, d. July 25 1942, on her farm near Richwood, O. She married, March 6 1906, Bert Carter, and had one child, Clyde, b. Oct. 25 1914.
vii. Vella, b. Oct. 27 1876, lives in 1944 near Richwood, O.
viii. Otis Morgan, b. Feb. 2 1881, near Richwood ,O., married, Sept. 21 1904, Annette McCurdy, at Greencamp, Marion County, O. Dr. Young graduated from the University of Indiana in 1904 and practiced dentistry at Marion, O. until retirement in 1945. He bought his father's farm near Richwood but is living in Marion. No children.

345 RILEY PARKER YOUNG

born, Feb. 17 1840, near Galena, O., died, Aug. 26 1926, at Fremont, Ind., in the home of his son John. His parents sold their farm in Delaware County, O., April 17 1854, and moved to Indiana (Delaware Deed Bk. 39, p. 611). Riley served as Corporal during the Civil War. He married, Aug. 14 1869, Cordelia O. Trowbridge, at Fremont, Ind. She died in 1913 and was buried at Fremont. Riley married, 2nd., Ida, widow of James Barney, at Fremont, Ind. There were 11 children by the first marriage, none by the second.

i. Florence M., b. 1869, d. Feb. 14 1891, age 21 yrs. 8 mos. 3 days (Fremont, Ind. cemetery gravestone). She md. J. L. Kenyon, and had one child, Rollo Kenyon, who was a printer at West Unity, O.

ii. Girt B., b. Oct. 23 1873, at Camden, Mich., d. Feb. 9 1923, at Buffalo, N. Y. where he was buried. He was interested in horses. He md. 1st., ——— Thursa, and had one child James Russell Young, b. Apr. 30 1895, at Paris, Ill. He md. 2nd., Molly Murphy, July 4 1898, at Philadelphia, Pa. One child, died in infancy.

iii. Ethel, no record

iv. William Perry, b. May 5 1875, at Camden, Mich. He md. 1st., July 25 1896, Edna Gertrude Myers, b. March 31 1878. There were 3 children: (1) Carl Myers, b. Feb. 23 1897, at Fremont, Ind., d. Aug. 23 1915, at Angola, Ind. (2) Ruth Elizabeth, b. Mar. 30 1899, md. Sept. 10 1930, Valmore Carlton Snyder, at So. Bend, Ind. Mr. Snyder d. Feb. 27 1943. No children. (3) and Roscoe Dunbar Young, b. Apr. 3 1902, at Fremont, Ind., md. Jan. 6 1926, Gladys Mildred Little, at Sturgis, Mich. One child, Nadine Joanne Young, b. Aug. 18 1927, at Kendallville, Ind. where the family lives.

v. Frank Wallace, b. Apr. 1 1877, in Camden Township, Hillsdale County, Mich., farmed for some years in Branch County, Mich., is now living near Coldwater, Mich. He married, May 26 1901, Gertie Maude Clingan, at Fremont, Ind. She was born, Feb. 21 1881, at Angola, Ind. Four children: (1) Leona Belle, b. Apr. 18 1902, in Steuben Co., Ind., md. Apr. 5 1919, Walter J. Zurrbrugg, at Coldwater, Mich. Five children, Margaret Ann, b. Nov. 9 1925, at Elkhart, Ind., Phyllis Jane, b. Nov. 9 1925, twin of Margaret, Sonia Marie, b. June 19 1933, at Quincy,

Mich., Frederick John, b. Jan. 16 1935, Quincy, Mich. and Charles Virgil Zurrbrugg, b. Sept. 23 1936, at Battle Creek, Mich. (2) Dessa Arline, b. May 14 1904, in Kinderhook Twnshp., Branch Co., Mich., d. Nov. 24 1906, Girard Twnshp., same county. (3) Wayne Franklin, b. July 31 1907, md. July 3 1944, Bertha Adamson, at Idaho Falls, Idaho, where he is chef at the Bonneville Hotel. (4) Lyle Edward Young, b. Jan. 7 1917, Branch Co., Mich., md. June 26 1938, Marjorie Van Orman, at Tekonsha, Mich. and lives at Battle Creek, Mich. Two children, Janet Ellen, b. Mar. 18 1939, and Richard Frank Young, b. Aug. 1942, at Battle Creek, Mich.

367. vi. Otis Jay, b. Apr. 23 1880

vii. Maude L., d. when 15 years of age.

viii. Mabel B., d. Dec. 16 1895, age 11 years (Gravestone, Fremont, Ind.

ix. John K., b. May 4 1888, md. Lela H. Kaiser, and lives at Coldwater, Mich. He served in World War I.

x. Ralph, d. Apr. 10 1892, bur. Fremont, Mich., age 10.

xi. Ruth C., d. in youth.

346 DANIEL YOUNG

farmer, born, Oct. 27 1813, in Pennsylvania, died, April 18 1850, in Adams County, O. He married, March 9 1831, Clarinda Brooks, b. Mar. 9 1811 d. Sept. 14 1860. She came to Ohio from Chemung County, N. Y., and was a sister of Elizabeth who married John Young, brother of Daniel. After the death of Daniel, Clarinda married John Scott. There were seven children ("Ike," Isaac Young, Blue Creek, O.).

i. Wesley, served in the 85th Ohio Reg. during the Civil War, died while on furlough.

ii. Thomas, served in the 70th Ohio Reg. during the Civil War. Buried at Corinth, O.

368. iii. John Brooks, b. Feb. 1 1839

iv. Francis Marian

v. Daniel Clark, md. and one of his children was Hendrick Young whose widow, Mrs. Frances Belcher, lives in West Union, O. Three of Hendrick's children were Russell, Geneva and Adrian Young.

vi. Sally Ann, md. James Woodworth

vii. ——— md. "Alick" Ralston

347 JOHN YOUNG

born, March 17 1816, died in Adams County, O., where he farmed. He married, Oct. 18 1834, Elizabeth Brooks. Nine children.

369. i. Leonard, b. Jan. 22 1841
ii. Alaniah, b. Nov. 19 1844, d. Sept. 26 1901, md. Angeline Compton. Seven children: Jane, Ella, Lizzie, Ottie, Manford, Mary and Belva Young.
iii. Ann E., b. 1846, d. Mar. 23 1906, at Oakwood, O., md. James K. P. Shiveley. Six children: Ida, Madlin, Effie, Hamar, Della and Ida Shiveley.
iv. Margaret E., b. 1849, d. 1928, md. James K. Ellis.
370. v. Isaiah, b. Dec. 12 1851
vi. Daniel C., b. May 9 1854, md. Mary McDermott. No children.
371. vii. John Hamar, b. July 29 1856
373. viii. Newton, b. May 15 1858
372. ix. Mary Minerva, b. Nov. 1 1860

348 THOMAS YOUNG

died at Mt. Tabor, Green Township, Adams County, O. in 1890. He married in 1854 Jane Copas. The records at West Union, O. show that they sold land on Brush Creek Feb. 4 1854. The name of one child has been found.

374. i. Melvin Nelson Young

349 FOSTER YOUNG

married, first, Jane, sister of Ellen Morrison, who married Patterson Young (Rec. 355). One of Foster's children was Marion, died 1939, married Elizabeth Flaugher who died in 1941. Marion and Elizabeth Young had 3 children: Samuel Foster, who lives in Portsmouth, O. and has a son William, born 1932; Emma, married Hugh McGorkle and lives in Portsmouth; and Grace, married ——— Suter. Foster lived in Green township, Adams county, O. He married, second, Catherine Charles.

350 JOSEPH YOUNG

died at Beaseley Fork, Brush Creek, Adams county, O. about 1910. He married Betsy Jane Miller, a sister of Rachel, who married Hosea Young.

Joseph and Elizabeth sold land, June 15, 1833, to David Young. Most of the vital statistics of Adams county were destroyed by fire in 1910. Five children. (Mrs. S. M. Cooper, Clarksville, Ia.).

375. i. Lewis Sidney, b. Nov. 15 1854
ii. George
iii. Roxy
iv. D. Turner, lived in Manchester, O.
v. William

351 RHODA YOUNG

had a daughter Mahala who married Charles Stevenson. Charles and Mahala had two children: Clia B., married Charles Holliday and had a daughter Nellie who married Roby Young, son of Melvin (Rec. 374); and Louella Jane Young, b. March 17 1863, d. Nov. 18 1942, md. J. Hamar Young (Rec. 371).

352 PARKER YOUNG

was born about 1827 in Adams County, O. He married Mary Jane Anderson, an aunt of Mary Anderson who married George, son of Patterson Young. Parker was buried in Ralston cemetery, Poplar Ridge, West Union, O. Two children are known (Della Belle Young).

i. Polly Ann, b. Feb. 7 1848, md. Joseph Trotter.
376. ii. David, b. Feb. 26 1850

353 SUSAN BELLE YOUNG

born, July 21 1829, near West Union, O., by her marriage to John G. Young ("Ivory"), son of John and Jane (McGarah) Young, united two branches of the Young family (Rec. 76).

354 LAFAYETTE YOUNG

born, July 23, 1840, in Adams County, O., died, Feb. 15 1870. He married Harriet Malone, sister of Patterson who married Harriet Young. After Lafayette's death, Harriet married, second, Mr. Russell (1841-1880) and had a son, Fred Russell. Lafayette and Harriet had 3 children.

377. i. Alice, b. June 20 1870
ii. Mary
iii. Son, died in infancy.

355 PATTERSON YOUNG

born, Sept. 1826, Brush Creek, Green Township, Adams County, O., married Ellen Morrison, b. Feb. 7 1834, daughter of Joseph and Betty (Baldwin) Morrison, at Brush Creek. Both were buried in Foster Cemetery. Nine children.

i. George, md. Mary Anderson. Of their four children, only one survived infancy, Wilma, the second child. She married Homer Grooms and has a daughter Mary Ellen Grooms.

ii. Rillie K. (Corilla), died Nov. 27 1945, age 71, at West Union, O., md. William Cooper.

iii. Joseph Eylar, b. 1857, d. Oct. 1938, Adams County, O. where he was a farmer. He married, May 16 1884, Mary Minerva Young, ("Little Mary") b. Nov. 1 1860, d. June 10 1946, in her home near Lynx, O. No children.

378. iv. William Jaspar, md. Mary Jane Satterfield, daughter of Benjamin and Lydia (Black) Satterfield, and sister of Frank C. Satterfield who md. Maude Young.

379. v. John, b. Jan. 11 186-.

vi. Alice, md. Frank Grooms.

vii. Louisa, md. Jack Hayslip.

viii. Margaret, md. Jake Taylor.

380. ix. Mitchell Morrison, b. April 23 1854

356 HOSEA MOORE YOUNG

born, Nov. 3 1830, Adams County, O., died, April 17 1905, and was buried at West Union, O. Hosea farmed for a short time in Kansas and in Clinton County, Ind. He married Rachel Ann Miller and had six children (Mrs. Miner McAdow, West Union, O.).

i. Mahala, d. in infancy.

ii. Harvey Martin, b. Aug. 7 1867, Adams County, O., md. Pearl McPherson. Three children: Leslie, Kathryn, and William Young.

iii. J. Ollie, b. Apr. 3 1870, Clinton County, Ind. did not marry.

iv. Mary, b. July 31 1872, Clinton County, Ind., d. June 6 1942, md. Charles Bayless. Five children: Ocie Anna, Harry Joseph, Clyde, Charles and Elizabeth Bayless.

381. v. William H., b. Jan. 8 1875

382. vi. Hannah, b. Oct. 17 1876

357 RHODA YOUNG

born, Jan. 4 1836, near West Union, O., died, March 20 1912, at Los Angeles, Calif. where she was buried. She married at West Union, O., in Sept. 1861, Jacob Easter, born in Adams County, O., June 20 1835, died, Nov. 20 1898, at Lebanon, Mo. where he was buried. The family moved to near Mattoon, Ill. in 1867, and to Lebanon, Mo. in 1893. Mrs. Easter went to Los Angeles in 1903. Five children (Mrs. Lillie (Easter) Kanzig, Los Angeles, Calif.).

i. Clara Albertina, b. July 5 1862, Adams County, O., md. William McGirk, at Mattoon, Ill.
ii. George Wesley, b. May 19 1864, Adams County, O., md. Anna White, at Mattoon, Ill.
iii. John Wheeler, b. Nov. 8 1868, at Doran's Crossing, Ill., md. Margaret Reams, at Mattoon, Ill.
iv. Walter Addison, b. Oct. 3 1871, at Doran's Crossing, Ill., md. Anna Frolick, at Los Angeles, Calif.
v. Lillie Bell, b. Apr. 7 1878, at Doran's Crossing, Ill., md. Oct. 6 1897, Thomas Austin Kanzig, at Lebanon, Mo.

358 HENRY YOUNG

was born, May 3 1838, in a log cabin on Brush Creek about 12 miles southeast of West Union, O. He died, July 29 1927, at Los Angeles, Calif. and was buried in the Odd Fellows Cemetery. He married at Rome, O., March 13 1867, Amanda Melvina Kerr who died at Lincoln, Nebr. in 1890 and was buried there. The family moved to Missouri about 1880, and from there to Lincoln, Nebr. Henry went to California about 1900 and there married, 2nd., Elizabeth Barwell. Henry and Amanda had 7 children (Mrs. G. D. Young, E. Los Angeles, Calif.).

i. George Wiley, b. Dec. 28 1867, Adams Co., O., d. Sept. 1 1941, Los Angeles, Calif., bur. Odd Fellows Cemetery. He md. Oct. 26 1907, at Baker City, Ore., Mary Kanada, d. Aug. 28 1946. No children.
ii. Lenora Jeannette, b. Oct. 21 1869, d. about 1889, at Grant City, Mo. where she md. Harvey Waugh.
iii. Samuel Oscar, b. March 11 1873, went to Mo. with the family.
iv. John Wesley, b. Oct. 11 1878, md. and lived at one time near Wichita, Kan. Three children, Christine, Gerald, and Olive Young.
v. Elizabeth Demnie, b. March 28 1880, d. and was buried at

Geneva, Nebr. She md. at Seward, Nebr., Dec. 31 1899, Fred Ford, b. Nov. 3 1874, d. Nov. 17 1943, at Seward. Two children: (1) Ethel Sullivan, b. Dec. 22 1901, Seward, Nebr., md. Sept. 14 1931, Vern N. Miller, at Geneva, Nebr. and has two sons. (2) Paul Seward Ford, b. Jan. 11 1913, Geneva, Nebr., md. Sept. 14 1940, Mary F. Frederick, at Elko, Nev. and lives at Stockton, Calif. He is in service 1943.

383. vi. General Dix, b. Sept. 12 1882, at Grant City, Mo.

vii. Jennie Murphy, b. Apr. 1 1886, md. John C. Wulf, and lives at Nyssa, Ore.

359 MARY EVALINE YOUNG

"Eva" was born, Sept. 22 1845, in Adams County, O. She married, June 23 1864, near West Union, O., Isaac Newton Denning, b. Jan. 10 1844, d. May 9 1928, at Mattoon, Ill. where the family was living. Six children (Elizabeth F. Denning, Mattoon, Ill.).

i. Wiley B., b. June 29 1865

ii. Minnie Alice, b. Dec. 2 1867, d. March 12 1894

iii. Elizabeth Florence, b. July 29 1871, lives at Mattoon, Ill. where she cared for her aged parents, and now is caring for her blind brother, William.

iv. David Elmer, b. July 27 1875, d. the same year.

v. Rosa Maude, b. Oct. 7 1879, d. March 27 1884.

vi. Wm. Otis, b. Apr. 24 1884

360 ADDISON NEBLIK YOUNG

born, Sept. 19 1847, in a log cabin, some 12 miles from West Union, O., married, Nov. 24 1870, in Adams County, O., Ella Jane Holliday, born in Lawrence County, O. in 1852. They moved to Mo. in 1877, and to Northwest Kansas in 1886. Both are burried at Bogue, Kan. Eight children (Minor H. Young, Omaha, Ark.).

i. Frank G., b. Aug. 25 1871, d. Sept. 11 1934

384. ii. Minor Holliday, b. Oct. 10 1873

iii. Laura I., b. Sept. 6 1875, d. Sept. 30 1880

iv. Elizabeth M., b. Apr. 23 1878, in Worth County, Mo., md. James T. Lavell, at McDonald, Kan.

v. Ella M., b. May 9 1881, Worth County, Mo., d. July 26 1908

vi. Homer A., b. Dec. 22 1883, Worth County, Mo., md. Ethel Cook, and lives in Bogue, Kan.
vii. Minnie B., b. Oct. 10 1887, Norton County, Kan., md. M. Earl Kelly, and lives in Manhattan, Kan.
viii. Winnie D., a son, twin of Minnie, d. Oct. 18 1888, Norton County, Kan.

361 HOWARD YOUNG

born, Jan. 1 1856, near Galena, O., died in 1916, at Columbus, O. where he was buried in Union Cemetery. He married Louisa Jane Miller, daughter of his father's second wife. Five children, Maude and Mabel, twins, did not marry. They are buried at Columbus, O. (Mrs. Mildred Young Minugh).

i. Charles N., b. Nov. 23 1883, Delaware County, O., md. Haidee C. Price, at Ellensburg, Wash. where Mr. Young is with the Aetna Insurance Co. No children.
ii. Mildred Louise, b. Aug. 14 1896, at Columbus, O., md. Oct. 6 1926, William Arthur Minugh, of Monmouth Beach, N. J., at Columbus, O. He died, July 8 1939, and was buried at Columbus.
iii. Howard Miller, b. Feb. 25 1899, at Columbus, O., md. 1st., Wilma Mendenhall, of Parkersburg, W. Va. He md. 2nd., 1933, Mary Fontelle Harper, of Glouster, O. One child by the first marriage, Robert Mendenhall Young, b. Sept. 28 1920, at Springfield, O., is serving in the U. S. Army, 1942, and one child by the second marriage, Newton Douglas Young, b. Jan. 4 1939, near Lexington, O. where the family is living.

362 DURELL YOUNG

born, Sept. 15 1858, near Galena, O., died, April 12 1934. He married Ada Armentrout, born Dec. 10 1866, in Madison County, O. One child, Ivy G. Young md. William Harsh, and had one son, Fay Ivan Harsh, b. July 30 1909, at Chuckery, Union County, O. Fay married Gladys Klontz, and had one child, Gladys Maxine Harsh, b. near London, O.

363 CLARISSA M. YOUNG

born, May 31 1871, near Galena, O., is living at Columbus, O. She married, March 24 1897, Walter Bidwell, at London, O. Two children.

i. Marguerite, b. Aug. 24 1902, md. March 28 1929, Roscoe C. Pendelton. Two children, Roger Dean, b. Apr. 2 1931, and Nancy Ann Pendelton, b. Jan 28 1934. Family lives in San Antonio, Texas, 1944.

ii. Frances Jo, b. Aug. 18 1905, near Plain City, O., md. Dec. 26 1926, J. Price Neff, at Covington, Ky. Five children, all born at Columbus, O.: Wayne, b. Feb. 2 1927, d. Jan. 30 1943; Richard Lee, b. May 3 1928; Bradley Lynn, b. June 7 1932; Sharon Ann, b. Aug. 23 1938; and John Paul Neff, b. March 21 1940.

364 WILLIS E. YOUNG

born, June 19 1864, near Richwood, O., d. Aug. 21 1942, at Akron, O. where he was in the printing business. He married, May 21 1890, Mary Belle Benedict (b. Feb. 13 1870, d. Mar. 22 1946, bur. East Akron, O.), at Richwood, and they celebrated their Golden Wedding anniversary in 1940. They moved to Akron in 1891, after living a year in Shelby, O. One child.

i. Helen Louise, b. June 6 1909, at Akron, O., md. Feb. 1 1947, Clyde Mott Poulson, at Akron, O.

365 LUTELL YOUNG

born, Nov. 1 1867, near Richwood, O., died in 1902, and was buried at Richwood. He married Alice Cox (1872-1923). There were four children. After the death of Lutell, his widow married ——— Murphy.

i. Harry L., md. Aug. 21 1913, Minnie May Wallace, at Richwood, O. where the family lives. Two children: James S., and Harold Young. James was born, May 26 1914, at Richwood.

ii. Bertha, b. Nov. 22 1895, Richwood, O., md. July 3 1919, at Columbus, O., Dr. Marion L. Scott, a Veterinarian, who is now Meat Inspector at Akron, O. Two children: Marjorie, b. Apr. 27 1922, is a student at Akron University, and Barbara Scott, b. Jan. 1 1925.

iii. Willis, md. and was living in Springfield, O. in 1942.

iv. Robert, was killed in a street-car accident, 1904, at Akron, O.

366 EDWARD D. YOUNG

born, Aug. 5 1871, died, Nov. 13 1931, at Marion, O. and was buried in Price Cemetery, Essex, O. He married, March 19 1895, Orpha M. Blue, at Essex, O. She was the daughter of Michael and Catherine (Axten) Blue and was born, Aug. 25 1875, in Union County, O., died in 1934 at Marion. Four children.

i. Nellie May, b. Aug. 18 1896, Union Co., O., md. 1st., May 1 1918, Lloyd Dickason who d. in 1920. One child, Dorothy J. Dickason, b. May 1 1919, at LaRue, O., md. June 10 1936, at Covington, Ky., Frank Bevis, and has one child, Huberta Bevis, b. Aug. 2 1937, at Richwood, O. Nellie md. 2nd., Nov. 2 1921, at Marysville, O., Sherman Cowgill. One child, Edward Cowgill, b. Dec. 20 1922, at Richwood, O., is serving in the U. S. Army, 1943.

ii. Lucille, b. May 30 1898, near Essex, O., md. Sept. 15 1942, Paul Simmermacher, at Cleveland, O. and lives at Willard, O. where Paul is in the insurance business.

iii. Myron E., b. Dec. 1 1899, Essex, O., md. Nov. 4 1924, Zella Seiter, at Marion, O. and lives at Akron, O. No children.

iv. Arthur Morgan, b. Sept. 7 1901, Essex, O., md. June 12 1935, Birdell Houser, at Marion, O. He is a railway engineer. No children.

367 OTIS JAY YOUNG

born, April 23 1880, in Hillsdale County, Mich., is living with his son Robert at Kendallville, Ind. He married, Dec. 17 1904, Norma Odell Teeters, at Fremont, Ind. She died, June 8 1939, and was buried at Pleasant Lake, Ind. Eleven children, the first three were born at Fremont, Ind., the others at Kendallville.

i. Rollo Otis, b. Nov. 3 1906, md. Wilma Smith, at Kendallville, where they live. Two children: Lois Ann, b. 1941, and Joyce Ellen Young, b. 1942.

ii. Arla Margarite, b. May 3 1909, md. 1st., Earl C. Kellenberger, and had one child, Deloss Earl, b. March 11 1928, at Kendallville, Ind., md. 2nd. Clarence Medlem.

iii. Kenneth Deloss, b. March 3 1911, md. Myrtle Stewart, of Elgin, Ill. where the family is living. Four children: Norma Lynn, b. 1931; William Spence; Richard Deloss, b. 1941; and P. Ann Young, b. 1942.

iv. Riley Donald, b. Feb. 23 1913, md. Ruth Miller, at Garrett, Ind. where they live. One child, Dean Allen Young, b. Dec. 1942.

v. Otto Edward, b. Apr. 14 1914, md. Dolores Strouse, at Kendallville, Ind. where the family lives. He served in World War II. Two children: William Edward, b. Mar. 29 1937, and Susie Ann, b. Oct. 1942.

vi. Theresa Ruth, b. Mar. 14 1918, md. 1st., George Paul Miller, of Lagrange, Ind. They separated and she md. 2nd., Leslie Willington Yeske, of Oak Park, Ill. where they live. One child, Beatrice Ann Miller, b. Aug. 14 1937, Elgin, Ill.

vii. John Franklin, b. Jan. 9 1920, md. Mary K. Roberts, of Garrett, Ind. He served in World War II, now lives at Kendallville, Ind. One child, Nancy Lee Young, b. Apr. 13 1942, Kendallville, Ind.

viii. Max Earl, b. Mar. 2 1921, md. Bernice Stewart, of St. Louis, Mo. and lives in Ft. Wayne, Ind.

ix. Willard LeMar, b. June 12 1922, md. Mary George Elgin. One child, Willard Lee Young, b. July 1943, Kendallville, Ind.

x. Inez Eileen, b. Sept. 20 1924, d. Apr. 7 1925, at Avilla, Ind.

xi. Robert Lewis, b. Nov. 26 1929, lives with his father.

368 JOHN BROOKS YOUNG

born, Feb. 1 1839, in Jefferson Township, Adams County, O., died suddenly, March 11 1908, in Wamsley's Chapel while attending a revival service with his daughter Sarah. He lived with his great uncle George Young from the age of 11 until 16. He was granted a certificate to teach in 1859 and taught in Jefferson Township. He enlisted for Civil War service in 1862, served in Co. H., 81st, Reg., O.V.I., and was mustered out, July 13 1866, at Louisville, Ky. For years he was Chaplain of the Wm. M. Bailey Post, G.A.R. He was a member of the Ohio State Legislature in 1884. His ancestry back to his great grandfather is recorded in Evans and Stivers, "History of Adams County, O.," p. 291. He married, Aug. 16 1862, Diademie Thompson, at Black Oak, Ky. Ten children (Isaac D. Young).

385. i. Isaac D., b. 1867

ii. Edmund Lee

iii. Clement L.
iv. John Henry, b. Apr. 14 1871, on Churn Creek, Adams Co., O., d. July 13 1943, in the home of his sister Mrs. Anna Haines, of Dayton, O. He spent much time promoting the welfare and happiness of his community. He was Ruling Elder and Superintendent of the Sunday School for 36 yrs., served as Town Clerk, and as a member of the Board of Education. He md. March 1 1896, Margaret Staten and had one child, Aubrey who is md. and has a son Jack Young.
v. Clarinda (Inda), md. William Copas and lives at Earl Park, Ind.
vi. Thomas M.
vii. Thomas E., md. Cora Heilbromer and lives at Wheat Ridge, O.
viii. Sarah, did not marry.
ix. Mary, md. the Rev. Roy Lucas.
x. Anna, md. Oren Haines and lives in Dayton, O.

369 LEONARD YOUNG

born, Jan. 22 1841, at Sandy Springs, near Rome, O., died, Dec. 17 1915, at Dunkinsville, O., and was buried in the I.O.O.F. cemetery as West Union, O. He served as Corporal in the Civil War, taught school in Adams County, O., and was Recorder of Adams County from 1886 until 1897 at West Union, O. He married, March 24 1870, Hannah Kesiah, daughter of Simon and Mary Ann Osman, of near Lynx, O. Ten children.

i. Minnie Josephine, b. Jan. 18 1871, d. Nov. 13 1920, md. Mar. 9 1892, Charles F. McCoy, Lawyer, son of Chas. A. One child, Bernice G. died in infancy.
ii. Demarius, b. June 11 1872, d. Mar. 22 1931, at Dunkinsville, O.
iii. Orzo, b. June 3 1873, md. Ann Coates (1872-1921). Five children: Leonard Emerson, b. 1897, d. Mar. 16 1928, md. Evalyn Pence; Harley, b. Oct. 3 1900, farmer, md. Mary E. Davis, of Cherry Fork, O. and has 7 children, Myrtle, b. Dec. 31 1930, Rosa Mae, b. Oct. 27 1932, Wilma, b. 1936, Wanda Young, b. Mar. 12 1939, Orzo, b. 1942, Alma Louise, b. Nov. 17 1944, Robert Eugene, b. May 24 1947; Summer, b. Aug. 11 1905, d. Apr. 8 1908; Helen, b. Oct. 3 1908, d. June 29

1909; Melba, b. May 10 1903, md. Dec. 20 1920, Noble E. Matthews.

iv. John Franklin, b. Sept. 6 1875, d. May 5 1938, md. Jan. 1904, Agnes Wolf, and had three children: Eustace Lee, b. Oct. 17 1907, md. Ora Bartholomew, daughter of Ammon, of Seaman, O. and has 3 children, Willa Dean, b. Dec. 6 1932, Carrol Lee, b. Nov. 9 1935, and Gail Ann Young, b. Sept. 2 1937; Glenn, b. July 25 1910, md. Apr. 1 1932, Winona Hanes, of Cincinnati, O. and has 2 children: Ronald, Aug. 5 1937, and Roger Young, b. Oct. 16 1941; and Clarine Young, b. May 21 1913, md. Clyde Manker, of Sabina, O.

v. Clara Estella, b. Jan. 25 1877, d. June 8 1933, at Wilmington, O., md. May 23 1898, at West Union, Charles Lee Parry, druggist at Peebles, O.

vi. Charles Homer, painter, b. July 6 1878, d. Oct. 8 1915, at Peebles, O. He md. 1905, Ione Hanes, of Peebles. A son, Paul, b. Nov. 6 1905, md. Reba Lloyd.

386. vii. Curtis Lamar, b. Feb. 8 1880

viii. Rodney Arthur, b. Feb. 3 1881, d. Aug. 17 1918

ix. Edwin Stanton, b. Sept. 11 1885, d. May 13 1947, at Dunkinsville, O. He served in the local and county Board of Education and in the State Highway Department.

x. Donna Maria, b. Dec. 21 1886, at West Union, md. Dec. 26 1922 Walter Mattingly. A son, Lamar Mattingly, b. Jan. 26 1924, md. July 1 1945, at Mayville, Ky., Dora Belle Sheppard, of Manchester, O.

370 ISAIAH YOUNG

born, Dec. 12 1851, in Adams County, O., died there in 1917. He married, Dec. 20 1874, Mary Alice Shiveley. Three children.

i. Claracy Maudest, md. Franklin Coates Satterfield (1859-1943), son of Benjamin and Lydia (Black) Satterfield, as his second wife, Sept. 7 1898. Two children: Raymond I. and Adrienne Satterfield. Adrienne, b. July 28 1905, md. Dec. 25 1931, Houston Newman. She died, Jan. 28 1944, at Milford, O.

ii. Effie Ann, md. J. L. Treftz and had three children: Vernon, Wayne and Nell Treftz.

iii. N. Watson (Watt), lives at May Hill, Seaman, O., md.

Mamie Piatt and had two children: James Brennan and Margery Berry. Brennan had five children: Paul Morris, Robert Dale, James Kent, Janet Carol, and Daniel Brent Young, b. Jan. 5 1945.

371 JOHN HAMAR YOUNG

born, July 29 1856, Adams County, O., died there in 1922. He married, June 12 1894, Louella Stevenson, b. March 17 1863, d. in Dec. 1942, in the home of her daughter Betty at Portsmouth, O.(Rec. 351). Two children.

i. Elizabeth (Betty), md. Leslie McGovney and lives at Portsmouth, O. Two children: Roy and Ernestine McGovney.
ii. Albert Oakley (Bert O.), lives at Beasley Forks, Monroe Township, Adams County, O. He md. Mary Schultz, daughter of Edward and Emma J. Schultz. Five children: Howard S. who served as S/Sgt. in World War II; Martha, Geraldine, Edward; and Grace Young.

372 MARY MINERVA YOUNG

born, Nov. 1 1860, died, June 10 1946, in her home near West Union, O. "Little Mary," as she was called, married Joseph E. Young (Rec. 355). Her family Bible supplied data for these records.

373 NEWTON YOUNG

born in 1871 in Adams County, O. farmed near Lynx, O. He married Emaline Pence. Four children: Hartzell, md. Belva Stewart; Harley, md. Flora Pollard and has two sons, John Hamar and Wilbur Young; Sampson, md. Rhoda Young. Ola, daughter of Newton, married Floyd Young.

374 MELVIN NELSON YOUNG

born, June 6 1857, spent his life farming in Adams County, O. and died there in Feb. 1940. He married Mary Ellen Easter, of Dutch origin, in Adams Co. She died in April 1946, aged 87 yrs. in the home of her son Connor, on Brush Creek, near West Union, O. Eight children:

i. Maurice Melvin, b. 1877, md. Laura Crummie, and had two children, Stella deceased and Bennard Young, of

Seaman, O., md. Ada Baldridge, and had 4 children: Paul, Dale, Frank and Janet Young.

ii. Roby C., b. 1879, md. Nellie Holliday (Rec. 351) and has 6 children: Edna, Harrison, Martha, Fred, Robert and Richard S. Young. Richard was awarded the Purple Heart for service in World War II.

iii. Charles E., b. 1882, md. Susan Nesbit and lives near West Union, O. Four children: Ray W.; Mary who md. Maurice Grooms; Harry E.; and Anna Lou Young who md. Harry R. Roush.

387. iv. Connor Wilson, b. Oct. 2 1885

v. Icie, b. May 2 1887, md. Connor Satterfield and had five children: Ethel, Mabel, Mary, Ralph, deceased, and George Satterfield.

vi. William Nelson, b. 1889, is md. for the third time. Four children by his first wife are: William N. jr.; Carol, md. Vaughn Chesterman; Mary Helen; and Gail Young.

vii. John O., b. June 21 1895, md. at West Union, O., Mae Thompson. He is a merchant at Seaman, O. One child, John, jr., b. Sept. 10 1921, Cedar Mills, O., md. Jan. 27 1943, Memita Kelley, at Marsgall, O. He served in the Air Corps in World War II, and is now associated in business with his father.

viii. Robert Bruce, b. 1898, md. Mary McNeilan. One child is Ruth Young.

375 LEWIS SPIRES YOUNG

born, Nov. 15 1854, in Monroe Township, Adams County, O., died in Oct. 1930, age 75 yrs. 11 mos. 18 days, and was buried in the Odd Fellow's cemetery at West Union, O. (Gravestone rec.). He married at Brush Creek, West Union, O., in 1879, Dorothy (b. 1860), daughter of John B. and Susanna (Young) Fleming. She is living, 1947, at Manchester, O. Eleven children, of whom seven died in infancy. (Mrs. Benjamin Blythe, Manchester, O.).

i. Earl, b. Nov. 11 1880, md. Phoebe Chamblin and has 5 children: Russell; Mabel, md. ——— Grooms; Patty Ruth; Mancel; and Lucille, md. Robert McCarty.

388. ii. Edward Cleveland, b. Dec. 10 1885

iii. Mae, b. May 15 1895, md. Benjamin Blythe, at West Union, and lives at Manchester, O.

iv. Liddy, b. May 8 1902, md. Lloyd Molen, lives at Manchester, O.

v. Homer, died in 1920. He md. Minnie ———, and had two children: Theodore, md. Nell Lumbleson and has 3 children, Thelma, Shirley and Donald Young, all born in Manchester, O.; and Lillian, md. Harry Smith and lives at Manchester, O. Three children: Wyvetta, Wayne and Delmar Smith.

376 DAVID YOUNG

born, Feb. 26 1850, farmed in Tiffin Township, Adams County, O. where he died, Jan. 5 1935, and was buried in Foster cemetery. He married, Rebecca Jane Monroe, born, Aug. 10 1855, in Adams County. Six children. They also raised J. Arthur Young.

i. Della Belle, b. Sept. 22 1876 on Poplar Ridge, West Union, O., is living there.

ii. William

iii. India

iv. George, lives near West Union, O. Three children: Mable, Hubert A. and Kenneth Young. Hubert, b. 1922, md. Sept. 27 1945, Eva Jean Minton, at West Union. He served in the Army in World War II. Mabel is now Mrs. Ray Mason.

v. Jennie, md. Wesley Satterfield and has a daughter, Mrs. Wm. Lafferty.

vi. Stella, md. and had a daughter, Mrs. Verlin Swearingin.

377 ALICE YOUNG

born, June 20 1870, in Adams county, O., daughter of Lafayette Young and Harriet Malone, married her second cousin, John Young, son of Patterson (Rec. 379).

378 WILLIAM JASPER YOUNG

born, Oct. 17 1850, in Adams county, O., died there, March 27 1932. He married, May 26 1887, Mary Jane Satterfield. One child.

i. Alva Latin, b. May 1 1890, near West Union, O., d. Jan. 26 1932, and was buried in the Odd Fellows cemetery. He married, Nov. 4 1909, Edna Moore, daughter of Andrew C., at Maysville, Ky. Five children: (1) Mary, b. Jan. 26 1912, md. Feb. 1932, Ora Crawford, at West Union, O. (2) Bonnie, b. Oct. 18 1914, md. Dec. 8 1934, Marlin Young, a distant cousin, at Vanceburg, Ky. They have raised and educated Bonnie's sisters, (3) Bernice, b. Dec. 28 1919, (4) Ruby, b. Nov. 16 1927, md. Aug. 25 1945, Richard Dean Rogers and has a dau. Sharon Dianne, b. Sept. 11 1947; and (5) Roxie Ellen, b. Oct. 4 1930. The family lives east of West Union, O.

379 JOHN YOUNG

born, Jan. 11 186-, in Adams county, O. He married Alice Young, born, July 20 1870, daughter of Lafayette (Rec. 354). She lives at Mowrystown, O. Nine children.

i. Walter L. b. Dec. 18 1889, md Elizabeth Osman, and lives at Russellville, O. Five children: (1) Robert Coleman, b. July 5 1909, d. June 18 1945, and was buried in the I.O.O.F. cemetery, near West Union, O. He md. Sept. 7 1933, Mary McKenzie. One child, Carole Young. (2) Curtis, (3) Richard, (4) Verda, md. ——— Grooms, and (5) Leona Young, of Russellville, O.

ii. Ernest Frank, b. Nov. 30 1891, md. Dec. 8 1917, Rebecca McCarty, at West Union, O. and is farming near Satterfield Chapel. Two children: Robert Charles, b. Aug. 13 1922, served in the U. S. Army in World War II, and Berlyn Glenn Young, b. Oct. 23 1934.

iii. Harry O., b. Nov. 24 1893, is farming at Mowrystown, O. He md. Edna M. Grooms, at West Union, O. Five children: Jessie L., b., March 25 1915, md. Feb. 25 1933, Vernon Edgington, at Maysville, Ky. and lives at Mowrystown; John S., b. Dec. 8 1916, d. Apr. 1917; Grace, b. June 10 1918, lives in Dayton, O.; Raymond O., b. Sept. 10 1921, is serving with the U. S. Army; and Harold Young, b. July 5 1925, in Highland county, O.

iv. Laura, b. Nov. 2 1895, md. Samuel Mahaffey, and lives at West Union, O.

v. Ruth, b. Oct. 1 1898, md. Joseph Mahaffey, and lives at West Union, O. Six children.

vi. Goldie, b. Aug. 1 1900, md. Floyd Morrison, and lives at West Union, O. Five children.

vii. William, b. Sept. 8 1902, md. Identie Morrison, at West Union, and lives at Mowrystown, O. Two children. Pickard E., b. Feb. 2 1931, at Peebles, O., and Dale C., b. Dec. 3 1934.

viii. Fred, b. May 3 1904, works at the Post Office, Hillsboro, O. He md. July 14 1926, Mary O. Piatt, at Vanceburg, Ky. Three children: Betty Jean, b. Nov. 14 1926, in Brown county, O.; Marjorie Laru, b. Apr. 24 1928; and Patty Lou Young, b. Nov. 3 1935, in Highland county, O.

ix. Mildred, b. May 16 1906, md. Albert Kratzer.

380 MITCHELL MORRISON YOUNG

born, April 23 1854, in Adams county, O., died, Feb. 8 1942, and was buried near his wife in East Liberty cemetery in Adams county. His farm was part of an original grant to Nathaniel Massie and was once owned by Morgan Young (Rec. 9) who was a neighbor of William Young, grandfather of Mitchell. The Youngs helped to form a "Jersey Settlement" in Adams as they did in Knox county. The first and second names of our subject are colonial N. J. names. Mitchell received his farm from his blind uncle Mitchell, who had it from his father, William. Our map shows the land was part of the Northwest Territory which became the Virginia Military Lands.

Mitchell married, April 30 1876, near West Union, O., Sarah Jane Hayslip, born, July 25 1855, died, June 11 1932, daughter of Thomas Hayslip and Elizabeth Rothwell, and a sister of Jack who married Louisa Young, sister of Mitchell. They had six children, all born on the old homestead in Brush Creek township.

i. Melvin Eylar, b. Aug. 31 1877, d. Jan. 19 1947, on the homestead. He did not marry.

ii. John Wheeler, b. May 31 1879, now, 1947, living on the homestead.

iii. Minnie Ellen, b. Oct. 14 1881, md. Sept. 9 1898, Edward T. Grooms, the son of Wm. Jackson and Jane (Radar) Grooms and lives at West Union, O. Nine children.

389. iv. William Hoadley, b. Oct. 7 1883

390. v. Inez Elizabeth, b. Oct. 25 1885

vi. Enna Ethel, b. Oct. 14 1888, md. Dec. 19 1919, Samuel Drenan Baldwin, at Maysville, Ky. and lives at Manchester, O. Two children: Virginia R., b. Feb. 2 1920, md.

Apr. 28 1942, Lloyd Berry, at Maysville, Ky., and Alma Grace Baldwin, b. Apr. 27 1923, md. Apr. 15 1939, at Morehead, Ky., Martin Meyers.

381 WILLIAM HENRY YOUNG

born, Jan. 8 1875, in Clinton county, Ind. where his parents lived a short time, died, April 23 1943, at West Union, O. where he was a Justice of the Peace. He was buried in the I.O.O.F. cemetery. "Gus" was a veteran of the Spanish-American War, having served in the 2nd U. S. Inf. He married at West Union in 1903 Hetty A. Nixon, b. March 7 1881, d. June 13 1936. Their six children were all born at West Union, O. (W. H. Young)

i. Julius Stroman, b. Oct. 12 1904, d. Sept. 11 1905.
ii. Eva M., b. May 17 1906, lives in Bellevue, Ky. She md. Mar. 26 1926, Alfred E. Newman, and has 2 children: Juanita Jean, and John Thomas Newman.
iii. Norma Lucille, died in early youth.
iv. Margaret, died in infancy.
v. Cora Rachel, b. Mar. 23 1916, md. Apr. 21 1941, John Dee McClurg.
vi. Edna Fay, b. Aug. 27 1922, lives at West Union, O. She md. Nov. 3 1938, Harold Hanson and has 4 children: William, James, Thomas, and Johnda Sue Hanson.

382 HANNAH YOUNG

born, Oct. 17 1876, in Illinois, when her parents were returning to Ohio after a brief sojourn in Kansas, lives in West Union, O. and has appreciably aided in this compilation. She married, Dec. 14 1914, at West Union, Minor McAdow, and has one child, John McAdow. John was born Sept. 26 1917, and served in World War II, in radar service in the Pacific area. He married, June 3 1939, Evelyn Graybill, at Carlisle, Ky. and has a son, Kenneth Harvey, born, Feb. 24 1940, at Mayville, Ky. Residence, Dayton, O.

383 GENERAL DIX YOUNG

born, Sept. 12 1882, at Grant City, Mo. lives at East Los Angeles, Calif. and works for the So. Pacific Ry. He married, June 12 1907, at Springview, Nebr., Florence Alida Webster, born, Oct. 4 1882, at Oil City, Pa. Three children.

i. Benjamin Arthur, b. March 29 1910, at Enterprise, Nebr., d. July 30 1918, at Los Angeles, Calif. where he was buried in the I.O.O.F. cemetery.

ii. Marion Alice, b. June 30 1912, at Enterprise, Nebr., md. Aug. 30 1936, Irl Eugene Joyce, at Los Angeles, Calif. He was killed in action in the So. Pacific, Feb. 26 1945.

iii. Elva Grace, b. March 31 1914, at Wewela, S. Dakota, md. Nov. 13 1937, Varlie J. Gordon, at Los Angeles, Calif., and has one child, James Allan Gordon, b. July 20 1942.

384 MINOR HOLLIDAY YOUNG

was born, Oct. 10 1873, in the same house in which his father was born, on Brush Creek, about 12 miles South-east of West Union, O. He married, Jan. 16 1907, at Bogue, Kan., Ethel Jane Long, and is living, 1945, near Harrison, Ark. where they have a Novelty Shop. Six children, all born at Bogue, Kan. (M. H. Young).

i. Vernita Vaden, b. Jan. 26 1908, md. Apr. 4 1931, at Stockton, Kan., Harvey Rash, and lives in McPherson, Kan.

ii. Lodema Jane, b. Feb. 5 1909, md. Oct. 20 1934, at Hays, Kan., Milton Beach, a lawyer, and lives at Oskaloosa, Kan. They have two children: Jane Lynn, b. Oct. 21 1938, and Michael James Beach, b. Aug. 7 1941.

iii. Robert Millard, farmer, b. June 17 1910, md. Feb. 2 1941, at Forsyth, Mo., Maxine Logan, lives near Omaha, Ark. Three children: Sharon Lee Young, b. Apr. 3 1942, Wm. David, b. Apr. 21 1943, and Karrel Anne, b. May 12, 1945.

iv. Alvin Addison, b. Sept. 30 1911, md. Nov. 6 1936, at Osborn, Kan., Cleo Brinkmeyer, and has one child, Jo Ann Young, b. May 4 1941. Alvin had served 9 yrs. in the Marine and Army Services in 1943, and was a M. Sgt. Radio Operator on a plane that was lost in the South Atlantic.

v. James Herbert, b. Feb. 6 1913, served as 1st. Lt. in World War II, was returned wounded from France in 1945. He md., Sept. 9 1945, Mary Alice Westcott, R.N. and has one child, Patricia Anne, b. July 9 1946. Family lives near Harrison, Ark.

vi. Chester Lewis, b. Nov. 20 1916, md. May 2 1942, in Ill., Jane Brooks, and lives at Danville, Ill. Served in World War II.

385 ISAAC D. YOUNG

born, April 29 1866, in Jefferson Township, Adams County, O., died there at Blue Creek in the home of his daughter, Mrs. Nell Copas, Jan. 18 1945, age 79. He married Rosetta Kratzer. The order of birth of the known children is uncertain.

i. Nell, md ——— Copas
ii. Stella, md. ——— Harris, and lives at Blue Creek.
iii. Ethel, md. ——— Harper, and lives at Columbus, O.
iv. Brooks, lives at New Boston, O.
v. Lee, lives at West Union, O.
vi. Robert Burton, lives at Blue Creek, O.

386 CURTIS LAMAR YOUNG

Druggist at Peebles, O., was born, Feb. 8 1880. He married, March 25 1913, at Cincinnati, O., Ethel Rose Jackson, born, Sept. 20 1890, dau. of Jos. P. Jackson, brother of Mary Wasson. Three children, all born at Peebles, O.

i. Eunice Annabelle, b. Oct. 5 1913, at Peebles, O., md. Sept. 17 1946, Thomas O. Mahaffey, who served as Pvt. in the U. S. A. in World War II.
ii. Clara Josephine, b. Oct. 6 1921, at Peebles, O., md. July 4 1942, Robert R. MacDonald, Lt. U. S. A. in World War II.
iii. Betty Louise, b. May 4 1926, lives with her parents.

387 CONNOR WILSON YOUNG

born, Oct. 2 1885, near West Union, O., is farming near there at Cedar Mills. He married, Nov. 5 1908, Bertha, daughter of John and Alice McClaren Knauff, at West Union. Six children, all born at Cedar Mills.

i. John Melvin, b. Sept. 2 1909, is teaching in the Public Schools of Cuyahoga County, O. He md. June 28 1939, Bernice Covert Harte, at Cleveland, O. One child Frances Jane Young, b. May 1 1940, Cleveland, O.

ii. Donald, b. Sept. 16 1911, md. 1935, Pauline Bennington, at West Union, O. where he is living. Two children, Shirley Ann, b. Feb. 10 1937, and Linda Lou Young, b. 1942.

iii. Julius, b. Aug. 26 1913, md. in Dec. 1942, June Bennington, at West Union, O. Two children: Janet Ruth, b. 1944; and Brenda Joyce Young, b. Dec. 1946.

iv. Dorothy, b . May 21 1916, md. May 1934, Curtis Clark, at West Union, and is living at Manchester, O. Three children: Roger, b. March 1935; James, b. 1939; and Michael Clark, b. 1947.

v. Marjorie, b. May 14 1920, md. 1939, Edgar Grooms, son of Otis, at West Union, and lives near there. Five children: Ethelene, b. 1940; Carol Lee, b. 1942; Nancy Ann, b. 1943; Dennis, b. 1944; and Jerry Grooms, b. 1946.

vi. Lawrence, b. Oct. 1927, has been in the U. S. Navy since 1945.

388 EDWARD CLEVELAND YOUNG

born, Dec. 10 1885, at West Union, O., married there Bertha, born, Jan. 20 1891, daughter of Edw. M. Shultz and Emma Jane Anderson. Six children, all born at Manchester, O.

i. Edward Pershing (Perk), b. Nov. 21 1918, md. May 27 1945, Kathryn F. Bartholomew, and has a son Chester Lee Young, b. June 29 1946, at Manchester, O. He served as Sgt. in World War II.

ii. George Arnold, b. Dec. 3 1920, md. Jan. 23 1942, Garnet Lumbleson, and lives in Cincinnati, O.

iii. Margaret, b. Nov. 1 1922, md. May 3 1946, ——— Greenlee, at Maysville, Ky. and has a daughter Andria, b. at Manchester, O.

iv. Betty Lee, b. Jan. 29 1925, md. Sept. 29 1945, George St. Mary, at Maysville, Ky. One child, Judith Ann St. Mary, b. Aug. 24 1946, at Saginaw, Mich. where the family lives.

v. James Rufus, b. Nov. 10 1926

vi. Mildred Eileen, b. Nov. 30 1929

389 WILLIAM HOADLEY YOUNG

born, Oct. 7 1883, in Adams county, O., is farming there near West Union in 1947. He married, April 6 1905, Rillie Conn, at Lynx, O. They have six children, all born at Lynx.

i. Lesta, b. June 3 1908, md. June 28 1929, Floyd Shivener, and has a son, Lorin William Shivener.
ii. Otis Sherwood, b. March 11 1926, is living with his mother.
iii. Marlin, b. March 17 1910. See Rec. 378.
Vanceburg, Ky.
iv. Harold, b. March 15 1917, md. Apr. 27 1942, Cordia, daughter of Arthur and Mary (Copas) Grooms, and had 2 daughters, Helen and Wanda.
v. Treber, b. Nov. 25 1921, d. Sept. 13 1937.
vi. Lewis, b. July 17 1926, is living at home.

390 INEZ ELIZABETH YOUNG

born, Oct. 25 1885, in Adams county, O., lives at Lynx, O. She married, Oct. 13 1907, at Rome, O., Frank Seward Campbell (son of John M. and Mary Jane (Rothwell) Campbell) who died, May 19 1926, and was buried in East Liberty cemetery. Four children, all born at Lynx, O.

i. Othel Myrl, b. Aug. 16 1908 md. Eugene Ashenhurst, and has a daughter Shirley Ann Ashenhurst.
ii. Icy Jane, b. Sept. 28 1910, md. Shelby Pollard, and has a son Roy Eugene Pollard.
iii. Treber Mott, b. Jan. 8 1913, md. Vernie Pollard, and has 2 daughters, Mildred Jean and Sandra Fay Campbell.
iv. Otis Sherwood, b. March 11 1926, is living with his mother.

INDEX OF NAMES

A name often appears more than once on a page.
(Numbers refer to pages)

Daniel Beers	2/ 24, 1866	2/ 24, 1866	
Charity Ann	10/ 30, 1869	10/ 7, 1870	

Alvina E. Potter	1/ 18, 1851	1909	Lived at Toulon Ill. Died at Bowie, Tex.
	Married 12/ 5, 1867		
George S. Lawrence	6/9, 1836		Died at Bowie, Tex.

Children of Alvina E. Potter and George S. Lawrence.

Abigail Young	11/ 2, 1868	About 1950	Married J.Frank Ziegler. No Children.
Bessie	5/ 31, 1870	1953	Married Charles A. Foster.One son Lawrence C. Foster. who married Seba Slaughter. Four daughters. Bowie Texas.

RESIDENCE

FAMILY	Folio	m. Marriage	b. BORN	d. DIED	REMARKS
		CHARITY ANN YOUNG	2/ 25, I829	I2/ 5, I896	Pioneer residents of Kewanee. Built first house in Kewanee. Now owned by Kewanee Chapter D. A. R.
			MARRIED 3/ 27, 1849		
		John Philo Potter	3/ 26, I823	I0/ 23, I898	
		CHILDREN OF JOHN P. AND CHARITY YOUNG POTTER			
		Alvina E.	I/ I8, I85I	I909	Married George Lawrence.
		Emily Rosalia	I/ 2I, I853	8/ I90I	Unmarried
		Bessie Young	4/ 26, I855	I/ I939	Married Herbert Green.
		Lucy Jacobs	I0/ I857	I0/ 9, I858	
		Noble Elbert	II/ 2I, I859	II/ 7, I950	Married Emma L. Massey of Virginia Illinois

Clyta Gertrude Lovejoy	Married 8/ 3I, I947 to I2/ I7, I9I9	Corp, Water Division, in South Pacific . Lt. Commander. Graduate University ofIllinois.

Son of Bessie Lawrence and Charles A. Foster

Lawrence C. Foster	9/26, I896	Lives at Bowie, Texas.
Seba Slaughter	Married to Seba Slaughter I930. 6/ 2I, I90I	Daughter of Geo. C. Slaughter.

Children of Lawrence C. and Seba Slaughter Foster.

Jane	I/29, 3I	Married Edgar W. Brash 6/I4, I952 at Carmel, Cal.
Lois	II/ 27, I933	Married M. E. Campbell 8/ 7, I955, Bowie, Texas.
Frances	9/ 27, I936	Married James McCarty 7/3, I955, Bowie Texas?
Virginia	4/ 4, I938 –	" Wayne Ellis " "

RESIDENCE

FAMILY	Folio	m. Marriage	b. BORN	d. DIED	REMARKS
		Bessie Young Potter	4/ 26, I855	I, I939	One son John B. Green. Died 1949. No issue.
			Married to (I885)		
		Herbert L. Green			
		Noble Elbert Potter	II/ 2I, I859	II/7, I950	Mfg. Brick and Tile. Kewanee, Ill.
			Married Io, 20, I886 to		
		Emma Louise Massey	5/9, I860	II/ IO, I926	One daughter, Charity Martha.
		Charity Martha Potter	7/I9, I887		
			Married 2/2I. I9IO to		
		Smith Leroy Heaps	9/ 26, I887		Son of Samuel Lloyd and Ann Eliza Ludlum Heaps.

Son of Charity M. Potter and Smith Leroy Heaps.

Printed in the USA
CPSIA information can be obtained
at www.ICGtesting.com
LVHW012146261223
767492LV00005B/47